Governance, Regulations and Powers on the Internet

Digital technologies have prompted the emergence of new modes of regulation and governance, as they allow for more decentralized processes for the elaboration and implementation of norms. Moreover, the internet has been raising a wide set of governance issues, since it affects many domains, such as individual rights, public liberties, property rights, economic competition, market regulation, conflict management, security and the sovereignty of states. There is therefore a need to understand how technical, political, economic and social norms are articulated, as well as to understand who the main actors of this process of transformation are, how they interact and how these changes may influence international rulings. This book brings together an international team of scholars to explain and analyze how collective regulations evolve in the broader context of the development of postmodern societies, globalization, the reshaping of international relations and the profound transformations of nation states.

ERIC BROUSSEAU is Professor of Economics and Management at the University Paris-Dauphine and at the European University Institute in Florence. He is a member of Dauphine Research in Management, which is affiliated with the French National Scientific Research Centre (CNRS). He is also involved with the Global Governance Programme at the Robert Schuman Centre for Advanced Studies, based in Florence. He is the Director of the European School on New Institutional Economics.

MERYEM MARZOUKI is a senior researcher with the CNRS and currently works at the Computer Science Laboratory of Paris 6 (LIP6).

CÉCILE MÉADEL is Professor of Sociology at the Ecole des Mines de Paris and a researcher at the Centre de Sociologie de l'Innovation, a joint research center between MINES ParisTech and the CNRS.

Governance, Regulations and Powers on the Internet

Edited by

ERIC BROUSSEAU, MERYEM MARZOUKI
AND CÉCILE MÉADEL

CAMBRIDGE
UNIVERSITY PRESS

CAMBRIDGE UNIVERSITY PRESS
Cambridge, New York, Melbourne, Madrid, Cape Town,
Singapore, São Paulo, Delhi, Mexico City

Cambridge University Press
The Edinburgh Building, Cambridge CB2 8RU, UK

Published in the United States of America by
Cambridge University Press, New York

www.cambridge.org
Information on this title: www.cambridge.org/9781107013421

First published 2012

Printed in the United Kingdom at the University Press, Cambridge

A catalogue record for this publication is available from the British Library

Library of Congress Cataloguing in Publication Data

Governance, regulations and powers on the Internet / edited by Eric Brousseau, Meryem Marzouki, Cécile Méadel.
p. cm.
Includes bibliographical references and index.
ISBN 978-1-107-01342-1
1. Cyberspace–Government policy. 2. Internet–Government policy. I. Brousseau, Eric. II. Marzouki, Meryem. III. Méadel, Cécile. IV. Title.
HM851.G68 2012
303.48′330973–dc23
2011029388

ISBN 978-1-107-01342-1 Hardback

Contents

Figures

Contributors

The editors of this book would like to pay homage to James Rosenau, who passed away on September 9, 2011. His innovative way of thinking about international dynamics influenced many scholars and will certainly inspire the future of global governance.

CHRISTOPHE AGUITON is a researcher at Orange Labs, working on internet social networks, new models of innovation and geolocalization, and an activist who participates in all the World Social Forums. He lectures about the internet and social sciences at the universities of Paris-Sorbonne and Paris-Est Marne-la-Vallée.

MADELEINE AKRICH is Director of the Centre for the Sociology of Innovation at Mines ParisTech. She has devoted most of her work to the sociology of technology, with a specific focus on users. In the past few years her work has primarily concerned medicine. In collaboration with Bernike Pasveer she compared obstetrical practices in France and the Netherlands. She has been working with Cécile Méadel on internet discussion groups in the health field (patient groups, professional groups). With Vololona Rabeharisoa, she is currently coordinating a European project on patient organizations and the governance of knowledge.

NICOLAS AURAY is Assistant Professor of Sociology at Telecom ParisTech and a member of the LTCI (the joint laboratory of the CNRS and Telecom ParisTech). His work focuses on the articulation between professional belonging and amateur practices through involvement in computer-mediated communities. He has coordinated researches on online gaming, free/open-source software and social support websites.

ERIC BROUSSEAU is Professor of Economics and Management at Paris-Dauphine University and in the Global Governance Programme at the European University Institute in Florence. He is the director of the European School on New Institutional Economics. He was the director of EconomiX, a joint research center between the CNRS and the University of Paris Ouest, from 2005 to 2011. He also coordinated the CNRS's Research Consortium "Information and communication technologies and the society" (GDR TICS) from 2002 to 2009. His research agenda focuses on the economics of institutions and on the economics of contracts, with three main applied fields: the internet and digital economics, innovation and intellectual property, and the environment. Besides his academic publication, he has been involved in researches for the French government, the European Commission, the US National Science Foundation, the United Nations and the Organisation for Economic Co-operation and Development.

HERBERT BURKERT is President of the Research Centre for Information Law at the University of St Gallen (Switzerland), where he teaches public law, information and communication law. He is also a Senior Research Fellow at the Fraunhofer Institute for Intelligent Analysis and Information Systems, St Augustin, Germany (currently on leave of absence).

DOMINIQUE CARDON is a sociologist in the Laboratoire des Usages of Orange Labs and an associate researcher in the Centre d'Etudes des Mouvements Sociaux (Ecole des Hautes Etudes en Sciences Sociales – EHESS). He lectures about the internet and social sciences at the universities of Paris-Sorbonne and Paris-Est Marne-la-Vallée. He is currently working on the use of social media in different contexts: blogging, Wikipedia, Facebook and Flickr. He recently edited two thematic publications of the journal *Réseaux*, on "Les réseaux sociaux de l'Internet" (no. 152, December 2008) and "Web 2.0" (no. 154, March 2009).

TOM DEDEURWAERDERE is Research Director of the Biodiversity Governance Unit of the Centre for the Philosophy of Law and professor at the Faculty of Philosophy, Université Catholique de Louvain. He is a graduate in engineering and philosophy, with a Ph.D. in philosophy. His main research focus is the institutional analysis of the governance of genetic resource commons and the global knowledge commons.

BRUNO DEFFAINS is a professor of economics and Director of the Law and Economics program at University Paris 2 Panthéon Assas. Prior to arriving at Paris 2, he was professor at the Universities of Paris X and Nancy 2. For much of his academic career he has focused on the interactions between law and economics, especially in the fields of business law, civil liability, conflict resolution and comparison between common law and civil law systems; he is the author of many books and papers on these subjects. He is a member of the board of the European Association of Law and Economics. He also teaches law and economics as Adjunct Professor at the European Business School in Wiesbaden.

SÉVERINE DUSOLLIER is Professor of Law at the University of Namur (Belgium), where she mainly teaches intellectual property rights (IPR) and information technology (IT) law. She has been the head of the IPR department at the Research Centre on IT and Law since 1998. She received her doctorate from the University of Namur. Her current research focuses on copyright in the information society, public domain and the intellectual commons, copyright and authorship in art, digital rights management, software patents, IPR and competition law. She has carried out research in several European and national projects and has been an advisor to the World Intellectual Property Organization, the Council of Europe, United Nations Educational, Scientific and Cultural Organization and the European Commission. She was a research associate at the University of California, Berkeley, in 2001 and a Jean Monet Fellow at the European University Institute in Florence from 2005 to 2006.

NIVA ELKIN-KOREN is the Dean of the Faculty of Law at the University of Haifa and the Founding Director of the Haifa Center for Law and Technology. She has written extensively on copyright law and information policy. Her research focuses on the legal institutions that facilitate private and public control over the production and dissemination of information. She earned her S.J.D. from Stanford Law School in 1995, her LL.M from Harvard Law School in 1991 and her LL.B from Tel Aviv University School of Law in 1989. She has been a visiting professor at leading law schools in the United States and in Europe.

BENOÎT FRYDMAN is Professor at the Law School of the Université Libre de Bruxelles (ULB) and Director of the Perelman Centre for Legal Philosophy, where he leads the research programme on "Global law." He used to be a Visiting Research Fellow at the Programme of Comparative Media Law and Policy at Oxford University.

JEAN-MICHEL GLACHANT has been Director of the Florence School of Regulation and Holder of the Loyola de Palacio Chair in EU Energy Policy at the European University Institute in Florence since 2008. He took a Ph.D. in economics and then became Professor in Economics at La Sorbonne. He left La Sorbonne for University Paris Sud in the autumn of 2000, where he took the head of the Department of Economics and founded a new research team "Groupe Réseaux Jean Monnet." He has been an advisor to several directorates-general (DG TREN, DG COMP and DG RESEARCH) at the European Commission and to the French Energy Regulatory Commission. He has been coordinator or scientific advisor of several European research projects (SESSA, CESSA, Reliance, EU-DEEP, RefGov, TradeWind, Secure, Optimate and THINK). He is a research partner of the Center for Energy and Environmental Policy Research at the Massachusetts Institute of Technology, the Electricity Policy Research Group at Cambridge University and the European Energy Institute at the Catholic University of Leuven.

LUDOVIC HENNEBEL is a Research Fellow at the National Fund for Scientific Research (Belgium) and affiliated with the Perelman Centre of Legal Philosophy of the Law School of the Brussels University. Until 2008 he was a Global Research Fellow affiliated with the Law School of New York University. He is a lecturer at the Law School of the University of Brussels and at Sciences Po Paris, where he teaches global justice, transnational law and human rights law. He is the Executive and Faculty Director of the Magna Carta Institute, an independent research institute based in Brussels, which specializes in human rights and international law. He holds a Ph.D. in law, an LL.M in international human rights law, an MA and a BA in law, and the René Cassin Diploma in international human rights law.

CHRISTINE HINE is Senior Lecturer in the Department of Sociology at the University of Surrey, based in Guildford. Her main research centers on the sociology of science and technology, combining ethnographic and historical approaches to understanding the role of information and communication technology (ICT) in scientific research. She also has a major interest in the development of ethnography in technical settings, and in "virtual methods" (the use of the internet for social research). In particular, she has developed mobile and connective approaches to ethnography that combine online and offline social contexts. She is the author of *Virtual Ethnography* (2000) and *Systematics as Cyberscience* (2008) and the editor of *Virtual Methods* (2005) and *New Infrastructures for Knowledge Production* (2006). Christine was President of the European Association for the Study of Science and Technology (EASST) from 2004 to 2008.

GREGORY LEWKOWICZ is Professor at the ULB and affiliated with the Perelman Centre for Legal Philosophy. He has taught at Lille University and Sciences Po Paris. He is the Co-Director of the Magna Carta Institute, based in Brussels, and of the Bruylant book series "Magna Carta." His research focuses broadly on the intellectual history of international law and relations and the contemporary development of international law and governance with specific respect to globalization.

MERYEM MARZOUKI is a senior researcher with the CNRS, and is currently with LIP6. She holds a Ph.D. in computer science and an "Habilitation à diriger des recherches," both from the National Polytechnic Institute of Grenoble. In 2002 she started PolyTIC, a multidisciplinary research activity dealing with relationships between ICTs, public policies and the public space. Her current research interests include internet governance and the transformation of the rule of law, privacy and personal data protection issues, and usages in mobile and broadband communications. As part of her volunteering activities, she has also been actively promoting human rights in digital environment since 1996 at the national, European and global levels, including at the World Summit on the Information Society (WSIS) and the Internet Governance Forum (IGF).

CÉCILE MÉADEL is Professor of Sociology at the Ecole des mines de Paris and researcher at the Centre de Sociologie de l'Innovation, a joint research centre between MINES ParisTech and the CNRS. She has devoted most of her work to the uses of communication technologies. Originally trained as a historian, she focuses on the genealogy of the media, broadcasting, internet applications, all devices that allow mutual adjustment between a means of communication, the professionals specialized in it, its resources and its users. Her current research is in e-health and peer-to-peer technologies and explores questions raised by such architectures in terms of uses, technologies, rights and norms.

PIERRE MOUNIER lectures in digital humanities at EHESS and is the Deputy Director of the Center for Open Electronic Publishing. He is the Editor-in-Chief and author of "Homo Numericus," a blog focused on digital technologies. He has written a book on the political history of the internet (*Les Maîtres du Réseau*, 2002) and another on digital publishing (*L'Edition Electronique*, 2010).

MILTON L. MUELLER is Professor at Syracuse University School of Information Studies. Mueller received his Ph.D. from the University of Pennsylvania in 1989. He founded the Internet Governance Project, a consortium of university scholars working on global internet policy issues. His widely read book *Ruling the Root: Internet Governance and the Taming of Cyberspace* was published in 2002. His new book *Networks and States: The Global Politics of Internet Governance* was released in 2010. Mueller has been active in the Internet Corporation for Assigned Names and Numbers, WSIS civil society and the new IGF.

JAMES N. ROSENAU passed away while this book was under revision, having retired in 2009 as University Professor of International Affairs at the George Washington University (GWU). He was the author of many books, including *Along the Domestic–Foreign Frontier*, *Distant Proximities* and *Turbulence in World Politics*. He also co-edited the book *Information Technologies and Global Politics* with J. P. Singh. His most recent book, *People Count! The Networked Individual in World Politics*, was published in 2007.

YVES SCHEMEIL is Global and Comparative Politics Professor, Institut Universitaire de France and the University of Grenoble. He also teaches or has taught in the United States, Japan and Switzerland. His recent publications include "Expertise and political competence: consensus making within the World Trade and the World Meteorological

Organizations," in *Decision-Making within International Organizations* (edited by B. Reinalda and B. Verbeek; 2004), "From mutual denegation to mutual recognition: NGO/IGO partnership in trade and atom," *Cosmopolis* (June 2009) and "Dynamism and resilience of intergovernmental organizations in a world of persisting state power and rising non-state actors," in *The Ashgate Research Companion to Non-State Actors* (edited by B. Reinalda; 2010).

MILES D. TOWNES is a doctoral student in international relations at GWU, where he worked as Research Assistant to Professor James N. Rosenau. Prior to enrolling at GWU, he earned an M.Litt. from the University of St Andrews, Scotland, in international security studies, with distinction in the dissertation.

JANE K. WINN is Charles I. Stone Professor and Co-Director of the Law, Technology and Arts Group at the University of Washington School of Law. She received her bachelor's degree in economics from Queen Mary College, University of London, and her law degree from Harvard Law School. She is the author of the leading US reference book on electronic commerce law as well as writing many articles and book chapters on electronic commerce law developments in the United States, European Union and China. She has served as a Fulbright Scholar in China, as well as an advisor to the American Law Institute's Principles of Software Contracts, and a member of the EU ICT Standards Board. She is a Senior Fellow in the Melbourne Law School Masters Programme. Her current research interests include information security law, e-invoicing, global production networks and the impact of trade policy on ICT standards.

Introduction

1 Governance, networks and digital technologies: societal, political and organizational innovations

ERIC BROUSSEAU, MERYEM MARZOUKI AND CÉCILE MÉADEL

1.1 Introduction

Digital technologies play a major role in the profound changes that characterize political and economic regulations both within nation states and in international relations. They often provide the conditions for these evolutionary processes by means of new modes of information circulation, of interactions between individuals and of collective organization. They have also prompted the emergence of new modes of regulation and governance.

In addition, they raise qualitatively new issues, since global information networks affect the performance of information-based activities, the organization of related industries and coordination between all kinds of stakeholders whose interests are impacted by the rise of the information society.

As a result, technical governance and political governance are becoming more and more intertwined. There is therefore a need to understand how technical, political, economic and social norms are articulated, as well as to understand who the main actors in this process of transformation are, how they interact and how these changes may influence international rulings in terms of individual rights, public liberties, property rights, economic competition, market regulation, conflict management, security, state sovereignty, etc.

This contributory volume aims to address these related issues from a truly international perspective, with views from different academic cultures and backgrounds. Although the role of digital technologies is highlighted, other factors that are driving our rapidly changing world are also considered. How collective regulations evolve is analyzed in the broader context of the development of postmodern societies, of globalization, of the reshaping of international relations and of the profound transformations of nation states.

This book thereby aims to improve our understanding of the interactions between the evolution of collective governance principles (at all levels from community to global) and the diffusion of digital technologies, which lead on to the development of information-based activities, the initialization of new social practices and the rise of new modes of governance.

Indeed, on the one hand, digital technologies tend to influence governance mainly through two channels. First, digital technologies facilitate the management of the innovative processes of elaborating norms and standards. This is illustrated, for instance, by the practices of the World Social Forum (WSF). Information technology (IT) provides the flexibility to aggregate information without imposing the classical constraints of collective debates on the management of agendas and processes in order to reach consensus or a majority of votes. Digital technology makes possible the dynamic management of archives, tracks, forking (i.e. the emergence of new debates or a new line of analysis), etc. This may lead to new types of norms. Adhesion and compliance can be "negotiated," in the way that agents can decide whether they fully comply or not.

Second, as pointed out in particular by Lawrence Lessig (1999b), digital technology provides a relatively cheap and convenient means to implement norms. Indeed, the control of access and "code" makes it possible to monitor how information and virtual spaces are accessed and used. This is well illustrated by digital rights management (DRM) technology, which facilitates the implementation of barriers allowing owners to charge for or to control the uses of digitized works of creation. Users often challenge these technological hurdles. Regardless of whether they are considered as unfair, useless or more generally illegitimate, the mass of lay users may well overwhelm the barriers after "hackers" have broken through them. Technology provides most users of information systems with a relatively costless capacity to implement norms, however. Governance can thus be more decentralized – i.e. both in the hands of individuals and organizations – rather than being the unique prerogative of governments at various levels.

On the other hand, social changes are responsible for many of these new practices. The development of democratic forms of governance, even if they benefit only a minority of the global population, leads to a more decentralized design of systems of norms. There is, in effect, a strong tendency to evolve from representative formal democracy, based on the delegation of regulatory power by citizens to representatives, toward multiple forms of more participative and more decentralized processes to elaborate norms. Different types of stakeholders (citizens, experts, professionals, organized groups, etc.) are included in the processes of ruling characterized by consensus-building and negotiations. The resulting norms range from self-regulations to public/state-backed regulations, but they are all characterized by a high degree of involvement on the part of "users" in the process of their elaboration.

This leads to the coexistence of different types of norms elaborated in contrasted types of forums at different levels. Such a trend is well illustrated by the emerging environmental regulations aimed at dealing with climate change. Indeed, legally enforced nationwide regulations result from the recommendations and analysis put forward by the experts of the Intergovernmental Panel on Climate Change (IPCC), on which potential intergovernmental agreements are based. Before becoming legally enforceable, implementation is "negotiated" with the various stakeholders at the national level. National legislation is therefore no longer the result solely of the process of discussion and negotiation in national parliaments.

The processes of the elaboration of norms go hand in hand with new forms of norms implementation. The state is no longer the monopolistic provider of the means of enforcement. Public–private partnerships characterize an increasing number of functions related to the provision of public order. In certain circumstances, the state even retreats from its core "regal" functions. This is well illustrated by the development of video surveillance, of security companies, of gated cities and, more generally, the "enclosure" of public areas. Of course, the magnitude of such trends differs from one country to another, and the ability of nation states to monopolize and take care of enforcement alone has proved far from perfect in many historic periods. In fact, it is largely a nineteenth- and twentieth-century phenomenon. There is unquestionably a move by the state to withdraw from trying to control enforcement alone, however, and to subcontract or negotiate enforcement with all types of stakeholders. For instance, it is clear that the European Union has been promoting "new" approaches to the regulation of economic activities, based not only on stakeholder involvement in the design of these regulations but also on self-enforcement.

In this context, what is happening with the governance of digital technologies in general, and of the internet more specifically, is of central importance – and is particularly radical. There are three reasons for this. First, the transborder nature of the internet and its integration have made it a global infrastructure around which all kinds of conflicts of norms – of legitimacy, of power, of culture – develop. These conflicts are either out in the open or hidden. There is, however, a sort of de facto multi-purpose competition between conflicting norms at the global level. Think of the principle of free speech, of the various interpretations of the public domain, of the right to privacy, of the right to voice by minorities or opponents, etc. The multifunctional nature of the internet has also enabled it to transform itself into an essential infrastructure for a wide set of social, cultural, economic and political activities and sectors. The stakes are huge, and exacerbate conflicts among nations and domains alike. Beyond the regulation of information flows and of access to network resources lies the actual content of civic rights, consumer protection and competition regulation, as well as the conditions by which knowledge is accessed, cultures are maintained and developed, communities are organized, individuals participate in collective decision-making, etc. Lastly, the "end-to-end" architecture of the network – i.e. its distributed architecture – favors the development of decentralized collective action, since the internet provides all kinds of communities and leaders with the ability to organize themselves and to benefit from the distributed intelligence that lies in the network's structure.

The regulation of the internet is, therefore, an arena in which all the technical and societal trends highlighted above are mutually reinforcing. Digital governance is thus an essential domain of interest, on account of the range and the centrality of human activities that are impacted by the internet, and because the regulation of the internet relies on innovations that turn its governance into a laboratory from which many lessons can be drawn.

This introductory chapter is structured along four tracks. First, we highlight how the technology, and beyond that the development of a knowledge-based society, are reshaping macro-governance. In a nutshell, the fast pace of innovation permanently challenges collective rules and norms while, at the same time, the information infrastructure provides society with enhanced capabilities to identify issues and manage them. Second, we focus on the mechanisms by which the technology transforms the individual's capability to influence the building and the implementation of collective norms. We highlight, in particular, the fact that, in an increasingly complex world, technical capabilities are the source of new legitimacies and new capabilities, and, hence, new potentialities and needs in matters of the organization of governance. Third, we show how digital technologies impact self-governance capabilities. Indeed, self- and community-based governance is not new. Traditional societies and even modern societies rely extensively on the governance provided by all types of communities. What is new with the internet, and the underlying social trends, is the fact that these communities are loosely connected internally and based on non-exclusive membership. This results in a complex combination of fragmentation and general interdependence within society. Fourth, the technology impacts on the relative costs of private/self-regulation as compared to public/state-based regulation. A society increasingly based upon self-regulatory mechanisms raises new needs in matters of public governance, since the properties of private regulations differ from those of public ones.

As argued before, a backdrop to the analysis of all these issues is provided by the idea that major societal trends, and, in particular, the empowerment and autonomization of individuals, are drivers of the observed practices that are far from simple "impacts" of technological development.

1.2 Macro-level transformations: digital technologies and governance

1.2.1 Innovation, empowerment and collective decision-making capabilities

Innovation, empowerment and decision-making may be identified as the three fundamental processes in which digital technologies have been instrumental, leading to major transformations in the political, social, cultural and economic realms. Far from being technological determinisms – a point that has been refuted by Manuel Castells – these changes are themselves included in broader developments of the global polity at multiple levels, which impact in their turn the governance of digital technologies and networks (Castells, 2001; Cowhey and Aronson, 2009).

Permanent innovation characterizes the knowledge-based economy and the information society. Innovation operates at all levels: technological, industrial, organizational and commercial, as well as uses. Most of them are endogenous, as we are reminded by Milton Mueller (Chapter 2), in the context of the evolution of the nature of property rights over information and key network resources, and by Eric Brousseau and Jean-Michel Glachant (Chapter 3), in the context of network services. Constant innovation leads to an increased and renewed complexity of relationships and transactions between different actors and stakeholders, who are forced to develop agile strategies. Flexibility makes it possible to meet the new requirements permanently in matters of coordination.

Seen as knowledge management and coordination technologies, digital technologies are the means of *individual and collective empowerment*. They lower collective action costs and delays and overcome territorial boundaries, leading to changes in individuals' relations to authority, as well as political and social reconfigurations, as stated by James Rosenau and Miles Townes (Chapter 5). Although these skills and organizational revolutions are still far from permitting the formation of a global polity, or even of a "global civil society," some non-governmental actors – anti-globalization movements, as well as business networks – have been experimenting with new, alternative models of networked coordination at the global level.

The means of *collective decision-making* are also being transformed, and traditional political institutions are no longer the sole methods of managing such processes, which leads to a shift from government to governance – that is to say, the exercise of authority relies on informal instruments, tradition, norms, habits, etc. (Rosenau and Czempiel, 1992). As a result, the modalities of democratic control are themselves being reconfigured and restructured in the particular contexts of globalization and the development of a global information infrastructure. This leads to the need to reorganize appropriate checks and balances in the global information society, as analyzed by Herbert Burkert (Chapter 4), in a cyclic way, which may be summarized as follows: digital technologies allow for decentralized control and individual action, leading to more inclusive and participative policymaking; that technologies be open and neutral are necessary conditions, however, which in turn requires political oversight over networks and technological development.

This generic, cyclic process may be achieved through various global digital technologies and network governance dimensions – access, content, privacy, security, cultural and linguistic diversity, intellectual property, domain names, etc. – as can be seen in the discussions conducted during the two phases of the United Nations' World Summit on the Information Society (WSIS), in 2003 and 2005, and the subsequent follow-up processes. The three main governance issues regarding digital technologies are: the regulation of networks; the political oversight of this regulation; and the conditions for a democratic oversight.

1.2.2 The mutual dependence of democratic governance and the openness of networks

"Openness" is the keyword for the effective regulation of networks, defined as both openness of networks (see Chapter 2, by Milton Mueller) and openness of the regulation process (see Chapter 3, by Eric Brousseau and Jean-Michel Glachant).

One of the key elements for openness is *interoperability*, or the capacity to extend the network to new services and new players through a "plug-and-play" process. The main issue of network openness, however, is illustrated in the current fierce debate on the network neutrality principle. The debate, in a sense, may be seen as a "remix" of an earlier debate on the common carriage principle, which developed in the early 1990s after the break-up of public monopolies and the privatization of telecom operators. This principle, which played an important role in the development of transport and communication networks, implies that the licensed carriers provide "service on a non-discriminatory basis, neutral as to use and user" (Noam, 1994). Despite fundamental differences in the architectures and protocols of the internet and of the telecom networks, the network neutrality principle elaborated for the former corresponds to the common carriage principle applied to the latter.

Most vertical or quasi-vertical integration in the network industry (think of mobile phone operators, on the one hand, and Google, on the other) in terms of content and applications, coupled with the development of new technologies, protocols, services and applications – such as peer-to-peer (P2P), Voice over Internet Protocol (VoIP) or internet protocol television (IPTV), etc. – have raised concern about the *openness of competition* in the internet industry. Following the idea that vertical integration threatens the internet "end-to-end" principle (Lemley and Lessig, 2001; DeNardis, 2009), many authors have elaborated on the network neutrality concept, a term coined by Tim Wu (2003a). Practical cases of network neutrality breaches by major network operators occurred, bringing the debate to the political arena, most notably in the US Congress and, more recently, within the institutions of the European Union or EU governments (Marsden, 2010). The non-discriminatory provision of services remains the main concern of network neutrality advocates, even if important nuances are still to be clarified (van Schewick and Farber, 2009).

Such debates are influenced by the uncertainties and risks characterizing this rapidly evolving domain. They need to involve many players, including the average user, both to take into account the multiple developments and because the interests and well-being of all are at stake. Regulators and other decision-makers therefore develop a multiplicity of *"participative debates"* and *"soft regulation"* instruments that might enrich or divert the production of public legitimacy, as highlighted by Eric Brousseau and Jean-Michel Glachant (Chapter 3).

Private actors and, to a certain degree, civil society are thus increasingly encouraged to meet and confront views, to coalesce, collude or compete through a number of tools.[1] Discussion forums, public hearings, ad hoc expert groups and consultations organized on white or green books tentatively framing a given issue are open to various communities, interests, groups, lobbies and, more generally, all types of stakeholders, allowing them to contribute to these "open debates" and to participate in "collective" decision-making.[2] Such tools and processes lead to information-sharing and capacity-building. At the

[1] This raises many question about the consequences for political life and democracy, the transformation of the public sphere and the functioning of social movements. Andrew Chadwick (2006) and Matthew Hindman (2008) warn about the myth of digital democracy, underlining the persistent role of the elite in the shaping of political information and debate.

[2] This proliferation of "new" public policy instruments and arenas has even led some authors to formulate the hypothesis that "it may relate to the fact that actors find it easier to reach agreement on methods than on goals – what are instruments for some groups might be goals for others" (Lascoumes and Le Galès, 2007).

global level, one example of such capacity-building is the United Nations' Internet Governance Forum (IGF). On more focused domains of competence, but with the notable addition of recommendation or decision-making capacities, the "London Action Plan," dealing with internet security issues (Brown and Marsden, 2007), and the French "Internet Rights Forum" (Marzouki and Méadel, 2006) constitute two good examples of this type of forum.

These new public policy processes and instruments raise the fundamental issue of the *political oversight* of the design of the regulations they might define or induce (Coleman and Blumler, 2008). Mainly at stake is the need to take into account the common interest, and to avoid the capture of the regulatory game by the main economic players or by technological experts. A straightforward but wise course lies in the "Back to basics!" principle – that is, Baron de Montesquieu's democratic division of powers and its system of checks and balances – as we are reminded by Burkert. Political hazards and disparities cannot be entirely avoided when traditional constitutional tools are relied upon, however. On the one hand, the executive shows a greater degree of agility than both the legislative and the judiciary. On the other, private sector players and non-governmental organizations (NGOs) have gained influence in this game – though certainly not to the same extent.

A citizen's watchful eye over the information infrastructure of his or her society is in itself, however, a necessary condition for a real democratic oversight of that polity. A really open information society is, indeed, necessary in order to guarantee freedom of speech and the actual freedom to access and release information. These rights and guarantees set the condition for a true citizen's control of politicians and of the formal and legal order. This requires that a certain effort be made in terms of empowerment and capacity-building, as called for by Rosenau and Townes.

1.2.3 In search of new forms of legitimacy

These necessary transformations of governance tools and practices are not specific to the information society. They are driven and accompanied by larger societal trends, as shown in the rise of new forms of democratic governance. In his recent work, Pierre Rosanvallon (2008) analyzes the crisis of democratic legitimacy through the crisis of its two main bases so far: the majority and the general interest principles. He shows how they have been confusingly mixed up with the concept of democratic election, despite their difference in nature, the general interest being a "justification principle," while the majority is a "decision-making technique" (p. 10). He further identifies and elaborates three new forms of legitimacy – the legitimacy of *impartiality*, of *reflexivity*, and of *proximity* – and proposes a "new grammar of democratic institutions" to embody them (p. 23).

The *legitimacy of impartiality* is embedded in the development of control, regulation and arbitration authorities. Their institutional form varies from country to country (board, council, commission, independent administrative authority, etc.), but their functions are similarly defined and the expectations they generate are equally high. Data protection authorities are the typical means used in the information arena.[3]

The legitimacy of reflexivity has been theorized, mostly on the basis of the seminal works of Jürgen Habermas and Ulrich Beck. Society's increasing complexity prevents the establishment of a complete, "just-in-time" and direct democracy. Reflexive third parties and deliberative forums have developed to reflect the diversity/fragmentation of the social reality. Rosanvallon identifies constitutional courts as the best embodiment of such third parties, with their "judicial review" capacities (p. 218). Although less institutionalized, other third parties, such as civil society organizations, social movements and scholarly associations, also play their role in the reflexive democracy field. Such a reflexive democracy perspective should not be confused with the so-called "multistakeholderism," however, as defined in the internet governance field during the WSIS and tentatively implemented by the IGF (Malcolm, 2008; Mathiason, 2008), or even earlier, by the Internet Corporation for Assigned Names and Numbers (ICANN) (Antonova, 2008). Multistakeholderism refers to stakeholders – understood as governments, the business sector and civil society – entering into a bargaining game with their own stakes and policy priorities. Reflexivity, by contrast, refers to facilitators such as hybrid forums and other dialogic democratic tools (Callon, Lascoumes and Barthe,

[3] According to Herbert Burkert, they have gained a true legitimacy in the European Union. In some countries their existence has even led to an erosion of the sense of privacy on the part of the population. Citizens entirely rely on them for the protection of their rights.

2009). As a result, it is not restricted to experts, stakeholders and "policy entrepreneurs" having found their "window of opportunity" (Kingdon, 1995) in the crisis of the nation state. According to Rosanvallon (2008: 237), it should be understood as "a larger vision of citizen participation and public deliberation."

As a consequence of and in close relation with the participation issue, the third concept identified by Rosanvallon is *the legitimacy of proximity* (or "closeness"). It is characterized by citizens' claims or communities' calls for the recognition of their specific concerns. It is noteworthy that it comes together with a demand for greater transparency and accountability on the part of political institutions. Citizens' adhesion to public policies is hence directly related to their perceived equity, which means that everybody has a voice. This applies in particular to normative institutions, and, as highlighted by Rosanvallon, to procedural justice (p. 270). It is not just the content of the norm that should be subject to social consent but its process of elaboration as well.

On the one hand, there is an increasing need for participation, permanent deliberation and consensus-building. On the other, transformations occur from a clear hierarchy of general norms (embedded in the principle of the rule of law; Chevallier, 2003) to a multiplicity of juxtaposed norms addressing various particularities, characterized by the plasticity of the forms they could take.

The conjunction of these developments, in line with globalization in all sectors, leads to the concept of multi-level governance. This should be understood not only from the local to the global levels but also as new or remade connections between different actors. It implies the reshaping of the international relations system, with an increasing, and sometimes redefined, role for intergovernmental organizations through specialized agencies (thoroughly analyzed in the information and communication technology [ICT] sector by Drake and Wilson, 2008). In addition, complex "trans-governmental networks" (Slaughter, 2004) develop. Beyond interactions between heads of state and ministries, a dense web of governmental authorities and powers at all levels are rebuilding international relations, international norms and practices. These macro-level transformations translate, in terms of domestic and infra-domestic regulations, into important roles for non-state actors and non-democratically controlled entities.

1.3 Micro-level transformations: digital technologies and regulations

1.3.1 Technical regulation as a source of fragmentation

In his acclaimed *Code and Other Laws of Cyberspace*, Lessig (1999b) shows how "architectures" or "codes" need to be considered as sources of regulation, together with legal, behavioral and market norms. As Lessig himself points out with historical examples, regulation and control by architecture, design and urban planning is not new, but with this book he elaborates, after Reidenberg (1998), how this also applies to cyberspace.

Going further than Lessig's concept of code as a compliance mechanism to law and regulation, Wu argues that code could also be used as a means of non-compliance or avoidance – in other words as an "anti-regulatory" mechanism – aimed at decreasing the costs encompassed by a given law to certain interest groups (Wu, 2003b). He documents the way that technology and the law are instrumentalized by various groups. Intellectual property right (IPR) holders, for instance, desperately try to maintain old economic arrangements despite the fact that technological evolution has led to new social usages, and thus, potentially, to new economic models (Curien and Moreau, 2007). This has led users of protected works of authorship to develop strategies to bypass legal lockers. P2P software and platforms, for instance, have been designed to exploit the loopholes, ambiguities and vulnerabilities of copyright law. The legal regime based on intermediaries or gatekeepers allowed the distribution of copyrighted work on a mass scale. The new software has simply removed the need for such intermediaries, thus "leaving primary enforcement against end-users as the only option" (Wu, 2003b). The fact that DRM technologies have later been developed and implemented, as analyzed by Séverine Dusollier in her contribution (Chapter 14), and have even been further complemented by anti-circumvention legislation, which she describes as "law (copyright) – technology (DRM) – law (anti-circumvention), a three-tiered protection scheme", is entirely compatible with Wu's argument, the protection (or compliance) scheme becomes intertwined with the avoidance scheme as "(copyright) law – (P2P) avoidance technology – (DRM) compliance technology – (DRM circumvention) avoidance technology – (anti-circumvention) law."

The same phenomenon is observed in the case of personal data protection, in which privacy rights are threatened by electronic commerce and advertising methods using personal data as the main resource. In a harsh critique of Lessig's thesis, Marc Rotenberg (2001) demonstrates that, by advocating the use of technology platforms such as the Platform for Privacy Preferences Project (P3P), developed by the World Wide Web Consortium (W3C) as a technology enabling users to choose how their personal data may be used by commercial websites, Lessig acknowledges the establishment of property rights on personal information. He highlights a "law becomes code becomes law" scheme. The example of the 1997 German multimedia law exhibits a "three-tiered protection scheme" in the privacy arena: privacy and fair information practice law – anonymity technology – anonymous payment services requirements law. In this case, the anti-regulatory mechanisms are not developed by final users and citizens but, rather, by organized economic actors (especially advertising companies). Here, again, there is an intertwining of avoidance and compliance not only through technology but also through formal and informal norms in an endless succession: privacy and fair information practice law – personal data collection by commercial companies' avoidance technology – social call for comprehensive privacy legislation against unfair commercial practices compliance behavior – P3P and other "notice and choice" platform avoidance technology.

Rotenberg thus reinforces Wu's thesis. When a law is disagreeable to a stakeholder group, and when the cost of legal and formal ways of amending it (e.g. through lobbying or other means of political influence) is high – either because compliance is based on social norms or because the group is disorganized (e.g. P2P users in copyright cases) – then the "code" or the technology becomes a viable means of law avoidance.

As the technology is both a compliance mechanism and an avoidance mechanism, technical regulation defines the space where alternative orders apply as well as the space's gatekeepers. Addressing the specific question of legitimacy in internet governance and building on Pierre Bourdieu's theory of legitimation and domination, Pierre Mounier (Chapter 8) shows how the internet is then fragmented into a myriad of small semi-private spaces in which governance is administered within restricted areas of legitimacy. This fragmentation is enabled and sustained by stakeholders' ability to self-regulate the semi-private space under their control – that is, to design norms and implement them at the same time. The underlying conditions for this ability to be realized, however, are the existence of multiple legitimacies and multi-level governance capabilities, instead of a single global legitimacy that would exert a hierarchical power to organize them.

1.3.2 Heterarchic governance, co-elaboration and the reordering of norms[4]

This fragmentation and the absence of hierarchy do not mean anarchy. Self-regulated spaces and actors do interact, if only by their respective strategies of compliance/avoidance, as discussed above. They thus constitute a heterarchic governance system (Jessop, 1998). They cannot entirely escape from the law, however, nor from other public regulations (Padovani and Pavan, 2009). As shown by political science research into the development of private and mixed public/private networks, the public authorities and formal regulations are not losing control (Mifsud Bonnici, 2008). Instead, they are exercising control through modified forms (Mayntz, 1998), over entities operating "in the shadow of hierarchy," to use an expression popularized in the literature on governance (Scharpf, 1999).

Moreover, the networked heterarchy is composed of more than just self-regulated spaces and actors. It also includes privately regulated public spaces. The particular and pivotal position of some actors as gatekeepers makes them able to act as control points in the internet space or as governments' instruments of law enforcement. ICANN, a key gatekeeper, has a central authority over the internet through its management of the domain name system (DNS) and internet protocol (IP) addresses – a critical resource (DeNardis, 2009). In addition to the ICANN case study included in his contribution, Milton Mueller comprehensively identifies and discusses the democratic issues involved with such a centralization of power and control exerted by a private organization under contract with a single government over all internet users (Mueller, 2002). Other important gatekeepers include network

[4] A heterarchy is a system of organization replete with overlap, multiplicity, mixed ascendancy and/or divergent but coexistent patterns of relationships. The concept of heterarchy was first employed in a modern context by Warren McCulloch (1945), to examine alternative cognitive structures and point out, in particular, that the human brain is not organized hierarchically. This has been widely used since then in the fields of artificial intelligence and computer design (Crumley, 1995).

operators, internet service providers (ISPs), search engines and, most recently, companies owning social networks.

The complexity of this heterarchy defines multiple orders, leading to the need to organize their self-organizations (Jessop, 2003). This implies *mutual recognition and mutual legitimation* between all actors, leading to a reordering of the process of norm-making, and *defining new patterns of interactions*, through cooperation, co-elaboration and other forms of interaction between the whole range of social and political actors (Kooiman, 1993, 2003). In the field of internet governance, two main ordering principles are witnessed: on the one hand, through the acquisition of new legitimacies, and, on the other, through reflexive governance.

New forms of legitimacies are acquired or regained through the *mutual recognition* of different actors or norm designers. Such a process has most notably been undertaken by intergovernmental organizations (IGOs) and non-governmental organizations. As demonstrated by Yves Schemeil (Chapter 9) in a broader perspective than the sole regulation of the information society, IGOs and NGOs are both experiencing "the strength of being weak" in the current crisis of democracy, representation and legitimacy faced by nation states. Although IGOs cannot claim representation and equal participation in the same way that nation states do, they stress accountability, transparency and openness as their main democratic principles. This allows them to continuously expand their domain of claimed competence. NGOs, for their part, are demanding more consideration for their competence. With IGOs and NGOs both attempting to reinforce their legitimacy, a "win-win strategy" operates, in which "both actors need cross-validation to fill the gap between their initial mandate and their actual impact." This process of mutual reinforcement by recomposing the political space is visible not only at this macro level but also at the micro level of online communities, as analyzed by Mounier.

Bob Jessop (2003) theorizes this understanding of governance as "the reflexive self-organization of independent actors involved in complex relations of reciprocal interdependence, with such self-organization being based on continuing dialogue and resource-sharing to develop mutually beneficial joint projects, and to manage the contradictions and dilemmas inevitably involved in such situations." *Dialogue* thus appears as an essential element in the governance process. Its reflexive and procedural rationality, with negotiated consent as its criterion of success and the network as its typical form, makes it the privileged principle for new ordering and for building new forms of legitimacy.

This is especially well illustrated through the post-WSIS process of the Internet Governance Forum. Indeed, the IGF has prevented itself until now from reaching any formal outcome, and even from making any recommendation. In its attempts to arrive at a consensus, however, its deliberative procedures impact the models and practices of representation, the forms of conflict and controversy resolution and even modes of public action. Although its mandate is, *inter alia*, to "discuss public policy issues related to key elements of Internet governance," it reproduces the functioning of the previous United Nations Working Group on Internet Governance (WGIG), which was constituted by forty members from governments, the private sector and civil society in a range of countries, "who all participated on an equal footing and in their personal capacity" (WGIG, 2005) for the elaboration of consensus. As previously mentioned, this non-constraining feature of the IGF makes it a perfect capacity-building instrument. It would certainly appear to be close to Habermas's ideal model of learning through procedures and argumentative logic, if only it did not raise calls for more openness and civil society inclusion, as attested by the proceedings of its first two years of discussions (IGF, 2008).

The IGF experience might be confirmed by other examples. On the basis of cases of environmental, biological and scientific resource management, Tom Dedeurwaerdere (Chapter 7) shows that subpolitic processes, by which non-state actors solve social problems through direct negotiations, tend to be more appropriate than processes of political cooperation and compromises among representative authorities, especially when global problems are addressed.

1.3.3 Normative consequences of privatization, proceduralization and prevention

Governance arrangements may therefore encompass various and complex forms, especially when they are focused on technical regulations and the subsequent strategies of compliance/avoidance, leading to the fragmentation of the internet. These fragmented spaces may redefine their own orders, and may interplay following different scenarios: antagonistic mechanisms of law compliance or avoidance, co-elaboration through mutual recognition, consensus-building through rational dialogic processes, or power relations confronted in agonistic arenas. The resulting heterarchic system itself requires a meta-heterarchic level (Jessop, 2003) to manage the interactions between components of this complex system.

Such a meta-heterarchy is mainly – but not only – organized on the internet by governments acting on the main control levers, which are the gatekeepers of the sub-spaces, especially ISPs. Procedural arrangements with them have important normative consequences.

In fact, although internet governance is a concept that has emerged only relatively recently in the public sphere, many of its involved issues, policies and arrangements have been discussed since the mid-1990s, when the internet became accessible to a larger and more heterogeneous public. This included discussions in various national, regional and international forums (Poullet, 2004), most notably on how to regulate content and identify liabilities on the internet (Marzouki, 2008a). It was the huge literature on internet regulation regimes – including the grey literature – that finally came up with the concept of "co-regulation." This, as analyzed by Benoît Frydman, Ludovic Hennebel and Gregory Lewkowicz in their contribution (Chapter 6), is a regime in which either regulation is co-elaborated and co-operated by a mix of public and private actors, or the state voluntarily delegates all or part of these activities to private parties. Internet governance is thus an extension of the concept of internet co-regulation as it was originally understood. This has been summarized in the WSIS's "Tunis agenda for the information society": "Internet governance is the development and application by Governments, the private sector and civil society, in their respective roles, of shared principles, norms, rules, decision-making procedures, and programmes that shape the evolution and use of the Internet" (WSIS, 2005). As so defined, the concept leads to three forms of meta-heterarchical arrangements: proceduralization, agencification and privatization.

Proceduralization has been theorized by Habermas as the means to reach legitimate decision-making, grounded on rational discourse and deliberation (Habermas, 1996). It also aims to achieve efficiency in terms of law and regulation in the framework of a shift of legitimacy from an input – democratic conditions – to an output – efficient results – orientation (Scharpf, 1999). These output-oriented criteria characterize the concept of "good governance," particularly as it has been defined at the European Union level, encompassing the five principles of "openness, participation, accountability, effectiveness and coherence" (EC [European Commission], 2001).

Proceduralization is also a means to achieve impartiality (Rosanvallon, 2008), and thus goes hand in hand with *agencification* (Christensen and Lægreid, 2006) in the move toward the regulatory state. In the field of digital technologies and internet governance, such agencies have proliferated, either as purely public ones or, more and more, as co-regulation public–private agencies. One of the identified characteristics of law transformation in a globalization context is the increased use of procedural rules instead of substantive rules (Frydman, 2004). Such a proceduralization trend is developed by Frydman, Hennebel and Lewkowicz in their chapter, most notably through their analysis of the "notice and take-down" provisions of the 2001 European Directive on Electronic Commerce, in terms of limiting the liability of ISPs hosting unlawful content on their servers. This delegation of law enforcement, once the "regal" function of the state, to private parties is also witnessed in other areas of internet governance, and has been identified, for instance, as one of the main trends in ICT-based public security policies (Marzouki, 2007). In the case of the internet addressing system, the transfer of the control of the root of the system in 1999 from the US government through contractual agreement to a private entity, ICANN, has been analyzed as a delegation of powers violating the US Administrate Procedures Act and the US constitution (Froomkin, 2000b).

This movement toward *privatization* is further developing in less "regal" areas. There is an increasing promotion of alternative dispute resolution (ADR) mechanisms, especially when implemented in online form (e-ADR). Although ADR traditionally concerns disputes that are not subject to judicial decisions, such mechanisms have proliferated, including in fields normally subject to legal litigation, with the aim of avoiding court battles (Schiavetta, 2004). Codes of conduct and other such incitements to specific behavior have gone further than simple charters or collections of "best practices." They have become part of contractual obligations, especially for ISPs, promoted at the national level by law or at the regional level, for instance, through European Union directives (Marzouki, 2006). In the field of copyright law, access to user-generated content is more and more governed by various private licensing, such as the Creative Commons licenses. As analyzed by Niva Elkin-Koren in her contribution (Chapter 15), such a development of private arrangements through contracting, sometimes without actual oversight by the legal authority, leads to an increase of private ordering in the governance of digital networks.

These developments bring about important normative consequences (Marzouki, 2006). The weakening of so-called "guarantee rights" – that is, the right to equality before the law, to an effective remedy, to a fair trial, to habeas corpus and the principle of no punishment without legal ordering – leads to serious impacts on the substance of fundamental rights and freedoms, on democracy and on the rule of law. The massive use of technical mechanisms, in particular the ex ante recourse to technical means to avoid infractions (and, more generally speaking, *to prevent any "deviating" behavior* before it can even be committed), instead of ex post enforcement leads to an entire reversal of perspective and values – and, incidentally, increases the complexity of the architecture, with consequences in terms of costs, transparency and reliability (Clarke, 1997).

There is a clear novelty here with respect to the early analyses, most notably those developed by Lessig. Although we are witnessing the changing nature of the state and the rising importance of private orderings, these movements have encountered important technical progress, whereby gatekeeping mechanisms (not only of contents, but also of protocols, bandwidth, data packets and other space gatekeeping means) have become central. Beyond the central role of gatekeepers (which is discussed further in section 1.4), Matthew Williams (2004) highlights that "[t]he effectiveness of technology as a regulator lies in its ability to alter behaviors, its ability to be shaped, its rapid adaptability, its ex ante approach, its wide reaching scope, its sensitivity toward criminal and sub-criminal activity, and its less visible approach to social control." Gatekeeping and automated enforcement thus threaten the democratic and legal means of control of public and private regulators that have been developed for the last four centuries, at least in most advanced countries.

1.4 How technologies transform the forms of self-governance

Among the various existing spaces, online communities have developed particularly innovative forms of self-governance relying on technical means, and these are worth analyzing in detail. IT has enabled people to meet in new ways, through online communities that organize the production, consumption and dissemination of information. The nature of what brings people together through digital technologies is, however, still so ambiguous that the abundant literature on these collectives has produced only vague or polysemic definitions that highlight different aspects (Proulx and Latzko-Toth, 2005): simply the co-presence long enough of the actors to form personal relationships (Rheingold, 2000); the stability and permanence of the group; the nature of shared activities (Gensollen, 2006); the uses of the medium (Amin and Roberts, 2008); the formalization of rules (Preece, 2000); and so on. It appears difficult to qualify the online social groups, all the more so when the metaphor of virtual community could be considered as "inadequate to characterize the panoply of social interactions, processes, and human sharing occurring in cyberspace" (Fernback, 2007). This diversity increases with the growing heterogeneity of internet users because of the massification and globalization of digitization (Zittrain, 2008). Actually, these online communities are characterized by the fact that different information technologies link up distant contributors from diverse backgrounds around a common interest, condition or project. These contributors' attachments to the collective vary widely, but often they are limited, or even very loose.

If community-based governance is not new, we analyze how digital technologies impact the capabilities of self-organization. This raises a set of questions, from how these groups, whose distance activity is mediated by technical artifacts, organize themselves to how they set their rules and manage their conflicts. One may wonder, in particular, whether technologies transform the governance of the groups that mobilize them. How do digital technologies impact on the actors' capacity to organize collective action? How do "scripts" (Akrich, 1992a), embedded in technology, achieve relationships between actors, role-sharing and the distribution of competences? Finally, how does technology empower collectives? Christine Hine (2000), for instance, shows that the resources allowing a specific group to be convincing and to attract an audience depend not only on the public's responses and the transmitter's contribution but also on the group's technological choices.

In what follows, we show that, even if a small group of "inventors" and "first users" happens to master the main technical options, users keep a wide plasticity in their technical choices. They impact therefore on the techno-organizational dynamic of alternative communities.

1.4.1 *The automation of governance*

The governance mechanisms of online communities are no more "spontaneous" than those of offline communities. Contrary to the libertarian utopia of the internet (Barlow, 1995; Turner, 2006b) – an extension of the mid-1990s hackers' ideology (Turner, 2006a) – e-communities are very well organized, and their regulation relies on systems or rules organizing problem-solving and interactions, and conditions for participation and conflict resolution. Even in communities that are sometimes considered transgressive or marginal, such as sex picture traders or queer groups, a social order, mediated by technological options, is established that necessitates formalized rules and forms of policing (Slater, 2002; Nip, 2004).

Because they are ICT-mediated, though, these groups have different characteristics from those that are offline. Apart from the extreme diversity of e-communities differentiated by their medium, size, subject, members' equipment, and so on, their performance on the basis of digital technologies alters their ways of constructing and applying these rules, especially because they are *delegated to automated devices*. Pointing at those devices does not mean that technology has to be considered as an autonomous form of regulation; technology is intricately connected with other modalities, such as legal and social norms (Callon, Law and Rip, 1986; Hosein, Tsiavos and Whitley, 2003).

The regulatory tasks assigned to robots concern different aspects of regulation. First, these automatic devices can be given the job of protecting the community against attacks that could endanger it or against various kind of vandalism: either attacks of a general nature, such as spam, or specific ones, such as messages from trolls. They may also, more simply, combat the inadequate use of common resources or deviant behaviors.

Second, automatic devices organize collective action. Indeed, they support or facilitate the division of labor, by articulating tasks and distributing competences (Akrich, 1992b). Certain tools, for example, serve to coordinate the group's work by allowing the merging of outputs, while avoiding inconsistencies (Iannacci, 2005). They may define the participants by establishing the conditions of entry and the authorized formats of intervention, by setting up automated procedures for the qualification of participants and participation. This is the purpose, for instance, of the "stars" and other means of recognition given to the most active members of online forums, the profiles of evaluation on eBay, the contributors to Wikipedia, etc. (Lampe and Resnick, 2004; Méadel, 2006; Auray, Poudat and Pons, 2007). They can also be mobilized to collectively govern the community, as exemplified by the sophisticated voting mechanisms described by Nicolas Auray (Chapter 10). Designed *a minima* as a coordination tool, technical artifacts can be seen as organizational solutions to implement new decision-making processes in communities that are difficult to regulate because of their fragmentation and heterogeneity, especially when the reasons for members' mobilization and involvement are uncertain (Wright and Street, 2007).

The delegation of all these tasks – which most of the time could be performed by an administrator or an authority – to an automated mechanism is not only or exclusively chosen for efficiency (even if it may make "policing" tasks simpler and more effective), as shown by Christophe Aguiton and Dominique Cardon (Chapter 13). Automated procedures seem to *create trust*, because they ensure equal treatment for all contributors, reduce arbitrariness and allow for the participation of strangers or anonymous participants. This is precisely the case when, after the participants have been consulted on the internet, the choice of topics selected for the debates is delegated to a lexicographic robot reputedly capable of respecting the constraints fixed by the organization (openness to all, a refusal to delegate and decisions based on consensus).

The use of automated governance tools can also favor the implementation of all kinds of *democratic mode of organization*, such as those constrained by consensus. This form of governance is based both on the denial of delegation to representatives and on open and free participation. Decisions can be taken only at the end of a (long) process (relying on "time, bargaining and negotiation," as Aguiton and Cardon put it) to end up with a statement to which no one is directly opposed, *hic et nunc*. This makes the problems of policing even more complex, since any capitalization or control has to reach a consensus (Papacharissi, 2004).

The delegation to these tools is therefore believed to introduce neutrality into the procedures of group management. This is not a matter of generalized equality, however. These same tools develop procedures of qualification, for example, according to the intensity of individuals' contributions or their degree of competence as evaluated by the other members.

The reliance on technology does not totally prevent arbitrariness and power relations, however. The communities may be reflexive, but the rules are not discussed in their entirety. The increasing weight of proceduralization demands that a choice be made between the transparency of decisions and their production. Authority cannot be delegated entirely to robots (Akrich and Méadel, 2007). Even when rules have a large degree of formalization (which is by no means always the case), they are not sufficient to regulate the group. Designers of the system and early adopters often have a strong influence on the regulation of these groups and communities. The constitution and perpetuation of collective spaces stem from the informal activities of support for the group and of conflict management – activities that are distributed between some participants, especially the most active of them, who then generate a strong political influence on the dynamic of the group, its regulation and its production.

1.4.2 Characterizing online communities by their purpose

To what extent do technical artifacts, automated robots or, more generally, systems for managing online collectives transform and format communities? Does the elimination of the physical or geographical constraints and the removal of social barriers enable free participation in the activities of a collective?

Differentiating between e-communities according to whether they exist offline or not could yield a first answer on the basis of a contrast that is very often made in the literature (Kollock and Smith, 1999; Papadakis, 2003; Nip, 2004). This would imply that, on the one hand, there are communities that are created online and whose entire activity, at least in the initial phase, takes place on the internet. The link between the members then exists only via the artifact, or at least is formed through it. On the other hand, there are the communities that first existed offline, and then redeployed (all or part of) their activity onto the web, with the offline part imprinting the group's governance (Baym, 1995). How do the norms of these groups change when there is a redeployment of the online activity? Christine Hine (Chapter 12), Nicolas Auray and Pierre Mounier point out that the external constraints, such as legal regulation, social status or scientific reputation, are not made operative in the same way in these two types of community. They impact strongly on the norms of both, nevertheless, without clear and distinct differences between pure online and other communities. Most communities are, indeed, embedded in social and political spaces that transcend offline/online boundaries. As the case studies show, it is impossible to establish a strong differentiation either among their procedures of regulation or in the degree of intervention of technical artifacts.

The differences between communities probably lie in a more structured way in the differentiation between stable groups and ephemeral ones, or groups whose constituency is permanently evolving. Indeed, the groups constituted offline tend to be more stable. The *instability of the community*, in terms of members' renewals, poses specific problems of continuity in terms of common norms and practices. It therefore imposes constraints on the organization of the collective, as shown, for example, in the comparison made by Hine between marginal sex picture traders and networks of biologists. Although digital technologies support, in both cases, reflexive debates on goals, principles and practices, the role granted to automated regulation seems to be more structuring in unstable communities.

This sustainability of the collectives is directly related to the object that brings the members together and binds them (Shirky, 2008). The community is defined by its form of regulation and its procedural mechanisms, as well as by the nature of its production and activity, and by the way in which members contribute to the construction and life of the collective. We propose a typology of online communities that takes into account what they produce, both for the individual and for the collective. Four types can therefore be distinguished: *exchange, empowerment, consensus-building* and *collective work communities.*

Exchange communities: above all, the members exchange information and/or goods. Commercial exchange is simply one of the possibilities in this type of community, and transactions a possible outcome among others. The model is that of exchange, with the expectation of quid pro quo, whether it be of a good or information. The exchanges of information in Usenet forums, of assessments on eBay and of information goods on file-sharing platforms, and the cases discussed by Auray and Elkin-Koren, constitute various examples of such communities. Is this a "true" community when what brings the members together is very limited: a common consumption activity? As with the case of the mass media, it creates, nonetheless, a sort of "imagined community" (Anderson, 2006). The platform, the technical artifact, sets up a public space in which the individuals enter into relations with others who resemble them, and with whom they can mutually compare their behaviors.

Empowerment: here, too, the members of the collective exchange information and data, but their contributions provide them with more than simply something known and expected in return. The member contributes to the collective activity without expecting an immediate return, apart from the debt that the collective may feel it owes him/her, or a symbolic reward in terms of recognition and reputation. The participation contributes to increase the competence of the members of the group, and to improve their level of information, as illustrated by the case study of biologists (see Hine's chapter).

Consensus-building: through its exchanges the community tries to construct a collective agreement, a common contribution on the theme or in the field that binds members together. Its unity no longer depends solely on a shared interest; it produces a conception of the world (even its own world) endowed with some coherence, and exportable to other spheres. The group can therefore become visible from the outside as such, even if it does not necessarily stand for this aim. A typical example of such communities, analyzed by Aguiton and Cardon, is the one formed by participants in the World Social Forums.

Collective work: the members of the collective come together to generate a real, programmed and formalized common output. This corresponds to the emblematic image of software developers working on open projects. In this case, the degree of integration achieved by the members is high, because the collective is identifiable as such as a creative entity. The collective may also be more fragmented, however, for example when the actors contribute freely to the common project, with relatively few barriers to entry, as in the case of contributors to Wikipedia.

1.4.3 Technical artifacts, deliberation and self-policing

Of course, these are ideal types. In many cases the activity of communities belongs to more than one of these types. As shown for instance by Madeleine Akrich and Cécile Méadel in their contribution (Chapter 11), some patient communities may answer the questions of new patients (empowerment), establish and adopt collective positions on their health problem in the public sphere (consensus-building), and produce common tools, for example for monitoring their pathology (collective work).

In each of these ideal types, technical mechanisms have different structuring power, and the share left to automated regulation varies, as shown by Mounier. In addition to the stability of the group, mentioned above, another criterion seems to come into play: the intensity of the debate on how the group defines itself, its objective, its rules and its modalities of exchange. This definition could be argued to be at the heart of the process of common production, and to become the most significant and discussed part of the exchange, as in the consensus-building type, or to a lesser extent in the empowerment communities. It could be limited to certain aspects of the self-definition, as the content of the common project in the collective work communities. Conversely, it could be well known and indisputable, as in the exchange communities, in which every member is loosely involved. A structural laxity of the common definition creates a convergence of thought around it, allowing for the most diverse appropriations, and enriches the range of valid contributions; valid, but unhelpful for the purposes of automation. The more the production of the group is complex and continuous, the more the group is stable, and the less the regulation of the group is delegated to machines.

In fact, the regulation of these communities can be conceived either as a collective task on the basis of consensus or as a higher principle – which can, of course, be circumvented or disregarded, but which can in no way be ignored. When regulation is a collective task, which corresponds primarily to the exchange and empowerment types of communities, policing is constantly under negotiation, transformed and debated. These very debates enable the collective to be defined and perpetuated. When regulation is a higher principle, which relates essentially to the consensus-building and collective work communities, policing is not intangible, but is transformed through decisions at a higher level, which may be triggered by suggestions or transgressions at grassroots level. This second model is not necessarily less democratic than the first; there may be consultation between the members or delegation to representatives. The point is, again, that the more intensive the orientation toward collective/joint production, the less governance tends to be delegated to artifacts. Even in spaces such as that of Wikipedia, in which many tools frame participation, much room is left for discussions on the encyclopedia's main options (especially everything concerning the verification of content), as pointed out by Mounier. When regulation is not delegated to automats, regulation and the definition of collective work are negotiated at the same time.

Finally, an important common characteristic of these groups is the *participants' "goodwill."* No matter how sophisticated the regulatory tools and how inventive the "political" procedures organizing decision-making may be, the existence of the group and its development stem above all from the free participation of the parties. This comment weighs the role of ICT governance insofar as it is not imposed on members unless they agree, at least by default. This is somewhat specific to online communities, as they form or are joined on the basis of individuals' will to participate.

This by no means applies to all fragmented spaces, however, especially those resulting from norm reordering that is increasingly based on private, or privatized, orders. These new orders apply de facto to individual participants, with or without their adhesion or consent, and redefine the balance between public and private governance.

1.5 A renewed debate on public versus private governance

As highlighted in particular by Lessig (1999b), one of the fundamental features of digital technologies is that they allow the decentralized implementation of coding and norms. By coding digital sequences, individuals can easily make any rule about their condition of access and use self-enforceable. As pointed out by Eric Brousseau (2004) and others, in particular Mark Lemley (1998), this ability to control access to and the use of digital goods is, in fact, extended to many activities that are not fully digital, as the same capabilities of erecting digital fences and tracking uses can be used to monitor digital spaces on which coordination is organized. Those in control of these spaces – whether they are market places, "communities," commons, collective repositories of information goods or whatever – can de facto exclude or include relational networks, which allow the imposition of norms of behavior both online and offline if access to offline activities is conditioned by online participation (think, for instance, of a market place). The result of these technological developments is, in economic terms, a substantial fall of the relative cost of self-regulation, as compared to public or state-based regulation.

1.5.1 A shifting balance of powers

The result is a substantial shift in the balance between public and private regulations. Traditionally the extent of private/self-regulation is bounded by the poor enforcement capabilities of private regulators (Brousseau, Schemeil and Sgard, 2010; Brousseau and Raynaud, 2011). Self-regulations are based on adherence. Members of a self-regulated community compare the costs of compliance with the benefits they draw from the collective regulation. They are free to opt out of the system. The only cost is that they thereby lose the benefits associated with the self-regulated community, whatever they are – reduced transaction costs, a lower level of risk, access to pooled resources, risk-sharing, etc. Because private regulators usually do not have strong means of retaliation to hand, (or the established legitimacy to use them), they are unable to deter all types of opportunistic behavior. This explains why public regulators are often involved in the oversight of the behavior of self-regulators. The latter need to be recognized by the public regulator in order to enhance their enforcement capability. In that case, the public regulator can make compliance with the self-regulation mandatory. Recognition establishes a balance between self-/private regulators and the public regulator, which allows the latter to impose on the former constraints linked to the "general" interest (that is, when the public system of regulation is itself designed to guarantee that the collective interest, and not only the interest of a clique in power, is taken into account in public decision-making). In turn, the public regulator benefits from the expertise and the potentially lower costs of regulation by private regulators.

This traditional balance is strongly challenged today. There are two reasons for this (Brousseau, 2007). First, with the globalization of many issues, the ability of public regulators to impose credible threats and to uphold the general interest is weakening as a result of their national scope. Second, the decreasing cost of decentralized enforcement arising from digital technologies' capabilities boosts the capability of self-regulators to regulate without relying on national state enforcement capabilities. If access to information spaces can be controlled technically, then the need for last-resort "physical exclusion" from the social game decreases.

It is important to point out that this shift toward a higher relative intensity of private and self-regulation as compared to public regulation is due both to decreasing costs of private enforcement and to the decreasing legitimacy of public regulators to establish the general interest. At the same time, private/self-regulators remain poorer holders of the general interest than public ones. This is a result simply of their having less diversity in their constituency. By virtue of their constitution, public regulators receive a mandate from a wider diversity of stakeholders than private regulators do (Brousseau, Schemeil and Sgard, 2010). Consequently, with the extension of the relative scope of private regulations as compared to public ones, there is a high risk of collective regulation capture, to the benefit of some, which would be especially detrimental for those who are marginalized with the rise of the globalization and of the information society.

Both issues are well highlighted in the contributions by Dusollier and Elkin-Koren. The former points out how DRM technologies lead to a reshaping of the balance between copyright holders and users, to such an extent that it has become problematic. This is also an argument made by Lessig (2004), who highlights how DRM systems turn most of the cultural public domain into private property. This leads to a massive transfer of wealth, which benefits those who hold the rights. Moreover, given the non-rival nature of information goods, the efficiency of this new "enclosure" movement is questionable. The usual reply to this last comment by those who applaud these developments is to point out that, if a lower degree of privatization is more efficient, then it should come as a result of open competition. They see in the growth of free/open-source software and Creative Commons licenses an unprompted reply to this enclosure movement. For those goods to which the "tragedy of the anti-commons" would apply, the spontaneous solution of society should be the organization of self-governed communities involved in the provision and consumption of club goods, the access to which is largely open if no congestion constraints occur.

Elkin-Koren shows, however, that the efficiency of "laissez-faire" policies in matters of regulation is not totally convincing. By focusing on the Creative Commons licensing regimes, she makes the nice point that decentralized regulations do not always have the same properties as centralized ones, even if the former are attempting to mimic the latter. To put it another way, Creative Commons licenses do not reproduce the public domain. They introduce transaction costs, and, since various regimes of licensing coexist, they may result in inconsistencies in the rights that are circulated among agents.

The optimal balance between public and private regulations is complex in a global and innovation-based society, however. Indeed, as pointed out above, and in many publications on global governance (e.g. Brousseau *et al.*, forthcoming), the bodies and channels necessary to build and protect the collective interest at the global level are lacking. National governments tend to defend their sovereignty above all, and, in the best cases, the interests of their national stakeholders (Deibert, 2009). Private and self-regulation are built in narrow domains in the interests of the club members, without consideration of the generated externalities. In a context of permanent innovation – both in matters of technology and of uses – the traditional orders are often no longer able to reach their goals and ensure a sustainable level of stability, security and efficiency, thus threatening the collective confidence and potentially hindering the diffusion of innovations and their benefits. This is why private actors might have incentives to provide regulations and norms that consider the collective interest.

This is well illustrated by the contribution by Bruno Deffains and Jane Winn (Chapter 16), who compare the contrasted path of development of e-commerce on both shores of the Atlantic Ocean. According to them, the European Union's attempt to protect consumers in order to boost the development of e-commerce has failed to provide the incentives to private operators to enhance the quality of their services. In the United States, the responsibility for developing trust in e-commerce has remained in the hands of online sellers and platform operators. This has led them to compete in this field, and the authors consider competition to have had a doubly positive effect. First, it has led to services that efficiently protect consumers. Second, this has boosted creativity on the e-commerce providers' side, resulting in a strong competitive advantage for US-based operators compared to their foreign competitors.

It should not be automatically concluded, however, that the absence of public regulations always leads to efficiency. In the specific case just mentioned above, many other factors are at play. For instance, the early and strong development of the internet in the United States, the weaker concentration of the US population as compared to the European one, which favors the development of remote sales, and the size and homogeneity of the US consumer market as compared to the fragmented and multicultural one in Europe all help explain why the dynamics of e-commerce emerged and developed initially in the United States (Kraemer *et al.*, 2006). Moreover, in addition to competition, the US liability laws and the related high level of judicial conflict explain why there were incentives to deal efficiently with the security of transactions and with consumer protection. The incentives might have been different in Europe. Thus, this example is neither a demonstration of systematic regulatory failure nor proof of public regulation inefficiency. It is simply a reminder of the well-known fact that public regulations can lead, in some circumstances, to undesired results.

1.6 Conclusion: toward guarantees provided by the open dynamic of governance processes

Digital technology provides its users with information management capabilities – especially in matters of instantaneous exchange, large-scale sharing and long-term memory – that allow for a greater decentralization, flexibility and adaptability of governance. The technology is neither the main cause of nor the solution to governance issues, however.

Indeed, technology is opening options, not guaranteeing results. The "code" does not substitute for the "law." Circumvention/anti-circumvention techniques and the loop they generate demonstrate that codes of conduct and conventions – which are norms guaranteed by mechanisms of retaliation in case of deviation – have to shape the use of the technology in order to guarantee the proper operation of the latter. More generally, all kinds of organizational and institutional patterns interact with the development of the technology to make possible new practices, which in turn raise new challenges in terms of governance. An open-ended dynamic results from this, by which new governance mechanisms are experimented with and implemented by all types of communities and actors.

These practices and related tools are appropriated by a wide diversity of stakeholders in the context of a more general call for more participative governance. This call is largely the result of the weakening of national governments (whose capabilities are diminished by globalization) and of their decreasing legitimacy (largely linked to citizens' calls for more open societies). The rise of the knowledge-based society, characterized by a rapid pace of innovation, is also relevant, since most norms and, more generally, the established (economic, social, political) orders are challenged by new technical capabilities, social practices and people's ability to coordinate. This results in the combination of decentralized collective action (at the infranational level) and global networks, which in turn initiates head-on competition between large numbers of producers of norms.

These developments, together with the decreasing cost of private regulation – essentially thanks to technical enforcement – change the balance of power between private and public regulators. The ability of the latter to oversee the former declines. As a result, a clear hierarchy of norms, as well as consideration of the interests of all stakeholders in society, can no longer be guaranteed by a central and dominant actor/organization, widening the potential for private capture and inefficient foreclosure. In such a context, the collective interest is better served by open competition (and cooperation) among regulators, since network users benefit from exit options and checks and balances among authorities. This leads to a regulatory landscape with neither a clear hierarchy of regulators and norms nor a clear division of powers to guarantee efficient and balanced governance.

At the same time, the needed plasticity of governance mechanisms (to adapt to innovation and the evolution of collective preferences) and the empowerment of individuals and communities in matters of governance call for political oversight of the technological infrastructure of governance so as to ensure openness and neutrality. Political oversight cannot rely on participatory processes only, however, because of their manipulability and the high potential for capture by special interest groups. A well-functioning government with a division of powers *à la* Montesquieu is also needed, therefore. The insufficient flexibility of parliament and the courts, as well as the possible non-neutrality of the executive, call for a second level of oversight by citizens, however, whether organized or not, conditioned by the transparency guaranteed by a free press and the development of information networks. The three principles of governance highlighted by Rosanvallon – namely impartiality, reflexivity and proximity – characterize nicely the sources of a renewed legitimacy of political governance that would fit with the possibilities opened up in this respect by digital technologies.

All these trends suggest a fragmentation of the collective space into heterarchic systems of governance, more reticulous and biological than hierarchic and designed. They are characterized by redundancies, resilience and checks and balances, and are also difficult to control and optimize. This is why the resulting order does not draw on rational design but, rather, on strategies of leadership, either political or technological. A key issue for all kinds of actors is accordingly to become "gatekeepers," able to structure communities given the strong "first-mover" advantage and the "winner takes all" effect that characterize competition in an innovation-based and networked society and economy. In this competitive framework, strategies of mutual recognition/legitimation among gatekeepers is also essential, contributing to the heterarchization of governance. A consequence of these developments is the "doomed to failure" character of attempts to build a totally consistent and rational governance framework (*à la* Montesquieu), either on a public (the United Nations, the United States) or on a private (Microsoft, ICANN) basis. On the one hand, governance is inherently characterized by inefficiencies, on account of overlaps, missing links, redundancies and maladjustments. On the other, the fear of a "big brother" able to monitor the system, whether benevolent or not, is a mirage.

In this context, in which there are always all kinds of exit strategies available and a balance of power, consensus-based modes of regulation become central. Consensus brings the notion of veto, hence adhesion. Norms cannot be totally binding. They are permanently being negotiated and challenged, and thus they are open to evolutionary change. Norms become references rather than rules. This situation allows innovation, but it also raises a security issue: the non-stability and "fuzziness" of norms continually challenge investments and status. This is the reason why the process by which norms evolve becomes central. Procedures frame the process of norm development, and then provide guarantees to the various stakeholders. Digital technologies play a key role here, since they provide tools not only to facilitate but also to guarantee ongoing negotiations, to enforce and check compliance with the procedures and to dynamically implement norms. They also contribute to guarantees as to the fairness and "neutrality" of theses processes, hence generating trust, both by automating procedures and by keeping track of all actions.

These new modes of governance, relying on consensual, evolving and soft norms, apply even to the way that states attempt to oversee the evolution of the key resources of the internet. Weakened governments – characterized by restricted technical capabilities in the face of the cloud of innovators, of the global and decentralized character of the internet and of their shrinking legitimacy to watch over information exchanges – rely increasingly on externalization and cooperation to keep control of the information infrastructure, whether their intentions are to guarantee liberal and democratic constitutions or to exercise despotic control. This translates into multiples interactions with firms, NGOs, IGOs and all types of communities, which both bound their governance capability and constitute ways to divide power so as to guarantee checks and balances. Guarantees and capabilities tend to depend upon the multipolarity of governance and upon negotiations between "power-poor" rulers.

In a public versus private perspective, the current trends raise important issues. Indeed, the increasing "privatization" of governance has two effects. First, it promotes the development of "prevention" (digital fences, the switching of users, etc.), in order to punish potential deviancy before any deviation occurs. This might become a powerful obstacle to innovation, and then threaten one of the pillars of economic growth and social evolution. Second, the clear need for conflict resolution mechanisms can be seen to be emerging, since decentralized innovation leads to all kinds of maladjustments. This results in a weakening of existing rights, because they tend to become "fuzzier" if there are uncertainties in conflict resolution and interdependences.

PART I

The Evolution of Regulatory Frameworks in Perspective

2 *Property and commons in internet governance*

MILTON L. MUELLER

2.1 Introduction

The construction of a global governance regime for the internet is taking place alongside, and is intimately connected with, a radical reappraisal of the nature of property rights over information and networks. An intellectual and political movement has emerged to challenge exclusive property rights over informational goods and to promote the concept of openness in communication information policy (Kranich, 2004; Benkler, 2006). The free/open-source software movement can be considered the grandfather of this tendency. Since the early 1980s it has pioneered new forms of collaborative, non-hierarchical organization for software production (Raymond, 2001; Benkler, 2006) while creating a new legal institution, the General Public License (GPL), to protect its jointly developed software products from exclusive appropriation (Gay, 2002; Weber, 2004). These precedents later converged with intellectual and political resistance to extensions of copyright and trademark protection into the digital domain (Boyle, 1997a; Lessig, 1999a). The copyright resistance has produced its own alternative institution, the Creative Commons license, and its own political movement in national legislatures and international organizations focused on preserving the public domain.

From the same political roots has grown a movement for network neutrality (Lemley and Lessig, 2001; Wu, 2003a) and support for unlicensed radio spectrum (Werbach, 2004). In their rejection of exclusivity and support for openness, the net neutrality (NN) and unlicensed spectrum advocates take the logic of the "commons" into new territory. Its political demands pertain not to pure informational goods, such as software and digital content, but to networks and bandwidth – resources that, unlike software or digitized information, are subject to physical scarcity and are not nonrival in consumption.

All the same, the ethic, the policies and the politics of open-source software, network neutrality, opposition to excessive copyright claims and software patents, etc. reveal a striking family resemblance: a reliance on commons over private property rights for certain kinds of resource allocation; and a valorization of openness and freedom over exclusion. The dialogue on internet governance participates fully in the ongoing debate over "commons" and "property" in communication information policy.

This discourse tends to dichotomize private and common property radically, however. The two property regimes are counterposed as hostile and mutually exclusive. On one side of the debate, "the commons" (note the definite article) is presented as something large, public-spirited and inclusive while the role of private property rights is either ignored or denigrated as enclosed, restrictive, selfish. On the other side of the political spectrum, "commons" is equated with an all-embracing economic communism or overbearing regulation, and "the market" (note, again, the use of the definite article) defended rigidly as if it were the answer to all problems.

This chapter reexamines the property/commons dichotomy as it applies to internet governance. Its main point is that commons and property are not mutually exclusive, totalizing principles for economic organization but merely distinct methods of organizing access to resources. The two methods can and do coexist, and are often interdependent and mutually reinforcing. I argue that we need to deromanticize the idea of the commons in our debates over information policy and internet governance. Progressive intellectuals should not be seduced by the warm and fuzzy communitarian overtones of the commons ideal; pro-market liberals need to overcome their association of commons with "communism" and heavy-handed regulation. Both need to engage with the myriad ways in which commons and market interact. Both must accept the commons' actual nature as just another method of organizing access to resources.

As an extension of this approach, I pay careful attention to the specific political economy factors that sustain or advance commons-like arrangements in telecommunications and internet governance. On examining the actors and interests involved in promoting (or opposing) and constructing (or disassembling) commons arrangements, a pattern is discovered. The commons as an institutional option is rarely implemented as the product of communitarian compacts or a sharing ethic. It is more likely to be an outcome of interest group contention. In this view, a commons is a way for an alliance of non-dominant actors to "neutralize" a strategic resource that is, or might be, controlled by a dominant actor.

The chapter begins with a conceptual discussion of commons and exclusive property in informational and network goods. Next I examine four case studies involving the interaction of commons and private property. The first case is about equal-access arrangements in long-distance telephony in the United States; the next is about the internet protocols and the end-to-end principle; the third is about network neutrality; the last is about domain names and IP address governance. Three of these four case studies were selected because they cover the three fundamental areas in which policy issues related to exclusive rights might arise in internet governance: the open or proprietary status of the core internet standards (the TCP [transmission control protocol]/IP case); the open or proprietary status of the internet's bandwidth (the net neutrality case); and the property status of critical internet identifier resources (the ICANN case). The telephone long-distance case, on the other hand, provides a useful historical contrast to the more contemporary internet cases. It proves that many of the same policy issues and economic relationships arise in different technological and historical contexts, while revealing how the relationship between property and commons changes dynamically over time. The institutional arrangements in this case also parallel certain features of the domain name market in the ICANN case.

It would have been possible, of course, to document many other instances of the interdependent relationship between property and commons. Research on local music scenes in Brazil, for example, have explored how the absence of copyright on music leads to a robust private market for live performances and self-produced CDs (Lemos, 2007). There is a growing body of research on the diffusion of hybrid business models that mix the offering of open-source software with the provision of proprietary software or software-related services (e.g. Bonaccorsi, Giannangeli and Rossi, 2006). Given the theme of this volume, however, I have chosen to concentrate on cases directly relevant to global internet governance.

2.2 The interdependence of commons and property rights

Commons may be thought of as resources upon which every member of a community has an equal claim. In the special case of an open-access commons, the community is unbounded, allowing any individual who comes along to appropriate some of the resource. More frequently, the community is bounded, and the common ownership rights apply only to a specified group. Elinor Ostrom (1990: 30) defines common pool resources as a "natural or man-made resource system that is sufficiently large as to make it costly (but not impossible) to exclude potential beneficiaries" from appropriating resources.

Interestingly, it is virtually impossible to define what we mean by a commons without referring in some way to private use or appropriation. An open-access commons may allow any individual (within a possibly bounded group) to withdraw resource units from the relevant resource pool at will. Alternatively, it may establish, through some collective governance process, generally applicable rules restricting the time, manner, volume or type of appropriation among the members. A private property regime, in contrast to a commons, parcels out the resource into independently administered units, and gives owners the right to exclude others from appropriation. Access to the resource is regulated through the interaction of buyers and sellers in the market. Thus, far from being diametrically opposed to private appropriation in principle, a commons is simply a different principle for governing or regulating private appropriation. Nonproprietary status can, furthermore, stimulate private productive activity by eliminating the need for strategic behaviors designed to avoid or preempt free-riding by competitors. Producers become more willing to share labor, knowledge and resources in productive ways if they know that the shared resources cannot be appropriated by others and used against them. Everyone's right to appropriate is equalized.

Not only are commons and market related in terms of their purpose but, empirically, it is clear that they coexist and are almost always interdependent and interacting parts of a wider economic system. Resources governed as commons are usually adjacent and linked to processes that involve private ownership and market prices. The herder whose livestock grazes on the common field nevertheless owns the cows and is often interested in selling them or their milk in a market. The Wi-Fi user who avails him-/herself of public internet access has exclusive possession of his/her computer terminal and may be using it to sell his/her services or to buy services from others. Free software for web servers supports private networks and privately developed websites that engage in e-commerce. As Ostrom (1990) has written, "In field settings, public and private institutions frequently are intermeshed and depend on one another, rather than existing in isolated worlds."

How can we understand this interdependence better? Why do we get specific mixtures of the two in specific components of the economy? There are two theoretically grounded methods for answering this question. One relies on the physical characteristics of resources; the other relies on transaction costs. Both identify important considerations, but, I argue, neither is sufficient to explain empirically either the political demand for a given commons–market complex or the actual results that are implemented. The most important factor determining where commons are located in relation to exclusively owned resources in a specific historical context, I maintain, is interest group contention.

One simple and commonly held idea is that a resource's status as a commons is defined by its physical-economic characteristics. Information, for example, has special economic characteristics as a nonrival resource. Resources are said to be rival in consumption when my use of it precludes your use, or my consumption "uses up" some of the resource. Nonrival resources, such as certain kinds of information or digitally encoded software, do not diminish in quantity or value when one person consumes it. Since physical scarcity is often thought to justify exclusive ownership and use of resources, the absence of such scarcity might indeed make it inefficient and wrong to create exclusivity by assigning property rights to information. This is the approach taken by some in the free software movement (Gay, 2002).

The simple fact that information is nonrival, however, doesn't necessarily eliminate all normative justifications for exclusivity, nor does it explain, in a positive sense, whether institutions emerge to define and enforce exclusivity. The persistence of copyrights and patents for centuries shows that social institutions can and will create exclusivity whether or not the resource involved is nonrival in consumption. Almost everyone would recognize the normative right of people to exclude others from access to information they have in certain circumstances. I have, for example, thousands of document files on my computer. If anyone were to demand a right to copy all of them (or any one of them), I would be justified to refuse, even though giving out such copies would not diminish my ability to use them. My refusal might be based on a number of factors: personal privacy, a desire to withhold from public view writings too embarrassingly bad to see the light of day, or a desire not to let others benefit from hours of work unless I received appropriate payment or recognition.

This logic works both ways. Just as it is easy to find instances of, and justifications for, exclusion from access to nonrival resources, it is not that unusual to find public policy decisions to create nonexclusive access to resources that are rival in consumption. Think of public park lands, primary education or universal health care. In their discussion of public goods, Inge Kaul and Ronald Mendoza (2003) make the point that one cannot derive the actual regime used to produce and deliver a good a priori from the characteristics of the good. They call this the distinction between the resource's "basic properties" and its "socially determined status" and note that "the properties of (non) rivalry and (non)excludability only signal a good's potential for being (public) private – not its de facto provision status." This argument opens up new possibilities in terms of treating objects as public goods, but it also could be used to justify moving in the opposite direction.

Transaction cost theory is another way to attempt to explain why we might get a particular configuration of commons–property interdependences. Coasian theory suggests that, if the costs of defining, monitoring and enforcing exclusive rights are too high, then either an absence of exclusive ownership or an institutionalized commons might become the preferred solutions to the problem of regulating private appropriation. This works, up to a point. Empirically, the ease or difficulty with which people can be excluded from access to the resource does seem to be an important factor affecting the nature of resource regulation regimes, as Ostrom's work demonstrates. One important limitation, however, is that classical transaction cost theory does not address the complementary relationship between a private good and a commons; it tends to look at specific resource regimes in isolation. In addition, the minimization of transaction costs does not always explain outcomes. For example, in the first case study below, I show how the US regulatory system willfully incurred enormous transaction costs in order to create an equal access "commons" regime around the interconnection of long-distance carriers and local exchanges. The important question in this case is not whether the transaction costs were high or low but whether the actors involved thought the transaction costs incurred were worth the benefits they believed the regime would deliver.

Transaction cost theory predicts that one will get a commons arrangement when the value of a resource is so low and contention for it so limited that it makes no sense to incur the expense of creating private property rights. One may also get an institutionalized commons, however, when the resource is a widely shared input central to an industry, its value is extremely high and contention for it is so intense that only a commons arrangement can provide a political-economic equilibrium. An example of the latter is the "tragedy of the anti-commons," which refers to the proliferation of private ownership claims in a resource space to such a degree that control becomes so fragmented and the degree of exclusivity so unclear that economic activity is immobilized. In such cases private ownership claims negate, rather than enhance, the productivity of the resource.

The "tragedy of the anti-commons" provides an important clue as to how commons can support markets, and vice versa. Robert Merges (2004) notes that "firms and individuals are increasingly injecting information into the public domain with the explicit goal of preempting or undermining the potential property rights of economic adversaries." In particular, he discusses the use of "property-preempting investments" (PPIs) in biotechnology and open-source software. Firms in biotechnology have invested in the creation of public domain databases that can prevent other firms from asserting exclusive rights over inputs that are critical to pharmaceutical research. IBM's support for open-source software is cited as another example. Merges (2004) concludes that "strong rights lead to investments in the public domain" and that these represent a "private ordering response to the phenomenon of the anti-commons." In the case of software, it is not just the possibility of an anti-commons that has led to the embrace of open-source software by the likes of IBM, Sun Microsystems and other major IT interests; it is also (if not primarily) the market dominance of a rival firm, Microsoft.

Merges' concept of a PPI shows that major economic actors can have a strong interest in creating and preserving an unowned space. A commons preserves and advances certain strategies for private market development and private appropriation, by institutionalizing a more open and nondiscriminatory form of access to resources. It is not just any resource that gets this treatment but all those required by a wide number of market actors as a critical input to their products and services. In the case studies that follow, we see this pattern repeated in various forms. It is precisely the contextual interdependence of private property, markets and common resources that makes it difficult to predict or specify, a priori, which resource will be or should be a commons. This is because it is the strategic status of the resource in relation to other resources and to market actors and their private appropriation strategies that will determine its status.

2.3 Case 1: equal access in long-distance telephony in the United States

An example of the dynamic interplay between privatization and common spaces in telecommunication regulation occurred with the introduction of competition in long-distance telecommunications in the United States. The 1984 divestiture broke up what was at the time the largest company in the world, the American Telephone and Telegraph Company (AT&T). AT&T, which integrated the supply of local and long-distance telephone services and telephone terminal equipment, was split up into a nationwide long-distance company and seven regional operating companies. Over the next decade the long-distance market was largely deregulated with respect to prices and services. The regional local exchange companies (LECs), which continued to hold monopoly or near-monopoly power over access lines, remained highly regulated.

One might view the introduction of less regulated, competing long-distance telephone companies as the ultimate in creating a privatized market. Indeed, in the aftermath of the divestiture more than one leftist critic expressed nostalgia for the "public service" ethic of the old, vertically integrated monopoly system (Stone, 1991). What the advocates and critics of market competition both often failed to notice, however, was that the introduction of long-distance competition was predicated upon the construction of an "equal-access" regime at the interface of the long-distance and local telephone systems. The post-divestiture telecommunication regime granted long-distance competitors nondiscriminatory interconnection rights to the local exchange facilities of the regional telephone companies, and provided uniform, regulated rates governing what the regional companies could charge for originating and terminating long-distance calls over their facilities. The purpose of the equal-access regime was to create the proverbial "level playing field" that competitors in the market place often demand. By increasing the certainty and uniformity of long-distance carriers' relationship to the local exchange bottleneck, the equal-access policy fostered the construction of private, competitive networks in vertically related segments of the market. Secure in their ability to access local exchange bottlenecks, the competing long-distance carriers could invest in and build out private, exclusively owned long-distance network facilities (Brock, 1994). For about fifteen years a highly competitive market thrived on the basis of this combination. Prices for long-distance usage quickly plummeted, investment in new long-distance facilities and technologies soared and usage grew at double-digit annual rates. The incumbent local exchange carriers did rather well, too, charging regulated tolls on the growing volume of long-distance traffic originating or terminating on their local lines.

Consider now the political dynamics that produced the regime. Equal access was created because a politically powerful coalition of interest groups recognized the existence of a strategic bottleneck, namely the monopolistic local exchange facilities controlled by LECs. These facilities were essential inputs into their businesses but would have been prohibitively expensive to duplicate. Prospective long-distance competitors demanded that the facilities be governed by an equal-access regime in order to protect themselves from the market power of a dominant player (the local exchange monopolies) and to prevent any of their competitors from leveraging that dominance to create a strategic advantage. The interest groups involved were the competing carriers and the major business users of long-distance services, with some support from consumer groups. Equal access or a commons, in this case, came about not as a result of a sharing ethic, or even because of its optimal economic effects; it happened because there was a coalition among a group of peers who confronted a "common" enemy.

Although this was successful in many ways, one must not overlook the costs and problems associated with instituting the equal-access regime. It was, to begin with, very expensive to implement. The dismemberment of AT&T and the definition and monitoring of the borderline between LECs and inter-exchange carriers occupied millions of billable hours for lawyers and regulators alike and required new physical facilities as well as tariffs and organizational structures. Its segregation of the market for voice telephone services into "local" and "long-distance" segments required the definition of politically negotiated territories, called local access and transport areas (LATAs).[1] Some economies of scale and scope were lost as a result of the division between "local" and "long-distance" companies. As a consequence of its arbitrariness, the regime had difficulty adjusting to techno-economic change. The regime was predicated on the assumption that local exchange service was monopolistic, but the growth of mobile telephony introduced serious competition into local access. When mobile telephone companies started offering distance-insensitive nationwide calling plans that integrated local and long-distance service the old regime rapidly became irrelevant. The specialized, stand-alone long-distance carrier had ceased to exist by 2001, with the main long-distance carriers taken over by the major LECs (e.g. SBC took over AT&T, Verizon took over MCI, etc.). The advent of VoIP, usually through cable television companies in the United States, further undermined the need for an equal-access regime. The federal regulations regarding equal-access interconnection probably still exist, but they are no longer relevant to most of the market.

The next three cases deal specifically with internet governance. We see common elements with the older telephony case, however. Political pressure for creating or maintaining institutionalized commons comes from alliances of many competing peers against a common entity that holds dominant control over a resource that they are all dependent upon.

2.4 Case 2: internet (TCP/IP)

The internet protocols and the end-to-end architecture upon which they were based is a more successful and longer-lasting example of the

[1] LATAs had no pure relationship to "local" versus "long-distance" service but were a politically negotiated compromise on how to structure the market. A separation based on the actual technical characteristics of the network would have created something like 10,000 local exchange companies and required all traffic between them to be handed off to long-distance carriers. That would have been fantastically inefficient and would have made it difficult for fledgling long-distance carriers to interconnect with all locations. Instead, LATAs were defined roughly on the basis of population, such that, for example, the entire state of Wyoming, comprising hundreds of square kilometers, was one LATA and the 20 km areas surrounding major metropolitan areas also constituted a single LATA.

dynamic interaction of commons and private markets. The internet is based on global and nonproprietary standards that can be freely adopted by anyone. These standards constitute a global commons. The primordial *situs* of internet governance, the internet technical community and its Internet Engineering Task Force (IETF), was one of the first functioning open-source software collaborative communities. From the early 1980s the IETF and its predecessors developed standards and protocols by means of open working groups and unincorporated collaborative networks. Its standards were self-consciously nonproprietary and public. Eventually they were copyrighted by the Internet Society to preserve their openness, just as free software's GPL uses copyright law to preserve the openness of its products.

The TCP/IP standards on which internetworking is based can be appropriated and used by anyone, without the need for licensing or paying a fee. Of course, since the standards are information and the protocols that implement them are software, their appropriation by one user does not diminish the availability of the resource to any other user. The standards development community, centered on the IETF but also including the World Wide Web Consortium, strives to ensure that the core internet and web standards are unencumbered by restrictive intellectual property rights. Patented technologies are unwelcome in both the IETF and the W3C.

Unlike the standards and software protocols, however, the networks connected by IPs are not open, nonexclusive and nonproprietary. The internet is a network of privately owned and administered networks. The networks so connected are heterogeneous; some belong to households, some to small businesses, some to large enterprises, some to nonprofit organizations, and many to the (usually privately owned) commercial networks of ISPs. The bandwidth resources supplied by these entities are not nonrival.

By facilitating the interoperability of heterogeneous networks, the internet protocols allow for the privatization and decentralization of network operations and policies. They also facilitate the development of private, decentralized software applications and information content. Open standards and private networks are linked together via the end-to-end argument, one of the internet's few general architectural principles (Saltzer, Reed and Clark, 1984). It means that the design of the network is not optimized for any particular service or set of applications; the network provides basic data transport only, leaving the implementation of user-specific applications to devices attached to the ends of the network. This permits the network to serve as a relatively neutral and transparent platform for the widest possible variety of applications and services, including services never anticipated by the network protocol designers. The end-to-end principle is believed to promote innovation, network growth and market competition by reducing barriers to entry. No one need ask for permission to offer a new application or service on the internet. One might say, then, that the connectivity resources of the internet constitute an open-access commons (albeit restricted, of course, to those who purchase internet access).

Standards commons, privately administered networks and the end-to-end argument are not three distinct principles, but they are closely interrelated, and they can be seen as a philosophy for articulating commons and the market. At the end points, the internet is private and exclusive; at the core standards level, it is nonproprietary and open. The end-to-end principle was an attempt to ensure that private market and public commons complement each other. The market in internet-related applications, content and networking requires public, neutral coordinating mechanisms that enable interoperation. With the end-to-end principle, the sharing and coordinating mechanisms are deliberately minimized so as to provide maximum scope for initiative and innovation at the end points. There is a clear separation between the parts of the system that are subject to private initiative and control and the parts that are subject to global coordination and nonexclusive access. Thus, new applications, such as the World Wide Web in the early 1990s, or the real-time voice capabilities of Skype, can be implemented without the permission, or even the cooperation, of the network providers. Any willing end user and supplier can take basic transport for granted and build on it using applications at the end points.

How did the backers of TCP/IP succeed in getting this dynamic integration of commons and market globally adopted? What were the political and economic preconditions? The story is complex, but on the whole it fits with the argument of this chapter. A TCP/IP commons emerged as a kind of equilibrium point among powerful contending interests. The internet protocols were developed in an environment in which nearly everyone was searching for a common data communication standard that would provide an escape from the dominance of data networking by IBM and its proprietary protocols.

IBM at the time had a status as reviled monopoly equivalent to that of Microsoft around 2000. Second, as products of government research, the IPs could be copied and adopted for no charge, which gave them a superior ability to overcome the critical mass problem associated with the generation of network externalities. Once a substantial user base had committed itself to it, its value as a potential global nexus for compatibility became clear and its adoption gained momentum. Third, the IPs served a very useful function for the United States and its industry by providing a viable alternative to the standard-setting efforts of the International Telecommunication Union's (ITU's) CCITT (Abbate, 1999). The rest of the world acceded to the IPs and the IETF as the de facto platform for standards development because it provided the United States, Europe and Japan with an acceptable way to avoid wrangles over industrial policy. Once again, we see a kind of power equilibrium among peers. As Peter Cowhey and Milton Mueller (2009) put it:

> [R]etaining the IETF as the locus of [internet] standards governance allayed the worst fears of the three major industrial regions. For the US Government, the worry was that the European Union or Japan might belatedly become tempted to engage in industrial policy to overcome the de facto boost to the US computer industry emerging from the Internet computing revolution. For the EU and Japan, the IETF was an instrument for keeping the computer industry away from the consolidated dominance of Microsoft.

Even allowing for the path dependence inherent in achieving standards dominance, the internet's unique mixture of open, nonproprietary standards, private networks and private content, applications and services was welcomed because it offered a more open and neutral alternative to powerful and potentially threatening actors such as IBM, Microsoft and the ITU.

2.5 Case 3: net neutrality

The net neutrality debate reflects a crisis of confidence about the future of the end-to-end principle in a broadband, digitally converged world. It signals a major renegotiation of the relationship between what is private, differentiated and managed and what is uniform and common on the internet. Here, the critical resource around which debates over property and commons revolve is bandwidth.

The policy conflict is prompted by three important changes in the market for internet services: digital convergence; the emergence of a broadband telecommunication infrastructure; and the existence of competition between broadband networks. In the old, narrowband internet, the internet was confined primarily to asynchronous data communications. A large number of competing ISPs could rely on a common, regulated and monopolistic telephone company to provide universal connectivity on basically equal terms and conditions. The broadband internet, in contrast, carries real-time voice and video as well as e-mail and web traffic. It relies on a smaller number of competing bandwidth suppliers, because of the capital-intensive nature of the alternative infrastructures; hence the market for local access bandwidth is usually oligopolistic, with as few as two or as many as four or five suppliers. In thinner markets there still may be only one supplier.

Two related regulatory decisions in the United States contributed to the emergence of the net neutrality debates. First, the United States rejected the unbundling of the telephone and cable companies' broadband access lines. In most other Organisation for Economic Co-operation and Development (OECD) countries, the telephone companies are required to make their broadband access facilities available for lease by competing ISPs. (Note that unbundled local loops make the physical access facilities an open-access commons, similar to the equal-access regulations discussed in case 1.) The intent was to encourage facilities-based competition rather than competition based on shared utilization of the incumbent's facilities. Second, the US regulatory framework differentiates "information services" (which are unregulated) from "telecommunication services" (which incur common carrier obligations). In 2005 a Federal Communications Commission (FCC) decision classifying cable modem-based internet access services as "information services," and thus exempt from common carrier obligations, was upheld by the Supreme Court.[2] The combination of no unbundled local loop and the absence of common carrier obligations led to fears that bandwidth suppliers would become vertically integrated into the supply of content and applications, and that that integration would give them incentives to discriminate against independent suppliers (Reynolds, 2007). Under

[2] *National Cable and Telecommunications Association* v. *Brand X Internet Services*, 545 US 967 (2005).

these circumstances, net neutrality – the demand for turning bandwidth into a commons – became the rallying cry of many public interest groups and internet companies. As one advocacy group has argued in debates before the US Congress:

> IP-layer neutrality is not a property of the Internet. It is the Internet. [. . .] The heart of the Internet protocol is the agreement that all data packets will be passed through without regard to which application created them or what's inside of them. This reliable, uniform treatment of packets is precisely what has made the Internet a marketplace of innovation so critical to our economy.[3]

Opponents of net neutrality, on the other hand, see bandwidth as a private resource, one that is supplied most efficiently if exclusive owners take responsibility for managing and conserving it, and are able to optimize its value by exerting control over the content and applications it conveys (Yoo, 2006a).

The NN debate is often framed as a clash between advocates of "regulation" and advocates of a "free market." It is true that NN advocates are more willing to impose certain rules or constraints on network providers, but it is also true that the policy is motivated by their belief in a complementary relationship between nondiscriminatory treatment of packets by internet bandwidth suppliers and a robust, unregulated private market for content, services and applications on the internet. Lessig (1999a) and Wu (2003a) both invoke the end-to-end principle as the inspiration of their net neutrality concerns, while recognizing, with Blumenthal and Clark (2001), the growing tendency of the broadband internet to deviate from that principle.

In fact, Wu (2003a) grounds the case for network neutrality in a Schumpeterian or even Hayekian theory of how the open markets built around nondiscriminatory access to critical inputs will spur technological and business innovation. A bandwidth resource pool that is allocated in a nondiscriminatory manner lowers barriers to entry and prevents errant central planners from imposing their mistakes on the greater economy:

[3] Dynamic Platform Standards Project, "For real 'network neutrality'"; www.dpsproject.com/twotypes.html. This group advocates prohibiting non-neutral networks from using the term "internet" when advertising and marketing their services.

> Speaking very generally, NN adherents view the innovation process as a "survival of the fittest" competition between developers of new technologies. They are suspicious of models of development that might vest control in any initial prospect holder, private or public, who is expected to direct the optimal path of innovation, minimizing the excesses of innovative competition. The suspicion arises from the belief that the most promising path of development is difficult to predict in advance, and the argument that any single prospect holder will suffer from cognitive biases (such as a predisposition to continue with current ways of doing business) that make it unlikely that he/she will come to the right decisions, despite his/her best intentions. (Wu, 2003a: 145)

Opponents of NN policies also invoke "innovation" and "free markets" as critical values. Focusing more on competition and innovation in the provision of networks, however, they predict that NN policies will have negative effects. Regulations that "neutralize" networks impose upon them a standardized uniformity that preempts competitive differentiation, and may even undermine the incentive to invest in the construction of competing bandwidth facilities (Yoo, 2006a, 2006b). They tend to see deviations from NN as justifiable forms of vertical integration, and call upon traditional competition policy law and economic analysis as guidelines for policy. Vertical integration, they claim, can yield a number of benefits, including economies of scope and an easing of compatibility across the components of a technical system. It should not be prohibited in principle unless there are clear signs that it harms competition. Their most direct rebuttal to the NN advocates, however, is that consumers value the wealth of information available on the internet, and therefore competition between network providers will prevent arbitrary deviations from nondiscriminatory access to content, applications and services. "Walled gardens" lost the competition for consumers in the first-generation, dial-up internet, and there are signs that attempts by wireless service providers to maintain vertical ties to and restrictions on web access are breaking down as well (Hahn, Litan and Singer, 2007). This chapter need not take sides in this debate; the point here is simply that the debate is not about "commons" versus "market" but about the interdependence of the two and the role of an open-access commons in preserving or advancing innovation and competition in adjacent markets.

If agitation for network neutrality reveals political demand for some new kind of commons, where is that demand coming from? The appeal of ideas, especially to intellectuals and regulators, cannot be overlooked; nor can the agitation of public interest advocacy groups. A great deal of the political impact of the network neutrality campaign in the United States has depended on the support of major internet content, application and service providers, however, such as eBay, Google, Amazon, Microsoft and Yahoo, and the device manufacturers organized under the Consumer Electronics Association. These participants in the internet economy perceived themselves as being heavily dependent upon a broadband duopoly to reach customers, and did not want control of bandwidth to be leveraged in ways that could impair their businesses. In other words, we have the now familiar pattern of a large, heterogeneous collection of economic actors mobilizing themselves to secure stabilized terms and conditions of access to a strategically central resource upon which they share a common dependence.

2.6 Case 4: internet identifier resources

Domain names and IP addresses are the unique identifiers that direct the movement of data across the internet. The policies governing the allocation and assignment of these identifiers are a critical part of internet governance. Coordinating the uniqueness of internet identifiers is vital if the internet is to remain globally compatible. Because of the requirement for global uniqueness, both domain names and IP addresses must be exclusively assigned to particular users. A domain name or IP address occupied by one person or organization cannot simultaneously be advertised by another without disrupting operational compatibility. Thus, the internet's identifier resources are rival in consumption.

Currently, the institutional mechanisms for internet identifier governance are centered in the Internet Corporation for Assigned Names and Numbers. ICANN is a California-based nonprofit public benefit corporation that is recognized and supervised unilaterally by the United States Department of Commerce. Like the basic TCP/IP standards discussed in case 2, the ICANN regime is global in effect. In the ICANN case, we again see how concerns about neutralizing a strategic resource that is a critical input across an entire industry led to the institutionalization of a commons governance regime. We also see how the actual rules and procedures used to manage the commons can facilitate or impede private appropriation strategies and competitive markets, and how commons-based governance regimes suffer from certain problems.

ICANN administers the root of the domain name system and the root of the internet addressing system. Both these virtual resources – names and numbers – are delegated to private users in a hierarchical fashion. Thus, whoever stands at the top of the hierarchy holds a kind of first-order control over the possession and use of identifier resources by all users further down the hierarchy. This means that the problem of coordinating uniqueness is complicated by its frequent intersection with larger economic and political issues (Mueller, 2002). By withholding or granting conditional access to these resources, a root-level governance authority can enforce a variety of policies that are unrelated to the problem of technical coordination. It can control market entry, the prices charged by service providers, dispute resolution policies, and so on. The consequences of such decisions are significant, in economic and political terms alike. The domain name registration market is valued at about US$3 billion per year, and IPv4 address blocks, though not traded in a market, are probably worth many times more.

The combination of political and economic power inherent in control of the root convinced the US government and most influential parties in the emerging internet industry that control of the root should not be concentrated in the hands of a single, commercial private actor. The entity that raised these concerns was not a gigantic AT&T, Microsoft or IBM, however; it was a small firm known as Network Solutions, Inc. (NSI), which in 1991 was awarded a contract by the National Science Foundation to operate the basic domain name registry functions. Its authority over the root servers was shared with Jon Postel, another US government contractor and the chosen agent of the Internet Engineering Task Force to perform the identifier assignment functions.

It is not possible here to describe in any detail the operational and historical facts about the relationship between the US government, NSI and the informally organized internet standards community during the critical period between the commercialization of the domain name registration services in 1995 and the creation of ICANN in 1998. Suffice it to say that, in 1997, NSI's and Jon Postel's contracts with the US government were both due to expire. At that point, had it been willing to adhere to a truly private market-oriented transition, the United States simply could have let the contracts expire, walked away and let the private actors sort it out themselves. This was perceived as undesirable by many, if not most, of the influential actors, for reasons that should already be evident from the other case studies.

If the United States had walked away, it is likely that NSI would have inherited de facto control of the DNS root. That scenario alienated many key actors (though see Gordon Brady, 2003, for a case in favor of it). The IETF feared that it would lose a great deal of its influence over the course of the internet's name space. Trademark owners feared that a commercially driven NSI would permit many new, unregulated top-level domains (TLDs) and increase their problems policing trademarks in the domain name space. Potential competitors feared the opposite: that the need for NSI's approval and cooperation would block domain name registries that wanted to compete with NSI's ".com," ".net" and ".org" top-level domains. Still others feared that competitors would avoid NSI's power over the legacy root by creating alternative, competing DNS name spaces, which could lead to the fragmentation of the internet. Moreover, NSI itself was less than excited about taking on the responsibility for controlling the content of the root zone, because it feared that it might incur liability under the antitrust laws. NSI seemed to prefer shifting that liability to a quasi-governmental entity (Froomkin and Lemley, 2003).

ICANN was therefore created as a common, "neutral" coordinator of domain name allocations. The root of the domain and address spaces was recognized as a commons or "public resource" in which no private property rights inhered. Indeed, ICANN, corporate trademark holders and governments insisted that top-level domain delegations were trusteeships and not private property rights.[4] ICANN was required to create processes for representing stakeholders and for bottom-up policy development by affected stakeholders. A similar

[4] The Governmental Advisory Committee (GAC) operating principles, adopted May 25, 1999 (see www.icann.org/committees/gac/operating-principles-25may99.htm), declares that "[t]he Internet naming and addressing system is a public resource" and that "[c]ountry code top level domains are operated in trust by the Registry for the public interest." An August 1999 GAC communiqué declared that "no private intellectual or other property rights inhere to the TLD itself nor accrue to the delegated manager of the TLD as the result of such delegation"(www.icann.org/committees/gac/communique-24aug99.htm). Likewise, trademark owners, while keen to claim property rights in the second level of the domain name space, insisted that no such rights could be claimed in top level domains. See McCarthy (1996, 2000: sect. 7:17, 7–27); see also Mueller (2002: 260–2) for a more detailed discussion of this.

pattern was followed in the IP address space. Address space assignment authority was delegated to nonprofit entities known as regional internet registries (RIRs), which were collectively controlled by a membership consisting primarily of commercial ISPs. No private market for addresses was permitted or encouraged; instead, a regional central planning regime was put in place. The RIRs coordinated among themselves the basic policies for allocating and assigning addresses.

In the domain name market, two distinct commons were created. One, at the root level, gave ICANN authority over the delegation of top-level domains and the distribution of the root-zone file to the root server operators. In addition to that, an equal-access regime was created to govern the registration of second-level domain names. Using a policy that was very similar in intent and implementation to the equal-access regime for the interconnection of long-distance and local telephone companies, the US Commerce Department required NSI to allow any company accredited by ICANN as a registrar to sell domain name registrations under the ".com," ".net" and ".org" TLDs. By the end of 1999 it had installed a regime of multiple, competing registrars, all with the same technical interface and the same fixed price for accessing and selling second-level domains. Registrars were given equal access to all unregistered names in the ".com," ".net" and ".org" top-level domains operated by the dominant NSI registry. The purpose of this policy was to undermine the market dominance of NSI.

In both domain name levels (the root level and the NSI top-level domains), instituting a commons form of governance was a response to political demands from market actors. In both cases, the intent was to facilitate, rather than replace, effectively functioning private markets. Collective governance at the root level was intended to provide a neutral institutional platform for making decisions about the addition of new top-level domains (thus adding competition to the market) and for developing policies for the global regulation of domain name registries and users. The accreditation of registrars and the granting of equal access rights to the dominant registry (".com," ".net" and ".org") was intended to pave the way for a competitive market in domain name registrations at the second level, reducing the exclusivity of the dominant actor's property right over the TLDs it operated. Similarly, in IP addresses, treating addresses as a centrally allocated common pool was intended to avoid dominance and create a neutral platform for coping with complex coordination issues related to the aggregation of address blocks.

Of these experiments in commons governance, the results have been mixed. Registrar-based competition has been an unqualified success at fomenting price competition in the sale of second-level domain name registrations and at eliminating the dominance of NSI (which is now known as VeriSign). This short-term success suffers from the same problems as equal access in long-distance telephony, however. Once the market dominance upon which it was predicated had been eliminated, the rationale for the equal-access regime eroded. The compulsory registrar/registry split may even become an impediment to additional market entry and new forms of competition. For small, specialized, new top-level domain registries, for example, being forced to interface with customers through ICANN-accredited registrars is counterproductive and costly. The equal-access regime, if consistently carried out, would also prevent major registrars from entering the market for new top-level domains, yet those firms are undoubtedly willing and the most capable of competing in this market.

At the DNS root, the ICANN solution has not been that successful, unless trademark protection is taken as the only criterion of success. Despite a widespread consensus on the need for managing the root of the name space as a commons, the ICANN case has shown that establishing new, commons-oriented global governance arrangements for virtual resources required the creation of new representational mechanisms, accountability and review procedures and policy-making processes. This has proved to be extraordinarily difficult, time-consuming and contentious. Such a politicized process can be dominated by rent-seeking interest groups (such as the intellectual property interests) that can use collective control over the resource in a protectionist manner. The need to set policies through collective action has mostly resulted in stasis and gridlock. As an example, ICANN's mandate to develop a policy for adding new top-level domains, mentioned in the very first (1998) policy statement and reiterated in successive memorandums of understanding with the US government, took ten years to complete, on account of disagreements between constituency groups. The institution of multilingual domain names has been stalled even longer. The inability of ICANN, with its public governance regime, to introduce non-Roman scripts into the domain name market contrasts strongly with the rapid progress made in websites, where content in nearly all languages is available. The difference between private initiative and collective action should be evident: in the case of websites, the voluntary adoption of compatible standards by private actors in the market has produced a plethora of multilingual sites, whereas ICANN's reliance on global governance agreements subjects every decision to political and economic contention, and produces no results.

Collective governance at the root level has suffered from an even more fundamental problem. In a global context, the unilateral oversight powers of the US government undermined the perceived neutrality of the governance authority, triggering geopolitical contention during the World Summit on the Information Society (2003–5). The issue of political oversight is still not resolved, nine years after ICANN's formation and two years after the close of the WSIS (IGP [Internet Governance Project], 2006). The IP address commons is also about to be sorely tested. As the IPv4 address space nears exhaustion, RIRs are being forced to consider permitting a market for address blocks to develop so as to provide strong incentives for hoarders to release unused address resources and move them to higher-valued uses (van Beijnum, 2007).

2.7 Summary of the case studies

The preceding case studies suggest three main conclusions.

The first is that, in all these cases, the existence of a commons regime is either intended to, or actually does, contribute to a more robust and competitive private market in adjacent areas. In the telephone case, nondiscriminatory access to local origination and termination services produced a level playing field for competing long-distance carriers, thereby encouraging investment in new inter-exchange network facilities and producing lower prices for long-distance calls. The standards commons at the core of the internet has succeeded for nearly two decades in facilitating a robust private market for devices, applications and services that can be developed and implemented by any network participant. This was a deliberate aim of the end-to-end argument. Similarly, whether rightly or wrongly, the advocates of net neutrality believe that nondiscriminatory access to bandwidth and content in the broadband internet era will preserve and enhance diversity and competition in the market for broadband content, applications and services. ICANN's registrar market intervention, which created an equal-access regime for competing registrars in the dominant ".com," ".net" and ".org" top-level domains, made domain name registration services much more competitive and vastly expanded the market. Although the commons at the root level has encountered numerous problems, it was created with the expectation that its effects on the market for internet services would be superior to the options of either monopoly control of the root by a private actor or a fragmented name space produced by competition between private actors. In short, the picture of an ideological and institutional clash between "the" commons and "the" market is a completely false one. If one examines real institutions and markets, one sees a vibrant interaction between open, commons-type property regimes and private, exclusive appropriation.

The second conclusion pertains to the nature of the political demand for commons regimes. A commons can be seen as an outcome of interest group contention. It is an equilibrium, in which a large group of heterogeneous actors seek to establish some kind of stable, level playing field in which they can contend fairly. Their ability to coalesce around a commons solution is usually facilitated by the existence of a single, commonly feared dominant actor – an AT&T, an IBM, a Microsoft, a Network Solutions. A commons is a way for one set of nondominant actors to stabilize and "neutralize" a strategic resource controlled by a dominant actor, or to prevent a critical resource from becoming monopolized by an unforeseen actor that might parlay it into dominant status in the future. There is little support here for the more romantic and communitarian conceptions of commons politics, which contrast the sharing ethic of the commons with the supposedly selfish and individualistic promoters of private property.

Third, the case studies suggest some tentative insights into how we might seek to optimize commons–market arrangements and relationships. Firmer conclusions would require more formal modeling and more extensive empirical research, of course. At this point, though, it appears that the most successful and enduring instance of a complementary commons–market relationship is the TCP/IP case. The defining characteristic of this case is that the commons was based on a nonrival resource: a nonproprietary, open standard. Efforts to make rival resources such as broadband networks or internet identifier resources the basis of a commons have raised more difficult issues. In these cases, contentious collective action is required to establish the policies needed to ration the resource and to work out the distributional effects of sharing policies. Nondiscriminatory access arrangements seem to succeed best when there is a single, clearly identifiable dominant actor, such as AT&T in the equal access case, or NSI in the domain name registration market. When there are multiple competitors, as in the NN case, the application of nondiscrimination standards is more complex and contentious, and the jury is still out on their effectiveness. It is also evident that equal-access arrangements face the risk of becoming obsolete over time. At best, they simply become irrelevant and disappear from view; at worst, they become permanent distortions in the political economy that prevent industry evolution, by erecting barriers to entry or privileging a certain caste of businesses that benefit from the regime and refuse to let it depart.

2.8 Conclusion

A strategically located commons can be a vital part of preserving the viability of private markets, and can actually increase the opportunities for efficient private appropriation. Conversely, private property's well-established ability to liberate individualized production and innovation from collective restraints and to incentivize production and efficiency provide a vital escape from the potentially deadening, overly political nature of certain kinds of commons governance. Properly linked, private property can enhance the value and importance of the commons, and vice versa. Thus, there is – or should be – an important place for both commons and property in internet governance, and it is unwise to emphasize one to the exclusion of the other. Indeed, the very structure of the internet, which combines exclusive, private network facilities and services with open, nonproprietary standards, is a prime example of this interdependence. Balancing the two may be complex and difficult, but movements for freedom of information and communication must recognize the potentially complementary nature of the two property regimes.

3 *Regulating networks in the "new economy": organizing competition to share information and knowledge*

ERIC BROUSSEAU AND JEAN-MICHEL GLACHANT

3.1 An economy based on knowledge and modularity

The regulation of network industries has been profoundly transformed in the past twenty years. First, the "object of regulation" is no longer the same. Network industries have been opened to new dynamics, which have overwhelmed their industrial, technological and marketing frameworks. The relationships between players, of whom there are now significant numbers, and the interaction between users and suppliers have been totally reshaped. Beyond economic structures, these industries have been involved in significant societal changes. In short, networks are the infrastructure of our postmodern societies, the necessary conditions for the provision of a large set of "facilities" that form the foundation of both the economy and sociability. Second, "practicable" regulations are no longer the same (Laffont and Tirole, 1993; Armstrong, Cowan and Vickers, 1994; Joskow, 2002). In a knowledge-based economy, characterized in particular by extensive innovation, regulatory models designed in the nineteenth century to manage investments and the pricing of transportation infrastructures are no longer relevant. They are unable to handle the new central issues: the interactive dynamics of innovation in the areas of technology, uses and markets (Noam, 2001; Langlois, 2002). Third, Western societies have been evolving dramatically. Governance, specifically, has become more interactive, as suggested by the development of both lobbying and "public opinion" tyranny, which, to a large extent, are both symptoms and causes of the crisis facing traditional representative democracy.

In this chapter, we suggest that the regulation of network industries is no longer a question of "command and control," in which the main issue for the regulator is to design "optimal" regulations, given information constraints both ex ante (when rules have to be designed) and ex post (at the implementation stage). Instead, it has become an issue of knowledge-sharing and the alignment of stakeholders' perspectives to guarantee a "satisfying" level of interoperability within a system decentrally managed, open to continuous innovation and characterized by strong systemic consistency constraints. In such a context, the regulator's role is to promote the sharing of knowledge among market participants, both to favor the spontaneous matching of plans and to limit monopoly capture, the latter tending to be more problematic on account of asymmetries of cognition between suppliers and users, leading competitors and followers, and suppliers and regulating entities.

To identify the "new" logic characterizing the regulation of networks more clearly, we compare past and present approaches to the organization of network industries. To allow for and stimulate constant innovation, and permit a more effective adaptation to users' diverse needs, the supply side of networks and most industries has been reorganized around interacting modules that can be assembled through standardized interfaces. The modular conception of production processes allows the coordination of a wide number of agents, both in static situations (service provision) and in dynamic circumstances (innovation). This is the heart of the new paradigm of "mass customization" that has replaced the "Taylorist–Fordist" model (Aoki, 2001; Baldwin, 2008). It provides the basis for a flexible organization of the industry at the global level (because of the parallel dismantling of barriers to trade).[1] This new model is both the cause and consequence of two sets of radical changes in the organizational foundations of network industries. First, technologies have been becoming intelligent and flexible. The combination of the massive recourse to ICTs and technical innovation in all domains (containers,

[1] This model is not restricted to network industries. It is the model around which most industries are organized today. If the "new economy" does exist, it is certainly characterized by the reorganization of entire productive systems around the triptych "innovation–modularity–globalization." Energy, transportation and information networks, therefore, appear to be central, since they are the enabling infrastructures of the reorganization of the whole economy. There are, thus, essential challenges behind their regulation. Moreover, the regulation of information networks is of particular importance, for two reasons. First, information and communication technologies are the support technologies of these reorganizations of the economy. Decision-making, new management methods and the flexible coordination of complex systems are based on ICTs. Second, many of the regulatory models that are implemented were first developed and tested in the telecommunication industries.

gas power stations, etc.) has completely broken down the old notion of economies of scale and the strong links between physical infrastructure and service. Second, because of the increasing difficulty that public authorities faced in finely and efficiently monitoring industry players' behaviors, a revolution in the beliefs of most national elites occurred. Following the logic of Ronald Coase (1960), the way to fix "market failures" is no longer seen as "command and control" regulation, because of bureaucratic failures. The combination of these two movements totally reshaped the basis for the regulation of network industries.

In this chapter, the notions of "regulation" and "regulator" are understood in a very broad sense. Both are black boxes. Regulation stands for all rules established by the state to organize/frame economic activities. In concrete terms, regulation encompasses all sets of laws and administrative regulations that affect network service providers' activities. Along the same lines, the term "regulator" is used for public authorities in charge of designing, enforcing and reshaping public rules that frame the activities of economic agents. The legislature, the government, the judiciary and even "regulators" and "regulatory authorities" are grouped under this category. We do not discuss the details of the hierarchy of legal norms, or the complex machinery of lawmaking and implementation bodies, as analyzed, for instance, by Peter Cameron (2005). This is consistent with the level of our analysis, which addresses the question of the approach of public oversight of network industries, no matter the peculiarities of various national institutional frameworks and each specific industry.

From this broad perspective, we consider that the regulation of networks has (and has always had) to deal with "five" central issues. First, there is the distribution of fixed costs, which consists of dealing with the "natural monopoly" issue. Second, the establishment of property rights results in a distribution and level of incentives to invest and to innovate. Third, the management of negative network "externalities" consists mainly of addressing the issues of quality and security. Fourth, positive network effects depend upon the proper management of interconnection and interoperability so as to guarantee that networks reach an efficient size and scope.[2] Fifth, the notion of "public/general" interest has to be defined, because it is anything

[2] All these issues related to externalities are "externalities " only when interacting suppliers provide the final services (or sets of services). In vertically integrated

but "natural." In addition, there are conflicting claims when public goods are impure in the sense that there is some rivalry in the use of resources. Therefore, there are conflicts between stakeholders in society to define either the notion of "public interest" (and the related fundamental private and individual rights) or the scope and possible use of the "public domain." In any regulatory process, there is, therefore, lobbying by interest groups to sponsor the definition of the public/collective interest at the "generic" level (Noll, 1999).

We start by digging deep, in an analysis of the new economic conditions in which the regulation of networks has to be considered in the present day (section 2). Then, in sections 3 to 7, we examine how the five domains of regulation are transformed. We subsequently determine the consequences of designing a regulatory framework (section 8), before briefly concluding with a discussion of the new nature of regulatory entities and public governance (section 9).

3.2 The three transformations of the economics of regulation

Three fundamental transformations are impacting the economics of regulation, in the sense that they are transforming the ability of public entities to oversee and organize industries while, at the same time, new industrial and competitive contexts generate new needs. First, by decreasing information costs dramatically, information technologies allow for the creation and oversight of a wide diversity of markets. Second, the perpetually increasing pace of innovation constantly renews the knowledge base necessary to understand the functioning of industries. Third, the modularity of industries turns the design of interfaces between modules into a crucial and central issue.

3.2.1 The increasing verifiability of transactions and processes

ICTs are becoming the support of a systematic, just-in-time and multi-criterion tracking of industrial processes and transactions (Brousseau and Rallet, 1999; Brousseau and Curien, 2007). This has a serious

industries, the issues behind them are addressed thanks to technical constraints imposed by the regulator on the operator to guarantee a minimal availability, level and security of service. At the same time, since networks are always interconnected, such externalities arise/arose even in "traditional" networks.

impact on the economics of transactions among economic agents, learning capabilities, and strategies (Brousseau, 1993). The "market failures" of the microeconomic theory of the past (symbolized by the theory of market equilibrium, as established for the 1880–1980 period) focused on the many obstacles to the establishment of the market and the performance of commercial transactions: whether it was a question of externalities, technological inseparabilities or strategic interactions when there are small numbers of players. Today, the informational wealth generated by ICTs allows us to envisage implementable Pareto-enhancing arrangements to overcome most market failures. The creative domain of "market design" aims at implementing solutions based on private arrangements and competition in order to avoid replacing market failures by bureaucratic ones (Newbery, 2000; Wilson, 2002; Buchner, Carraro and Ellerman, 2006).

In the electricity industry, for instance, the general wisdom twenty years ago was that the costs of gathering and the delays in computing information on all the inflows and outflows of power in a network prevented the implementation of any wholesale market. Today such markets operate on a daily basis and are quasi-integrated between Belgium, France, Germany and the Netherlands. More generally, ICTs allow agents to design and implement all kinds of highly complex contractual arrangements and markets, including sophisticated tools to arbitrate on an intertemporal basis. At the same time, since ICTs underlie all these arrangements and markets, they enhance public authorities' potential level of information considerably. Beyond ideological and political evolution, ICTs have certainly been contributing to the rise of a new way of providing public goods on the basis of outsourcing to private operators (Saussier and Glachant, 2006). Public authorities could therefore concentrate on their essential missions: setting collective objectives and checking that populations effectively benefit from the best quality and accessibility over cost ratio in the matter of access to services of "general interest."

3.2.2 Expansion and fragmentation of the knowledge base

At the same time, a second trend is seriously hindering the capability of public authorities to oversee businesses and regulate their activities: the trend of constant innovation. This is not merely a question of technical innovations. In the Schumpeterian tradition, we look at the transformation of organizations, marketing techniques and users' practices (Schumpeter, 1954). Moreover, these innovations are not driven solely by the supply side; users play an active role (Von Hippel, 2005). In addition, innovations are spreading across industries, since many new practices are attributable to fresh opportunities arising from innovations made elsewhere (Foray, 2004). This enduring and widespread process of innovation permanently transforms cognitive frameworks and accelerates the pace at which the existing stock of knowledge becomes obsolete. The notions of tacit knowledge, epistemic community, network forms of organization and localized innovation highlighted in the literature on innovation combine to indicate that the rapid pace of innovation and the evolving nature of the relevant knowledge – which is constantly under construction and being tested – requires close interactions between all the actors involved, whether in research-oriented activities or in actual practices (Foray, 2004; Cohendet and Amin, 2004). Specific cognitive frameworks are developed within the resulting communities to update the required knowledge, individually and collectively. The consequences are that those who are not involved in these cognitive communities experience difficulties in interpreting and grasping the very meaning of what they can observe from outside. This is exactly the situation of the regulators. Public authorities, and more generally those involved in public decision-making, have difficulty following the transformation in practices, and even more in anticipating new strategies.

This makes regulation a challenge (Laffont and Tirole, 2000; Littlechild, 2006). Beyond that, it generates legal uncertainty. Indeed, those in charge of settling conflicts are hardly aware of the evolution of practices and the issues at stake. Even when they are fully informed, because the competition between conflicting parties leads to widescale revelation, judges and regulatory commissions have difficulty making decisions and implementing appropriate responses.[3] Moreover, this uncertainty increases lobbying and opens the door to the strategic manipulation of information, especially information about trends, which has a cumulative effect on the difficulty of interpreting observed paths of evolution and overseeing economic practices.

[3] This cognitive issue is to a large extent one of the drivers of the increasing privatization of dispute settlement through the explosion of alternative dispute resolution mechanisms.

3.2.3 The centrality of interfaces

The third fundamental transformation is linked to the increasing modularity of industrial structures (Baldwin and Clark, 2000; Baldwin, 2008). On the one hand, it allows for the autonomous evolution of the various modules, and dealing with them separately, which is one way of coping with the above-discussed fragmentation of knowledge. On the other hand, the management of interfaces – whether technical standards, platforms or gateways – becomes an essential issue. In particular, in dynamics, interfaces play a key role in limiting the ability to innovate within modules, and in allowing or preventing a dynamic adaptation of the system. Indeed, the diffusion of waves of innovations across modules and industries is strongly dependent on the "openness" of the management of interfaces (Langlois, 2002). Second, the evolution of these interfaces may be needed to implement more systemic changes than "local" ones.[4] Competition between industry players to master these interfaces is, therefore, very strong, with a considerable risk of the "winner takes all" effect. This opens a new domain for public intervention and regulation. From a normative and collective welfare point of view, regulating the competition that takes place to master these interfaces is essential, because they are the way to control the process of competition and, potentially, to reach a long-lasting position of dominance. This is exactly what the *European Union* v. *Microsoft* case is about (Gilbert, 1995; EC, 2004).

From a positive political economy viewpoint, this is a domain in which governments can benefit from recognized legitimacy, in particular by citizen-consumers, new entrants and followers, against the domination of incumbents. At the same time, the management of interfaces and their evolution is a fundamental cognitive challenge, since efficiency would require the reassembly and reorganization of the fragmented knowledge that is teeming along specific paths within

[4] It is worth noting that the modular organization of industry, and therefore of innovation, might increase uncertainty (González-Díaz and Vázquez, 2008) and slow the process of change (Hogan, 2002). The autonomy of innovation in each module, although there are in practice all kinds of technical, economic and psychological (etc.) interdependences between them, generates risks of inappropriate coevolution, which in turn may induce various strategic behaviors – from wait and see to alliances among actors across modules – that result in a slowing down of the process.

all modules. Although the management of interdependences between domains reinforces the legitimacy of public oversight of competition and public goods provision, the necessity of mastering the complexity of systemic evolutions limits their ability to do it efficiently.

The challenge, therefore, is to identify and implement a new regulatory mix that combines the new economy informational wealth with the cognitive poverty of public authorities to apply a regulatory process that might be imperfect, but is still viable and Pareto enhancing compared to the absence of regulation. In a sense, the challenge is to revive the tradition inaugurated by John Maurice Clark that, sixty years ago, reconciled the issues raised by market failures with the administrative capabilities of the welfare state through the principles of "workable competition."

3.3 Dynamic uncertainties when dealing with fixed costs

3.3.1 The challenges of fixed costs distribution

From the end of the nineteenth century until the 1980s the economics of fixed costs have provided the rationale for regulating and managing infrastructure networks (John Stuart Mill, Jules Dupuit, Augustin Cournot, Alfred Marshall, John Bates Clark, Clément Colson and Léon Walras). This basis was enriched during the twentieth century by several revolutions, such as the generalization of marginal welfare analysis in partial and general equilibrium, or the second best approach taking into account information and incentive constraints faced by public authorities (Arthur Pigou, Harold Hotelling, Abba Lerner, Maurice Allais, Marcel Boiteux, Kenneth Arrow, Gerard Debreu, Jean-Jacques Laffont and Jean Tirole). For the last twenty years the implementation of digital technologies in all infrastructures has been raising hopes for the advent of an era of "smart" regulation, based on a combination of transparency in the uses of infrastructure and the ability to manage them "just in time." The power of databases and computing capabilities makes it possible, for instance, to assess marginal costs almost in time for electricity networks on a wide scale (as, for example, on the French and German grids).

These advances are far from allowing a perfect and neutral (purely techno-economic) management of networks, however (Green, 2003; Joskow and Tirole, 2005; Joskow, 2006). This is due to the short-term horizon of assessment methods, on the basis of which just-in-time marginal costs of existing infrastructure use are computed. The contributions of the various layers of past investments to present alternative uses of networks are unknown, raising the issue of fairness toward past investors, and therefore incentives for future investment. Moreover, short-term marginal costs do not take into account and do not help to compute long-term marginal costs of development. These costs are highly dependent upon forecasts of future volumes of alternative services, deriving from scenarios of alternative paths of technological development, evolution in demand and the competitive process. Uncertainties about the outcome of technological competition and user demand diminish the reliability of these predictions. In vertically integrated industrial structures, this lack of information and the uncertainties matter, but to a much lesser extent than when the industry is modular. Think, for instance, of mobile phone service providers. Since "big players" own the infrastructure, they internalize most of the costs due to errors in prediction, and, obviously, can cross-subsidize among the various services to cover these costs. In contrast, in industries in which there is a separation between the management of infrastructure and the provision of services, investments made by the infrastructure manager impact on the future ability of service providers to offer alternative services, and therefore affect competition (Léauthier and Thelen, 2009). Auctions to allocate present and future capacities (the "open season" for gas transporters and storage managers), as well as the development of secondary markets for capacities, lead to the possibility of transferring investment decisions to service providers (to a certain extent).

Neither mechanism, however, changes the fact that decisions made by infrastructure managers – who are, or should be, profit-maximizing entrepreneurs – have structural consequences, though they may lack the knowledge and incentives to make decisions maximizing the collective interest. The latter might themselves be difficult to anticipate because of the considerable development of alternative uses of networks.

3.3.2 The many uncertainties about cost functions

As can be seen, the combination of abundant information due to ICTs and new regulatory principles on incentives does not solve the problems of allocating fixed costs, and the correlative distribution of investment incentives. Indeed, the structuring impact of decisions by infrastructure managers is hardly addressed by the design of incentive regulations, because of the public regulator's inability to anticipate both the required capacity and the preferred technologies (Helm, 2004). This lack of information is demonstrated by the need to renegotiate when public authorities contract with private firms to develop all kinds of infrastructures (Guash, Laffont and Straub, 2003; Guash, 2004; Brousseau and Saussier, 2009). The issue is magnified in a competitive context in which providers have strong incentives to lobby (the regulator and the infrastructure manager alike) to influence the future competitive game, however. Lobbying is intensive, both because technological choices might prove to be irreversible in the future (reflecting network effects) and because interconnection charges or auctions might fail to guarantee ex post an efficient and fair distribution of costs and benefits (Laffont and Tirole, 1996).

As pointed out by David Sappington (2005), permanent changes in the structures of infrastructures, as well as the unanticipated addition or removal of components, tend to prevent the computing of "objective" access tariffs. Accordingly, lobbying can prove to be highly profitable, because it can lead to obtaining the preferred infrastructure without paying its costs.

The divestiture of the formerly integrated network operators and the development of competition and permanent innovation have combined to reinforce the need for an efficient regulation of the allocation of fixed costs. Information asymmetries, which were the main issue dealt with in the past, have tended to be replaced by knowledge asymmetries. In the short run the regulator lacks the required knowledge to compute interconnection tariffs fairly. These tariffs should be flexible, in order to take innovation and the viability of the competitive process into account. In the long run the fact that tariffs can change boosts firms' incentives to compete, by manipulating the knowledge basis on which technical and pricing decisions are made. Since the regulator tends to be unable to develop the necessary knowledge to regulate "efficiently," its new role should be to attempt to oversee the game of influence played by coalitions to structure the "knowledge basis" on which investment decisions are made. In particular, the aim should be to oversee the establishment of interconnection rates (in a context of permanent innovation, additions to the network, and turnover) so as to guarantee a distribution of long-term infrastructure costs that hinder neither investments nor innovation.

3.4 The dynamics of the re-establishment of property rights

3.4.1 The unbundling of network components

Regulating is establishing property rights, in the sense of Yoram Barzel (1989); i.e. establishing and distributing the right to make decisions over economic resources. Traditional regulations in network industries were based on the exchange of exclusive rights to serve a market in exchange for certain commitments (essentially in the areas of quality of service, access and pricing). The regulator's role was both to design the appropriate rights (duties) and to decide who should be granted them (i.e. to implement a system to grant licenses for "public" service). Opening this up to competition totally transformed the principles by which property rights are determined, as well as those governing their distribution.

More precisely, in the first phase of the deregulation of network industries, the conventional wisdom was that it was possible to design a new set of property rights and then to let actors in the industry negotiate according to a Coasean logic (Coase, 1960). In other words, there were hopes that, once a new set of property rights had been established, essentially by dismantling the formerly bundled and exclusive property rights over components of the networks, the industry would spontaneously reorganize itself efficiently thanks to competitive pressures. Hence, there was a focus on antitrust policies in the early phase of the so-called "deregulation processes," to ensure, first, that new entrants could credibly challenge an incumbent and, second, that they would not collude once established in some market niche. This was typically the logic of the New Zealand experience in the late 1980s and early 1990s (Mueller, 1994; Vickers, 1997; Kwoka and White, 2004). It was expected that there would be an in-depth restructuring of industries on the model of air transportation, in which mergers and acquisitions, alliances and a revolution in the business models ended in favoring a considerable fall in prices and strong development of the market. It incorrectly predicted the consequences of this generalized bargaining, however. Indeed, it assumed that the new set of property rights was established once and for all, and that therefore private renegotiation could easily solve most problems of reallocations. Consequently, it ignored two strong movements that pushed for a further (and permanent) redistribution of rights.

3.4.2 Strategic games to reshuffle property rights

First, as has been pointed out, in particular, by Gary Libecap (2002), there is a strong tendency to renegotiate the current delineation of rights when agents are involved in bilateral negotiation. A contract is nothing but an agreement to rearrange rights (usually considered temporary and reversible). As pointed out by transaction cost economics (Williamson, 1985), parties play strategic games during the life of the contract because it is always incomplete. There are ex ante constraints of design and ex post limits to enforcement on account of information costs and bounded rationality. Negotiations about the actual definition of parties' rights occur and might lead either to conflict or predation. Interconnection agreements in the telecommunication industry illustrate this perfectly. New entrants have to fight continually with incumbents in all markets, because ambiguity in the definition of property rights enables the latter, de facto reluctantly, to open their networks to competition. The "devil is in the detail," as usual, and incumbents took full advantage of a wide range of possibilities with respect to the management of priorities, access to physical facilities for operational maintenance, the availability of connections, etc. Beyond legal principles and pricing issues, these permanent minor conflicts led regulatory or competition authorities to redesign the rights of the various parties, most often when they had to settle conflicts to allow for the development of standardized transactions on a broad scale.

Second, technical and marketing changes have also largely been unanticipated, as illustrated by what happened with the increasing digitization of communication networks and the correlative development of "triple play" packages to access broadband internet, telephone and television services simultaneously. The provision of these services to end users demanded the "unbundling" of the local loop, while most processes of opening up telecommunications had previously considered the local loop as a "natural" monopoly. It is only with the development of compression technologies and with major advances in the ability to manage broadband services efficiently that the logic of the vertical unbundling of network services was pushed the furthest.

In practice, the change resulted from two movements. In industries in which new infrastructure had to be built or when it was possible to duplicate infrastructure at reasonable costs (long-distance telecommunications or liquefied natural gas terminals), the rights to build and operate infrastructure were distributed to all (or a limited set) of claimants. In industries in which it would have been too costly to develop new infrastructures (typically the local loop in most network industries, but also hubs in many transportation systems), the solution was to define new rights of access for third parties. In both cases, however, there are the same results, since the production capabilities of competitors have to be interconnected and operate jointly, which presupposes agreement on common rules. Incumbents lack positive incentives to negotiate efficient rules, resulting in strategic behaviors during the process of negotiation (in order to delay any agreement) and at the implementation stage to maintain their competitive advantage. Hence the necessity for regulation and the initiation of a complex game between the regulator and incumbents, which continuously invent new ways to maintain their dominant position.

Not only is this strategic maneuvering constantly adjusted in an endless "war game" approach but it is also made permanently more complex. First, the game is a multi-player one. In practice, the opening of networks to competition relies on the attribution of new rights, not only to new entrants but also to existing users (Goldberg, 1976; Hirsh, 1991). Since they are themselves diverse (e.g. large versus small, professionals versus households, etc.) there is a wide variety of dynamics of negotiations and conflicts, leading to a tangle of rights. Second, the increasing technical flexibility of infrastructure networks multiplies the uses, and thus the battlefields, on which appropriate property rights have to be (re)established.

In summary, three interacting dynamics affected the establishment of the durable, clear and non-renegotiable property rights characterizing network regulation in the past. Innovation generates much myopia as to the efficient way to unbundle property rights, which also depends on the logic by which technology develops. The diversity of players and their number also lead to uncertainties regarding the dynamic of their service needs and techno-economic solutions proposed by the supply side. Indeed, this largely depends upon the competitive selection process, which is quite difficult to anticipate. Lastly, the diversity and technicality of interactions among service providers, as well as transactions between providers and users, make third-party verification quite difficult. Compliance is imperfect, reinforcing incentives to develop conflict strategies that make property rights yet more uncertain. In this context, the regulator's challenge is to maintain an ability to permanently redesign the second best possible system of property rights. Clearly, the goal cannot be either to guarantee stability – which would be the Cosean suggestion – or to implement optimal incentives to invest (both in infrastructure and in innovation), as they appear to be two partially conflicting goals that are, in addition, seriously affected by uncertainties. The goal of the regulator should be a "third best" one: to limit the scope and scale of conflicts and to allow the dynamic coordination of players in the industry so as to limit delays and serious incorrect decisions in investment and research and development (R&D) strategies. At least, this is how the minimization of social costs should be understood in the context of such great uncertainty.

3.5 Fixing congestions and security issues: the necessary coordination

3.5.1 Optimizing in a context of fragmentation

Externalities are the consequences of imperfection and incompletion in property rights systems. Three phenomena combine to aggravate the issue of negative externalities in the "new economy" of networks. First, as just pointed out above, the unbundling of previously integrated networks combined with the permanent regime of innovation increases the ambiguity of property rights. Second, the modularization of service provision multiplies the number of actors transforming past technical interdependences in today's inconsistencies in network management. Third, continuous innovation leads to the creation of new demand for access or for functionalities that might negatively infringe on actual capacities and capabilities.

The increasing fragmentation of the supply side, the widening scope of the delivered services and the multiplication of the production processes implemented in most networks significantly increase the risks associated with congestion and security. This is well illustrated by incidents and accidents in the British railway system, electricity blackouts and the lack of confidentiality and massive cyber-attacks on the internet.

On the one hand, the "deregulation" process enabled network suppliers and users to implement market-based means to deal with these issues. For instance, in many circumstances, congestion has been dealt with on a local basis, thanks to various mechanisms valuing the capacity use at peak hours (e.g. firms' long-term rights of access, and auctions). The creation of new operators – namely the managers of physical infrastructure – also allowed for the development of explicit new markets aimed at dealing with these issues. Indeed, these later operators are responsible for providing capacity and security to the flows of services they monitor. At the same time, recourse to economic tools to manage congestion and security is efficient (Ehrenmann and Smeers, 2005; Glachant and Pignon, 2005) when a minimum level of stability and predictability is reached, so that contracts and markets can be designed (Brunekreft, Neuhoff and Newbery, 2005).[5] Otherwise, a regulator is needed to establish rules to set priorities to allocate access to scarce resources and standards of interactions – that is, constraints on the content of transactions and the nature of agreements – to manage security issues.

3.5.2 *The logic of "ex post regulation"*

The challenge is, of course, that, in an economy based on innovation, establishing harsh and fixed rules hinders innovation – and establishing efficient, flexible regulation is constrained by the regulator's ability to access the relevant knowledge. In practice, then, the regulator may have to transform its modus operandi. Instead of setting ex ante rules of priority and standards of interaction, it can be more efficient to oversee private interactions with the goal of learning from them. There are two complementary ways to adopt this approach. Public

[5] Network operators can design and exchange user rights/rights of uses only for predictable congestion (or security issues). Vectors of potential uses of the network can be designed and, given alternative use of network rights to be served, can be guaranteed. This allows for the management only of structural congestion. Random congestion and the unpredictable nature of the demand cannot be dealt with.

authorities can oversee markets and check whether minimal standards of performance are met. Either crises or low performance reveal malfunctioning, and can lead to the development of regulations. In addition, public authorities can be responsible for conflict resolution. Conflicts between users and providers or between competitors are mechanisms that reveal information, since parties have an interest in providing information to the third "judging" part. Regulation can then follow to avoid repetition of the conflict.

Such logic of "ex post regulation" is, in a sense, "revolutionary." The aim is not only to design traditional regulations (i.e. sets of general constraints on property rights to avoid "failures" in satisfying the general interest) but also to involve market players in the prevention of failures. First, the fear of regulation (which may be justified by its negative impact on innovation, and therefore on the ability to compete and create new businesses) can lead market players to develop de facto or de jure self-regulations. Created by players and innovators themselves, they have more chance of being suited to actual and evolving problems (Ogus, 2000; Glachant, Dubois and Perez, 2008). The concern is to avoid the "capture" of this self-regulation by private interests, however, for instance to foreclose access to markets or to favor technical solutions owned by a player able to price them at a monopolistic rate. Consequently, a regulatory authority must oversee self-regulators (Brousseau and Raynaud, 2009). Second, precedents, whether in conflict resolution or in the management of crises, can be relied on to progressively close loopholes in the definition of property rights – and, therefore, limit the scope and scale of externalities. Here the logic is to apply the principle of liability by identifying those responsible for a lack of capacity or security and having them pay for it. Therefore, ex post, their incentives are more aligned with the collective interest, since they know they will have to internalize (some) collective losses in cases of inadequate behaviors. The actual extent of property rights being better known, behaviors should tend to be more appropriate.

There are two sets of remaining barriers to efficient regulation, however. First, whether it is ex ante or ex post, the nature of the economic regime characterized by innovation leads to no clear optimal criteria. The ideal tradeoff between the short-term constraints of the efficient use of existing capacities and the long-term incentives to invest (already mentioned in section 3) remains to be determined.

Reinforcing this, there is a tradeoff between freedom in implementable uses that favors innovation and the level of security. The second factor that affects the adequate management of negative externality is the disjuncture between the scope of markets and the extent of regulatory authorities' jurisdiction (Katz and Shapiro, 1985). Most networks today are interconnected across national boundaries. Many security issues – whether related to systemic risks, such as electricity, or to more private ones, such as privacy and data integrity on the internet – exist because of a lack of consistent practices and coordination between the regulatory authorities. Moreover, many capacity constraints would be better addressed at an international level. This is clearly the case, for instance, in Europe for air transportation, energy networks and the radio spectrum. Nation states consider all these resources de facto strategic and basic components of sovereignty, however, resulting in discrepancies between the scope of operations and that of regulations, although, as pointed out by Pigou in 1920 in his *Economics of Welfare*, they should be coordinated.

3.6 Tradeoffs in managing interfaces to maximize network effects

3.6.1 The centrality of interfaces

The breaking up of past monopolies and the unbundling of network operations into independent modules (or layers) has been the cornerstone of most so-called "deregulation" policies in network industries. Although the transition to the new regime was often characterized by a period of significant failures in terms of interconnection and interoperability among services provided by alternative users, norms and platforms rapidly developed to provide standardized interfaces. The latter boosted the exploitation and benefits of network externalities, as it became easier for service providers to rely on facilities and functionalities provided by third parties. Consequently, end users experienced access to wider arrays of services, enabling them to benefit from a supply finely adapted to their needs. The network's openness has yielded both diversity and innovation in the provision of networks and network-supported services. As pointed out earlier, however, innovation requires the evolution of interconnection/interoperability techniques (Awerbuch, Crew and Kleindorfer, 2000; Chao, Oren and Wilson, 2008).

Since it is admitted that any regulator would lack the required knowledge to efficiently and neutrally manage the evolution of interfaces among modules alone, their management has been left in the hands of market players, mostly on a competitive rather than on a cooperative basis. Indeed, technical standards of interconnection, as well as platforms of interoperability, are primarily provided by firms in the framework of a competitive process (with the exception of the internet in ICTs). Two major issues thus arise for market players and regulators. First, how can they maintain consistency in the evolution of the interface system (so as to dynamically ensure interoperability)? Second, how can they avoid the capture of interfaces by private interests? This last question is a consequence of the specificity of technological competition (David, 1985; Farrell and Saloner, 1986; Arthur, 1989; Liebowitz and Margolis, 1994; and see Geroski, 2000, for a survey). It is characterized by path dependence and "winner takes all" effects when network externalities play a role. Those players controlling interfaces – either because they are the designers of a technical standard of interoperability or because they provide platforms impassable by other market players – benefit from a dominant position that is subject to abuse. This is well illustrated by the Microsoft case. Being both the designer of interfaces and a market player, Microsoft can manage the release of the technical evolution of its interfaces so as to advantage its (and its allies') products. This is a way both to maintain its leadership position in the competitive race and to benefit from monopoly rents in the market. Even when such a technological competition in the definition of standards does not take place, there can be domination. In transportation and energy, the dominant player can manage interconnection arrangements for its own benefit, by reserving priority access to the best portions of the network or to services associated with the network, such as storage capabilities in energy (EC, 2004, 2007b).

3.6.2 Guaranteeing evolution and openness

In such a context, the role of the regulator is to support the openness of processes of standardization and to try to control any abuses of a dominant position. This is clearly a complex challenge. Beyond the problem of access to relevant information and knowledge, the point is that processes for the standardization of interfaces and the supply of platforms can be de facto rather than de jure. Technical standards and norms of behaviors can emerge from spontaneous recognition of and adherence to common principles. A central and unique platform of interconnection/interoperability may result from a competitive process (or from users choosing satisfactory solutions that do not leave any room for new entrants), as illustrated by the process by which Google has been becoming the central information platform. Key interfaces were not created by the law or administrative decisions (e.g. a delegation contract) that could be rewritten. Legal tools have to be instrumental to deal with the issue, which means, in practice, deciding which is responsible among the various components of the state (the executive, the legislature, administrative commissions in charge of different industries or different issues, etc.) and on what grounds public intervention is legitimate.

The other potential difficulty is the interplay between legal tools and, therefore, rights. This is the case, in particular, of intellectual property rights, as they are a matter of innovation. Beyond this, however, there is the more generic interference between the property rights of economic agents and pro-competition principles. Indeed, success in innovating and in developing a commercial supply may result in a monopoly, or, at least, a dominant position, which is even legally legitimate in the case of IPRs. The grounds on which it is possible and legitimate to intervene to limit the behavior of a successful entrepreneur are few and very restricted. At the level of principles, the issue is to balance the negative and redistributive effect of dominance, with the benefits of a system of incentives and selection that leads a supplier to propose solutions adapted to users. In other words, the question to be addressed is whether better alternatives exist, and whether the dominant firm hindered the emergence of an alternative solution. Moreover, the ability to design regulations that would not hamper possibilities for future evolution is also a concern. At the pragmatic level of implementation, there are a number of issues highlighting the difficulty of intervening efficiently. Is an interface really locking in a solution and to what extent does dominance matter? Should an antitrust suit be launched, or should other means, such as public support for competitors, be introduced? Should the interface manager be sanctioned or simply forced to guarantee fair access, and how can compliance be ensured? These are only some of the issues, and they all raise questions about the general ability of public authorities to efficiently oversee and monitor a highly complex and rapidly evolving system of strategic players.

Whatever the answers to these questions, it is clear that the role of the public regulator is totally new in this domain. In the past the maximization of network effects was largely determined by the organizational arrangement in each nation by which a national equipment manufacturer was quasi-integrated with network operators. In the new context, national regulators have to guarantee openness and avoid market foreclosure, especially by ensuring the revelation of information at an early stage to permit actual upstream competition in the setting of standards and downstream competition at the implementation stage (Twomey *et al.*, 2005; Gilbert and Newbery, 2007). One of the difficulties is that large market players are simultaneously in several regional or national markets, while regulation capabilities are still organized at an irrelevant level. Intergovernmental cooperation is therefore needed (Eberlein, 2005).

3.7 The permanent renewal of norms of "collective/public" interest

3.7.1 Uncertainty and the difficulty of setting objectives

As pointed out earlier in this chapter, the vertical and horizontal unbundling of network industries combined with the regime of intensive innovation, which multiplied the scope of services delivered by networks, made the role of regulators much more difficult, as they now have to deal with a considerably greater level of complexity and uncertainty than in the past. In addition, the criteria according to which a regulator has to make decisions are also complicated. In a stable and single service context, the objective function of a regulator is relatively simple: to optimize the quality/volume of service and design a pricing scheme guaranteeing access to the widest share of the population (or all, when a service is considered "universal" – i.e. as a component of the "package" of rights and services to be delivered to any citizen). In the new context, this objective function is less clear, since elements of dynamic efficiency have to be combined with static ones. As pointed out above, several somewhat contradictory objectives must be pursued by any regulator seeking to maximize collective welfare. Interoperatibiliy is required to guarantee the modularity of the network system. At the same time, it can hinder innovation. The intensity of competition between service providers has to be balanced with the need to guarantee security and quality. Open competition can lead to domination, while short-term and long-term consequences can diverge because of the potential strategic reactions of competitors, in particular with respect to questions of innovation. At the same time, cumulative effects may appear in the long run. Thus public regulators are not only constrained by information asymmetries because of strategic games played by operators (Laffont and Tirole, 1993; Smeers, 2005); they are also held back by lack of knowledge about the future dynamics of the complex system they oversee, which in concrete terms translates into a lack of criteria by which to assess the desirability of alternative techno-economic options and decide whether a particular firm's strategy works against the public interest or not. In short, many situations are very problematic.

At the same time, it must be recognized that "players" face uncertainty and undecidability as well. The strategic moves of their competitors, and also of partners, or of entrepreneurs interested in a distant module, obscure their decision horizon, because interdependences are multiple and complex. Technological change and innovation in utilization exacerbate this situation. Consequently, they lack knowledge when they have to decide on investments, R&D orientations, pricing and marketing policies, alliances, etc. Even "day-to-day" management is affected. Methods to allocate costs between the present and the future, or to deal with externalities, cannot be optimized so long as scenarios on the evolution of the industry cannot be established (Rious *et al.*, 2009).

3.7.2 Lobbying and forums to share information

In such a context, a convergence of interests might exist between regulators and regulated players. The former can attempt to build arenas and forums to gather information, knowledge and new perspectives from the players. The latter have an interest in both lobbying the regulator and sharing knowledge and views with competitors and other members of the industry.

Regulators – in our broad understanding of public authorities in charge of setting the rules of the game in a particular industry – have always been lobbied by particular interests seeking to influence the design of the regulatory framework. As pointed out by Pablo Spiller and Sanny Liao (2008), lobbying can be considered as welfare-enhancing when the regulator is able to balance the biased messages received with alternative information received from other stakeholders. Moreover, the day-to-day practice of regulatory authorities consists of investigating cases and confronting alternative assessments of a given situation. Controversies between stakeholders are a powerful means of acquiring information. Thus, although there are always risks of the "capture" of the regulator by operators, especially the dominant one (Levine and Forrence, 1990; Laffont and Tirole, 1991), an adequate design of the process of information-gathering can be an excellent means of enhancing the regulator's information and knowledge.

For their part, although they always have incentives to play "strategically" and therefore to bias or hide information, players have an interest in participating in such processes of information-sharing and revelation, because they can understand these as forums in which information is shared between market players on the basis of barter. They might be encouraged to display relevant information, because it is necessary to urge other market players to do the same. Since they are involved in business and social networks, the need to build trust, to maintain a reputation and to develop credibility contributes to limiting the tendency to lie. Sharing information has two advantages from a player's point of view. First, it is a way to get a better understanding of many relevant issues, and in particular technological and market developments. Second, it allows market players to share beliefs and reach a common vision of the future. Indeed, in a world characterized by uncertainties because of the possibility of alternative technological paths, convergence of beliefs by market players may be a way to select one equilibrium (one path) among possible alternatives. Market players understand very well that, if they all invest in compatible plans of R&D and investment, it is very unlikely that an alternative scenario will develop, because their independent decisions based on shared beliefs will be mutually reinforcing and serve to become self-fulfilling prophecies.

Lastly, competition between players is a factor contributing to making accurate information public in the framework of a process "arbitrated" by a regulator. Indeed, the messages sent to regulators can be challenged by competitors or users that have an interest in avoiding the single sourcing of information. The regulator can thus play on adversarial relations in order to make sure that the information it gets is challenged and therefore tends to be accurate, even if the information is incomplete. It might be necessary for competitors to complete it to avoid biases.

3.8 Regulatory frameworks as an open arena

3.8.1 Regulation by consensus and competition for knowledge provision

On account of the evolving issues and challenges raised in this chapter, the role of the regulator, as well as the means of public regulation and the nature of regulations, are subject to fundamental transformation. To be able to oversee network service providers efficiently, to guarantee the sustainability of the competitive process among them (which is a strong factor policing their behaviours) and to allow self-organizing to guarantee the dynamic consistency of networked systems, regulators have to organize informational arenas. These arenas should be public and open. The aim is to allow information-sharing and common knowledge-building between market participants and between the latter and the regulator. Their ability to reveal relevant information and ensure a convergence of vision should be based precisely on the public nature of the information revealed so as to guarantee that the information is subject to scrutiny (Graham, 2006; EC, 2007a; Waddams Price *et al.*, 2007).

Posting information is the key to a process of continual amendment, and therefore it guarantees adaptability. It is essential both to make information public and to build common beliefs. Of course, attempts to manipulate collective processes of information-sharing are likely to occur. Two mechanisms can limit their impact. First, competition between stakeholders limits the ability to brainwash the other players de facto. In the traditional lobbying system, messages exchanged are private, so that other stakeholders do not immediately challenge them. In an organized forum, public posts are immediately challengeable by all. Second, a regulator (that is, an entity that has the ability to impose constraints on market players and even to punish them) arbitrates the process. Manipulating information too explicitly is dangerous, either because the regulator could retaliate, or because it would no longer trust the company. In addition, the regulator can stimulate the emergence of alternative sources of information to balance the influence of dominant players. In particular, the regulator can open the regulatory arena to fringe and small stakeholders. Groups of consumers, citizens and activists can be empowered to ensure better access to hidden information.

Another problem might arise, however, in the context of uncertainty about the transformation of usages and technology. In a process very similar to the "winner's curse effect" that characterizes auctions, a convergence of beliefs can focus on collectively incorrect predictions. The 1999–2001 internet bubble comes to mind. An open and arbitrated process of information-sharing should serve to favor the disclosure of relevant and accurate information, however, potentially avoiding the development of fallacies. In a comparable way to the "republic of science," regulatory forums should organize collective skepticism and allow for reflexiveness. Indeed, sharing information and knowledge can have a different dynamic from competitive information bidding and claims. Forums can indeed become arenas for the emergence of an evolving consensus.

The goal of these forums is not only to build a common vision but also to agree on common rules. The model for these rules differs, nonetheless, from traditional formal regulations. Since they need to adapt to modifications and are progressively discovered thanks to actual experiments and knowledge development, a formal process of lawmaking does not create them. Instead, they are progressively constructed through amendments and complied with on the basis of consensus (even if there is a permanent threat that the regulator exercise its power to enact them and ensure mandatory compliance). This "semi-formal" character of regulation by consensus allows for continual evolution though progressive amendments. It also favors evolution through experimentation. Competitors and network users can implement innovation, the impacts of which are scrutinized by other stakeholders, the regulator becoming an arbitrator in the case of the infringement of preexisting rights, or becoming an antitrust authority in the case of a threat to the competitive process.

The introduction of heated and constant debate among stakeholders changes the nature of the regulator. It becomes a type of "common law" judge, which progressively establishes rules on the basis of precedents. It must be clear, however, that the regulator is not – and should not be – purely passive in the context of this process. Of course, it must react to suits or claims raised by parties that consider others' behaviors as problematic. It should also play an active role, nevertheless, in favoring a convergence of visions and beliefs. Its role is, therefore, to anticipate issues and organize debates favoring the emergence of consensus, and information-sharing, at least on existing alternatives and possible evolutions. Consequently, as an agenda setter, it has a soft power.

3.8.2 A platform combining the three powers

This leads directly to the concrete organization of public authorities. Up to this point, we have referred to a disembodied functional notion of "regulator." What has just been written about the role of the "regulator" explains why the regulatory authority increasingly needs to be organized on the (now established) model of an independent administrative authority, with a special status between that of the executive, the legislature and the judiciary. This is a key issue, both to legitimate its role and to provide it with the ability to exercise it (McCubbins, Noll and Weingast, 1987; Spiller, Stein and Tommasi, 2003). First, the authority needs to borrow from the government an ability to anticipate by setting the agenda. It must also react quickly in case of crisis (especially because systemic crises must be avoided). Second, the authority needs an ability, like that of the judiciary, to solve disputes, in particular because they highlight loopholes in the existing body of rights and rules. The need to react rapidly explains, moreover, why a specialized entity is required. Its role in terms of a knowledge platform and its established information networks are essential to resolve disputes more quickly and relevantly than a standard court, which suffers from obtaining its knowledge from industry, including that on the issues at stake and players' patterns of behavior. Third, this authority, like the legislature, is granted the right to enact rules.

Obviously, any authority should act under the last-resort control of the established and legitimate power that oversees it. Government has the ability to limit players directly and more severely. It can employ much more powerful instruments. Above all, it can influence the authority itself. This is dependent upon the political climate and the constitutional regime. Decisions of the authority may be appealed against in regular courts, and the legislature has the ability to pass legislation and even to reshape the authority's competences. This role of intermediary between the three powers also impacts the regulatory authority's internal organization. To guarantee legitimacy and efficiency in its ruling, the authority should, for instance, adopt the practices of the legal system, in the sense that investigation should be public and open to claims and its decision should be subject to appeal (both internally and in the courts; Stephenson, 2005).

Its "central" role also explains why the regulatory authority should combine the management of the public good supply with oversight of the competitive process (Perrot, 2004). As a regulator, it should favor cooperation and coordination in the industry, while, as a competition authority, it should avoid the drift toward implicit or explicit collusion (in addition to the exercise of monopoly power). This is a direct consequence of the fact that the regulator becomes a societal regulator arbitrating between various stakeholders trying to influence the setting of public norms (Prosser, 2005).

3.8.3 A "public" authority to manage dynamic consistency

The central role of the regulator explains why she should emanate from the public sphere, even if she is dependent upon the information and knowledge provided by private stakeholders. Indeed, there is a permanent risk of the regulator being captured by the dominant players. In a context of self-regulation, the risks of the emergence of a club of dominant players forming a coalition to regulate in their best interests would be high. The public status guaranteeing the regulator's strength and independence is the first level of collective protection. It is insufficient, however, as dominant players also benefit from having more means to develop the relevant knowledge, technology and facilities that are necessary to manage interoperability. The regulator could easily be dependent upon these resources to be able to regulate, which would provide major players with a means of influence, if not more than that. The fact that the regulator is an "agenda setter" – deciding how and when to organize debates, and designing the scope of the debatable issues – provides her with the means to partially counterbalance the major players' capability of influence. Moreover, the fact that debates result in an amendable set of rules open to modification as a function of its actual performance, the possibility of enhancing it and the necessity to adjust it to innovation means that the effects of a potential capture of the regulator at a particular point of time are subject to ex post revisions. This dynamic context explains why it is essential for the regulator to be in charge of the resolution of conflicts from the first instance. Conflicts reveal maladaptations, and responsibility for their settlement conveys the relevant information to the regulator.

The role of the regulator is to become that of a "platform," as is highlighted in the "two-sided markets" literature (Rochet and Tirole, 2003, 2007), in the sense that she is responsible for managing externalities among market players. It is not a question here of the network and service externalities discussed earlier in this chapter. This refers instead to externalities linked to the production of a common institutional framework needed to operate in the industry. First, its role is to align the participation constraints of stakeholders, both in the "market" and in the "process of reform." Indeed, one of the roles of the regulator is to guarantee the network's openness. From this perspective, the regulator has to manage reforms so as to guarantee that new entrants and small players are not expelled from the market. In addition, she has to make sure that small stakeholders can have a voice in the process of regulation-making. From this perspective, she has to be able to organize cross-subsidization among stakeholders given their "willingness to contribute." For instance, the infrastructure owner might be asked to contribute to the needed adaptation of the infrastructure to allow the organization of a competitive retail market. Service providers could also be requested to contribute to funds aimed at subsidizing user associations. Indeed, the latter have to build competences to be able to influence the regulatory process.

Second, continuous adaptation of the regulatory framework is needed because of permanent innovation. Regulatory changes have a cost for market players, however, since they lead to the writeoff of all kinds of investments. The regulator's role is to manage the resulting costs for players (which have to be balanced with costs associated with the status quo) dynamically. It can take the form of cross-subsidies among stakeholders to organize the compensation of losers by the winners in a Hicks–Kaldor approach. It can also rely on the speed of implementation of changes so as to smooth the timing of the scrapping of past investments as a function of the standard obsolescence delay in industry. A way to do this, without hindering supplier or user initiatives, is to allow the emergence and testing of new practices, and managing the processes of adaptation for generic rules when these new practices are stabilized. More generally, taking into account the participation constraints of stakeholders leads to calls for progressive processes of change. Incremental changes allow "players" to learn and to adapt. They also provide them with a foreseeable horizon. Knowing that changes are implementable over time, they can adapt their decision-making processes and investment decisions to a pace of evolution they can anticipate, even if they cannot foresee the nature of the evolution. This calls for favoring some over others, reversibility, revisability and flexibility.

3.9 Conclusion: soft and reflexive regulations

In this chapter we highlight the necessary evolution of the notion of regulation in the context of an economy based on innovation and on a modular organization of production. It is both impossible and inefficient to implement a "command and control" regulation, and even to design an optimal incentives scheme aimed at leading network operators to maximize collective welfare. The definition of the criteria of desirable performance, the permanent rate of innovation, the complexity of modular networks, etc. work together to prevent any public regulator from designing and implementing satisfactory solutions. At the same time, in industries characterized by fixed costs and network effects, a dominant position can become established and unchallengeable for very long periods. Since network industries provide public goods that are the essential infrastructure of modern economies, self-regulation could lead to very unsatisfactory results. Private regulations could be captured by dominant players, with a major risk of collusion translating into a slow rate of innovation and significant transfers of rents in favor of dominant competitors.

New forms of public regulations have two principal characteristics. First, they are soft regulations. They are based on a decentralized process of emergence, either by negotiation or on the basis of case law, which means that they are constantly evolving. They result from public consultations, hearings, conflict settlement, green books and White Papers, and result in principles of fair practices, guidelines, public commitments, letters of intention, etc. Of course, some rules are enacted and made enforceable in the framework of the formal legal order. Many of the rules have a softer – and more ambiguous – nature, however, and are complied with because of concerns about reputation and individual interests in not deviating from expected standards. One of the important consequences of the constantly evolving character of network industries is that players have an interest in reducing the level of uncertainty; as a result, one can understand consensus regulations based on the logic of the focal point. One of the interests of the common framework is that it allows for the convergence of anticipations, and facilitates the adoption of consistent/compatible behaviors.

The second characteristic of the new form of regulation is that it is (and must be) reflexive, in the sense that it should be constantly revised as a function of the development of knowledge. All players are aware that the regulatory framework is to be revised as a function of innovation, whether technological or in terms of practices. In addition, they have incentives to share information and knowledge, because they need to guarantee the viability of their practices and investments, while at the same time learning from others in order to anticipate future evolution. Although there are always threats of a cognitive capture of the public regulator by private interests, the adequate organization of debate and of information release allows for information disclosure and knowledge-sharing.

Despite its soft and evolving characteristic, the new, reflexive regulations are powerful tools for addressing the many issues that regulators face, namely the definition and implementation of the public interest, the distribution of fixed costs, the establishment of a property rights system and the management of the remaining externalities. The public release of information and sharing of knowledge allow for coordination of behavior. Learning allows the regulator to establish new norms and to check compliance, moreover, whether these norms are formal or informal.

In such a cognitive context, the role of regulators is essentially to manage information disclosure. The forums they organize are open processes of lobbying aimed at making information public through competition between stakeholders. This need to organize competition justifies the specific status of the regulator, balanced between the legislative power, the executive power and the judiciary. The resulting regulations are based on the principle of evolving compromises, rather than on the sovereign enactment by the government of collective objectives and rules.

It is worth pointing out that these new forms of regulations are consistent with the necessity to adapt the scope of regulations to that of economic activities. Since networks are de facto increasingly cross-border (such as communications and media, and electricity and gas), common principles of regulation and coordination among jurisdictions are needed. At the same time, it is difficult for states to delegate public prerogatives on the matter to a supranational level, because the services delivered by telecommunication, energy and transportation networks are considered as essential to the national sovereignty and components of the "social contract." Equally, national regulators have incentives to coordinate among themselves. Indeed, they must avoid being cognitively surpassed by major players that benefit from various "regulatory games" in each national market. Sharing information among regulators is a way to balance this and to restore public abilities to regulate. Consequently, far-sighted national sovereignty is compatible with open international cooperation.

4 *Balancing informational power by informational power* or *Rereading Montesquieu in the internet age*

HERBERT BURKERT

4.1 Introduction

"In every government there are three sorts of power: the legislative; the executive in respect to things dependent on the law of nations; and the executive in regard to matters that depend on the civil law" (Montesquieu, 1941 [1748]: 152). This is the English translation of the beginning of Montesquieu's famous chapter 6, "De la constitution d'Angleterre," in his treatise *De l'Esprit des lois*. To today's readers this passage is a little cryptic, particularly if they are not familiar with the terms used in English law. Montesquieu himself goes on to clarify the issues for his French audience (p. 152, para. 2):

> By virtue of the first, the prince or magistrate enacts temporary or perpetual laws, and amends or abrogates those that have been already enacted. By the second, he makes peace or war, sends or receives embassies, establishes the public security, and provides against invasions. By the third, he punishes criminals, or determines the disputes that arise between individuals. The latter we shall call the judiciary power, and the other simply the executive power of the state.

In short, what Montesquieu is describing as the English system and prescribing for political governance systems in general is what has become the classical triad of the legislative, executive and judicial powers – powers that, as Montesquieu then goes on to prescribe at length in this chapter 6, have to be kept separate and have to balance each other if the liberty of the citizens is to be preserved. Even if there are doubts as to whether Montesquieu had delivered an accurate description of the British constitutional system of his day, the normative force of the "three powers" model has remained undiminished, still challenging the legitimacy of deviations or alternative constructs and serving as a model and benchmark for new and emerging democracies.

In the course of political and constitutional history this ideal-type model has seen many variations in the real world of democratic political systems.[1] It has been observed, for example, that the system of political parties has been stratifying political power across the boundaries between the three separate powers to an extent that the separation of powers seems to have been replaced by a "separation of parties" model (Levinson and Pildes, 2006). The classification of such a development as a deviation, however, is quite an indicator that the model itself retains at least some of its normative force. Indeed, the notion of the separation of power has remained largely unquestioned in legal and political theory in recent decades (Kropp and Lauth, 2007).

This chapter discusses a different challenge to this model, and discusses it from an "information" perspective. How far have changes introduced with the advances in (modern) information and communication technology changed the functionality of the separation model? Is a sort of separation of informational power model developing that mirrors the traditional separation of powers model?

I argue that the ICT advances have largely favored the executive power, to the detriment of the two other powers and to the detriment of the model itself, affecting its functionality as a power-restraining device. This disequilibrium cannot exclusively be attributed to information and communication technologies, nor to the specific role of the executive in the three powers model, but must also be attributed to the strategic behavior of the executive.

The chapter goes on to ask if there are other transformations visible that might produce a functional equivalent to the structural safeguards provided by the separation of power. I search for such changes within the confines of the three powers model, looking first at how the other powers seek to keep up with the shift of informational power. I then examine the executive itself to see if internal changes can be observed that may produce at least an internalized system for the control of informational power. Finally, I address some changes that have been affecting the democratic environment

[1] Moreover, they have expanded internationally; see, for example, Prempeh (2006).

as such. To this end I discuss the emergence of new sites of policy-making and the appearance of new actors in these sites.

Evaluating the observations of these changes, internal and external alike, some common trends are apparent, indicating that informational power itself has a dialectic quality, which may not yet have produced an equivalent to the separation model but which will continue to influence the way in which the executive is able to execute its powers.

Before proceeding with this line of argument, some clarification would appear to be necessary. The focus on the executive power requires a terminological clarification: The terms "the executive" or "executive power" as used here are not identical with "government." The term "government" is used in many contexts: In the initial quotation from Montesquieu, for example, "government" referred to the combination of the three powers. The "government" is often referred to as that part of the executive that is subject to change by elections, however. To add to the confusion, in some countries this part of the executive is also referred to as the "administration," while other countries refer only to the other part, the bureaucratic organization, as the "administration." The term "executive," as it is used here, refers to this latter meaning, to the organizational complex, which continues administering when governments change.

The "informational view" – as the instrument of approach adopted here – derives from the school of legal analysis looking at the way in which rules and institutions legitimize and delegitimize and eventually seek to influence information generation and information handling in societies. This type of analysis and discussion has developed in line with the advances in information and communication technologies in the last six decades and the attempts to establish a normative language to describe and prescribe changes occurring with these technologies as a sort of legal science equivalent to systems analysis.[2]

Finally, "information and communication technology" is understood in its broadest sense, to comprise not only the technical inventions themselves and their implementation in economic, social and

[2] The term that seems to have established itself for this type of analysis is "information law," although the term is also used for all regulatory material that addresses information. For more details, see Gasser (2002, 2004). For an early informational analysis of the *legislative* power, see Krehbiel (1991).

political practices but also the desires and ideas that have helped to form these inventions, the economic, social, political and cultural conditions that have helped to ensure the transformation of such ideas into social practice, and the impact of the uses on these conditions.[3]

4.2 The executive, information governance and the informational separation of powers

The organizations of judiciary power decide cases when they are brought before them. By design, therefore, the judiciary avoids initiative. Parliamentary assemblies dissolve and reassemble. By design, therefore, the legislature is not built on personal continuity. It is only the executive that carries the burden of initiative and constant presence, and has to show its constant ability to act, or at least to react. It is the executive of the modern state that has inherited from the absolutist state the legitimacy of the monopolistic use of force, albeit this time legitimized by democratic consent. This inheritance is not just a privilege – it is an expectation: The executive has to be effective, and has to be seen to be effective, in directing this force at the right moment with the appropriate intensity to the proper place. Cybernetic theory calls this guiding capability "information" (Klaus and Buhr, 1974). In addition, as a resource, information is able to compensate for the lack of other resources, such as personnel, money and material. Finally, the ability to bind information to organizational continuity enables the executive to use force economically and thus to enhance and stabilize its legitimacy further. For military and intelligence systems, the importance of mastering information has been a truism since ancient times; for modern public administrations, governing by information has become a continuous learning process. The increasing reliance on information cannot solely be attributed to pragmatic reflections on the use of force; it equally reflects a more general belief that science, and with it systematic information collection and conscientious information analysis, are also useful for analyzing and predicting social interactions in general, and could thus be useful for administrative tasks.

[3] For a comprehensive definition of the technology and a description of the technological change in detail, see Volti (2006).

This belief in information has been reinforced further with the advances in information and communication technology. This technology finally seems to have provided the tools with which to master the quantities and the complexities involved in the handling of information in the modern state. The strong belief in information is strengthened not only by ICT (although the actual implementation may have taught many different lessons) but also by observable behavioral effects among those on whom information is being collected. Information-handling can therefore become a tool of guiding behavior even if it is not followed by action. Relying on the scientific improvability of executive power, trusting the behavioral effects of information, certain of the manageability of quantity and complexity with the help of ICT – all these factors are contributing to the conviction that governing by information is not simply a prerequisite to governing by action but is also able to substitute for governing by action, at least partly, in a more economical way. Last but not least, a reduced potential for the use of force as a result of governing by information would at the same time contribute to the legitimacy of governing.[4] If the process goes too far, this overreliance on information produces symptoms known by the phrase "surveillance state"; the term "state" instead of the "executive" seems justified here, because in such situations one can usually observe strong collaboration between the executive, the judiciary and the legislature.

Governing by information, or at least shifting greater attention to the informational elements of governing, has other pitfalls as well, however. Information has to be analyzed. Analysis is also a matter of perception and concepts filtering perception. Information and information analysis may spare actions, moreover, but they are no total substitutes for actions. Actions may also meet their own constraints, which do not always permit what information-gathering and analysis have been suggesting. Recent history has shown that the combination of surveillance and inertia may well produce self-destructive results for governmental organizations.

Against this background, executive dominance does not come about automatically nor is its continuity secure; it has to be reasserted

[4] On information governance with examples from environmental policies, see Mol (2006); more generally, on information governance (including technological aspects), see Mayer-Schönberger and Lazer (2007).

continuously, and requires the executive to use its structural position strategically. Arguing for the dominance of the executive follows a general pattern. It is usually by reference to something higher, more critical, that additional legitimacy is asked for to set aside the structural restraints imposed by the separation of powers model. The strategy that is currently predominant is reference to "crisis." Crisis establishes the link to the general self-perception of our societies as "risk societies" (Beck, 1986). Risk requires the constant management of risks, so "crisis" is the moment of the executive; only the executive – because it always stands to attention, in effect – appears to be able to mobilize and direct resources effectively and at very short notice. Crisis is the natural prerogative of the executive. It is by referring to crisis that the legislature can legitimately consent to the demands of the executive, and the judiciary can sanction this consensus.

Reference to crisis facilitates the solution of another informational problem of the executive: The "activist" status of the executive had granted informational privileges to the executive even before the governing process had become more information-conscious. The need for informational asymmetries in favor of the executive had been self-evident. Administrative secrecy had remained as sacrosanct as military secrets. The last fifty years or so have seen an erosion of the self-evident, however: informational asymmetries have become questioned – and not only in the public sector. Freedom of information laws have emerged that provide a general right of access to information held by the executive. Data protection (privacy protection) laws appeared that contained requirements to provide at least the persons concerned with information on the information that is being held on them. Both types of regulations contained numerous exceptions in favor of the executive that may not have fundamentally changed its informational prerogatives. What has changed, however, is the legitimacy default: although informational asymmetries in favor of the executive were taken for granted previously and forced opposing views to argue their case, the default has more recently been turning in favor of transparency, with asymmetries having to explain their legitimacy. It is in this context that the reference to "crisis" provides the necessary argument that – at least in times of crisis – the default rule has to be changed again to secure the informational advantages of the executive.

The situation is still precariously poised: at the current stage the executive may demand and command its unique informational position without too much interference from the other powers, to the extent that – in informational terms – there is no balance of (informational) power mirroring the traditional normative model of the separation of powers. At this "moment of the executive," however, the informational demands of the executive may well become perceived as "inflationary," in the sense of being too systematic and invasive a call/justification for governmental intervention on the grounds of "crisis" – as may be the constant reference to "crisis." In terms of efficiency, moreover, it remains open to question whether informational asymmetries may not prove to be counterproductive when searching for adequate responses to crises.[5]

At this stage, however, it is questionable whether a more balanced situation can be regained simply by waiting for such perceptional changes to take effect. It is also doubtful how sustainable this critical attitude will remain when new crises are being announced. Against this background, it seems useful to look for more substantial changes that may help to recapture the executive by improved structural safeguards to rehabilitate the normative essence of the model of the separation of powers, when necessary even with the help of functional equivalents.

Before searching for such equivalents, the traditional triad of the executive, the legislature and the judiciary needs to be re-examined. To what extent have the other two powers been able to make use of information and communication technology? Has this technology improved their ability to provide a balance to the expanding power of the executive? To what extent is the executive itself changing, perhaps by creating a system of internal checks and balances ? I then move from the traditional powers and address some more general changes to the democratic environment in search of evolving patterns for restraint that might be equivalent to the traditional model of the three powers.

[5] See, for example, with regard to the recent situation in the European Union, Temple Lang (2006: 128): "[T]he political safeguards in the EC system were well conceived and satisfactory but have weakened; and the legal and political safeguards in the Foreign and Security Policy 'Second Pillar' and the justice and Home Affairs ('Third Pillar') introduced by the Maastricht Treaty are not satisfactory." See also Bonner (2006: 47): "The overarching concern of this article is [. . .] with the legal accountability of the Executive branch, something particularly difficult in times of emergency or when the Executive intones the mantra of 'national security.'"

4.3 A future for the separation of powers model?

4.3.1 Changes within the separation of powers model

Information and communication technology has not affected only the executive. The *judiciary*, where the command of precedent is of essential importance, was an early adaptor, using this technology to prepare, store and distribute its decisions and to improve court administration.[6] Going through the literature of the early 1960s, with respect to computers and law for example, it seems that one of the many hopes at this time had been to employ computers in the task of legal decision-making itself[7] – a hope that remained alive with the artificial intelligence projects of the early 1990s and later[8] and that has seen a revival with the advent of formal document description languages (see, for example, Kotok, 2001). With regard to court administration, the use of ICT for the allocation of time, space and personnel, for the distribution of the case load and for communication between all the parties involved in a court case has become common practice. All such efforts have increased the productivity of the judicial branch and improved its information dissemination.

None of these measures can be said to have been aimed at actively and directly rebalancing the checks and balances system in favor of the judicial branch, however. To the contrary, in fact: quite often the judiciary viewed the productivity enhancement measures in its realm with some suspicion, wondering whether they had been an attempt to improve informational control over the judiciary for both the legislative and executive powers (for the discussion in Germany, see, for example, Schütz, 2005). In sum, ICT and improved information management have mainly had internal effects on this branch rather than extending or improving the judiciary's influence on the executive and legislative branches.

Legislatures, too, have profited from information and communication technology. This technology has greatly enhanced the inner

[6] See, for example, the overview of the literature on these subjects provided by Nagel (1990).

[7] One of the key articles on this issue at that time was that by Layman and Caldwell (1963).

[8] The journal *Artificial Intelligence and Law* first appeared in 1992, and it is still in existence today.

workings of the legislative branch just as it has with the judiciary. Administrative, archival, retrieval and text-processing activities, as well as the recordkeeping of sessions and voting procedures, have all been facilitated. Information exchanges between the legislature and the public have been improved, as have those between the legislative and the executive powers (for examples in the United States, see Reiman, 2000). Even routine tasks such as, for example, budgetary control would be almost impossible today for the legislature without the help of information technology, even if one might ask whether these improved possibilities have also led to greater scrutiny.[9]

The legislative branch recognized early on, however, that this technology might provide a way to reduce its dependence on the executive for the provision of information when such information was needed for legislative decision-making. It is a revealing story that the first data protection act worldwide, the data protection act of the German province of Hesse, formally introduced the issue of the informational separation of powers, both in a direct and an indirect way.[10] Indirectly, the separation concept was introduced by establishing the purpose limitation principle as one of the key principles of data protection,[11] allowing the processing of data (on persons) by an administrative entity only so long as this entity processed information only within the limits of its competence and the (predefined) purposes for which the data had been collected. In consequence, this principle was aimed at erecting Chinese walls within the executive defined by rules of competence and administrative purpose. This concept became known as the principle of the internal separation of informational powers (for a discussion of the doctrine in Germany, see Bull, 1979), and I return to it when I analyze internal changes within the executive.

More importantly for the legislative power, however, the Hesse act also addressed the separation and balance of power issue in its more traditional meaning. The legislature had observed that the use of

[9] See, for example, the papers of the conference on "Fiscal challenges: an interdisciplinary approach to budget policy," held on February 10 and 11, 2006, at the University of Southern California Gould School of Law, which are available at http://law.usc.edu/academics/centers/cslp/fiscal_06index.html (accessed December 1, 2007).

[10] Datenschutzgesetz. Gesetz- und Verordnungsblatt für das Land Hessen, teil I, 625f – published on October 12, 1970.

[11] See § 5 (2) of the Hesse act.

databanks, the key IT concept of the time, primarily benefited the executive. Consequently, the act – in its paragraph 6 – explicitly established an information right for the legislature against the executive. The then key provider of data-processing services for the executive was put under an obligation to provide access to and to run programs designed by the legislative body; not only was this right established at the provincial level but it was also extended to the representative bodies at the communal level for their centers of data-processing. With these regulations, the Hesse Data Protection Act established a comprehensive political concept for mastering the implications of ICT – a concept that went beyond seeing these technological advances as potential threats merely to the privacy of the individual.[12]

Only a very few of the data protection laws that followed the Hesse example addressed the separation of powers problem, however.[13] The separation of powers was still seen primarily as a somewhat old-fashioned constitutional law issue rather than a design concept that needed immediate attention in view of major technological change. Another reason for the lack of general attention may have been that, in practice, access to the executive's information was perceived mainly as a problem for opposition parties, while the governing party, with its

[12] This approach should have led the way to a more political understanding of data protection as a means to control informational power in a more fundamental way. Very few laws took up the challenge, however. It was several years later that the corresponding French act came to a similar political understanding by describing as the purpose of the data protection act not only the protection of privacy but the defense of all political rights and liberties against the risks of data processing ("Loi no. 78–17 du 6 janvier 1978 relative à l'informatique, aux fichiers *et aux libertés*: article 1er 'L'informatique doit être au service de chaque citoyen. Son développement doit s'opérer dans le cadre de la coopération internationale. Elle ne doit porter atteinte ni à l'identité humaine, *ni aux droits de l'homme*, ni à la vie privée, *ni aux libertés individuelles ou publiques*'" (emphasis added).

[13] The current Data Protection Act of Hesse still contains these requirements in § 38 (Hessisches Datenschutzgesetz in der Fassung, January 7, 1999, at www.datenschutz.hessen.de/hdsg99/Inhalt.htm; accessed December 1, 2007). The Data Protection and Access to Information Act of the Province of Berlin contains a similar reference in its article 1: "It is the purpose of this act [. . .] to protect the constitutional principle of separation of powers from dangers arising from automated data processing" (§ 1 (1) no. 2 of the Gesetz zum Schutz personenbezogener Daten in der Berliner Verwaltung, December 17, 1990 (GVBl. 1991 S. 16, 54), zuletzt geändert durch Gesetz, July 30, 2001 (GVBl. S. 305)), at www.datenschutz-berlin.de/infomat/dateien/blndsg/blndsg_04 (accessed December 1, 2007) (English translations by the author).

privileged link to the government of the day, could always ensure access to these information resources. The problem therefore resurfaced only in the context of blatant refusals of parliamentary minority rights. As a result, the informational efforts of the legislature do not seem to have led to the development of fully independent informational resources for parliaments, other than in areas in which the executive itself did not seem to have moved yet, because of their highly speculative nature or because of the emphasis on independent analysis, such as technology assessment or analytical services.

What has improved over time, nevertheless, is the legal position of the legislature when investigating the activities of the government of the day or administrative practices. In such cases, the separation of powers model still appears to be fully operational. Indeed, in such cases ICT has come in handy for the effective management of the information loads for legislative committees of inquiry. Practical experiences overall make it doubtful, however, if such activities can really be seen to constitute improved (informational) control over the executive. Such practices are all too often counterbalanced by the efforts of governing political parties to protect the government of the day.

When looking at the conflicts between the executive and legislative powers in the Hesse case, I referred briefly to the concept of the internal separation of (informational) power within the executive. It was noticed that this mechanism relied on the purpose limitation principle, introduced as one of the safeguards to protect privacy. While still one of the key principles of data protection regulation,[14] purpose limitation in practice has had very few limiting effects: In response to the principle, purpose tends to become defined rather broadly, in order to keep changes under the umbrella of the same purpose; in addition, purposes are still being changed afterwards, usually in reference to a new, upcoming crisis. Such changes may need more formal procedures of approval, such as legitimation by a formal law. In the crisis context, though – as outlined above – such collaboration between the legislature and the executive does not usually create a problem, and will only very rarely be corrected by the judiciary. This treatment of purpose

[14] See, for example, article 6 (b) of the Directive 95/46/EC of the European Parliament and of the Council of October 24, 1995, on the protection of individuals with regard to the processing of personal data and on the free movement of such data. *Official Journal of the European Communities*, November 23, 1995, L 281: 31.

limitation is not surprising. Although the context sensitivity of information (another data protection principle) may be acknowledged because it helps to improve data quality, purpose limitation in general is still perceived as an artificial barrier to precisely those aspects of ICT that the executive seeks to harness: the economic use of information for the optimal allocation of administrative resources through the seamless integration of information for multiple uses. In consequence, information systems, once dedicated solely to purposes such as financial reporting, traffic control and traffic flow monitoring, banking and credit information become extended and linked to early warning systems against undesirable social behavior and suspicious political and religious activities and are integrated into preventive intelligence and reactive enforcement systems. The purpose limitation principle may have survived as a principle, but as a principle without a purpose; and with it exited the concept of the internal separation of informational powers (for more detail, see Burkert, 2000).

Given this background, it is not surprising that reflections on how to rein in the informational power of the executive return to attempts at establishing additional institutions of informational control within the executive itself, building on traditions such as controlling money flows by comptrollers. Again, data protection and, to some extent, access to government information legislation has introduced such bodies combining elements of judiciary power (e.g. the power of independent inquiry) with those from legislative power (such as having leading officials of such agencies being elected by parliament and/or the duty/privilege to report directly to parliament). In the context of the European discussion, those outside "information control" agencies are mentioned with some pride, praising the "European model" of data protection (and access to information) agencies as an example of effective administrative oversight.[15] The EU "Data Protection Directive" of 1995 explicitly requires these agencies, so far as their data protection functions are concerned, to exercise effective control and enjoy an independent status similar to judicial bodies.[16]

[15] In the area of data protection, oversight very often extends to the private sector processing of personal data as well. Access to information legislation is directed only at public sector bodies and those bodies that, by virtue of the relevant definition of the respective law, are deemed to belong to the public sector.

[16] See article 28 of the directive (footnote 15).

Also beyond the confines of informational power, on a more general level, new designs are being discussed. In the US context, Neal Kumar Katyal (2006) has suggested designing a new executive system with internal overlaps of competence, with a more independent administrative staff protected by special status, with internal adjucating entities, with increased reporting requirements to the legislature and with oversight rights for minority groups as well in the legislature. As examples from recent reorganizations in this field – in this case in the United States – seem to indicate, such internal competition and rivalry can also be maintained even within purposely monolithic administrative structures (Thessin, 2003; Isbister, 2004).

Such constructs are facing the consequences of their hybrid design, however: built as part of the executive but with a mix of elements from the legislative and the judicial branches, these agencies have to manage *internally* what the separation of powers and checks and balances models have intentionally created as *external* mechanisms. In order to keep internal conflict in check, these supervising intra-agencies have to generate internal compromises, which in turn limit their capability for action. They are in constant danger of becoming hostage to the institutions they are intended to supervise from within. Although it seems difficult to assess the full extent in which such inbuilt mechanisms are indeed able to restrain executive power, these institutions at least contribute to the creation of new mechanisms of reporting, transparency and accountability.

4.3.2 Equivalents arising from changes in the democratic environment?

Although the observations above have remained within the confines of traditional systems of government (the term "government" being used here in its broadest sense), it needs to be acknowledged that these systems of government and the democratic systems in which they operate find themselves in processes of transformation that produce new modes of governance, open the entrance to new actors and shift the sites of decision-making. Such changes are addressed with terms such as "globalization," "self-governance" and "co-operative governance," "networking" and "informal decision-making." Whether it is possible to attribute all these changes exclusively to changes in (information and communication) technology is doubtful. These changes have occurred, or at least seem to have been accelerated, because of (modern) information and communication technology, however, and they have come to rely on the availability and functionality of this technology.

Two of these changes are discussed now so as to provide a summary examination of the extent to which the changes may produce equifunctional solutions: the change of site (or level) where executive decisions are being made, and the emergence of new actors competing with the executive for participation, at least, in decision-making.

Not only have ICTs shown effects within state systems but they have also contributed to a communication environment of exchange and communication between state systems. These new patterns of communication have intensified not just because of the technological availability of more, better and more time-saving ways of communication (and of mobility in general) but also because of the need to follow the extensions of economic, social and cultural exchange that the executive powers had to administer.

Legislative and judicial bodies followed this path of internationalization with a time delay and at different speeds. The institutional history of the European Union provides ample evidence of how executive cooperation helped to create a new powerful executive that was only eventually supplemented by judicial and legislative bodies. On the national level, of course, the expansion of the executive was accompanied by the necessary formal consent of the legislature, and in some cases of the judiciary. Legislative and even judicial intervention had mostly been binary and after the fact, however, either accepting or refusing forms of cooperation that the executive had already negotiated and concluded with other executive powers in detail.

Nevertheless, these forms of international cooperation at least exposed each individual executive power to competition with other executive powers. They also helped each executive power to maintain a maneuvering space with only limited oversight from the local legislature and judiciary, however. At the same time, this competition between executives was itself kept temporarily free from supervision for a time by internationally operating legislative and judicial powers. This situation – at least for some forms of international cooperation – seems to be slowly changing, however. Increasingly, the newly generated international forms of executive power – beyond the European example – are becoming surrounded by institutions of at least judicial power on the international level.[17] At the same time, however, the forms of multilevel governance provide plenty of opportunities for executive bodies to evade controls by oscillating between the local, provincial, national, regional and international levels. The executive power has become evasive (for more details on these phenomena, see Slaughter, 2003). Policies that are unpopular on one level can – in a sort of "policy-laundering" process, and provided sufficient competence can be constructed – be moved to a higher level where a more cooperative spirit seems to prevail, and then be reintroduced at the initial level as an obligation originating from the higher level. On these higher levels of cooperation, executive bodies sharing similar experiences with their respective judicial and legislative systems have come to regard each other as natural allies in defending themselves against such intrusions. Recent court cases and parliamentary debates surrounding the activities of foreign intelligence services in Europe are only some of the more spectacular examples of this general trend of executive powers resisting oversight at the national and international levels.[18]

Thus, although the new levels of interaction may have introduced a new type of competition between executive powers, they have also helped to create a new cooperative spirit among executives to ease the consequences of such competition. This eased competition, then, can hardly be seen as an equivalent to the separation of powers model. Rather, it seems to invite joint cooperative reactions from executive bodies at all levels against attempts from legislative and judicial powers to rein in their spheres of influence.

The lack of structural controls at the international level similar to those at least normatively provided by the separation of powers model has not been without consequences, and has created a legitimacy gap for the executive. Although some international organizations – as pointed out above – have tried to mirror national systems of checks and balances, international organizations and other forums for

[17] One example is provided by the International Criminal Court; more details can be found at www.icc-cpi.int (accessed December 1, 2007).

[18] See "Report on the alleged use of European countries by the CIA for the transportation and illegal detention of prisoners" (2006/2200(INI)), Temporary committee on the alleged use of European countries by the CIA for the transportation and illegal detention of prisoners; European Parliament Document FINAL A6–9999/2007, January 26, 2007.

international cooperation still largely see themselves bound to their national executive powers, with any requirements in terms of reporting or accountability directed exclusively to them.

With the establishment of the United Nations, however, a door was opened to new organizations entering the international arena that were not bound to national executive bodies: non-governmental organizations became officially recognized with article 71 of chapter 10 of the United Nations charter, although, in accordance with the political understanding of the time, arrangements with such national organizations could be made only after consultation with the member state concerned. These regulations were then superseded by Resolution 1996/31 of the United Nations' Economic and Social Council (ECOSOC), which now provides for a transparent procedure for NGOs to formally receive consultative status. For the region of the Council of Europe's member states, the European Convention on the Legal Personality of International Non-Governmental Organizations laid down similar rules in 1986 (for more detail, see Schwitter and Caoline, 2004: 6ff.). Today NGOs have become highly integrated actors in international policy-making. In their ascent they have been able, often more flexibly and more effectively than executive bodies, to harness modern ICT to organize themselves, to monitor the activities of executive powers, to create networks of expertise and political action among themselves and to communicate with their stakeholders and with the general public.

It remains doubtful, however, that NGOs have been able to generate an effective system of control that would be able to substitute legislative and juridical control. They have contributed to agenda-setting in international policy-making; they have provided new inputs for decision-making; and they have influenced communication policies and contributed to greater transparency in international policy making. They may also have introduced a consciousness of accountability that executive bodies can no longer neglect. In my view, however, NGOs have so far not been able to substitute for, or even to supplement, the control structures of a fully operational separation of powers model. In questioning the legitimacy of the international operations of the executive powers, NGOs are faced with the problems of their own legitimacy. They carry with them a constructional defect that is affecting their legitimacy. According to the accreditation rules set up by the ECOSOC and the Council of Europe NGOs have to have a certain range of operation (e.g. being active in at least three countries, as stipulated by the ECOSOC resolution, or in two countries, by the Council of Europe convention) and an internal democratic structure (demanded only by the ECOSOC rules) but they cannot claim to be representative. Their sources of legitimacy may be integrity, knowledge, concern and public opinion but not formal processes of legitimation beyond the consent of their members. The stability of NGOs remains fragile, and their organizational continuity cannot be taken for granted.[19]

4.4 Conclusion: the dialectic nature of informational power

Of the three powers of the separation of powers model, it is the executive that seems to have been able to make the best use of information and communication technology. It did so not only by implementing this technology but by adjusting its mode of governance to the technology's conceptual view of the world: governing as information and communication management. Neither the legislative nor the juridical powers have so far been able to develop structural control mechanisms to rein in sufficiently this newly found mode of governance. There are some indications that, for example, the parliamentary powers of inquiry or mechanisms of control and competition within the executive may at least contribute to a revitalization of checks and balances in the information age. As shown above, however, such mechanisms have their own constraints, which make it doubtful if they can fully reinstitute the traditional model's normative force. Nor can such a substitute be expected from changes in the general democratic environment: the internationalization of governance even seems to enhance the position of the executive, and the new actors on the international scene carry with them the burden of their own legitimacy deficit.

These observations appear to lead to the conclusion that the separation model as such has perhaps become obsolete. As observed in the introduction, however, the model is still being used for benchmarking new emerging democracies. It is still a principle that constitutional courts have to recall occasionally. This leaves us with two other possibilities. Either the executive power has reached a state in which it has

[19] The emphasis here is on international NGOs. National executives have to face national NGOs as well, of course. The observations on international NGOs also apply to national NGOs, however, and do not seem to change the national situation either.

finally escaped the systems of checks and balances altogether, at least for a good while (and there are indeed indications in the development of presidential democracies that seem to point into this direction), or the traditional three powers model is no longer able to sufficiently describe and effectively prescribe the constraints of the executive, and we have to look for a new model – perhaps a totally new model.

I find the latter conclusion more probable. I have already described how the executive is invoking crises to improve its informational position strategically. There has been reference to the NGOs; though not in a position to act as a legislative or judicial equivalent, they have at least strongly influenced the information and communication modes in international policy-making. There are other developments pointing to new types of governance that seem to bypass the separation of powers model designed for the public sector and that can only briefly be mentioned here: changes in the relationship between the executive and what is summarized as the private sector – changes that have led to new cooperative forms of governance, with a stronger emphasis on securing framework conditions rather than micro-managing relations, and developing a more extensive use of dialogue and persuasion, as well as reflecting the dependence of the executives themselves on particular private sector entities that operate globally. In addition, the relationship between the executive and citizens is slowly changing, with more modes of direct cooperation and deliberation, involving not only organizations of public interest but also the citizens themselves directly. Finally, we have to acknowledge the national and international role of the mass media, including new forms of mass media that make use of the different communication possibilities that internet technology offers.

Within the framework of this abbreviated analysis of the descriptive and normative validity of the separation of powers model, I have referred at various instances to the role of ICT and focused on what have been called informational power shifts. It might therefore be helpful at this stage to recall and restructure some of the observations of this analysis so as to make further forecasts as to where new restraints for the executive may come from and how they might operate beyond the traditional three powers concept. I have outlined how the reference to crisis has been used by the executive to strategically counter the development of sets of regulations on transparency and the protection of privacy. I have indicated that this reference to crisis is in danger of losing its appeal if it is used repetitively. It has also to be noted that, although the reference to crisis might have *reduced* the role of intra-executive "balancing" institutions such as data protection and information commissions, these organizations *are still here* and *have even increased* their international cooperation activities. Finally, we recall that NGOs have at least influenced, if not changed, the way in which international organizations and national policy-makers at the international level communicate with the public.

These observations suggest that the key to control of the power of the executive in the age of information and communication technology might be the very same resource that enhances the power of the executive: information and its supporting technology. With this observation the aim is not to revitalize the commonplace observation that ICT empowers not just the traditional operators of power but also those confronted with power. This – in my view – has always been too abstract a statement, which misses out on the conditions under which technologies can develop in societies. Rather, it seems that the social (and political) use of information is of a dialectic nature: requiring information as a power tool creates and exploits informational asymmetries. While such asymmetries cannot be avoided altogether, and perhaps even should not be, because of the possible beneficial consequences from the quest to generate knowledge in society, and while these asymmetries may even be justified in particular situations, such as – indeed – crisis situations, this asymmetry in itself can always only be of a temporary nature. Information has a tendency to flow; asymmetry management can therefore only ever be time management. As a result, informational asymmetries are constantly in need of renewed legitimation. In our current understanding of democratic systems – formed by the same experiences with ICT and its concepts as those executive powers that accumulate informational power – this legitimation can be provided only with the help of information itself, by information on the asymmetry itself and its procedures, as a sort of meta-information, and eventually by general transparency. Governing by exploiting informational asymmetries cannot escape the need for legitimation by information. It is within this perspective that new tools, sustainable organizations and modes of informational checks and balances might evolve that eventually, over time, may at least complement, if not substitute for, the traditional three powers model.

5 *People on the internet as agents of change*

JAMES N. ROSENAU AND MILES D. TOWNES

I am not educated, but I can think.

Meisie Ndlovu[1]

The tin line had been done two weeks now. Mr. James [the manager] did not fill out the forms properly for to get the foreign exchange to buy the material. It comes from Canada. The IMF [International Monetary Fund] man control the thing now, you know, so things have to be just so. And we workers suffer 'cause production shut down 'cause we need those things. And Mr. James, he's a fool to play with it. We ask him where the material, and he say it's coming. We know he mess it up. Jamaica doesn't have the money no more. Each factory must wait a turn to get the money. I hear the tin is on the dock in Toronto, waiting to be shipped here.

Unnamed Jamaican woman[2]

5.1 Introduction

It is not technological determinism to observe that the internet, mobile phones and a host of other recently developed means of communication have helped to unleash powerful forces that are transforming global politics. Of course, people can still choose to ignore or resist

This chapter was originally prepared by James N. Rosenau for the workshop on "Governance, regulations and powers on the internet," which was held in Paris on May 27 and 28, 2005. Parts of the chapter were drawn from two earlier papers: "Generational change and internet literacy," which was presented at the annual meeting of the American Political Science Association held in Boston on August 29, 2002; and "The skill revolution as a dynamic process," which was presented at the annual conference of the Future Society held in Washington, DC, on July 30, 2004. Both these papers were included in Rosenau (2006). The material was subsequently revised and expanded for publication by Miles Townes.

[1] Meisie Ndlovu is expressing skepticism about the future of her community in South Africa; quoted by Wines and LaFraniere (2004).

[2] Quoted by Alger (1988).

these forces, even as they shape and reshape the conduct of local, national and international life, but it seems clear nonetheless that change is occurring in the ways that individuals, communities and societies interact with each other. This, in turn, is largely a consequence of the fact that the internet and the other means of communication have recently become fixtures of daily life in much of the world.

Put differently, we live in an ever more complex world – one that is increasingly marked by the erosion of boundaries, time and distance. Technology reflects this, but to some extent also encourages it, as increasing complexity in human affairs spurs innovation and the spread of further communication – or, more correctly, information – technologies. That these are information technologies, instead of weapons or trade technologies, is an essential point, necessary to a sufficient understanding of the phenomena at hand. The transmission, exchange and control of information are crucial aspects of political and societal organization – so much so that any innovations affecting these activities will also have a significant effect on polities and societies. IT is therefore challenging, changing and sometimes threatening political organization globally.

We believe that decades, perhaps centuries, from now people will look back on our time as that in which the foundations of the order that marks their lives were laid. To be sure, there is much that is bewildering about the rapid transformations that we are sustaining and experiencing, and we do not know whether that order will seem better or worse in comparison to the recent past. At present, though, the cumulative effect of these changes is to place ever more of the burden of history on the shoulders of people as individuals, so that they stand at the core of contemporary political complexity, with increasing skills, engagement and resilience giving them the ability to shape the pace and directions of change. As the individual gains an enlarged capacity for activity in world politics, so he/she also gains increased authority within that sphere, effectively devolving and diffusing authority from its previous vessels – such as states – to new and nebulous collectivities as determined by the individual's engagement. The individual is thus both instigator and instrument of the momentum, able to resist it even as we are swept up in its dynamics.

Our exploration of these dynamics begins with the internet and related technologies that are facilitating these changes. We examine the specific properties of the internet that make it conducive to change in individuals' relations to authority, then discuss how individuals are taking advantage of these changes to increase their own skills, empowerment and engagement. This, in turn, is driving an organizational revolution with consequences for political and social authority at all levels. Finally, we offer some – admittedly speculative – suggestions as to the deep and enduring consequences of these twin revolutions, including a historical comparison to a previous technological revolution, to suggest that a proper understanding of the changes that are occurring now raises a very real possibility of epochal changes to come.

5.2 The internet as a medium of change

The internet is the most prominent of a number of technologies that have contributed to the changes discussed below; other technologies may be important, but the internet is pivotal. Because technology is essentially ideational, it is not often politically neutral. This is true of the internet in particular, because by its very design it privileges some people over others. The empowerment that the internet fosters is intrinsic to its component technologies, in that the network created by these technologies empowers its users over its owners. This is the consequence of a series of decisions made in the early stages of the internet's formation, compounded and reinforced by its growing popularity and eventual ubiquity over most other forms of computer networking (for more on this point, see Townes, 2011). For example, it was an early tenet among the architects of the internet (especially Louis Pouzin) that users should have far more control over the network than the centralized nodes (Abbate, 1999). Their motives may have been purely technical, but one of the consequences in delegating so much of the network function to hosts is that the network is far more resistant to centralized control. Lessig makes an even stronger claim: that the internet's architecture "reflects both a political decision about disabling control and a technological decision about the optimal network design" (Lessig, 1999b). Whether they arose from deliberate political motives or as an unanticipated outcome of technical design, the consequences are the same. A person developing a web page or writing an e-mail has far more control over the content of his/her corner of the internet than do the companies or governments that own the servers and fiber optics that make up that network.

This same structure is reproduced in other recent technologies, notably mobile phone networks, making them another technology whose growing popularity has profound consequences for people's lives.

This privilege is the basis of the internet's fundamental impact on politics and society. The strength of this dynamic has fostered an emphasis in the literature on the large extent to which people have been empowered by the internet and other recent communication technologies (Norris, 1999). These technologies grant users access to a vast wealth of information that previously would have been difficult to obtain or completely unavailable. It also allows them contact with people whom they might otherwise have never met, but who nonetheless impact their lives immeasurably. Much of this information and many of these people may be bogus or fraudulent, but most users will develop the judgment to discern the fraud as they progress. Meanwhile, their activities are no longer so tightly structured by the limits of their domestic society and government. As Lessig (1999b; emphasis in original) writes, "*[G]iven the architecture of the Net as it is*, it is difficult for governments to regulate behavior on the Net." Even with heavy censorship, the information available to people via the internet is likely to challenge the views and beliefs they might otherwise hold.

These dynamics are not limited to the internet alone. Wireless communications – cellular and mobile phones – are also facilitating an organizational revolution. One manifestation of this is sometimes called "smart mobs": "groups of people equipped with high-tech communications devices that allow them to act in concert – whether they know each other or not."[3] As of yet, wireless communications and the internet enjoy only limited overlap, but, as these technologies are further integrated and expanded, there will likely be a powerful multiplier effect from their convergence.

The proliferation of the internet, cellphones, satellite broadcasting and their spinoffs is facilitating a revolution in the capacity that individuals have to engage their world. These technologies are not the only source of this trend, but the new technologies provide people with the means and incentives to engage each other more broadly through participation in social networks without the constraints of existing political or cultural boundaries. E-mail, blogs, chat rooms,

[3] Schwartz (2002); his article anticipated the publication of the book on the same theme by Howard Rheingold (2002).

message boards, instant messaging, auction markets and text messaging are among the techniques that have expanded the channels through which people interact and thereby become more empowered. This trend promises to continue so that, in the words of one observer, "the person – not the place, household or work-group – will become even more of an autonomous communication node."[4]

5.3 The skill revolution

We summarize this transformation as a "skill revolution,"[5] but this label does not fully capture the variety of means and methods by which people can now engage in collective action. In effect, people are experiencing a multiplicity of skill revolutions amid a range of transformations, but none of these transformations is more profound than those that enhance the capabilities and skills of individuals around the world – be they young or old, rich or poor, South or North, rural or urban. Although these transformations include the increasing ability of governments, corporations and the other collectivities that comprise (macro-)institutions to direct and manipulate how people conduct their lives, these increases pale in comparison to the rapidly evolving range of skills that are unfolding at the (micro-) level of the person.

The epigraphs that began this chapter reflect the foregoing perspectives and highlight the central theme of this chapter; they illuminate the increasing capacities and skills of the individual and underscore the extent to which the world has entered the age of the person. There is a pronounced tendency on the part of many who stress the power of elites to downplay the capacities of ordinary people, to cite polls indicating ignorance of places and events, to downplay the skill revolution on the grounds that it encompasses only those with a university education, to dismiss as misguided the self-assessments of people such as Meisie Ndlovu (cited in the first epigraph). Skill is not confined to the educated elite, however; experience can be a great teacher, perhaps especially for those who have no other way of comprehending how the world works. Whether it be the Vermont farmer, the urban homeless,

[4] Barry Welman, quoted by Rheingold (2002: 57).

[5] The concept of a skill revolution has gone through a number of iterations; see, for example, Rosenau (2003).

the Chinese peasant or the dock worker in Jamaica, people everywhere are transforming a grasp of how the world works into working knowledge that helps them address their circumstances.

It is useful to conceive of the skill revolution as an evolving process, as consisting of a set of dynamic variables (rather than constants) that may prove to be powerful mechanisms for change. At the core of the process is the interplay between technologies, education and experience. All three of these dynamics elevate people everywhere onto a growth curve that incrementally – and sometimes swiftly – enables them to arrest the attention of leaders in positions of power. For those in the industrial world the process begins with formal education early in life, while children in the developing world start with experience, with the hard realities that attend getting from one day to the next. In both cases, what is learned is not so much a storehouse of information but a bundle of working knowledge, of premises and understandings of how things work, of when and how to apply the skills that working knowledge facilitates. In both worlds the sequence of skill expansion has quickened in recent years with the advent of the new microelectronic technologies. For many children throughout the world today, using the internet is as commonplace as skipping rope or playing in a sandbox. To be sure, what they learn at an early age involves games rather than surfing the web or reading about other cultures; but to manipulate games on the internet is to add to a working knowledge that can serve as a skill base for more sophisticated activities as maturation unfolds.

Of course, the acceleration of the skill revolution does not necessarily mean that people are experiencing a comparable growth in their readiness to engage in collective action. To have more refined skills at one's disposal does not ensure that one will use the expanded skills effectively. Nor does it guarantee that these skills will be used toward socially positive ends. For those who are criminals, terrorists or drug dealers, the acceleration of their skills will not moderate their greed or malice; rather, it will enhance their capacities to exercise their form of evil. There are, nonetheless, many reasons to welcome the continued acceleration of the skill revolution, unless one believes that most people intend to visit harm on others.

In short, the skill revolution is founded on an interactive sequence that lasts a lifetime, with each increment of experience, education and technological know-how building on the previous increments and resulting in more talented people. More than that, the widespread use of cellphones and the internet has accelerated the sequence at a stunningly exponential rate, and there is every reason to believe that it will continue to do so. To be sure, in many cases expanded skills may not lead to intensified political action. A host of factors, many beyond the control of even the most skillful people, can intervene to deny them political engagement. Even so, the skill revolution surely widens the pool of people upon whom the mobilizing elite can draw to apply their skills.

5.4 The organizational revolution

Some contend that the empowerment argument is misleading. People may be empowered by the new technologies, it is conceded, but what counts is the power wielded by elites and the deafness of their ears when it comes to acting on the messages articulated by the protest marches, letter-writing campaigns and other forms of collective action. In our messy, complex and nonlinear circumstances, it is further asserted, the ordinary person simply cannot keep up with either the pace or the content of the rapid transformations under way throughout the world. Thus, despite the efforts of activists who have mastered the art of mobilizing large crowds, ordinary folk are unable to carry the work through when dusk falls and the marchers disband. In effect, the argument concludes, social movements are transitory and unable to sustain the momentum necessary to impact meaningfully on leaders in a position to effect change.

This argument fails to appreciate the extent to which the skill revolution and associated technologies are also driving an organizational revolution, wherein people are coming together in new ways, in issue networks as well as broad-gauged and enduring associations, in horizontal as well as vertical structures of authority. The more skillful and self-aware people become, the more they are ready to join, form or redefine their organizations. Likewise, the greater the number and variety of organizations that dot the horizon, the more that people will be inclined to seek out like-minded others with whom to join in common endeavors. The self-reinforcing interaction of the two revolutions thus constitutes a powerful dynamic that seems bound to accelerate with the passage of time and the advent of new, more educated generations who travel more widely and who have been reared on the latest technological innovations.

The increasing capacity for collective action in countries around the world – even in repressive states – is one of the most obvious ways that these consequences are manifest. The seeming plethora of large numbers of diverse citizens protesting in various streets throughout the world is the result of people and organizations communicating with each other and spreading information by e-mail, text messaging, instant online messaging, blogs, fax, cellphones and teleconferencing as to the purposes, locales and timing of the protest activity (for a compelling example of this process, see Yardley, 2005). The size and frequency of such protests also trace a rising curve that derives its strength and growth from the empowerment of the participants, from their growing knowledge that micro-people can have macro-consequences if they act in concert. As new and nascent organizations bring pressure to bear on the established authority structures in the world, there is evidence that the targets of these protests are at least mindful of the policies the marching protesters seek to alter: there are good indications, for example, that this form of empowerment has been institutionalized, that crowds invariably gather to protest whenever the boards of the IMF, the World Bank and the World Trade Organization (WTO) hold their annual meetings at accessible locations. The recent pattern wherein the boards are convened at remote and inaccessible locations is surely an indication of sensitivity to the collective actions of empowered citizens. In some cases the citizen protests and demonstrations have toppled governments, as seen in the recent peaceful revolutions in Serbia, Ukraine and Lebanon.

Some argue that entrenched organizations – especially governments – will continue to assert their authority over the internet and other technology-mediated forms of communication. It is not surprising, given the inevitable tensions that the skill revolution creates between people and their governments, that some governments have indeed sought to curtail or constrain their citizens' access to the knowledge and technology underlying these changes. In Iran, China and other countries, internet access is limited or heavily monitored. In more regressive countries, educational opportunities are deliberately limited – especially for women. The problem for these governments is that the same skills that empower people to challenge their rulers also empower them to be economically, culturally and socially successful in an increasingly electronic world. Few governments are willing to remove themselves from world affairs, and those trying to straddle the line between engagement and disengagement find it increasingly difficult. In fact, it seems more likely that governments will be forced to expand educational opportunities as information technology diffuses around the world. This, in turn, is likely to encourage the development of emergent organizations of empowered individuals.

To be clear, it is a mistake to infer that all or most individuals are using their newfound capacity for wholly idealistic purposes – say, for example, to transcend territorial boundaries to form a genuine global polity. More often, people define collectivities that are in some ways narrower and more exclusive than their national loyalties or state citizenship, even though such loyalties may cross or ignore their territorial polity. Instead of a relentless push toward globalism, these twin revolutions are just as often driving a process whereby authority is disaggregated into smaller spheres. Decentralization and localization have become as central to the course of events as centralization and globalization; and the more the pace of disaggregation accelerates, the more central individual people are with their expanded skills.

This disaggregation will be both the central challenge and defining trend of governance in the internet age. Here – as elsewhere[6] – we draw a distinction between government and governance. Government refers to a formal mechanism of governance, usually defined and constrained by formal instruments such as constitutions, laws and regulations to exercise authority over a given populace or territorially bounded area. Governance is simply the exercise of authority wherever it occurs, by any number of formal organizations, including governments, as well as numerous and varied informal collectivities. When government depends on formal instruments, governance relies on tradition, norms, habits and a host of other informal means to define the extent and activity of the polity. Because governments are so bound to territorial areas, they are required to deal with a broad range of issues – essentially, anything that can happen within that territory. Governance can be specific to a given concern or issue, and in that sense much more limited in scope than a given government, while being more responsive and flexible within its particular area of concern.

The increased social complexity brought about by the skill and organizational revolutions also brings a commensurate increase in

[6] See, for example, Rosenau (2007: chaps. 13–17).

demand for governance. One might describe IT's role in this process as a vessel that can carry people to new areas of the social and political landscape, thus giving individuals new arenas and forums for their interactions. This landscape is often referred to as "cyberspace," but this term is perhaps misleading, in that it suggests something wholly non-territorial and incorporeal. It is possible, even helpful, to accept this space as real, in that, although people are increasingly drawn there for the sorts of interactions and activities that would not be possible in territorially bounded space, these activities are no less real for that limitation. That these are real people doing real things – even if only talking – is an important fact, because it allows for the possibility of government oversight of these spaces. Indeed, many aspects of this new social and political landscape do fall under the eye of governments. Censorship in authoritarian countries, as described above, is one such example. Another is the extent to which law enforcement officers in a number of countries have attacked online child pornography distribution over the last decade. Much of the early hyperbole concerning "cyberspace" has been belied by the often effective attempts of government to regulate and control aspects of it. Equally relevant here is the fact that government has ignored or delegated a wide range of issues concerning the internet, leaving them to be decided by informal governance mechanisms. For example, there was a series of efforts by government and governmental organizations in the early history of the internet to impose global standards on computer networks. Those efforts were ineffective, and ultimately they were overwhelmed by the growing popularity of the technology that is now the foundation of nearly all of the internet. Since then standards formulation and promulgation has been left to the Internet Engineering Task Force and other non-territorial, non-governmental bodies.

Another example is the Internet Corporation for Assigned Names and Numbers; in 1998 the US Department of Commerce entered into a joint project agreement (JPA) with ICANN to "effect the transition of Internet domain name and addressing system DNS to the private sector."[7] Recent changes to the JPA have sought to move forward on that transition, but these changes have been controversial. A public

[7] "Joint project agreement between the United States Department of Commerce and the Internet Corporation for Assigned Names and Numbers," www.icann.org/general/JPA-29sep06.pdf (accessed April 21, 2008).

comment solicitation drew dozens of responses from a range of interested parties, including corporations, think tanks, internet governance bodies, government ministers and unaffiliated individuals.[8] Many argued that the relationship established by the JPA should be retained for the immediate future, in order to give the internet better protection from government interference. Typical of such comments were those from the Center for Democracy and Technology (CDT), which stated that, "despite a few very unwise lapses, the US government has not harmed the core functions of the Internet...whereas other governments have made it clear that they would interfere if they could."[9] The CDT argued that ICANN had failed to develop "procedures or mechanisms that would ensure in the long run its procedural transparency or protect it against undue commercial or governmental interference," and that the JPA helped to ensure such transparency and protection in the meantime. The US government's involvement is valued specifically for its minimal interference and light-handed oversight, and the government is committed to devolving its authority to private actors.

Apart from direct government oversight, governance on the internet and related spaces is most likely to come from users as the ultimate source of authority. This emergent governance cannot appeal to sovereignty, historic authority or military force to legitimize its authority over the new landscape. Those seeking to govern amid disaggregated authority must instead justify themselves by other means, principally the effectiveness of their rule. Such justification may also come through popular participation, in that enough people believe the governance to be legitimate (even when not particularly effective). This may in turn be related to primacy, insofar as the first to describe an area of governance has some claim to govern it. The precise justification in each case is not as important as the general sense that legitimacy and authority emerge and appear in very different ways in this kind of informal governance from how they do in established governments. Again, the territorial dimension is important here, because in many instances the person can simply opt out of the new collectivity in a way not often possible with territorial

[8] See www.ntia.doc.gov/ntiahome/domainname/jpamidtermreview.html (accessed April 21, 2008).

[9] See www.ntia.doc.gov/legacy/ntiahome/domainname/jpacomments2007/jpacomment_006.pdf, p. 2 (accessed April 21, 2008).

jurisdictions. (The important exception to this is, of course, the internet – there is only one – but this and similar technologies are more important as the context for these interactions.)

That one need not participate in collectivities but does so by choice gives many of these a democratic inflection, and they are often more transparent or egalitarian than comparable governmental bodies. Just as often, though, the organizations themselves are not at all democratic, so that external "voting" *to participate* replaces the need for any internal "voting" *as participation*. As a result not all emergent organizations will be entirely democratic, transparent or egalitarian from the beginning, despite being seen as legitimate arbiters of authority by those who do participate. What enables compliance in these circumstances is the convergence of interdependent needs among actors, as opposed to a constitutionally specified hierarchy, but often this convergence permits a hierarchical scheme, as founding members typically exercise privileges above those of members who join later. These privileges may well be transient, however, as newer members' demands for more control over the organization often force the founders to renounce their privileges. If they do not, they risk losing members to other organizations, or allowing their own organization to become mired in procedural debates rather than substantive work on the original goal. Again, these technologies privilege users over owners and equality over hierarchy – but do not predetermine the exact resolution of these tensions, and allow a multitude of possible outcomes across the landscape. If readers find this messy and complicated and indefinite, they are likely very close to our intended point.

The threat to current governments is that many of the emergent organizations are in fact opposed to these very governments. For democracies this sort of opposition in not perilous, but it can lead to surprising results. For example, in 2004 a spontaneous text message campaign helped unseat the incumbent party in Spain, which had been widely expected to win the upcoming general election. Just days before the election 202 people were killed in bomb attacks on the Atocha train station in Madrid. The government immediately blamed the attacks on Basque separatists, despite evidence pointing to terrorists affiliated with Al-Qaeda; this sparked a series of demonstrations and the aforementioned text messages, bouncing from one mobile phone to another (Pfanner, 2004). On election day voters flocked to the polls, many of them angered by the possibility that the government was lying about the attacks to distract them from its unpopular foreign policy (Losowsky, 2004). The ruling party lost the election, and the use of mobile phones is widely credited as playing a key role in the defeat. In a less fraught example, the South Korean government's decision in 2008 to allow American beef into that country provoked mass demonstrations and petition campaigns, largely coordinated through the internet, that led the Cabinet to offer to resign en masse (Sang-Hun, 2008). These examples demonstrate how emergent organizations can undermine entrenched governance; insofar as democratic states facilitate competing ideas about political organization, however, these challenges tend not to threaten the state itself.

For authoritarian regimes the problem is more severe, and these governments must either ban or tightly regulate the internet and mobile phones to maintain their control. China, for example, has an extensive bureaucracy devoted to monitoring the internet and its users; the government also has strict rules to prevent the anonymous use of mobile phones (Callick, 2006; see also Pan, 2005). In Burma (Myanmar) in September 2007, networks of protestors coordinated via mobile phone and the internet to launch massive demonstrations against that country's military regime; these efforts in part reflected a deliberate strategy among some outside aid organizations to train opposition activists in the use of information technology. The protests spread across the country, and the authorities responded, belatedly, by shutting down the country's internet providers and confiscating cellphones and cameras (Mydans, 2007). Although the junta remains in power, the demonstrations and subsequent crackdown have led to new pressures from foreign countries, including the United States (*New York Times*, 2008), and have shown that the opposition possesses a sophisticated capacity to organize and coordinate actions in the face of repression. In effect, the opposition offers an organizational model that contrasts with the organization of the Burmese state. Where emergent governance provides a competing model against which to judge the entrenched organization – especially the state – this can feed the dissatisfaction that leads to opposition and protest. The problem for world politics is that nowhere in this landscape has there emerged a single form or even category of governance that promises to be a viable replacement for the nation state system, so that, although the disaggregation of authority suggests that the international system is facing tremendous change, there is still yet no clear picture of how that process will unfold.

5.5 Future frontiers in governance

Those wishing to estimate the ultimate impact of the internet often turn to the telegraph, the telephone and other advances of the nineteenth century for analogy. This seems reasonable as a lower bound; the internet is likely to be – and perhaps has been already – at least as profound a development as any of those technologies. There is also an upper bound on such an estimate, however, whereby a profound change in information technology leads to massive change in the political and social world. We agree with Geoffrey Herrera (2006: 199): "The technologies of the 'information revolution' are the next likely candidates to remake the international system." This is not to say that the internet will *necessarily* lead to massive change in the future, but that the possibility exists and merits consideration by anyone interested in the currently unfolding processes of change.

The analogy for this sort of change comes from the development of the printing press in late medieval Europe, more than five centuries ago. Europe at the time was undergoing a number of economic and social changes, including advances in business, warfare, art and scholarship. In particular, the modern scientific method developed in this period, which gave scholars new insight into and understanding of their world (Rice, 1970). It is entirely possible that these changes could have proceeded apace without major disruption, but the introduction of the printing press allowed for the diffusion of ideas and skills at an unprecedented pace, and printing technology itself spread quickly across the continent: "Unknown in Europe before the mid-fifteenth century, printers' workshops were to be found in every important municipal center by 1500" (Eisenstein, 1979: 23). This had a profound impact on individuals and collectivities wherever a press was established.

The impact on governance was especially profound. The feudal order to some extent depended on the Church's monopoly on knowledge and learning. Princes and lords employed clerics or church-educated scribes to help them compose the kinds of documents that were essential to their rule; this in turn bound the local rulers to the Church.

The fact that most printing presses were in the hands of lay entrepreneurs helped sever this bond, but also changed the way rulers governed: "Princes who had employed the cumbersome methods of manuscript to communicate with their subjects switched quickly to print to announce declarations of war, publish battle accounts, promulgate treaties, or ague disputed points in pamphlet form" (Eisenstein, 1979: 281). Meanwhile, printing allowed the Reformation to spread across Europe, giving rulers both a reason and an opportunity to depart the Catholic fold permanently, giving rise to the beginnings of the modern nation state. The instability this created in hierarchical relations across Europe, according to Elizabeth Eisenstein (p. 406), "took centuries to spin out." The most definite resolution of this process came with the Peace of Westphalia of 1648, which most political scientists recognize as the beginning of the era of international relations.

This is, of course, necessarily a brief and incomplete sketch of that period of European history, but it does suggest some relevance for IT in epochal change. Whether such change occurs with the spread and maturity of the internet remains to be seen, because that process is as yet incomplete (Herrera, 2006). As mentioned above, the skill revolution is likely to accelerate with the passage of time and the advent of generations reared on the computer. This possibility gives rise to a number of questions. Are the generations now in their early thirties or younger likely to differ from their predecessors by virtue of being the first to be fully comfortable and literate with information technologies – the computer and the internet, e-mail and search capacities – when they come to occupy positions of power and prestige in the decades ahead? Will their decision-making skills be more incisive, their grasp of complexity more substantial, their dexterity in framing and implementing policies more proficient, their respect for knowledge and expertise more secure and temperate, their talent for forming consensuses and reaching compromises more extensive, their attitudes more subtle and nuanced, their organizations more effective? In short, what follows from the fact that children today have been found to be "much heavier users of the Internet and all its services than were their parents" (Lewin, 2001)?

Even if we do not know the answers to these questions, we can point to specific phenomena as grounds for speculation. If, in the global future, the dominant information medium is the internet – not the printed word – then that future will probably reflect the ethos of this medium. Perhaps the best, though hardly the only, example of this ethos is found in the consideration of those who are often called "hackers" – persons skilled in the languages of computing and information technology.[10] Most hackers entered the computer world before they turned twenty years old, and virtually all of them are still under forty years of age, and by dint of their early exposure and continued study they are fluent in the medium beyond the competence of nearly all their elders. This fluency gives them a significant capacity for both constructive and destructive engagement via IT, and they tend to view the limits of technology itself as the principle constraint on their innovation. Much of their work is legal, even beneficial, but, in pushing the limits of technology, hackers sometimes collide with established laws, regulatory regimes or business practices – and, of course, they sometimes deliberately break laws or otherwise challenge authority.

The most interesting and relevant aspect of these challenges is that they are often condoned and even endorsed by hackers' peers, even those who are not specialists. Could it be that the hackers are an expression of a readiness on the part of the younger generation to challenge authority and thus contribute to the crises of authority that plague governments and non-governmental institutions throughout the world (Rosenau, 2003)? A related example arises in the tendency of the younger generations to reject or ignore attempts to make the internet and related technology conform to the established logic of intellectual property rights; see, for example, the success of music- and video-sharing networks such as Napster, Kazaa and YouTube. Yet another example of change involves notions of privacy. It too appears to be "undergoing a generational shift." Only newly aware that extensive information about them has made its way into databases on the internet, "those in their late 20s and 30s are going to feel the brunt of the transition" (Lee, 2002) to a world in which there are fewer and fewer secrets. In effect, the transition is difficult because they "grew up with more traditional concepts of privacy even as the details of their lives were being captured electronically" (Lee, 2002).

[10] For a cogent argument that the term "hacker" is an imprecise concept, that for hackers it is a term of respect, that hackers are often helpful to those who turn to them for assistance and that they "possess qualities that serve the public," see Gehring (2002) (quote from p. 25). See also Thomas (2002).

This generation may well view privacy as an unnecessary indulgence, however; witness the proliferation of autobiographical blogs and webpages on sites such as MySpace and LiveJournal. These are only hints at the possible world view of a generation that has grown up with the internet; if it is difficult to predict that world view, it is doubly difficult to predict the effect that it will have as these individuals mature and take on leadership responsibilities.

Another important aspect of this question arises when we look at the generational differences in internet usage in the developing world. Indeed, although the proportion of persons in the developing world who have access to the internet is substantially less than is the case for the United States and Europe, the concentration of users among young people in Asia, Africa and Latin America is probably greater than elsewhere in the world. Statistics on these trends are difficult to come by, especially concerning generational differences, but consider the relative levels of internet penetration and usage across the world. As of March 2011 there were already some 922 million internet users in Asia, more than in North America (272 million) or Europe (476 million), but Asian users represent only 23.8 percent of that region's total population. The proportion of users to population – that is, the penetration – is 78 percent in North America and 58 percent in Europe. Given the economic realities of information technology, it is unlikely that Asia will reach the same levels of penetration as North America, or even Europe, but just 23.8 percent penetration gives Asia nearly a billion users – outnumbering North Americans by three to one – with inevitable but unpredictable consequences for the internet. Likewise, plausible increases in Africa (118 million users: 11.4 percent penetration), Latin America (215 million: 36.2 percent) and the Middle East (68 million: 31.7 percent) could greatly increase the number of developing-world people with direct access to the IT driving the skill and organizational revolutions.[11] Intuition and previous research (from one of us: Rosenau, 2006) suggest, furthermore, that most of these users are under thirty years old, and many quite younger. In other words, not only is there a very real possibility that the developing world will claim a much larger share of the internet in twenty

[11] Internet World Stats, "Usage and population statistics," www.internetworldstats.com/stats.htm (accessed August 22, 2011).

years' time, but it is also possible that most of those users are not even adults yet. What will happen when these youths find themselves adults, empowered by IT to engage their peers in the developed world on a level playing field? How will their empowerment and engagement shape world politics? Will they assimilate among developed-world users, or will they hold their own distinct identities and values?

One observer argues that the diffusion and convergence of IT portends a shift "along the lines of those that began to occur when people first settled into villages and formed nation-states"; indeed, that, as a result of this shift, "we are on the verge of a major series of social changes that are closely tied to emerging technologies" (Schwartz, 2002). Put in more political terms, as whole generations possess the new equipment and acquire the habit of using it reflexively, the tensions between governments and governance, between individuals and organizations and between users and owners will become more conspicuous and acute and drive crises of authority throughout the world. It is much too early to assert with any confidence the ultimate resolution of these changes, however, because they are still under way; the internet-literate generation has yet to fully replace its predecessors, and even that may only be the first step. It seems likely, nonetheless, that, when those in the present younger generations enter the ranks of elites, activists and thoughtful citizens throughout the world, the nature of politics within and between countries will be, for better or worse, profoundly different from what it is today.

5.6 Conclusion: governance and regulation amid disaggregated authority

The brisk pace of invention and innovation in information technology is facilitating significant social change, both at the individual and the organizational levels of human affairs. For individuals, it is giving them the opportunity and ability to increase and refine the skills necessary to interact and engage with an ever more complex and messy world. For organizations, these technologies are encouraging the disaggregation of authority, creating a tension between governments that are no longer able to control new social and political space and the increased demand for governance within these spaces. The initial directions of these trends reflect the embedded political structure of the technologies behind them (that is, the privilege of users over owners, individuals over organizations), leading to novel ways of governing and organizing world affairs. What shape the ultimate resolution of these trends will take is difficult to assess.

Some might contend that any of the sequences of the skill revolution could be disrupted, even reversed, by authoritarian governments. It is surely the case, moreover, that most governments can prevent people from leaving or entering their country, just as they have developed means for exercising some control over the flow of information and ideas through the internet. Such reasoning underestimates the power of the skill revolution, however, sustained as it is by the expanding curiosity and tenacity of people everywhere and in every age group. Perhaps more than any other kind of revolution, past or present, the skill revolution seems likely to change the nature of societies and alter the course of history.

PART II

Reformulating the Fundamentals for Collective Regulations

6 Co-regulation and the rule of law

BENOÎT FRYDMAN, LUDOVIC HENNEBEL AND GREGORY LEWKOWICZ

6.1 Introduction

The internet defies the classic state law model, according to which the sovereign state makes and enforces the law on its territory, including by the use of force (Frydman, 1997; Svantesson, 2005). The required bond between state sovereignty, national territory and law is loose when dealing with internet regulation. In addition, international law does not answer the question of which court(s) should have jurisdiction over internet litigation and what law(s) should be applied (Berman, 2002; Svantesson, 2005). In other words, the internet engages regulators to use new methods of drafting and implementing legal rules. Co-regulation is one of the techniques that can be used. Despite the fact that defining "co-regulation" remains challenging and unsettled (Poullet, 2004; Lievens, Dumortier and Ryan, 2006; Hennebel and Lewkowicz, 2007), a theoretical sketch of what the co-regulation model entails can be produced.

For analytical purposes, it is convenient to make a distinction between regulators and what Jonathan Zittrain (2003) calls "points of control." Regulators are public or private bodies willing to influence the behaviors of actors in a field of action. Points of control are any public or private actors that, for any reason, play a strategic role in a particular area. Regarding internet regulation, the method used by regulators consists in leaning on these points of control as regulatory levers. The so-called "co-regulatory mechanism" must be understood in this chapter as a legal device designed to put pressure on the points of control to achieve some regulatory result.

The meaning of co-regulation is twofold. As a concept of legal theory, "co-regulation" is a legal model in which norm-drafting, implementation and enforcement are not under the sole authority of the sovereign ruler but, rather, spread – voluntarily or otherwise – among a number of players, both public and private. In a more rigorous sense, co-regulation embraces a new form of governance for public authorities (Schultz and Held, 2004), based on the voluntary delegation or transfer to private actors of the burden of all or part of the drafting, implementation and enforcement of norms.[1] This chapter refers mainly to this latter meaning of co-regulation, focusing on the strategies initiated by states.

In any event, it is necessary to tell apart co-regulation from the *regulation model* – the so-called "command and control" model – in which public authorities make the rules, enforce them and punish those who breach them. Co-regulation is also different from the *self-regulation model*, in which the players of a certain sector of activity make the rules and implement them collectively without any public intervention. Co-regulation is not just an "in between" model, however. Co-regulation is a legal model per se with its own rationale, based on the empowerment of actors to control one another.

The notion of co-regulation has been used with some success in the context of internet regulation because of what was called "a move to the middle" – an ever-increasing role for intermediaries in regulation (Kerr and Gilbert, 2004; Palfrey and Rogoyski, 2006). It has also been used in the regulation of other media (Hans-Bredow-Institut, 2006), as well as in other areas such as corporate governance, corporate social responsibility (Berns *et al.*, 2007) and environmental law. It may be seen as a general paradigm for global governance in the context of globalization (Frydman, 2004).

So far, most of the academic publications dealing with internet co-regulation have focused mainly on the question of the effectiveness of such a model of regulation. Although this chapter describes and scrutinizes the legal initiatives and set of tools developed by the United States, the European Union and China that entrust points of control to monitor the internet, it focuses more specifically on the impact of co-regulation on the rule of law (on internet regulation and the rule of law, see also Marzouki, 2006). It shows the emergence of different systems of internet regulation having an effect on international legal competition and compliance with the rule of law.

[1] Co-regulation in this sense refers to the main alternative mode of regulation as used and defined by the European Union (Palzer, 2003; Senden, 2005).

6.2 The United States: self-regulation with a taste of co-regulation

The US system of internet regulation has often been described as self-regulatory (on internet self-regulation, see Price and Verhulst, 2005), as opposed to the European system (Chen, 2004; Nguyen, 2004; Kesan and Gallo, 2006). The American system is not exclusively self-regulatory, however. In fact, because of a distinct legislative and legal history (Zittrain, 2006), the regulatory rationale of the internet in the United States takes the shape of a self-regulatory system based on a libertarian framework (see section 6.2.1). It is also in the United States, however, that co-regulatory mechanisms were first outlined to protect specific rights (section 6.2.2).

6.2.1 The American libertarian framework of internet regulation

Traditionally, US law distinguishes between the liability of the publisher and that of the distributor of litigious information. On the one hand, it engages the liability of the producer of unlawful information with that of the one who publishes the information. On the other, it immunizes the booksellers, libraries and other distributors insofar as they are unaware of and do not have reason to know about the offence (Lichtman and Posner, 2004). American courts applied this principle to the internet in the first lawsuits involving ISPs.[2] In 1995, however, the Supreme Court of the State of New York adopted a different position in the *Stratton Oakmont, Inc.* v. *Prodigy Services Co.* case.[3] It held that, when an ISP takes measures in order to monitor online content, it is to be regarded as a publisher. Hence, its liability could be involved. As a consequence, the paradox was that ISPs that had an editorial control policy were more at risk than the ones doing nothing in this respect.

According to the ISPs, this situation would end up undermining the system of internet self-regulation, and appeared likely to open the

[2] For example, in a textbook case, the District Court of New York refused to hold the technical intermediary liable for defamatory comments broadcast via its equipment. See *Cubby, Inc.* v. *Compuserve, Inc.*,776 F supp. 140 (SDNY 1991).

[3] *Stratton Oakmont, Inc.* v. *Prodigy Services Company*, 23 Media L Rep (BNA) 1794 (NYS Ct. 1995).

door to a mass of lawsuits and actions against them that could be a serious obstacle to the expansion of the digital economy. As early as 1996 Congress reacted by passing the Communication Decency Act (CDA). Section 230 sets up the so-called "safe harbours," which immunize all ISPs from any civil liability regarding the material made by others that they only stored or disseminated. Section 230 § 1 (c) states: "No provider or user of an interactive computer service shall be treated as publisher or speaker of any information provided by another content provider."[4] The US courts have applied this provision extensively. According to these rules, the hosting provider would not be held liable (1) even if it was aware of the unlawful character of the content; (2) even if it had been notified of this fact by the victim;[5] and (3) even if it had paid for the illegal data.[6] In addition, section 230 § 2 (a) states: "No provider...of an interactive computer service shall be held liable on account of any action voluntarily taken in good faith to restrict access to or availability of material that the provider...considers to be obscene, lewd, lascivious, filthy, excessively violent, harassing, or otherwise objectionable, whether or not such material is constitutionally protected,[7] and of any action taken to enable or make available to information content providers or others the technical means to restrict access to material."[8]

This latter clause, called the "Good Samaritan provision," shields ISPs that voluntarily monitor internet content and filter or restrict access to illegal, harmful or "problematic" material. In sum, these provisions shelter ISPs from any tort-based lawsuit whether they decide to do nothing or to edit problematic or controversial content (Frydman and Rorive, 2002a; Rustad and Koening, 2005). The immunity granted by the CDA covers only civil liability, however, and does not extend to criminal law. On the contrary, the CDA intended to criminalize the dissemination of any obscene or indecent message with full knowledge to minors of less than eighteen years

[4] 47 USC § 230 (c) (1).

[5] For a defamatory case, see *Zeran* v. *America Online, Inc.*, 129 F 3rd 327 (4th Cir. 1997). For a case dealing with advertisement for child pornography, see *Doe* v. *America Online, Inc.*, 783 So 2nd 1010 (FL 2001).

[6] For a defamatory case, see *Blumenthal* v. *Drudge and America Online, Inc.*, 992 F supp. 44 (DDC 1998). In this case, the defamatory statement was not anonymous but sent by a person with whom AOL contracted and paid a monthly fee.

[7] 47 USC § 230 (c) (2) (A). [8] 47 USC § 230 (c) (2) (B).

of age,[9] although affirmative defenses were provided for those who, in good faith, take effective action to restrict access to minors.[10] These provisions created a kind of mandatory self-regulation that could have formed the basis of a co-regulatory system. The Supreme Court of the United States struck down these criminal provisions nevertheless and applied the full protection of the First Amendment to internet content.[11] Despite the drafting of the Child Online Protection Act (COPA), which called for a similar mechanism to the one judged unconstitutional by the Supreme Court, the Supreme Court's ruling was reaffirmed.[12]

The conjunction of a *safe harbor* and the Good Samaritan clause provided by the CDA, on the one hand, and the full protection offered by the First Amendment to internet content as asserted by the US Supreme Court, on the other, characterizes the American system of internet regulation as a system of self-regulation. Indeed, the US internet regulatory framework, which immunizes ISPs against civil lawsuits, is based primarily on the voluntary ISPs' monitoring and drafting of codes of conduct.

6.2.2 A taste of co-regulation

Although the libertarian framework generally prevailed, American law displays a taste of co-regulation in three important areas: the protection of minors and the fight against child pornography, the fight against terrorism and the protection of copyrighted materials. In these areas, various legal patterns illustrate the "invisible handshake" (Birnhack and Elkin-Koren, 2003) between the state and private actors, such as ISPs, enlisted in the implementation of the law.

[9] The protection of minors against pornographic material published online is one of the main political objectives of Congress in the context of internet regulation (Wanamaker, 2006).

[10] 47 USCA § 223 (e) (5) (A) (supp. 1997). See also *Reno* v. *American Civil Liberties Union*, 521 US 844 (1997).

[11] *Reno* v. *American Civil Liberties Union*, 521 US 844 (1997).

[12] The long judicial history of the challenging of the COPA cannot be discussed here. The most important US courts ruling are *Ashcroft* v. *American Civil Liberties Union*, 535 US 564 (2002); *Ashcroft* v. *American Civil Liberties Union*, 542 US 656 (2004); and *American Civil Liberties Union* v. *Alberto R. Gonzales*, March 22, 2007, civil action n.98–5591, available at www.paed.uscourts.gov/documents/opinions/07D0346P.pdf.

In the highly sensitive issue relating to the protection of minors, initiatives were taken in order to share the burden of regulation with private actors (Wanamaker, 2006). First of all, at a criminal level, denunciation was made mandatory by the 1998 Protection of Children from Sexual Predators Act. It compels ISPs with knowledge of facts involving child pornography to report them to a law enforcement agency.[13] Failure to report may result in a fine of up to $50,000 in the first instance and up to $100,000 for any second or subsequent failures. Likewise, statutes such as the 2000 Children's Internet Protection Act (CIPA) – which exposes public libraries at risk of having their federal funding revoked if they made no effort to constrain and limit access to pornographic material viewed from their computers – were not held to be unconstitutional.[14] Such rules create incentives for ISPs and other internet players to act as law enforcement authorities by providing information to the government or by restricting access to controversial material.

Second, in the fight against terrorism, some law enforcement initiatives entitle ISPs to monitor internet communication. According to the Patriot Act – amended by the 2002 Cyber Security Enhancement Act – law enforcement authorities may urge ISPs to disclose information relating to an emergency matter. Moreover, "if the provider, in good faith, believes that an emergency involving danger of death or serious physical injury to any person requires disclosure without delay of communications relating to the emergency," it may pass on the content of a communication to a federal, state or local governmental entity,[15] and no cause of action can lie in any court against him/her for providing the information under such circumstances (Birnhack and Elkin-Koren, 2003: 103–5).[16] In this case, ISPs are encouraged to act as law enforcement authorities by enjoying immunity against lawsuits involving privacy and data protection violations.

Finally, in the field of copyright law, Congress drafted a special liability regime for ISPs (Manekshaw, 2005). In 1998 the Digital Millennium Copyright Act (DMCA) enacted in the Copyright Act the so-called "Washington agreement" between copyright owners and representatives of the e-business industry about infringing material online (Frydman andRorive, 2002b). According to the DMCA, an

[13] 42 USC § 13032.
[14] See *United States* v. *American Library Association, Inc.*, 539 US 194 (2003).
[15] 18 USC § 2702 B.8. [16] 18 USC § 2703 e.

ISP that is unaware that it is hosting infringing material and does not take advantage from the infringing activity cannot be held liable. When a copyright owner notifies the provider about the infringement, however, the ISP must remove or disable access to the material within ten days (*notice and take down*); otherwise it could be liable for damages. The ISP must also notify the content provider that it has removed or disabled access to the material.[17] The content provider may then dispute the validity of the notice and send a formal counter-notification to the ISP.[18] In this case, the ISP has to inform the author of the complaint that it will put the controversial data back online (*notice and put back*),[19] unless an action is filed against the content provider seeking a court injunction. In this way, ISPs play their part in the regulation of infringing material online. Thanks to the procedure of notice and counter-notice, however, they do not have to make decisions on their own in case of disputes.

In conclusion, although the US system of internet regulation is mainly self-regulatory, it uses some co-regulatory mechanisms to guarantee security (e.g. in the fight against terrorism) and specific rights (e.g. in the fight against pedophilia) and to protect specific economic interests (e.g. copyright protection). Co-regulation is the exception in the US model, nonetheless, and it aims to achieve very specific goals on certain issues. In Europe, though, co-regulation is the general and leading model for the regulation of internet content.

6.3 The European Union: co-regulation as a general paradigm

The European Union's system of co-regulation was set up by the Directive on Electronic Commerce, which came into force in January 2002.[20] The text provides a regime of liability limitations less

[17] 17 USC § 512 (g) (2) (A).

[18] To be effective, the counter-notification must meet the formal requirements set up by 17 USC § 512 (g) (3).

[19] 17 USC § 512 (g) (2) (B).

[20] Directive 2000/31/EC of the European Parliament and of the Council of June 8, 2000, on certain legal aspects of information society services, in particular, electronic commerce in the Internal Market ("Directive on Electronic Commerce"), *Official Journal of the European Communities*, July 17, 2000, L 178: 1–16, particularly articles 12–15. For a complete analysis of the content of the directive, see Strowel, Ide and Verhoestraete (2001).

favorable to ISPs than the United States' immunity clause in the CDA. It also leaves more room for state intervention – a position consistent with the European view that freedom of speech should be subject to certain restrictions, liabilities and penalties that justify the intervention of public authorities. Besides important differences that arise from its transposition into the domestic law of each member state,[21] the directive defines the main components of a general co-regulation model of internet content, and it favors the emergence of professional players entrusted to monitor the internet (see section 6.3.1). The European system may nevertheless appear *too effective* in its current configuration, and it lacks the guarantees needed to avoid the risks of massive private censorship (section 6.3.2).

6.3.1 A general co-regulation model: toward professionalization and proceduralization

Like the DMCA and CDA in the United States, the EU Directive on Electronic Commerce is aimed primarily at creating "safe harbors" for the sake of ISPs. The European approach differs from the American one, however, in terms of method. First, the EU directive creates conditional exemptions from liability at both civil and criminal levels. Second, whereas the United States favors a vertical approach to the regulation of legal issues related to the infringement of a specific right, Europeans have chosen instead – following the German model[22] – a horizontal approach, defining general rules applicable to any kind of illegal or damaging material: not only copyright infringement, but also defamation, disclosure of privacy, hate speech, incitement to violence, hard pornography, pedophilia, etc. The directive states, as a matter of principle, that ISPs are obliged neither to monitor the information that they transmit or store nor to actively seek out illegal activities on the network.[23] Member states may nevertheless compel ISPs to inform them about illegal data or infringements reported by

[21] For Belgium, for instance, see Montero, Demoulin and Lazaro (2004: 81). For the French implementation of the directive, see Sédallian (2005). For its implementation in the United Kingdom, see Hedley (2006).

[22] Informations-und Kommunikationsdienste-Gesetz – IuKDG vom 22 Juli 1997, *Bundesgesetzblatt*, 1997, teil I no. 52, Bonn, 28 Juli 1997, S. 1870.

[23] Directive on Electronic Commerce, article 15.1.

recipients of their services and the identity of their clients.[24] National courts and administrative authorities may also be entitled by national law to enjoin an ISP to restrict access to or to take down illegal, damaging or infringing material.[25]

Regarding liability, the directive makes an important distinction between access providers and hosting providers. The access provider is the ISP that provides the user access to the internet; the hosting provider is the ISP that stores the data provided by a content provider on its server.[26] According to the directive, the access provider will not be liable for the information transmitted if it plays only a passive role as a "mere conduit."[27] With respect to hosting activities, article 14 of the directive states that the provider will not be liable for the information stored if it is not aware of the illegal activity and, upon obtaining such knowledge, it acts expeditiously to remove or disable access to the information.[28] This clause implicitly leads to an informal "notice and takedown" procedure that, although not organized by the directive itself, is left to states or self-regulation.

These provisions frame internet co-regulation at the EU level and leave the door open for subsequent developments. The conditional exemption from civil and criminal liability granted to ISPs seems to be a solid starting point for the development of a system of co-regulation. Immunity, especially when it is subject to certain conditions, works as a covetable "carrot" that the industry is quite willing to run after. This is also why hosting providers play such an important role in the EU model of content regulation, rather than the access providers, which enjoy more or less full immunity and therefore feel less pressure to

[24] Directive on Electronic Commerce, article 15.2.

[25] Directive on Electronic Commerce, articles 12.3 and 14.3.

[26] The same ISP may, of course, sell both access and hosting facilities. In each case, the liability of the ISP will be determined according to the service that it performed in the transaction.

[27] This implies that the ISP "(a) does not initiate the transmission; (b) does not select the receiver of the transmission; and (c) does not select or modify the information contained in the transmission." Directive on Electronic Commerce, article 12.1.

[28] The directive says that "(a) the provider does not have actual knowledge of illegal activity or information and, as regards claims for damages, is not aware of facts or circumstances from which the illegal activity is apparent; or (b) the provider, upon obtaining such knowledge or awareness, acts expeditiously to remove or to disable access of the information." Directive on Electronic Commerce, article 14.1.

interfere with problematic content. As a result, hosting providers have been promoted, unwillingly, to the position of number one regulators of the information society in Europe (Verdure, 2005). In addition, the legal environment designed by the EU directive entails an increase of power on the part of other actors and intermediaries.

First, the informal notice and takedown procedure provided by the directive creates a major incentive to set a standardized procedure. Indeed, ISPs and hosting providers in particular are eager for a better management mechanism for the complaints that are lodged from various sources regarding controversial content posted on their servers by their customers. A standardized notice form would, moreover, allow the ISP to react to notices more accurately and more quickly. Standardization starts with the establishment of a standard notice form allowing ISPs to clearly identify the complainant, the controversial material and the URLs where it may be seen. These forms would usually require a formal statement by the complainant certifying the notice to be true and sincere, by which the complainant accepts that he/she will face the legal consequences of any malicious or wrongful notice. Such a standardization could be achieved in different ways through a professional organization or by each ISP individually, in partnership with public authorities or not, etc.

Second, standard notice and takedown procedures are quite demanding, and might deter most average end users from complaining to ISPs about illegal or harmful material they find online. This situation opens the way to another kind of professional intermediary between end users and ISPs, specialized in the processing of notices. Those intermediaries, known as "hotlines," bear a key role in the European co-regulatory landscape. Moreover, they are substantially funded by the European Union, at both the EU level and the national level. Since 1999 the European Union has funded the International Association of Internet Hotlines (Inhope), a network of twenty-five hotlines in twenty-three countries worldwide. Inhope is in charge of the transmission of notices to ISPs, the police or Inhope members. Between September 2003 and February 2004 the network claimed to have received 106,912 reports, including 54,242 related to child pornography.[29] In 2005 over 534,000 reports were sent to Inhope

[29] See www.inhope.org/en/news/stats.php?id=200309200402 (accessed April 7, 2007).

hotlines. Those reports paved the way for significant actions against child pornography. In Germany, for instance, "Operation Marcy," concerning some 26,500 internet users in 166 countries, was initiated after the transmission of a report by Inhope members to the German federal police.[30] In the United Kingdom, the Internet Watch Foundation (IWF) – the national hotline – reported that its partnership approach led to a reduction in child abuse content hosted in the country from 18 percent in 1997 to 0.4 percent in 2004. In 2005 more than 150 UK citizens were identified and reported to the British police by the IWF, resulting in fourteen arrests and assistance being received in over twenty police enquiries.[31]

Third, the notice and takedown procedure provided by article 14 of the directive calls for public and private internet watchdogs. Internet watchdogs do more than just report complaints made by others. They actively comb the internet, looking for the specific kinds of illegal material that they were set up to contend with. They are funded either by public authorities or by private parties, such as NGOs or business agencies. In fact, a number of hotlines also act as watchdogs, and vice versa. For instance, the German association Jugendschutz, created and funded by public authorities, actively tracks and reports "cyberhate" content to public agencies.[32] Between 2001 and 2005 some 750 extremist websites were shut down as a result of action taken by Jugendschutz.[33] On October 4, 2002, the International Network against Cyber Hate was created by Jugendschutz and the Magenta Foundation, in order to coordinate action internationally against hate speech on the internet. This network of watchdogs makes an active contribution to increasing notice and takedown practices concerning hate speech.

Finally, one might predict that notice and takedown would eventually open the way to online dispute resolution (ODR) mechanisms in order to settle disputes about the validity of material online.[34] At the

[30] See http://ec.europa.eu/information_society/activities/sip/news_events/success_stories/index_en.htm (accessed April 7, 2007).

[31] See www.portal.northerngrid.org/custom/files_uploaded/uploaded_resources/1880/IWFjune06esafety.ppt#16.

[32] See, for instance, Jugendschutz im Internet, available at www.jugendschutz.net.

[33] See International Network Against Cyber Hate [INACH] (2006: 23).

[34] Article 17 of the Directive on Electronic Commerce already provides that the states must favor "out-of-court dispute settlement," including by electronic means. The use of an online dispute resolution system, moreover, would be in conformity with the European Council's policy concerning the settlement of

moment the content provider and the petitioner have no choice other than to bring cases before the judiciary when they want to challenge the outcomes of the notice and takedown procedure. Courts are actually dealing with an increasing number of cases regarding internet content. The courtroom is not always the most suitable place for settling this kind of litigation, however: judicial proceedings are too lengthy and too expensive and judges are not necessarily experts in cyberlaw. The standardization of ODR could be the major next step in the development of an efficient European Union system of internet co-regulation (Schultz, 2005; Katsh, 2006), on condition that the fairness of the ODR – which is often an area of dispute (Geist, 2002a, 2002b) – is guaranteed.[35]

6.3.2 Dangerous effectiveness

Although the idea of regulating the internet appeared unworkable ten years ago, nowadays the system set up in Europe seems to be quite effective. Indeed, sometimes it is even so effective as to jeopardize freedom of speech and freedom of the press, in violation of the principles of the rule of law and, more precisely, of the standards of the European Convention for Human Rights (ECHR), based upon article 10 of the ECHR. Article 14 of the Directive on Electronic Commerce encourages hosting providers to take down controversial material stored on their servers as soon as they are notified by a public authority, a watchdog, a hotline, an NGO, a person claiming to be injured or any user alleging the material to be illegal, infringing or otherwise damaging (Frydman and Rorive, 2002b). The system appears to be quite unbalanced, moreover, since, although article 14 urges hosting providers to take such material down, it gives no incentive to put legitimate content back online. This can be explained by the fact that the directive does not provide a formal notice and take-down procedure, which must instead be set by national regulation or

commercial cross-border disputes (Council resolution of May 25, 2000, on a community-wide network of national bodies for the extra-judicial settlement of consumer disputes; *Official Journal of the European Communities*, June 6, 2000, C 155, 43: 1–2).

[35] The European Court of Human Rights provides some guidelines to ensure the fairness of ODR (Schiavetta, 2004).

self-regulation.[36] This regulatory pattern has negative side effects. The content provider has no formal right whatsoever to ask for a put-back, or even to be informed of the takedown. As a result, the ISP must decide for itself whether or not to comply with the notices (the accuracy of which may vary) that it receives on a daily basis. The ISP is then in the position of a judge, if not a censor (Frydman and Rorive, 2002b). In fact, recent academic surveys have convincingly demonstrated a growing trend for ISPs, especially in Europe, to take down legitimate content when a complaint is lodged, even when it is based on erroneous or misleading information.[37]

In sum, the European informal notice and takedown procedure appears unbalanced and wide open to massive private censorship. This situation could be solved through a legal procedure of counter-notice and put-back, similar to the DMCA model. Even better, a well-balanced system could be inspired by the Japanese model. Whereas the US copyright statute calls for an immediate takedown but allows the content provider to issue a counter-notice requesting a "put-back," the 2001 Japanese statute sets up the so-called "notice, notice and takedown" procedure, which requires the ISP to forward the notice to the content provider and wait for an answer before removing the notified data.[38] Such a system, which one might also call "reply and stay up," seems more suitable in terms of taking the interests of all sides into account, and it would relieve ISPs from the burden of making "rulings" that they have neither qualification nor legitimacy to issue. If such mechanisms could enhance the

[36] In its first report on the directive's application, the Commission stated that "at this stage [it] does not see any need for a legislative initiative"; see EC (2003: 16). On October 24, 2005, the Commission established an "expert group on electronic commerce" that it could consult, notably, on questions related to "notice and takedown procedures"; "Commission decision of 24 October 2005 establishing an expert group on electronic commerce," 2005/752/EC, *Official Journal of the European Union*, October 26, 2005, L 282: 20–1.

[37] Various experiments were undertaken by researchers to evaluate the perverse effects of this incentive, particularly in terms of limiting access to content on the public domain. The results of these experiments show the tendency of ISPs toward censorship, especially in Europe, of legal content on the basis of erroneous information (Ahlert, Marsden and Yung, 2004; Nas, 2004). For private censorship on the internet, see Kreimer (2006).

[38] See the Law concerning Limitation of Damages to Specific Telecommunications Service Provider and Disclosure of Sender Information; available at www.isc.meiji.ac.jp/~sumwel_h/doc/codeJ/provider-e.htm.

European Union's system of internet regulation, some states may, however, favor a system of co-regulation precisely because of its censorship potential.

6.4 China: from authoritarian co-regulation to an international struggle for law

Both the US and the EU systems show that co-regulation is an effective way to regulate the internet either for specific issues or as a general system. Co-regulation is nothing more than a method of regulation that may be implemented by any regulators with a disputable political agenda, however. Authoritarian states may use co-regulation to freeze out free speech, censor the internet and overpower the media. This is exactly what is happening now in China (see section 6.4.1) (Qiu, 2000; Reed, 2000; Lacharite, 2002; Cheung, 2006), resulting in an international struggle for law in the election of a global standard concerning internet regulation (section 6.4.2).

6.4.1 The evolving pattern of internet regulation in China

The Chinese authorities monitor internet communications to restrain controversial political and social discussions. At the same time, the internet is used to disseminate Chinese political propaganda, while its usefulness for carrying out business transactions means that the expansion of its reach in the country is being encouraged (McGeary, 2001: 219; Cheung, 2006: 1, 3). The Chinese government has set up a strict control and restriction system for access to the internet by building a virtual firewall that filters unwanted websites, such as human rights portals, and online newspapers, such as the New York Times, blocking access to them. Individuals or groups are not allowed to make a direct international connection and all internet access is controlled by the government (Qiu, 2000). The technology cannot ensure full control, however, and can be challenged by the use of technology itself. The enforcement of state censorship can be made extremely difficult, moreover, if it has to arrest, prosecute and condemn every single violator (Lacharite, 2002).

China consecutively used two methods to regulate internet content. First, since 1996, the Chinese government has regulated the internet through extensive legislation and official decrees (Newbold, 2003;

Cheung, 2006), which prohibit messages and conducts that may harm national security, disclose state secrets, endanger social stability or promote sexually suggestive material, etc. (Newbold, 2003; Cullen and Choy, 2005).

In addition, co-regulation mechanisms have been progressively set up to delegate internet monitoring to private actors and the business sector. In doing so, China has adopted a very effective and cost-efficient scheme of control that combines criminal sanctions and privatized enforcement (Boyle, 1997b), allying direct control and state censorship with surveillance by non-state actors, including foreign investors (Cheung, 2006). For instance, under the State Secrecy Law, a person who puts information on the internet is ultimately held liable for any unlawful dissemination of that information, even though information that is provided to or released on websites has to be checked and approved by the appropriate government authority. ISPs and users must put up management systems, and all entities or users that establish chat rooms or network news groups are subject to the examination and approval of government agencies. The providers of internet services and content are liable for any failure to monitor and supervise electronic activities conducted within their business sphere. The Regulations on the Administration of Business Sites of Internet Access Services,[39] passed in 2002, require ISPs to install tracking software, take surveillance and monitoring measures, report to the relevant authorities when someone uses the internet for illegal activities, keep records of each user's identity card and history of websites visited for at least sixty days and install software to filter out the banned sites that are considered subversive by the government (Newbold, 2003). The Interim Provisions on the Administration of Internet Publication of 2002 impose similar requirements on actors in the internet publishing industry, and various statutes and official decrees confirm that the provider must take steps to ensure effective control over the internet, such as deleting prohibited content, keeping records and informing officials of illegal activities (Cheung, 2006). Failing to take action is against the law and may result in a fine.

[39] Regulations on the Administration of Business Sites of Internet Access Services (promulgated by the State Council, September 29, 2002, effective November 15, 2002), LawInfoChina.

Finally, to control foreign investors, China initiated the voluntary Public Pledge of Self-Discipline for the China Internet Industry in March 2002, which requires signatories to "monitor the information publicized by users on web sites according to the law and remove the harmful information promptly," and prohibits "links to web sites that contain harmful information" (Newbold, 2003). US internet majors such as Yahoo! signed the public pledge and agreed to contribute to the Chinese government's content control management system of policing internet messages (Heffernan, 2006). Although it is unclear whether corporations that do not sign the public pledge will still be permitted to operate in China (Cheung, 2006: 33), it is interesting that China is using a co-regulatory mechanism to ensure internet censorship by "inviting" ISPs to organize it themselves. For instance, thanks to this method, the Chinese government was able to persuade Google to launch a censored search engine in the country (Kreimer, 2006). American ISPs are willing for business reasons to endorse the role of censor – for example, by signing and implementing the pledge, but also by selling the technology needed to enforce the Chinese filtering scheme or divulging private information to the Chinese authorities (Newbold, 2003; Heffernan, 2006). This raises the question of the complicity of internet corporations with authoritarian regimes.

6.4.2 *Ruling the rules: transnational struggle for law*

There are some boundaries, however, to governments' ability to use co-regulation to outsource the implementation of their national law, at least within their own territory. ISPs are global players indeed, and government law could have network effects. This global situation leads to a transnational struggle for law.

For instance, as a reaction to the policy of the Chinese government and that of other authoritative countries around the world (Kremer, 2006: 18), the US Congress is currently considering passing a statute to promote freedom of expression on the internet: the Global Online Freedom Act. This bill aims at establishing an Office of Global Internet Freedom in charge of drafting a list of "Internet-restricting countries." The bill states in section 201 that a "United States business that creates, provides, or hosts any Internet search engine or maintains an Internet content hosting service may not locate, within a designated Internet-restricting country, [any materials] involved in providing such search engine or content hosting service."[40] In addition, internet companies are compelled not to alter their search engines to "produce different search engine results for users accessing the search engine" from different countries.[41] Although the bill is unlikely to be enacted, it reveals another evolution in internet regulation: a cold war between states fought by internet companies. This trend underlines the global "struggle for law" that is currently emerging, with each state trying to impose its own standards on the others by using ISPs as soldiers for the defense of national values.

In this context, civil society actors also play a role, for instance by developing and adopting software, such as the Psiphon[42] software funded by the Soros Foundation and the University of Toronto, which enables internet users in internet-censored countries to access blocked sites. Along the same lines, the Voice of America broadcasting service, funded by the US government, contracted with Anonymizer Inc., the producer of censorship circumvention software, in order to provide Iranian citizens with access to information that was censored by their government.[43] NGOs may also play a part in the judiciary constituent of the international struggle for law. For instance, in April 2007 the US-based NGO World Organization for Human Rights filed a major lawsuit against Yahoo! based on the Alien Tort Claims Act in a US district court, accusing the Internet Corporation of having aided and abetted the Chinese authorities in the arrest and torture of a Chinese journalist. According to the petition, Yahoo! divulged, at the request of the Chinese authorities, the name of the journalist who was using a Yahoo! internet account to disseminate his calls for democracy in China. Such transnational litigation has the potential to add to the pressure on ISPs' shoulders and incite them to show more respect for basic human rights and democratic standards of free speech.

[40] Global Online Freedom Act of 2007, HR 275, January 5, 2007, section 201; available at http://thomas.loc.gov/cgi-bin/query/F?c110:1:./temp/~c110yo5Bpm:e388.

[41] Global Online Freedom Act of 2007, HR 275, January 5, 2007, section 202.

[42] Psiphon is a piece of activist software developed by the Citizen Lab. It is described as "a censorship circumvention solution" and contributes, of course, to the global struggle for law in contributing to getting around some national regulations. See http://psiphon.civisec.org (accessed April 7, 2007).

[43] See http://www.anonymizer.com/consumer/media/press_releases/02012006.html (accessed April 7, 2007).

6.5 Conclusion: internet co-regulation and the rule of law

This chapter has shown the differences between the regulatory solutions endorsed by American, European and Chinese regulators. In each case, some legal devices were implemented in order to press ISPs to control the internet. In the United States the co-regulatory model remains exceptional and is used only to achieve very specific goals, while in Europe and China co-regulation is the general and leading model. It is quite clear that, despite controversies concerning states' ability to control the internet, states are fully aware of the effectiveness and power of co-regulatory techniques, but co-regulation may jeopardize fundamental freedoms and basic guarantees of the rule of law. The chapter has underlined the Chinese use of co-regulation to support authoritarian policies, and shown the European system to be far from perfect itself, and lacking the requisite safeguard mechanisms to ensure full respect for the guarantees of the rule of law. Behind this can be discerned, in the absence of global standards to regulate the internet, a full-fledged competition between states, models and standards: a global struggle for law. Because of the impact that the regulation mechanism may have on the rule of law, it can also be seen that what are actually at stake are the fundamental freedoms. The question therefore remains: which model – the libertarian, the procedural co-regulatory or the authoritarian co-regulatory – will emerge triumphant?

7 Democratic governance and reflexive modernization of the internet

TOM DEDEURWAERDERE

7.1 Introduction

One of the main contributions of the theory of reflexive governance is to have shown the importance of new ways of building democratic legitimacy in global orders, by focusing on the transformation of the background beliefs that play a role in the behavior of actors and organizations. This approach has great potential for issues of global governance, in which no well-established collective preferences exist on many questions of common concern and where controversy over solutions is widespread. Not only are these challenges present in connection with the governance of the internet, but they are also prominent in other fields, such as environmental governance and the protection of fundamental rights. The debate on reflexive governance has been especially vigorous in the environmental field, however, in which social and scientific controversies surround complex issues such as global warming and genetically modified organisms. At the same time, it is a field in which truly global governance devices have been put in place, such as in the areas of carbon-trading and plant genetic resources.

In the context of this debate, two models of reflexive governance have been proposed for building democratic legitimacy in global orders. The first suggests how to organize reflexive governance in global centralized orders, and is based on the emergence of transnational civil society organizations; the second develops models of reflexive governance in global decentralized orders through so-called "subpolitics." Jürgen Habermas (1996, 2001) and Ulrich Beck (1992), respectively, elaborate these propositions in a set of seminal works.

The theory of democratic legitimacy developed by Habermas in *The Postnational Constellation* (2001) and in his earlier theoretical work *Between Facts and Norms* (1996) has been very influential. It was one of the first attempts to justify, from a normative point of view, the specific role of civil society actors in a post-conventional society, in which democratic legitimacy is no longer built on the basis of common conventions shared by a group with a common history at the level of a nation or a social class. Instead, democratic legitimacy is built through an agreement between state and non-state collective actors on the procedures for organizing open participation in the debates. This theory influenced experimentation with several deliberative processes, such as citizen juries, consultations with civil society organizations and participatory councils.

Habermas's analysis also demonstrates some limitations to the role of civil society. The first is the informational bias of civil society actors and problems in their access to information. According to Habermas, this bias calls for appropriate access to information, to be organized for citizens and stakeholder organizations, in the building of their preferences, and the necessity of filtering the propositions emerging from civil society through intermediary organizations before they are used in political decision-making. The second limitation is the possible lack of real influence on the part of civil society actors on decision-making, beyond the procedural guarantee of their participation in the public debate.

Another type of limitation in building democracy in global orders arises when the national or supranational entities have limited capacity to regulate the behavior of social actors. This can occur with unforeseen risks, or in highly technical fields such as the regulation of content on the internet. The second model of reflexive governance attempts to address the problem of a lack of legitimacy by organizing reflexive learning processes with different non-governmental actors that contribute to solving global governance problems in decentralized orders. This second model was studied by Beck in the context of his work on the regulation of ecological risks. According to Beck (1992), the building of efficient and legitimate rules for dealing with risks that might have important unanticipated side effects should involve subpolitics, in which non-governmental actors (including social movements) solve social problems directly in innovative ways without relying on the administrative state (Hunold and Dryzek, 2005).

Examples of subpolitics include direct negotiations between environmental associations and corporations to make corporate activities or products more sustainable, and the participation of representatives of indigenous peoples in meetings of the international organization for ethnobotanical research (such as that held in Belem in 1988) to reach common agreement on access to medicinal plants. In the field of internet governance, subpolitics occurs when authors decide to put their digital content in open-access repositories on the internet, and when they put pressure on publishers to authorize the self-archiving of published papers on their personal website or their research institution's institutional repository. An important strength of subpolitics is its direct impact on the strategic decisions of collective actors, without having recourse to global collective orders. An important weakness is the possible isolation of subpolitics from more encompassing issues and broader social groups.

The key lesson that can be drawn from these contributions by Beck and Habermas is the importance of reflexive processes in both global centralized and decentralized orders. This chapter reviews the research that has built upon these seminal analyses and compares basic features of reflexive governance in the fields of environmental governance and the governance of the internet. For this I use a broad definition of reflexive governance as the social process of the transformation of the cognitive and normative background beliefs that lead to and emerge from changes in the behavior of actors and organizations. In other words, I do not consider that reflexive governance can be reduced to the cognitive aspect only. Rather, reflexivity is analyzed as a cognitive process that emerges from, and is situated within, a social and political context. This chapter therefore also considers the extensive literature on governance in economics and political science, which has shown the importance of informal rules and beliefs in social orders. According to this literature, both formal (legal and contractual) and informal (social and normative) rules and beliefs are important in establishing global governance regimes (North, 1990; Ostrom, 1998). In particular, as stressed, for instance, by Robert Cooter (1994), the complexity of modern economies is so great that centralized lawmaking and regulation cannot effectively cope with the need to achieve normative regulation among communities of individuals who repeatedly face collective action problems.

In the first section of the chapter I analyze three main approaches to the explanation of the drivers of reflexive governance: the cognitive, institutional and experimental approaches to reflexive governance. For this the analysis relies mainly on the literature on global environmental governance, in which these approaches have been extensively debated in the context of both centralized and decentralized global orders. Then I assess the comparative strengths and weaknesses of strategies based on each of these three approaches to governance, showing that it is important to select the appropriate strategy depending on the characteristics of the context. Finally, in the third section, I illustrate my analysis with two examples of possible frameworks for reflexive governance in the field of environmental governance and internet governance, respectively, based on the lessons learned from the assessment. One of the main questions that I address in the discussion of these examples is when and how the cognitive approach to reflexive governance should be combined with institutional- and actor-centered approaches to foster the design and implementation of more effective global governance regimes.

7.2 Three explanations for the drivers of reflexive governance

The works of Habermas and Beck show that transnational civil society and subpolitics both contribute to building the legitimacy of global governance, through fostering reflexive learning in global centralized and decentralized orders. These studies mainly focus on reflexive learning on the basis of cognitive reframing by rational argumentation. This is only one strategy for reflexive governance, however, and other strategies for the revision of informal rules and their associated beliefs are also important, especially when the social and political dimensions of reflexive governance are considered. Because my goal is a comparative assessment of some of the main forms of reflexive governance, which also provide new insights for analyzing the governance of the internet, I do not provide a systematic overview of the different theories of reflexive governance (for an in-depth review, see Lenoble and Maesschalck, 2003). Rather, I contrast three complementary approaches to the explanation for the drivers of reflexive governance, capturing some of the main features of each. The models considered are the cognitive model of reframing, the institutional model of the social and institutional embedding of reflexive processes, and the experimental model based on the building of actors' capacities for reflexive learning. As I attempt to show, in order to address the challenges of legitimacy in global orders a combination of different models will be needed, beyond a simple focus on the cognitive model of rational deliberation in the public sphere.

In the cognitive approach to reflexive governance, the key driver for reflexive learning is a process of discussion about the rational acceptability of the beliefs. The main idea is that the revision of beliefs is the result of argumentation through open communicative processes. An important implication is that the communicative processes that are set up to question validity claims of all sorts must enable the participation of all affected and interested parties. Hence participation and deliberation are two sides of the same coin (Feindt, 2012). Reflexive learning through deliberation depends on some supplementary conditions to be effective, however. First, deliberation requires a political culture of open communication and the permanent questioning of normative and discursive backgrounds. Indeed, since participants bring along their discourses and experiences from outside the deliberative space, participants in the debate have to take a critical stance toward their own discourses and practices in which they and their social activities are embedded. Second, the usefulness of public deliberation depends on institutional guarantees that the results of the deliberations (with citizen juries etc.) are used in the revision of the collective rules in public decision-making. As a result, the scope for transforming background beliefs depends on the integration of the deliberative processes in the overall governance framework. This second condition is addressed in a more systematic manner in the second approach.

The second set of theories focuses on the dynamics of the social and institutional embedding of the process of revising beliefs. The main concern is with the role of reflexive governance processes in the effective social acceptance of new rule systems. This includes the rational acceptability addressed in the cognitive model, but in addition important social factors, such as the creation of social trust around the rules that result from the new beliefs, the creation of an appropriate institutional framework favoring the exchange of viewpoints and a permanent critical examination of beliefs in open knowledge societies (North, 2005).

This second approach to reflexive governance – which can be labeled the institutional approach – addresses the problem that rules that are designed in the framework of a certain belief system often have perverse effects when they do not take the existing action strategies that prevail in a given institutional and social context into account (Dedeurwaerdere, 2005). For example, under the United Nations Convention on Biological Diversity, new rules around the commercial use of biodiversity were adopted as a result of the consensus that emerged from the various deliberative processes organized in the preparation of the convention (Louafi, 2007). These rules have nevertheless led to very poor results, mainly because they were weakly embedded in the institutional and social reality of the local contexts of biodiversity conservation. In particular, profit-sharing mechanisms were envisioned as a tool for protecting biodiversity in the countries of origin. In practice, however, they have created perverse effects, in particular through the crowding out of intrinsic non-monetary motivations to preserve these natural resources.

In other cases, the dynamic change in beliefs, and the social embedding in the new rule system resulting from these beliefs, have been shown to be mutually supportive. For example, the seed exchange network managed by the Collaborative Group for International Agricultural Research (CGIAR) has adopted a set of core principles that promote open access (OA) and common responsibility in the preservation of the world's food security. The principles adopted by this group of non-state actors have proved to be an effective way to govern global food security. Their effect is to reinforce the informal norms of the research communities in a way that is compatible with the basic incentive structure of worldwide seed exchange. In particular, the informal norms are reinforced by the production of positive network externalities, such as the access of all players to the common pool, and the enhanced provision of collective goods such as basic research tools (databases, standards) that are shared among the network members.

The main driver of the revision of beliefs in this second approach is the creation of a mutually reinforcing dynamic between the changes in beliefs, on the one hand, and the institutional changes in the formal contractual and legal rules, on the other. Various factors contribute to this mutually supporting dynamic. Some important factors that have been addressed in the literature are inclusive decision processes in organizations, science-based knowledge generation and face-to-face communication. The first two play a role in broadening the available knowledge on solutions and changing the actors' perceptions of the opportunities generated by new rule systems (North, 1995). The third factor, which has been analyzed extensively in the context of community-based natural resource management, plays a role in building trust around new rules, which might in turn lower the compliance costs of institutional arrangements (Ostrom, 1990).

A major shortcoming of this model is its failure to address the conditions for the emergence of new beliefs and social norms in a forward-looking manner. Indeed, the set of available background beliefs is presupposed by the analysis, and the process of generating new beliefs is taken for granted. Its main strength, however, is that it explicitly considers the interaction between the new beliefs and the effective functioning of the rules in the social and institutional context. In particular, it draws attention to the possible synergies between certain belief systems and the set of informal and formal rules that generate productive outcomes in specific problem settings.

The third set of theoretical models addresses the problem of the building of the actor's capacities needed to enhance or generate reflexive change. An important example of this third approach to reflexive change is the model of democratic experimentalism (Sabel and Zeitlin, 2007). In this model, building capacities for joint experimentation is an important driver for reflexive change in situations in which cognitive processes do not lead to consensus, or institutional processes fail to accord with the available informal rules and beliefs in the social context. In general, this approach focuses on creating capacities for collective experimentation with a diverse set of action strategies resulting from a variety of cognitive frames.

The model of experimental open-ended learning process has been at the base of important policy innovations in the European Union, such as in the open method of coordination or the Water Framework Directive (Sabel and Zeitlin, 2007), and has also been implemented in other settings, such as natural resource policy in the United States and Australia (Gunningham, forthcoming). These examples of institutional innovation all have in common the establishment of procedures for joint experimentation, such as self-evaluation, reporting and the use of evolving outcome indicators. In this approach it is the proactive experimentation with various action strategies in a context of joint reporting and monitoring processes that leads to the successful governance regimes.

7.3 The use of the different strategies in building global democratic legitimacy

In the previous sections I have argued for broadening the debate on the legitimacy of global orders, beyond the focus on the cognitive model of the deliberative process in the global public sphere. First, new ways of establishing democratic legitimacy have emerged in global decentralized orders, through so-called subpolitics, in which actors contribute directly to the provision of collective goods without relying on the administrative state. Second, institutional models and actor-centered models have been proposed as an important alternative to the cognitive theory of reflexive governance. Reflexive change can be generated by a combination of mechanisms based on cognitive framing, the social and institutional embedding of new rules, and the building of actors' capacities for open-ended experimentation.

This section develops some general hypotheses that can guide the choice of strategies for reflexive governance in any given governance situation. In general, the choice of strategy depends on the characteristics of the governance. The openness of the political system to the participation of civil society actors, and the temporal dynamics of the process of change are both addressed.

First, the choice of appropriate strategies will vary with the openness of the political system to civil society participation. In this context, it is useful to adopt the distinctions between different types of political regimes established by Christian Hunold and John Dryzek (2005) and to adapt these distinctions to the governance of global orders. In their comparative research, Hunold and Dryzek distinguish between (1) active inclusive states, such as Sweden and Norway, which select civil society organizations and actively support their involvement in decision-making; (2) passive inclusive states, such as the United States, the Netherlands and Australia, which organize extensive public consultation but do not get actively involved in selecting and supporting civil society organizations; (3) passive exclusive states, such as Germany and Belgium, which have difficult access to state bureaucracies for everyone except corporate actors and the political parties; and (4) active exclusive states, which actively restrict the access of interests to decision-making or intervene to undermine the basis for the organization of social interests, such as contemporary China or, to a lesser degree, the United Kingdom under Margaret Thatcher's Conservative government.

These distinctions are directly relevant for the comparative assessment of the different modes and strategies of reflexive governance. For instance, subpolitics was effective in building an oppositional public sphere in the context of a passive exclusive state in Germany in the first half of the 1990s. It was this strategy of subpolitics that finally led to the adoption of new constitutional principles, such as ecological modernization and the precautionary principle. Another strategy, which played a role in the United States in the same period, favored the participation of moderate civil society organizations in the centralized state bureaucracy. It was this strategy that generated a major reconfiguration of environmental policy in the United States under the administration of Richard Nixon. Hence two very different strategies were adopted in these two cases, both of which led to successful policy innovations. As I go on to argue, similar differences in the openness of policy systems exist for global orders. An evaluation of the openness of the policy system will therefore also be highly relevant to the choice between possible reflexive governance strategies in global orders.

Second, the choice of strategy will depend on the temporal features of the process of change. Here a distinction can be made between temporary processes of reflexive change and more permanent reflexive processes. Reflexive governance processes will typically be temporary during the transition to a global order in which the benefits of coordination are considerable and the possibility of a consensus plausible. In such cases, the focus of the reflexive learning process will be on the transition to stable conventions that are expected to need little further adjustment. This temporary role of reflexive governance contrasts with the more permanent reflexive change that is needed when there is competition between different possible paths of development in situations of great uncertainty as to the possible outcomes. An example of the latter is trade in goods whose production has an undetermined, but potentially problematic, impact on health and the environment. Varying views on acceptable levels of risks circumscribe the circulation areas of such goods. Good examples are the different approaches of the European Union and the United States to genetically modified organisms and food safety regulations; no consensus seems likely to emerge in the near future (Godard, 2012).

On the basis of these distinctions, some of the advantages and disadvantages of the use of the various strategies of reflexive governance can be assessed. Cognitive strategies based on public deliberation are most useful in situations of possible consensus and when there are no major disputes over the adequacy of the knowledge claims (Rydin,

2007). In these situations the major issue is to remove the obstacles that block undistorted communication, by providing procedural guarantees for open and collaborative processes. As a result, cognitive strategies will be most appropriate in active inclusive political regimes, in which collaboration with civil society and other non-governmental collective actors is actively supported. An example of such processes in the field of environmental governance is the collaboration between the International Union for Conservation of Nature (IUCN) and the United Nations Environment Programme (UNEP) in writing the *World Conservation Strategy* (IUCN, 1980), which helped to build the consensus that led to the 1992 Convention on Biological Diversity (Louafi, 2007).

Another type of situation in which deliberative strategies might be useful is in passive exclusive political regimes. In this context, cognitive strategies have proved to be useful in building consensus in oppositional public spheres. For instance, an oppositional sphere emerged in the field of sustainable energy use in Germany in the early 1990s, with its own autonomous research institutions and service-providing organizations. In this case, deliberation in public forums proved very useful in building consensus about a possible alternative to the current public policy. Another example is the participation of representatives of indigenous communities in various forums before the Convention on Biological Diversity. Some principles that were elaborated in these forums, such as prior informed consent, did not receive a lot of attention at the time of the negotiations, compared to the principles of conservation and sustainable use. In the later implementation phase of the convention, however, they played an important role as guiding principles, and they are now at the core of the main policy advances in this area.

Institutional strategies for reflexive governance aim at adjusting the beliefs embedded in formal and informal rules to the institutional and social context. To be effective, these strategies depend on there being a certain degree of openness in political decision-making to the diversity of norms and institutions that operate in the social world. Hence they will be most useful in pluralist societies based on passive or active inclusive regimes, in which mechanisms exist to integrate new beliefs into the political decision-making processes.

This strategy is especially important when the embedding of the new rules in the social and institutional context is problematic, such as in situations of possible destabilization of the norms and institutions by new rule systems. For example, in the regulation of digital content on the internet, the declarations and guidelines issued by public research institutions have played an important role in enabling the rapid dissemination of research results in open-access repositories, in a context of enhanced pressure for potential commercial use and restrictive policies from the publishers. Institutional strategies are also important in situations in which formal rules are costly to implement and when the informal norms of organizations and communities play an important role in producing collective goods.

An important limitation on cognitive and institutional strategies is the difference in capacity between different actors. To be effective, these strategies often need to be combined with strategies oriented toward capacity-building. Democratic experimentalism aims to reinforce actors' capacities for reflexive learning through open-ended experimentation. This strategy is important when new capacities are needed to generate reflexive learning beyond the existing scope of possible consensus (in deliberative strategies) or beyond the existing scope of the current informal rules and norms (in institutional strategies). Capacity-building strategies are typically temporary, as they are oriented toward opening up new possibilities for reaching certain targets. They are complementary to other strategies, and are important tools in passive inclusive and passive exclusive regimes, in which not all the parties have sufficient self-organizational capacity to participate in the reflexive learning process in subpolitics.

7.4 Possible governance frameworks

The key message of this review of existing research on reflexive governance is the importance of combining traditional modes of governance, based on formal legal and contractual rules, with modes of reflexive governance, in centralized and decentralized orders alike. The review has also shown the complementary nature of current strategies of reflexive governance, based on cognitive, institutional and actor-oriented approaches. This section illustrates these two key messages with four examples in which reflexive governance has played an important role in global governance, two from the field of environmental governance and two from the field of internet governance. In doing so, the objective is to show how the governance models developed in the field of environmental governance allow the problems of global governance in the digital world to be better understood.

7.4.1 Reflexive governance in global centralized orders

7.4.1.1 The International Treaty for Plant Genetic Resources

A clear case illustrating the role of different strategies of reflexive governance in a global centralized order is the 2001 International Treaty on Plant Genetic Resources in Food and Agriculture (ITPGRFA). The treaty established an open-access regime for agricultural biodiversity, for a set of species considered essential for food security (such as wheat and rice). Two different reflexive strategies contributed to the elaboration of the basic principles that are the backbone of the treaty. These are conventional deliberative consensus-building, on the one hand, and institutional strategies in subpolitics, on the other.

As early as 1983 a mechanism for deliberative consensus-building on open-access principles was established by the Food and Agriculture Organization (FAO), through the creation of the Commission on Genetic Resources for Food and Agriculture (Halewood and Nnadozie, 2008). This deliberative process had some important shortcomings, however, including poor participation by civil society organizations. Moreover, the process had to face increasing commercial pressures stemming from the emerging globalized IPR regime. As a consequence, consensus was made more difficult.

Institutional strategies within the Collaborative Group on International Agricultural Research played an important role in providing an alternative strategy for reflexive learning. The strategy of the CGIAR was based on reinforcing the informal norms for the sharing of plant genetic resources through an agreement on a code of conduct, while at the same time continuing to provide advice to the treaty negotiators. Reflexive learning in the CGIAR in the 1990s is a good example of temporary subpolitics in a global centralized order, during a period when there were considerable difficulties in the deliberative processes. Now that the ITPGRFA has been adopted, there is again a level playing field for possible consensus, and deliberative processes have gained in importance. For issues that fall outside the scope of the treaty, however, such as relations with private seed collections, sub-politics in the CGIAR will remain important in further learning about new rules and opportunities for the worldwide sharing of plant genetic resources.

7.4.1.2 The open-access movement for digital publications

An interesting example in the field of internet governance, illustrating the use of reflexive governance in global centralized orders, is that of the open-access movement in digital publications (Comba and Vignocchi, 2005). In this case, gradual consensus was built through a series of international declarations establishing new norms and principles for digital publishing. At the same time (as with global environmental governance), this example illustrates the importance of combining cognitive strategies for reflexive governance (which characterize international declarations) with institutional strategies for embedding these new rules in the informal norms and practices of communities and organizations.

The open-access movement promotes open access to digital content, through deposits in repositories of digital pre-prints (early drafts of a published paper) and post-prints (the submitted or published version of the article). The system envisioned by the open-access movement would provide open access to all government-funded research, establish a common system of rules for certification of the quality of the research output and promote rapid dissemination with due attribution. The main hurdles for moving toward such a system are the current organizational rules of research funders and universities, which give priority to high-impact peer-reviewed journals (which are not usually open access), and the strong commercial publishers' lobby, which opposes the open-access movement. As such, it is an example of reflexive learning in a global centralized order, in the context of a highly conflicting social and institutional environment.

Consensus on the new rules for establishing open-access repositories has been built in a series of seminal statements and initiatives, of which the best known are the Budapest Manifesto in December 2001 and the Berlin Declaration in October 2003. The first promoted on a wide scale, for the first time, the idea of achieving open access to literature by self-archiving and publishing in OA journals. The second introduced these ideas into a statement, the Berlin Declaration on Open Access to Knowledge in the Sciences and the Humanities, which has since been signed by some 250 organizations – mainly academic and research institutions – worldwide. At the time of the Budapest Manifesto, self-archiving looked like a revolutionary, "anti-commercial-publishers" movement. After several years of debate, however, the supporters of opposing positions have been able to compromise and consider the tradeoffs. This can be evidenced by, for example, the recent establishment of the EU high-level group on digital publishing, composed of commercial publishers and prestigious research institutions.

Because of the highly conflicting social and institutional environment, it cannot be expected that the newly established consensus around digital publishing, even when endorsed by major governmental agencies, will automatically lead to a change in the publication practices of authors. Indeed, scientists are badly placed to adopt the new open-access principles in practice, because they are often themselves members of the editorial boards of the high-impact journals and are constrained by research evaluation practices that favor the (usually non-OA) established journals. It is here that coordinated institutional strategies for enforcing the new open-access norms and beliefs among scientists will play an important role.

The programs and activities of the Scholarly Publishing and Academic Resources Coalition (SPARC)[1] launched by the Association of Research Libraries (ARL) in 1998 and its European twin initiative, SPARC Europe, best embody and represent such an institutional effort to contribute to changing the present commercial publishing system. The research libraries are intermediaries between the authors and the publishers, and hence are well placed to reinforce the new norms and beliefs in a way that is compatible with the basic incentive structures embedded in the rules of scientific practice. Like the CGIAR, ARL provides an independent assessment of the socio-economic benefits of the open-access system and sustains a community-wide effort with important positive network externalities. Through these activities, the research libraries have had an impact on the background beliefs of authors and publishers alike. Today most journals allow self-archiving on personal websites and institutional repositories, and, increasingly, universities are demanding that research results be deposited in the central library's institutional repositories.

[1] These are available online at www.arl.org/sparc.

Finally, the main focus of this reflexive learning process has been on the social acceptance of the new rules for publishing in the digital age. Capacity does not seem to be the main concern. Some parallel efforts to build capacity have been made, however, through initiatives developed on the Sherpa web portal.[2] These include the RoMEO/Sherpa project, which develops and maintains a database that lists journals' and publishers' copyright agreements, and the OpenDOAR project, which is building an authoritative directory of worldwide open-access repositories.

7.4.2 Reflexive governance in global decentralized orders

As suggested above, reflexive governance also plays a role in global decentralized orders. This has been shown in the field of environmental governance, with the emergence of subpolitics, but increasingly it also plays a role in internet governance. For instance, decentralized orders arise when the formal and informal rules have to be tailored to the specificities of user and provider communities of digital content. To substantiate this argument, I first present an example of reflexive governance in the field of the environment. Then I compare this to a case of internet governance with similar features.

7.4.2.1 The Helsinki process in forest governance

A good illustration of reflexive governance in decentralized orders is given by the reporting and monitoring mechanisms established in the Pan-European Forest Process. This is an intergovernmental forum in which ministers and officials from the European Union and neighboring countries meet and establish common rules and guidelines for forest policy. The overall goal of the process is to move toward sustainable forestry, based on timber production and the preservation of the environmental and social values of forests. Major hurdles are the limits of command and control regulation for changing the management practices of private forest owners and the resistance to change of vested interests in the public administration of forests.

In the Pan-European Forest Process, consensus on the goals of forest policy was built through a series of common declarations and resolutions that were adopted at the meetings. An important resolution

[2] These are available online at www.sherpa.ac.uk.

adopted in 1998 established a common set of criteria and indicators for monitoring and evaluating sustainable forest management in Europe. These criteria and indicators are a translation into the European context of the criteria and indicators that came out of international debates after the United Nations Conference on Environment and Development, held in Rio de Janeiro in 1992, and they have been implemented in most national European legislations as the core standards for evaluating sustainable forestry.

Individual nation states have control over their natural resources. An effective transition toward sustainable forestry will therefore depend on initiatives taken at the national level. The criteria and indicators for sustainability cover only the economic, environmental and social dimensions of the forest in an abstract way, and, as such, they constitute no more than a scaffold on the basis of which further social learning can be organized. The need to translate the general principles to local contexts has led to major shifts in European forest legislation. New legislation has moved away from strict state control of forestry to new forms of joint management and collective learning involving forest owners, non-governmental organizations and public authorities (Schmithüsen, 2000). The new legislation sets out a framework for defining performance standards and supports efforts to develop cooperative forms of decision-making.

In spite of the progress that has been made by building these reflexive governance mechanisms into the legal frameworks, a major challenge remains, namely to broaden this approach to all forest owners. Indeed, the regime established by the new forest legislation still has to come to terms with the dominant trend in nature protection, which is based on investing in small but highly valued niches of biodiversity-rich forest reserves, with high payoffs for tourism and real estate value. In this context, the organization of a fully reflexive learning process among all the forest owners, as established by the joint management organizations, remains a challenge.

7.4.2.2 The Science Commons project on global data integration

An interesting example in the field of internet governance that illustrates some of the features of reflexive governance in decentralized orders is the Science Commons project on global data integration. In the Science Commons project, gradual consensus on possible rules of digital data-sharing has been built through a series of meetings with stakeholders involved in the specific subfield of medical research into Huntington's disease (although the objective is to build a prototype of global relevance). This project has also suggested a model for building capacity for further experimentation with the proposed new rules of data-sharing, through a common monitoring and labeling system for the various community-specific adaptations of the rules.

The Science Commons[3] is an organization that emerged from the Creative Commons movement. Its mission is to design strategies and tools for faster, more efficient, web-enabled scientific research. It promotes the use of open-access licenses and protocols within the current copyright legislation, in order to make it easier for scientists, universities and industry to use digital network infrastructures for sharing and integrating knowledge. The digital data-sharing project envisions large-scale machine integration and the user-based annotation of data made available through the internet. For example, life scientists have to integrate data from across biology and chemistry to comprehend diseases and discover cures, and climate change scientists must integrate data from widely diverse disciplines in order to understand the current state of the climate and predict the impact of new policies. Major hurdles for large-scale data integration are the wide variety of informal rules and practices that govern digital data-sharing over the internet and the legal uncertainty with respect to potential commercial exploitation of the databases and associated software in an open-access regime.

Consensus on the rules for data-sharing was reached through a set of stakeholder and expert group meetings. This resulted in the recognition of two basic principles: permission for full use and reuse of the contents of the database (for instance, through a broad waiver of all rights related to the database); and the need to preserve the reputational benefits of the database provider by giving due attribution of the original data source in all follow-on uses of the data.

In the discussion on the implementation of these rules and principles, it appeared that no formal contractual and uniform set of rules could be applied to all the communities. In particular, practices for due attribution of the use of digital data depend on the nature of the digital content and the norms of the communities. Archaeology data norms for citation will be different from those in physics, and different again

[3] See the website of the Science Commons Project, at http://sciencecommons.org.

from those in biology or in the cultural or educational spaces. The most practical way forward, therefore, seemed to be to allow community-specific adaptations of the data-sharing regime, by defining community-specific norms of attribution embedded in the specific beliefs and practices of each discipline.

The proposed Science Commons model stimulates experimentation by providing a common framework and a review mechanism of the results of the learning process. Any community norm providing full use and reuse rights and specifying a protocol for due attribution of data source can be reviewed by Science Commons. If it conforms to the basic principles, the organizations will be authorized to use a common digital label on their websites, called the Science Commons Open Access Data trademark. All websites using this label will enable machine-based data-mining and reuse, under tailor-made attribution rules and principles.

The key focus of this model is on building capacity for decentralized learning by means of monitoring and reporting mechanisms. Accordingly, the model allows some of the characteristics of the experimentalist approach to reflexive governance in the field of the internet to be illustrated. It also shares some features of the institutionalist approach, however. For instance, in addition to its role in monitoring, the Science Commons acts de facto as a trusted intermediary. It facilitates change in the informal rules by generating trust among the stakeholders, and provides independent assessment of the benefits of the proposed regime through expert consultation.

7.5 Conclusion

This chapter has discussed the role of reflexive governance in building democratic legitimacy in global orders. The argument has mainly focused on an analysis of reflexive governance as a cognitive process that emerges from, and is situated within, a social and political context. I have illustrated this argument with two important prototypes of reflexive governance in the field of digital content on the internet: the open-access movement in digital publications; and the Science Commons project on the global integration of digital data. An important lesson to be drawn from this analysis is the complementary role of reflexive governance in non-state organizations and communities, on the one hand, and more conventional public deliberation in transnational bureaucracies with the participation of transnational civil society organizations, on the other. In particular, global problems need not always be addressed by reflexive learning processes on a global scale. For instance, the analysis showed that subpolitics is often more appropriate for building social and political legitimacy in situations of transition or in contexts in which highly specialized communities use and produce the collective goods.

This chapter has adopted a modeling and design perspective to reflexive governance processes. It is from this perspective that I have analyzed the contribution of the cognitive, institutional and actor-based approaches to reflexive governance and assessed their strengths and weaknesses. From an epistemological perspective, however, the effective use of these models in real-world action situations will depend not only on their optimal adjustment to empirical reality (as in the modeling and design perspective) but also on the practical organization of epistemological inquiry into the limitations of the current models and practices of reflexive governance adopted by various actors in the face of collective action problems (Lenoble and Maesschalck, 2007). Theory, empirical evidence and practice all play important roles in enhancing the probability of selecting rules that will lead to better outcomes. Every institutional creation will remain a situated experiment that has to be evaluated and adapted over time through collective inquiry by those concerned.

8 *Internet governance and the question of legitimacy*

PIERRE MOUNIER

8.1 Introduction

As the history of the internet proceeds, developing more complex levels of communication and organization, the question of internet governance implies more and more actors and commentators. With more and more types of activities relying on the network, the social, political and financial stakes rise higher and regulation becomes critical. The discussions on this topic were always technical, but the technical dimension has changed with time: from Jon Postel's first organization of the domain name system to the highly complex reorganization plans under the ICANN structure, the topic is still highly technical, but differently so. Under these conditions, the actors implicated in the process show a tendency to evaluate the question solely from the point of view of efficiency: how can the institutions, processes and rules of internet governance be made more efficient, more reactive and, if possible, costless? This question is not to be ignored, but it should also be linked with another aspect, one that has always interfered with the concern for efficiency: legitimacy.

> Governments of the Industrial World, you weary giants of flesh and steel, I come from Cyberspace, the new home of Mind. On behalf of the future, I ask you of the past to leave us alone. You are not welcome among us. You have no sovereignty where we gather.
>
> We have no elected government, nor are we likely to have one, so I address you with no greater authority than that with which liberty itself always speaks. I declare the global social space we are building to be naturally independent of the tyrannies you seek to impose on us. You have no moral right to rule us nor do you possess any methods of enforcement we have true reason to fear.

"A declaration of the independence of cyberspace" (Barlow, 1996) one of the best known and popular expressions of political concern on this topic, whatever its validity or pertinence, grounds its sovereignty claims on a lack of legitimacy. At the moment, and for its author, John Perry Barlow, governments lack legitimacy to intervene in internet affairs. For others, the organizations, groups, technicians and self-proclaimed representatives that have mushroomed in cyberspace within the last few years cannot pretend to be more legitimate to govern or regulate the internet, as they are not elected or designated by governments to do so. Since the beginning of the internet, most circumstances of its history have shown that the problem of legitimacy has not been solved, at several levels: the legitimacy of institutions, first and foremost, is still pending. Among them, ICANN of course attracts the main bulk of the critics, but it should not obliterate, by its visibility, the importance of other governance institutions, of a more technical nature, such as the IETF and W3C. At another level, the legitimacy of rules is also at stake: the behavior of internet users in certain respects shows clearly that, for a large proportion of them, the laws they should obey, primarily because their representatives voted for them, just do not seem to exist when they are connected. Some laws, such as those pertaining to IPRs, do not seem legitimate in all circumstances.

In these conditions, should we consider the internet as a "legitimacy-free area"? It would mean that no governance is possible in this place, that it cannot bear any effective regulation – which is obviously not true.

Max Weber (1995 [1922]) has demonstrated that the key point of any political configuration is the kind of legitimacy it rests upon. Because legitimacy defines authority, it stands at the heart of the political process. Legitimacy should not be seen as a static concept, though. The ideal-typic presentation by Weber of his types of societies could be misleading in this respect. It certainly should be completed by a more dynamic approach in which legitimacy appears as a constant work in progress, the result of actions taken by different players on a limited playing field. Bourdieu's contribution to legitimacy theory is decisive. As Bourdieu integrates into his own theory the concept of "struggle" (1980), he can elaborate a representation of political order as a temporary stabilization of a balance of power between various actors. In Bourdieu's sociology, therefore, legitimacy is – and is only – the temporary result of legitimizing strategies along certain norms defined by the field in which they take place. The process is fairly complex, because actors when they try to legitimize their positions (re)define the norms of their field as much as they conform to them. The field in Bourdieu theory should be seen as a mix of an arena (in which people struggle to take each other over) and an agora (in which they cooperate to create a common space). Domination, as Bourdieu defines it, is the result of the mix; it's a legitimate takeover.

In many aspects, Bourdieu's theory of legitimization and domination is very apposite for an analysis of internet political history, as long as one does not consider the internet to be an already predefined field but as a space in which different actors try to elaborate and delimit fields within which they can establish their own domination. Much of the debate about internet governance can therefore be interpreted as a long struggle between very heterogeneous actors to define one or several "fields" (as Bourdieu uses this concept) within cyberspace; and the question of legitimacy – or, rather, of legitimizing strategies – is a key point in an understanding of this short stretch of history.

The aim of this chapter, in examining each of these aspects of the question, is to demonstrate that the question of legitimacy remains unsolved at a global level. In the first part, the role of ICANN is analyzed in the light of its failure to gain legitimacy in its efforts to build a global governance structure for the internet. In many respects ICANN's political history can be seen as an attempt to build a state-like configuration – an attempt that failed because it was unable to gain legitimacy. The second part of the chapter examines the lack of legitimacy of the rules relating to, for example, intellectual property rights, especially in peer-to-peer networks. This part is based on the importance of the "cyberspace" metaphor to explain why many users do not feel compelled to honour IP laws when they use the internet. The consequence of these first two arguments is that, as the question of legitimacy has not found yet a satisfactory solution at a global level, signs of fragmentation are beginning to become visible throughout the internet, resulting in limited areas of legitimacy. This point constitutes the final part of the chapter. If it is indeed the end of the internet "as we know it" (or dreamed about it), namely a common and public global space regulated by a more or less democratic governance structure, there are no indications that it is the end of internet communication; far from it. I conclude, therefore, by attempting to sketch out what life and activities (professional or otherwise) might be like in a space that is fragmented, unregulated at a global level and certainly not governed by a global democracy – primarily because there is no global society to sustain it.

8.2 Legitimacy of institutions

Among the galaxy of internet institutions, ICANN is undoubtedly the one that is most affected by the problem of legitimacy. Ever since it came into being the corporation has been continually criticized, on a variety of grounds: that it is flawed because of its origin, its composition, its decision-making process, its missions. Mueller (2002), for instance, surveys up all these criticisms and concludes that ICANN represents one of the prime historical examples of a socio-technical system stuck in a suboptimal configuration. The nub of his argument is that ICANN overstepped its primary mission, answering the simple need for technical coordination requested by the DNS, through an uncontrolled development process and a succession of unintended consequences of its acts. The result is a fundamental lack of legitimacy due to the introduction of a political model – the model of centralized power – in a context in which it was not needed. The criticism is radical because, in a way, it contests the legitimacy of any political control, conceived as political in nature, over the DNS itself. As domain names are names, and therefore are words, they are naturally abundant, and the scarcity of this kind of resource can only be the result of a conscious effort, exemplified by the behavior of ICANN.

Taking a different line, Jonathan Weinberg (2000) does not examine the (lack of) legitimacy of ICANN in such a fundamental manner. For this author, legitimacy is to be sought and obtained only through an elaborate construction. The position of ICANN in this respect is very close to the problem of administrative law. Unable to gain sufficient legitimacy from the process of its constitution, as a federal agency could, ICANN tried several techniques of legitimization. One of them was to try to inherit its legitimacy from the government that created it. In the case of ICANN, however, the way it was created by the US Department of Commerce, through the Green and White Paper process, blocked that route right from the start. Another way was to elaborate strict procedures of action: actions that comply with these procedures are accepted, and even approved, not because they are good or efficient but because they conform. Weber's rational-bureaucratic ideal type of state can be invoked here. Even so, it is not difficult for

Weinberg to explain that, despite a heavy bureaucratic apparatus that makes ICANN look like a sort of federal agency, the way it works in reality is radically different. The last possibility for an institution such as ICANN to acquire some legitimacy was to create a consensus from what can be called the internet society. The consensus method is interesting, because it has its roots in the way that the technicians and engineers of the internet (typically IETF working groups) work together, especially in the technical normalization process, for which it is required to validate important decisions. Consensus may possibly work when participants have the same professional background, the same knowledge and the same personal history and values, but experience shows that it cannot be obtained in heterogeneous organizations such as ICANN was planned to be. In the circumstances, consensus looks more like a deceit that barely conceals the underlying oligarchic configuration.

In fact, ICANN's difficulties in gaining legitimacy need to be interpreted and positioned within the context of all organizations relevant to internet regulation. The "rough consensus" method, which was used more or less from the beginning of the internet, for example in the Network Working Group (NWG), became progressively less efficient for the organizations that were set up subsequently to regulate different aspects of the internet: first the IETF, then W3C and, finally, ICANN. One explanation could be that these organizations deal with more and more complex aspects of the internet: at first the aim was to normalize the TCP/IP protocol; then there appeared the web and markup languages with more implications for the end user; finally, decisions had to be taken about the whole addressing system, which implied the existence of several "constituencies," several types of agent, all very different from each other. From the NWG to ICANN, the complexity of the objects to be dealt with rose higher and the actors became more heterogeneous. For example, consensus about domain name allocation cannot now be obtained so easily, because several dimensions of a potential name (as a character string, as an identifier, as a word, as a trademark) may conflict, as Joseph Liu (1999) explains.

Another way to consider the situation is to look at ICANN's legitimacy in terms of the state model of political organization. The literature about the relationship between ICANN and the state is often influenced by ideological questions. Should cyberspace be exempt from the power of the nation state? Is it necessary to create a new one to regulate it? How? Could ICANN become this state? Non-paradoxically, European and American scholars have often raised such questions and debated them. On one side, the emergence of new models of regulation supported by NGOs is interpreted as a marginalization of the state model of regulation (Froomkin, 2000a), while others want to "bring the state back in" (Drezner, 2004) in one way or another (H. Klein, 2002). This is another reason why ICANN can never gain clear and stable legitimacy: considered to be a threat because of some of its features, the corporation was seen as the gravedigger of the state by some, while another group of actors strove to transform it into a puppet manipulated by national interests. Historically, the failure of at-large elections to the board of directors, accurately analyzed by Françoise Massit-Folléa (2002), and the reform that followed, which was perceived by many as a coup, ended up depriving the organization of any possibility of seeking support for its attempts to acquire legitimacy from its users.

Therefore, rather than wondering if ICANN is a virtual state, or if the power of the nation state must apply to the internet, or even if cyberspace needs to get rid of all forms of state control, perhaps one should examine the configuration of the space to which these questions are addressed. The main contribution of Norbert Elias's (1990 [1939]) approach to state history is in demonstrating that the state should not be approached as an object but, rather, should be considered as a process with multiple factors. One of these factors is the constitution for some reason of a common, closed space to which several actors go in competition, sometimes reluctantly. In other words, whereas, in general, competition for domination is counterbalanced by centrifugal movements and a splitting of socio-political units, the sociogenesis of the state, as described by Elias, builds upon a common and relatively closed territory as a condition for a concentration of power. As the internet is not exactly the feudal France that Elias uses to build his argument, the comparison has to stop here. The important point, however, is that management of the root (i.e. the DNS) triggered the building of a common space (to be precise, a naming space).

The first hypothesis can therefore be proposed: that, at some point in its history, the internet presented some of the characteristics of a common space wherein the idea of a state constitution process could be discussed by the public, which was itself engaged in a process of constitution: the common space was the naming space created through the DNS; the ideas of state-like institutions were largely debated inside and about ICANN; and public opinion was nurtured and strengthened by the many discussions – undertaken through online forums, mailing lists, websites and so on, among professional and advanced users of the internet – about the policy of the DNS and the rules that should apply to domain names. A common space, common institutions, a common public opinion: every element appeared to be present, at least as a potentiality to foster the development of the legitimizing process of a state configuration. This chapter is not the place to argue the validity of such a hypothesis, but simply to propose it as a means to characterize the debates that flared around ICANN at this moment of its history. The rest of the chapter is based on the assumption that, although ICANN's legitimacy to administer the DNS is not reduced to zero, mainly because there is no alternative at the moment, its historical momentum has slipped away and other political trends of constitution (or, more likely, of disintegration) have taken command of internet history.

8.3 Legitimacy of rules

There is another debate about the legitimacy of rules that parallels the one about internet institutions in general and ICANN in particular. The issue of users' behavior on P2P networks and the lack of enforcement of IP laws in relation to the use of digital content also raises some interesting questions relating to legitimacy.

Many studies have confirmed what was clear all along to some observers: that most users of these networks infringe IP laws without feeling any culpability or even without perceiving the reality of infringement, as a report released by the Pew Research Center shows (Lenhart and Fox, 2000). It is far from sure, as some "copyfighters" like to think, that this behavior can aptly be interpreted as a revolt against copyright and its industry, rather than simply a lack of concern about the question. If IP laws are illegitimate for a whole range of users, this is in a different way from how ICANN is for some actors. This "illegitimacy by indifference" of IP laws inside cyberspace reveals some interesting phenomenon. Since Lessig's (1999b) book *Code: And Other Laws of Cyberspace*, an important part of academic literature has focused on the relation between law and technology (technical tools and technical architecture) (Wu, 2003b). In some cases, though and far removed from the way Lessig addressed the question, the discussion deals exclusively with the efficiency of law enforcement mechanisms. To copyright holders in particular, for whom the internet is no more than one distribution channel among others, it is often the only discussion acceptable: that the definition of copyright, negotiation, compromises and agreements between authors (and therefore publishers who claim to represent their interests) and consumers is to be set only outside the internet context, and independently from it. What can be negotiated is a mere adaptation of IPRs to the technical peculiarities of the environment in which they should be enforced. These adaptations have two sides: on the one hand, copyright holders agree to release their grip on the act of copying (for example, for technical necessities linked to network diffusion or in the case of backup copies); on the other hand, they want to control by themselves and a priori the way the law is enforced, through technical devices such as digital rights management systems. In a way, DRM technologies can be considered as delegates, representatives of copyright holders in cyberspace; they are here to enforce, in cyberspace, laws that were discussed, negotiated and voted for elsewhere.

What legitimacy can there be, however, with a law discussed, negotiated and voted for in one place and enforced in another place? How can a rule that has been conceived in one type of space (i.e. physical space, with its own qualities) be supposed to apply to another type of space (i.e. a virtual one, which has its own peculiarities)? The second hypothesis of this chapter advances the proposition that illegitimacy through the indifference to IP laws on the part of internet users can be attributed to the discrepancy between these two types of space and the blindness of lawmakers to this fact. It has been argued that considering the internet as a place is an illusion, which therefore leads to false conclusions, especially regarding IPRs; Dan Hunter (2003) in particular sustains this opinion. It seems to be a very effective illusion, however, given that it leads most people to behave as if the internet was actually a place, or at least a space different from the one in which they live.

"Cyberspace. A consensual hallucination experienced daily by billions of legitimate operators, in every nation, by children being taught mathematical concepts… A graphic representation of data abstracted from banks of every computer in the human system. Unthinkable complexity. Lines of light ranged in the non-space of the mind, clusters and constellations of data. Like city lights, receding" (Gibson, 2000). The cyberpunk movement, from William Gibson and Bruce Sterling to Barlow, cannot be reduced to marginality. It reflects to a considerable extent the experience of many internet users. It might be interesting to point out how the "spatial simile," which is the core of the cyberspace concept, runs as a red silk throughout the internet's history: from the MUDs (multi-user domains) to Second Life, from the Well to Myspace, it appears that internet users always need to ground their interpersonal relationships on a metaphoric representation of a common space.

When Barlow (1996) makes his claim for the independence of cyberspace, he considers the internet to be a separate space, in which digital objects have particular properties (they are nonrival and ubiquitous, for example). His approach to and definition of the internet can be criticized as a pure apology not based on the facts, that it looks more like a reflection of his wishes than the result of any analysis, but it can also be argued that his wish, his claim, works in the social space constructed by discourses on the internet as a self-fulfilling prophecy. The internet is a separate space to him (i.e. it influences his behavior) because he treats it that way. The same can be said about members of other private networks, such as the historical "Well," for example, or about any existing community on the net that considers itself to be building a new space. The same can surely be said, moreover, of members of P2P networks, who have to comply with the rules of the network (such as "Thou shall share," for instance – as Svensson and Bannister, 2004, show) rather than with a distant and global law subsequently fitted to their context.

The surge of judicial actions against file-sharers in P2P networks provides an opportunity to pose the question of compliance to rules in P2P networks as a conflict of loyalty problem for many users: which rule do they have to obey – the one that says that files must be shared, for the sake of the network itself, or the one that says it is illegal to share, for the sake of the law? It can be seen that resolution of the conflict will be influenced by the power of enforcement devices or techniques and by the legitimacy of conflicting rules. As to the first aspect, P2P networks have several technical devices that broaden or shrink the bandwidth allocated to a user according to his/her commitment to file-sharing. Ranged against this, a combination of DRM and judicial retaliations counterbalances the strength ratio. In terms of the second aspect, though, which rule seems the most legitimate to the internet user: the global prohibition from the Berne Convention or the local injunction from other participants, who are always keen to qualify offenders as "leechers"? It can be seen, therefore, that the second main model of internet governance (that is, governance through nation state laws enforced in cyberspace) is also flawed, as it gives insufficient consideration to the difficulty of transferring legitimacy from one type of space to another.

I talk about "types of spaces" and not about spaces; the nuance explains why the internet is more than a club in which special rules exist for some things but are always superseded by national laws. The space defined by a club belongs to the same order of space as the one a nation state controls. It appears that, space, as most internet users perceive it, belongs to another sort of "spatiality" than the physical space that states control. The objects it contains are digital objects, and, as such, because they have particular properties (such as nonrivalry), they are not subject to ordinary laws. The same thing can be thought of other criminal offenses. Video games, especially those that work with long-lived worlds, such as the Sims, offer fascinating cases to reflect upon: for example, could criminal offenses committed in the space of the game, between characters, be charged by a judge in physical space? The question remains open, and the way a player and his character articulate is worthy of serious consideration (Lastowka and Hunter, 2004).

It is very useful, however, to make distinctions between different levels of regulation. Norms and values, on the one hand, and rules and regulations, on the other, cannot be considered at the same level. For example, not abiding by IPR laws that forbid the copying and distribution of copyrighted materials does not mean that users do not recognize the principles of intellectual property. Above all, it does not mean that the concept of intellectual property is illegitimate to them; it simply means that the laws passed to implement it seem contradictory to the "physics" of the cyberspace – or, put another way, the "institutional ecology of [the] digital environment" (Benkler, 2006) they want to regulate. In his *Wealth of Networks*, Yochai Benkler demonstrates how the peculiar properties of informational goods require different forms of work organization and regulations but do not subvert the political and cultural norms and values shared within American society. In other words, analysts such as Benkler reinforce, from an economic point of view, the validity of the cyberspace metaphor, but in a much more precise way than Barlow: networks define a special space in which objects, persons and relations have peculiar properties that coerce users to behave differently from how they do in physical space. It does not mean that their values are different, but that these values apply differently. Intellectual property rights have been much discussed in this respect, of course, but one can also think of other subjects, such as privacy and freedom of expression.

The internet can be "a place," a space different and separated from the space of everyday life in some respects, even though it never had the capacity to structure a public debate on some of the main questions that could be discussed, such as IPRs. The concept of the "netizen," for instance (a term coined during the early years of the internet, which Michael and Ronda Hauben, 1997, describe and promote), reminds us permanently of the notion of a people of the internet. In the final analysis, however, "the" people of the internet have been constituted neither by political action nor by the formation of public opinion. The internet, often presented as an auto-organizing and self-regulating place, cannot fulfill its promises, because of the impossibility of collectively developing a set of rules that can be respected by all actors as legitimate. In other words, the netizen does not exist because there is no internet society; no society – but many communities.

8.4 Legitimacy within communities

Despite this, it works. For years we have heard recurring pronouncements about the death of the internet if no effort is made to regulate it beyond the minimal normalization of technical protocols and the continuity of the DNS. For years it was said that the internet had to be regulated, even at the level of its content, otherwise it would become a huge garbage bin for unwanted documents, opinions and behavior that would force the average user to leave. Some years afterwards it is clear to see that the internet has indeed become a huge garbage bin, but the average user has not left; far from it. Does this mean that the user can survive in a space that is totally uncontrolled and unregulated? The third hypothesis of this chapter makes the claim that the internet's space is fragmented into a myriad of small semi-private spaces in which issues of governance and legitimacy are treated locally. As studies on this subject inform us, the sociological constitution and structure of these semi-private spaces can be very different according to circumstances. One cannot be sure that the actual appearance of internet space is not determined by the evolution of sociological and communication studies on the internet, mostly constituted with case studies and ethnographic surveys. It should be possible, nonetheless, to neutralize the suspicion that the internet's appearance is profoundly influenced by the way it is studied, and to build propositions upon this representation.

The notion of a virtual community, thoroughly analyzed by Serge Proulx and Guillaume Latzko-Toth (2000), provides an efficient key with which to access and understand the configuration of internet space. The various studies on the subject indicate that virtual communities can be very different in size, lifetime, structure and procedures (Proulx, Poissant and Senecal, 2007). Free software virtual communities, for example, which gather programmers, designers and users around the creation of software, constitute a first group of virtual communities, among which some have a strong commitment to explicit and rigorous regulation. Other types of communities, structured around professional activity or hobbies, create social groups of different types. More recently, communication tools such as blogs, or socializing ones such as Friendster or Delicious, create more or less transient communities around persons – or, more probably, representations of persons (Boyd, 2002). Most studies suggest that these communities are strongly regulated, that regulation can use tools to become effective and that legitimacy (of organization, persons, decisions, actions), though differently incorporated in different communities, is often a permanent subject of discussion within them. It would be interesting to understand which resources members of these virtual communities mobilize in order to legitimize their mode of regulation. What can be said at this point is that they have a very large range of different tools: control of technical tools, historical commitment to the community, the use of different sanctions against offenders, behavioral conformance to an explicit or implicit "constitution" of the community, and judgment from other members, sometimes embedded in electronic voting systems. In addition, it is well known that several online communities design their regulation model in imitation of other communities or social groups outside the internet context.

The Debian community has been thoroughly studied by Nicolas Auray (2005). Debian is an operating system (OS) that is one of the most famous elements of Linux distribution. It is renowned for the quality of its code and has been developed by a very large and active community. Auray, having studied carefully the regulation mechanisms within the community, shows how elaborate institutions play a key role in conciliating the apparent contradiction between its goal, to produce the best-quality code ("the perfect OS"), and the means it can mobilize to achieve it: volunteering, for the most part. Debian policy (the constitutional mailing list of the community), bug-squashing parties (regular meetings "in real life" convoked to encourage developers to carry out what is very tedious work), the moderation of interpersonal relationships in mailing lists and differentiation in the distributed authority over the code are the main means of regulation the community uses to pursue its goal. Auray proposes that this political infrastructure should be categorized as a direct democracy characterized by a new form of "civic Puritanism."

More recently, Sylvain Firer-Blaess (2007) has studied the way the open and collaborative encyclopedia Wikipedia is regulated. Here, it is a case of being much the same question as it is for Debian: how to achieve good quality despite the fact that the contributors are non-professional volunteers. In the case of Wikipedia, the dangers are even greater, because many more people have an interest in writing articles that do not comply with the "neutral point of view" policy promoted by the encyclopedia. Firer-Blaess shows how, behind the apparent egalitarianism of the wiki editing process that allows everyone to modify every article, a very sophisticated machinery of regulation has developed, building a hierarchy between "editors," "administrators" (or "sysops"), "bureaucrats," "stewards," developers ("system administrators"), "check users" and, of course, "bots," whose behavior must conform to the "bot policy." Firer-Blaess's argument builds on the two concepts that Michel Foucault put in juxtaposition to describe modern political order: discipline and punishment. As to the punishment, we have seen how it is performed by an unequal distribution of power between very differentiated roles. Regarding the discipline, the Panopticon model described by Foucault has evolved toward a hyper-panoptic model in Wikipedia, in which surveillance is potentially taken charge of by everyone through the wiki mechanism (in a wiki, every modification is recorded with its time, date and author's name, nickname or, at least, IP address). The conjunction between (1) a formal right of participation given to anybody, (2) a hyper-panoptic technology, (3) an unequal distribution of power between differentiated roles and (4) the global but noninterventional supervision of the Wikimedia Foundation describes, in a nutshell, an institutional environment that is specific to Wikipedia and differentiates this community from everyone else.

Massive multi-player online game (MMOG) and online role-playing game (MMORPG) communities represent very interesting examples of political laboratory, in which different types of community governances are elaborated. Technological, sociological, economical and cultural approaches need to be combined to understand the phenomenon (Beau, 2007). For example, one could evaluate the role of professional "community managers" in these environments, assess the influence of political representations in fantasy literature on the governing structures that are designed in online games such as World of Warcraft or analyze the impact on the players' behavior of the arbitrariness of physics that rules these worlds. Interviews (Beau, 2007) with community managers suggest that the question of legitimacy is far more complex than one might think. Several examples show, for instance, that the corporation that owns the game cannot do whatever it wants. These games develop from the accumulation of millions of interactions between thousands of players and create their own type of legitimacy on the basis of several factors, such as skill, seniority and charisma, among others.

Debian, Wikipedia and the World of Warcraft are just three examples of online communities with different modes of governance. Potentially, there are endless possibilities for other examples. Linux, Facebook, Flickr, Digg: some of them having a strong hierarchy of status, others not; some are still under the power of the "benevolent dictator" who created them, while others regulate behaviors, with varying degrees of effectiveness, through automatic procedures, trials, reframings of interactions and controversies.

Finally, it should be pointed out that most of these communities overlap to some extent. As affiliation to them is nonexclusive, the same people can (and often do) participate in several communities at the same time, can shift rapidly and at low cost from one to another or even split and create their own community in minutes. This malleability and plasticity on the part of some virtual communities is important, because it has consequences for the way regulation is exerted in them and for the balance between legitimacy and constraint that supports it.

Historically, the structure of the internet space in communities is not new; communities were even one of the first imaginary representations related to the internet, as Patrice Flichy has shown (2001: 85–112). This representation corresponds, furthermore, to a technical organization of the network interconnected with preexisting networks, some of them defined as online communities. The online or virtual community as the most important level in the political structuring of the internet is not a new phenomenon; but this fact seems to have been blurred by the debate on internet governance, especially when it focused on the ICANN problem and IPR enforcement, in which the internet could be considered alternatively either as a common and unified space in which governance similar to that of a state-like organization was to be exerted or simply as a channel of diffusion for digital content protected by rights that were negotiated and defined elsewhere. Questioning these two representations by the yardstick of legitimacy can be proposed as a method that enables other models of political organization to be revealed with appropriate types of legitimacy.

8.5 Conclusion

If my argument has been accepted so far, a whole range of new questions arise that need to be investigated, all of which pertain to relationships between communities and the way they influence each other, at least in their mode of organization. How does this reciprocal influence evolve over time? Proceeding from the time when scientists and engineers used to influence the network by their model of regulation, can we see the influence of new models in the way virtual communities are managed? How do models of regulation "percolate" from one community to another? Are there key positions, at the intersection of several communities? Are there key persons, able to play several roles in different communities? More practically, can we imagine temporary coordination between communities, momentary gatherings to make a collective decision or settle a particular aspect of internet governance? In any event, if the two or three hypotheses proposed in this chapter are confirmed, it is more in this direction that a solution for internet governance should be sought: through a multi-local way rather than a global one.

In this respect, the notion of the "information society," heavily cited during the World Summit on the Information Society and subsequently, should be examined critically. Amar Lakel and Françoise Massit-Folléa (2007) observe the ambiguities that affected the construction of legitimacy, especially related to the representation mechanisms of civil society during the preparations for the summit. Seven years after the failure of the attempt to set up representation of the "internet society" through the at-large process at ICANN, the very existence of the so-called "information society" is still at stake. It is perfectly clear that the opposite is the case: that the community is the main model for social structure in cyberspace, as strongly today as in the past, or even more so (Delamotte, Lamarche and Prince, 2006). This notion of community refers to several practices of governance, sometimes very different from each other, but interconnected nonetheless, exactly as computer networks are interconnected in the internet. Consequently, the question of legitimacy should not be treated globally, as if it could be treated at one go, or even discarded and subordinated to efficiency. It reveals, instead, cyberspace as a nonunified space, populated by myriads of different groups knocking together their own peculiar models of governance from a large toolkit made up of habits, ideas, discourses, codes, observations, experience and traditions.

This diversity needs to be taken into consideration. The political consequences are clear: no global internet governance body will be able to accumulate enough legitimacy over such a heterogeneous world; nor can traditional nation states pretend to rule over it. Linux, Wikipedia, the World of Warcraft, Flickr, Facebook and many others are far more than the publications, services, games and communication facilities they profess themselves to be: they are huge, transnational communities, elaborating upon the unique domain name system and across national laws – governance structures supported by forms of legitimacy they have built through their own histories.

9 Global governance: evolution and innovation in international relations

YVES SCHEMEIL

9.1 Introduction

Following decades of top-down arrangements within an exclusive club of Western countries, the World Summit of the Information Society convened successively in Geneva in 2003 and in Tunis in 2005. It established the Internet Governance Forum, which was intended to foster an inclusive global architecture in information and communication technologies. In a world so far dominated by states and intergovernmental organizations, such an initiative introduced non-state stakeholders into the debate.[1] Despite great efforts to design participant-friendly procedures, however, it also signalled the return of big structures into the ICT game (IGF, 2008).

Such tension between decentralized and centralized governance raises doubts about the possible emergence of new multilateral regulation for cyberspace. Making forecasts requires making comparisons: will the future of ICT differ dramatically from models of institutional change that have already been tried elsewhere, or will it follow the same path? There are two schools of thought: scholars who insist on the libertarian characteristics of the internet predict that, once completed, its nascent organization will be truly *innovative*; new participatory designs will be invented in a sector that is, allegedly, more atomistic and less agonistic than, say, that of the telephone. According to the opposing camp, this promised regulation will, on

[1] The WSIS is a move "to build a people-centered, inclusive and development-oriented Information Society, where everyone can create, access, utilize and share information and knowledge, enabling individuals, communities and peoples to achieve their full potential in promoting their sustainable development and improving their quality of life, premised on the purposes and principles of the Charter of the United Nations and respecting fully and upholding the Universal Declaration of Human Rights" (WSIS, 2003a, 2003b).

the contrary, follow a well-documented pattern of *evolution*, toward tighter control by major governmental and intergovernmental actors. Whatever their divergences as to explanatory factors, one thing that all analysts point out is the degree of *self-government* reached in any emerging field, and that the internet is no exception. In spite of this, they also recognize that popular notions about ICT, such as "international regimes" and "global governance," were invented to depict some *global control* from major multilateral actors.

To assess how and to what extent the ICT order will fit into these two alternatives, this chapter is organized as follows. First, the problem is put into its theoretical context. A short discussion of the "international regime" and "global governance" concepts shows that both lack clarity. They are probably not the most capable instruments for arriving at robust explanations of current processes; a mixture of IGOs and NGOs may well suffice. Second, a new account of the current dynamics is made. It is clear that IGOs and their member states have developed adaptive strategies and updated management styles to such an extent that governmental actors are inevitably brought back in. Third, the most likely future of the ICT world is presented as a test of a broader hypothesis about the continuing empowerment of intergovernmental organizations since the end of the Cold War.

9.2 Varieties of international regulation systems

Regulation requires cooperation – a concept whose meaning is little explored in international studies. From the eighteenth century on, several concepts were formulated to explain international collaboration between stakeholders. From rudimentary, bilateral and voluntary *alliances* from which partners can pull out at any occasion to world *institutions* endowed with enforcement powers, technical arrangements and possible "defection" are on the softer side, while the triumph of high politics is positioned at the other extreme. During the last two centuries intermediate concepts were successively introduced to fill the gap between a lack of enforcement/regulation and full compliance/control; this is how "clubs," "concerts," "coalitions of the victorious," "unions," "international organizations" and "international regimes" became part of the overall international cooperation landscape. The last two fit the ICT field well. International institutions, in particular, seem to promise a bright future: with or without a theoretically certified "regime," they have enough flexibility to accommodate both the anarchical and the regulated aspects of the internet, as well as its bottom-up/top-down ambivalence.

9.2.1 *From anarchy to governance*

A profusion of concepts means regression in thought. In international studies, successive notions have lost clarity one after another. For instance, IGOs' "resolutions" – but not the treaties that established them, and those that they very rarely succeed in drafting – are less compelling than national "laws." In the same vein, international "regulation" is less effective than governmental "intervention." Matters are even worse with "regulation": that this soft, vague and ambiguous notion is currenly gaining momentum indicates resignation to anarchy rather than progress toward control over global transactions. As an understatement of "government," in turn, "governance" brings gains in promised implementation, which are immediately wiped out by losses in compliance. Convinced that an inherent contradiction between efficiency (decentralized governance) and domination (centralized government) could not be solved by the coining of a neologism, scholars eventually turned to less hierarchical terms, such as "steering" (Mayntz, 2003). The emphasis is now put on all possible regulatory processes and actors, not just traditional ones (such as alliances, functional organizations and regional integration) but also modern ones, with the emergence of new forms of regulations such as "international regimes."

9.2.2 *International regime in ICT*

As loose and incomplete structures regulating specific multilateral activities, "international regimes" compare well with the limited outreach of national institutions. In ICT, however, the United Nations, its world conferences and its specialized agencies concerned with information issues – the World Intellectual Property Organization (WIPO), the ITU and the United Nations Educational, Scientific and Cultural Organization (UNESCO) – have not yet succeeded in properly addressing such problems as copyright disputes, freedom of opinion, online decency and peer-to-peer encroachments on legality.

Reaching a more "*consistent*" and "*uniform* international system" without losing autonomy and flexibility is delicate (Sharrock, 2001; emphasis added). Although it is particularly constraining in the case of the internet, this institutional trap is universal. Internet end users could probably endorse without reservation statements made in global contexts, such as "Although institutions are essential for human life they are also dangerous" and "How can we gain benefits from institutions without becoming their victims?" (Keohane, 2001).[2] They would also agree on a soft conception of what "political institutions" are: "persistent and connected sets of formal and informal rules within which attempts at influence take place" (Keohane, 2001) – a definition that adequately fits the functioning of internet bodies.

Institutions could nevertheless be more compelling than in Keohane's view. International organizations' legitimacy actually relies on capacities that no other international bodies can match: they respect *principled beliefs*, disseminate *norms* and try to convert them into binding *rules*.[3] Following these lines, even the softer "regime" – conceived as a floor minimum – that may emerge in ICT would inevitably harm some stakeholders' interests. Its flexibility may help to overcome such resistance, however. Reaching a more encompassing and enforcing "governance" end game, in contrast, seems out of reach: because of a lack of agreement on basic principles, full control will not (Mueller, Mathiason and Klein, 2007) or cannot (Mueller, 2002) be achieved soon. Since a laissez-faire attitude is no longer acceptable, and tight supervision is not desirable, a middle-of-the-range mix of *incomplete regime* and *soft governance* solves the equation.

Some regulation of the internet is required: as no stakeholder would be prepared to pay the costs of collective action, free-riding and defections would in the long run tear the internet down. The right to live a decent private life, moreover, and be protected against undesirable interference from spammers, cybersquatters, hackers and online counter-terrorism requires norm production, rule enactment and the

[2] Robert Keohane also adds that, "[i]n thinking about a partially globalized world, one may be tempted to dismiss half the governance dilemma by pointing out that because international institutions are weak, they are unlikely to be oppressive."

[3] These are the basic ingredients for "governance," much celebrated worldwide (see WGIG, 2005, for a review of the various meanings of the notion brought to the WSIS discussion by its participants).

implementation of decisions.[4] This will take place nowhere else than within IGOs; being constrained by a "double-bind" – the need to *pool sovereignty* in order to deliver global public goods *without transferring excess power* to a supranational actor – states are paralyzed, whereas international agencies are free to establish themselves in the vacuum as the most capable instruments of intergovernmental policy. They were born precisely to accommodate tensions with greater flexibility than states can display: more receptive to participatory demands emanating from smaller partners, they are less reluctant to accept heated and interminable debate, contestation and amendment.

Theory predicts (Keohane, 2001) that international institutions combine rationally expressed interests (a state's function) with social norms such as trust, fairness and reciprocity (all of which are IGOs' ingredients). Empirical cases of emerging regulation also show that, to succeed, global regulatory action must link *economic* benefits with *security* guarantees (both on top of governments' agendas); it also has to combine these priorities with *social*, cultural, educational and medical considerations (which are high on IGOs' agendas). The future will therefore consist of collaboration between such "big" actors and most of the non-state actors that were present at the start of the internet. Will this, in turn, retain, or even accentuate, the democratic principles embodied in internet communities, or instead weaken this self-government aspect?

9.2.3 The democratic dilemma

The problems of democracy cannot be solved in the long run by the initial structure of the internet, since it possesses no adequate channel for the representation of the "demos." First, in international politics, interest aggregation is not transitive; current international gatherings are not domestic parties: WTO groups, for instance (the "22," the "77," the "8," etc., and also borne out in the more consensual WIPO),

[4] The internet relies on contradictory principles, to some extent, and has a scope that is never reached in other fields: (1) basic citizens' rights *and* state prerogatives (respectively, liberty and sovereignty) must be guaranteed; (2) other individual privileges that matter in Western societies can be both enhanced and threatened by nonintervention on the internet (WGIG, 2005). This will happen even if norm demand is alleviated by "customized" views on differential levels of protection reflecting group or individual preferences (Heller, 2002).

are neither *international political movements* nor heirs of the late "transatlantic," "socialist" and "non-aligned" *ideological blocs*. Second, representation is unbalanced, because so-called "civil society" does not exist at the world level. Recommending an internet election to endorse a new framework for a domain name dispute resolution (as Lisa Sharrock, 2001, does) is a welcome participatory means, but it will not save an ICT sphere populated with privileged "founding fathers" and first-movers from its dramatically undemocratic nature (Keohane, 2001).

This is where IGOs can give substantial help: on participatory issues, international institutions are less ambitious than nation states. Instead of targeting "equal participation for all," they stress, more modestly, "accountability" and "transparency." The scope of their action is also less extended than in full-fledged international regimes – a context that facilitates an open and focused debate among enlightened communities instead of diluting the cleavages in a huge network of excessively differentiated stakeholders. Finally, IGOs, not regimes, are the locus of norm-framing: new international norms that frame public and private activities are continually emerging via the IGO channel from the permanent activity of myriads of state, non-state and above-state actors – in ICT as in every other realm (Schemeil and Eberwein, 2008).

Consequently, there is no reason to suspect that scenarios that worked out successfully in the past cannot be copied in the future. At the very least, "international institutions" could regulate the internet without reaching the stage at which they operate within a well-established "international regime"; in other words, there could be "regulation" without "governance." At best, IGOs will cooperate in ICT as efficiently as they do in other sectors, so as to move toward tighter control of the internet. An organizational iron law may drive this: as major actors in the field are vying for survival, organizations of all sorts are both *expanding* (IGOs) and *networking* (NGOs). I now review the comparative advantages of the strategic alternatives of institutions active in ICT.

9.3 The strength of being weak: the empowerment of IGOs

Why should states invent international institutions and keep investing in them once the initial conditions of their creation have disappeared? Why do such agencies survive in the long run if they are either plagued with enduring inefficiencies, and therefore useless, or sufficiently successful to threaten their principals' independence? To test possible explanations of IGOs' unexpected resilience – along with their capacity to move back into a sector from which they were banned at its inception – it is necessary to review the adaptive strategies that are open to them. By looking at extreme cases in order to produce a convincing case with the internet, I examine how the weakest, youngest or most jeopardized organizations survived and even grew.

First, at the juncture with potential partners or potential adversaries, *four alternative strategies* can eventually empower institutions operating in the information field: *mandate enlargement*, *coalition and controlled overlap*, *nesting* and *mutual recognition*. Second, within their own boundaries, IGOs have no choice but to adopt *two deliberating systems*: the *duplication* of decision-making into formal and informal processes, on the one hand, and *cross-regulation* between bureaucratic and political circuits, on the other.

9.3.1 Cooperation and mutual adjustment

According to the minutes of their meetings, defining their mandate and limiting dysfunctional overlap with neighboring organizations are aims that are on the agenda of most IGOs. Accurately defined as "boundary decisions" in a pioneering analysis (Cox and Jacobson, 1974), the permanence of such minor issues – compared to the substance of their mission – underlines the dilemma with which IGOs are confronted: if they do not broaden their mandate, even at the expense of close allies, which may sooner or later become dangerous rivals and retaliate accordingly, they are condemned to lose relevance.

9.3.1.1 Mandate enlargement

The rationale for not keeping out of their neighbors' private domains is very easy to understand: IGOs were established to fulfill a specific function, such as bolstering education or freeing trade. If they succeed completely in this particular field, maintaining complex and costly machinery would no longer be useful. If they fail, by contrast, they should leave the place in favor of a more robust institution. Once their initial mandate becomes partially obsolete as a result of changes in their environment, moreover, IGOs have no alternative other than to launch new programs. This "race to the top" is inevitable, because the constituency of an international institution changes more rapidly than a domestic electorate does; whereas IGOs rely on their members' goodwill to survive, states have captive citizens – and voters, willy-nilly, elect governments. The founding fathers who at the outset considered it necessary to set up a new IGO to address emergency issues – whether it be providing relief, fighting pandemics, filtering immigration or whatever – cannot support indefinitely the same activities in the same field once they are assigned a lesser priority at home. This phenomenon is accentuated by the long delay that states face when they wish to create organizations: it is often the case that the birth of the new international actor coincides with a decline in the priority and urgency of its mandate; the WTO, for instance, may have appeared just after free trade was at its apex as a norm (Wallerstein, 1996).

To fight obsolescence, secretariats are always looking for new ventures. Most switch from one aging component of their mandate to a fresher one; a good example is the World Meteorological Organization (WMO), which progressively added to weather forecasting first the conservation of rare water and then, shortly afterwards, the mitigation of climate change. The road was rather long from the 1951 conference in Paris that created an independent international meteorological organization to the present "Weather, water and climate" section of the United Nations; but the legitimacy and popularity of the Intergovernmental Panel on Climate Change is incommensurate to the lack of reputation of the WMO. In this process, IGOs' secretariats – and some prominent member states – display a tremendously imaginative propensity to endorse emerging norms and apply them to their field. Examples abound, from the "precautionary principle" to "education for all," "food security," "creative heritage," etc. This is not just a matter of idiomatic and somewhat weird language; it is also preemption on a realm of competence, evicting slower contestants and disclaiming future competition. Norms help international institutions to redefine their goals, legitimize their mission and publicize their new identity. The "digital divide" and "shared" software, if not "peer-to-peer" practices, are good candidates to help ICANN, the ITU or WIPO overcome the electronic age challenges they are now facing.

9.3.1.2 Coalition

A second way to fight obsolescence if not dereliction is to manage a common project jointly with other IGOs. Instead of *going alone* against opponents, they may prefer to *go along* with allies. Weak institutions become stronger when they coalesce to deliver a new service. Punctual collaboration may take three forms: joint ventures, subcontracting and control overlap.

First, *joint ventures* (i.e. associating for a specific purpose) have many advantages: so long as engineers, economists, lawyers, educators and gender and health specialists just pool their skills to reach a common goal, the risks of being insufficiently endowed to solve a pressing problem or too redundant to be merged remain low. Entering such associations is a test of goodwill, and an opportunity to build new collective alliances and enduring interpersonal networks. The division of labor and its benefits are optimized, the more so when the main outcome is the provision of a global public good that no single institution would be able to provide. Information is, obviously, such a commons, as prominent organizations are assigned the delicate task of responding to the growing demand for free access to all sorts of news at a time when holding private information makes a considerable difference. Simultaneously, they must protect property and privacy rights. Fulfilling such a contradictory mission is not an easy task, but the very fact that cooperation between institutions is possible with or without visible outcomes already counts as performance. In fact, the provision of convenient venues for negotiations, agreed procedures of deliberation and neutral structures of cooperation is in itself a sort of "primary" global public good, conditioning the delivery of real, or secondary, goods – the very outcomes of the decision-making process. Aside from procedural learning, moreover, substantive knowledge is dramatically increased by the ability to exchange information and views about the issues under review, to such an extent that the only global public goods whose provision can be taken for granted are channels of learning and cooperative arrangements (Schemeil, 2002). In a way, the IGF itself is a good case in point.

Second, *subcontracting* also helps to fulfill a mandate, since the "agency" that meets the standards of the "principal" and accept its terms of reference is now in charge of the completion of a joint program, although its recommendations can still be turned down by the principal. For instance, the United Nations Development Programme (UNDP) manipulates the United Nations Development Fund for Women (UNIFEM) wherever there is a manifest linkage between gender (which belongs to the latter's constituency) and development (the stronghold of the former). Some agencies take greater chances than others to interfere with rival IGOs' mandates. Eventually, the rationale for a joint program well publicized by its participant agencies may become confused when the responsibilities for implementing it are too decentralized; each partner will tend to interpret the broader mandate in terms of its own culture. The risk is therefore great that each will try to achieve its own ends, with no consideration for the broader issue at stake. Something along these lines is at the roots of the relationship between ICANN and WIPO, although ICANN is not an intergovernmental organization.

Whereas plain overlapping implies duplication and waste, *controlled overlap* may eschew such difficulties. In this third alternative, mandate enlargement stops at the doorstep of the benchmark activities of potential partners. The WMO's enlarged mandate, for instance, includes water management but leaves out issues concerning river basins, as well as the depletion of non-hydraulic environmental resources, since powerful institutions or regional organizations claim responsibility in these realms. Within that line of reasoning, and as far as ICTs are concerned, it is legitamate to wonder if the ITU's drifting away from its initial mandates can be kept under control in the long term by this organization.

9.3.1.3 Nesting

The third grand strategy consists in detailing a small group of experts to another agency. UNEP used it recently in its relations with the World Health Organization (WHO). Subdivisions of the latter, such as "environmental health," are staffed with a couple of environment experts, to whom particular tasks are assigned by the Nairobi headquarters and supported by the UNDP. They have to persuade biologists to adopt UNEP's ecological views on environmental issues and sustainable development, rather than address these problems with economic and medical lenses; simultaneously, they also have to convince WHO's experts to launch pilot projects and test innovative hypotheses about possible linkages between ecological advancements, health improvement and budget cuts. In the ICT field, the WSIS has opened new avenues for such strategies since it legitimized the exchange of expertise and facilitated mobility from one organization to another.

9.3.1.4 Mutual recognition

The fourth consolidation strategy involves NGOs. As they were created in order to contest multilateral institutions' lack of transparency and poor enforcement, NGOs have few incentives to collaborate. Here again, however, the same process seems to be at work: whereas NGOs demand more consideration for their competence, IGOs try to enhance the legitimacy of their own decisions. The optimal solution is a tradeoff between the growing inclusion of NGOs in multilateral processes against their adoption of a more instrumental stance. IGOs open up their black boxes regardless, limit the number and strategic importance of closed sessions and pay the transaction costs involved in such a dramatic enlargement of the number of consulted entities. NGOs cease to express critical views, professionalize and try to contribute to the final decisions. As both actors need cross-validation to fill the gap between their initial mandate and their actual impact, there is room for a win-win strategy. Switching from a competitive to a cooperative game, actors that were once vying for power are now full partners on a more or less equal footing, and a new deliberative understanding of international democracy supersedes the traditional participation versus representation issue. In ICT, this strategy is illustrated by the smooth and growing involvement of some international NGOs in the IGF.

9.3.2 Deliberating processes

There is another recipe for survival: improve the management style, either through the *superposition* of *informal* and *formal* channels of decision-making, to facilitate adjustment, or via the *juxtaposition* at every level of *bureaucratic* and *political* leaders, to tie *transnational* elites and *national* representatives of their home state. These options are of the essence in internet governance issues, as they offer solutions to the ICT dilemma: institutions may well be less formal and bureaucratic than expected with UN standards in mind. To resist pressures, they may turn inefficient *waste* into efficient *slack*, and link reluctant stakeholders without tightening them.

9.3.2.1 Channel superposition and issue-splitting

Where might it be best to look for a model? The WTO seems by far the most advanced institution in terms of organization and management. It operates two parallel circuits, the official and the informal. Its "green rooms" have acquired a considerable reputation in recent years as a bone of contention between small powers and great powers, but they are not the institution's sole contribution to international negotiations. Less well documented is the convening of the "HODs," or heads of delegations' debriefings, with no legal existence, no official translation and no minutes of the proceedings (Schemeil, 2004). In order to identify and settle sensitive issues, delegates are invited by the director-general and the chair of the Council to exchange views as sincerely as possible on an informal basis before meeting officially as members of the plenary. Moreover, the Council, whose main goal is to rule the organization *politically*, may also be convened periodically as an *evaluation* body, the Trade Review Board; and, in a third guise, as a *tribunal* – the Dispute Settlement Body. Within the WTO, the formal/informal divide is equivalent to the checks and balances system that constitutionally organizes in each state the relationships between the legislative, the executive and the judiciary. In spite of the absence of an appropriate legal status, this duplicated system of decision-making operates at each level, from the top (the meetings of the permanent representatives in *four* different capacities, plus their potential participation in the green room system) to the bottom (the countless "workshops," "groups" and "seminars," outflanking the more official "committees"). These committees have a legal existence because they are the locus of coordination with other agencies.[5]

9.3.2.2 Duplication, co-decision and cross-regulation

This dual chart is implemented in a dualistic way: everybody has two heads, one functional and the other political. The "chairperson" is officially a permanent representative, and the "secretary" an administrative agent belonging to the staff who is competent on the issues under review. This tandem is efficient in searching the causes of potential or actual disputes, reviewing possible solutions and drafting

[5] Among them, the famous TRIPS, or "Trade-Related aspects of Intellectual Property rights," agreement is worth noting, with its impressive bureaucratic apparatus and its own communication policy.

feasible agendas.[6] Finally, to topple this elaborate policy design, the Council, which holds its sessions in Geneva with little recess, is itself duplicated by a ministerial meeting that convenes every two or three years in various venues. "Rounds" are launched every decade or so at this highly diplomatic level, while ordinary business is conducted at the headquarters of the organization.

One may object that the WTO is the most recent multilateral organization, and that its constitution has therefore significantly benefited from the experience accumulated in the world so far; alternatively, it can be argued that remaining outside the San Francisco/Bretton Woods agreements, in which blunt confrontation is frequent, explains such spectacular achievements. This may well be true, but duplicate systems of decisions and co-decision-making procedures also exist in older and less contested agencies, such as the sophisticated WIPO, with its twenty-three governing bodies and some sixty chairs, which meet separately to address specific issues before reconvening in a plenary to approve the budget. The closed-session meetings of the director and the prominent "group coordinators" resemble "green rooms." Because of these precedents, it is very likely that the same management style, made up of duplication, issue-splitting and co-decisions, will sooner or later characterize the ICT world order once it has consolidated. It may be argued, furthermore, that the internet provides a better test of cooperation theories than the WTO: it has not yet been toppled by a full-fledged global organization, offering a rare opportunity to observe institutional development from scratch.[7] The question whether these two hypotheses are confirmed by the evolution of the ICT field is worth examining.

9.4 An information and communication order rebuilt?

Which strategies and management styles discussed so far will be adopted by ICT stakeholders? It is most likely that they will opt for

[6] This replicates at the world level a "cross-regulation" process that was identified at an early stage in local politics by Michel Crozier and Jean-Claude Thoenig (1976); according to them, "French public affairs at the local level are managed by a complex, stable system of groups and institutions [...] which lends support to the contention that interorganizational relations are regulated by a complex, and more or less organized, system rather than by an interorganizational network."

[7] As Keohane (2001) says, "To focus only on existing institutions is to select the dependent variable... On the contrary, we need to explore situations in which institutions have not been created."

a subcontracting type of cooperation and a duplicate administration system of the cross-regulatory type, with the ITU and WIPO increasing their hold on the internet sector.

Many existing institutions came out of the interplay between *advocacy coalitions*, *epistemic communities* and *policy networks*. In terms of internet governance issues, these collective actors were at the roots of the "root," and participated in a "multi-stakeholder dialogue." In the IGF, they figure as "dynamic coalitions" or clusters of half a dozen to a dozen accredited entities (see the insider view on the IGF's website), though evidence of a real commitment to reform, either by NGOs or participating governments, is lacking. This is the proof that the most adamant adversaries of a regulated order can be integrated into a new governance system – as predicted by the "mutual recognition" model: the internet may not lag behind other sectors in this regard for long.

How will its possible regulation be positioned on a decentralization/centralization axis? Politically, the libertarian origins of the root will sustain individualistic demands. Mechanically, the needs for *connectivity* and *interoperability*, in turn, will inevitably bring more *standardization* – a process that is closely associated with the most powerful standard makers, such as the ITU and WIPO, plus the International Organization for Standardization (ISO). Moreover, organizational creation is conditioned to *leadership*: launching new programs, such as an "Arbitration and mediation cennter" (WIPO), the "portable Internet" or the "multilingual internet" (ITU), helps enhance the influence of big organizations.

9.4.1 Less centralization?

What can stop the centralization of decision-making in the ICT field? Not the power of the people, as already mentioned, in spite of statements beginning "We the representatives of the world," which undoubtedly give a deep constituent flavor to WSIS meetings.[8] The

[8] In fact, participants at the WSIS lack the ideological and selective incentives to combine their efforts in order to solve ICT issues jointly (for an opposing view, see Goldsmith, 1998). Although individuals may each be empowered by the use of the internet and other cyberfacilities, they display little propensity for collective action. Admittedly, collective action may be accelerated and accentuated by the internet, as in the case of mobilization against financial

paradox associated with collective action (i.e. increasingly centralized decision-making in ideologically decentralized groups) may be still more stringent in the information world than in domestic issues, since the internet's leaders cannot easily externalize the cost of collective action to the browsers and developers scattered over the whole planet; nor can they capture the profits associated with a leading position. This, in turn, generates few incentives at the user's end to dedicate time and money to the improvement of the global system.

The logic of collective action is therefore complicated by the tension between the technically required centralization of the root system and the decentralization of the numerous stakeholders, who are endowed with the capability to change its running procedures or its operating rules. Those who can balance the power of ICANN are not numerous; they are poorly organized, and their various components are autonomous. On top of that, institutions dedicated to regulate the internet are still in the offing. Although these contests seem aggregating, they come from such different structures (free software groups, consumers associations and alternative DNS experiments) that they are very unlikely to coalesce.

Consequently, ICANN is still the major operator of the ICT world.[9] *Technically*, it is involved in permanent bargaining with NSI, now VeriSign, to develop tradable products; it is also harassed by countless end users, all determined to keep the internet as decentralized as it was at the onset – with the Department of Commerce as an arbiter of these conflicts (Mueller, 2002). *Diplomatically*, ICANN debates its key multilateral position with the usual stakeholders of any international venture: the European Union and other national governments, of Brazil, Australia, etc.; regional bodies

summits, such as the G8 or WTO ministerial meetings. This much-celebrated performance is limited to big events, however, and works mostly to bring people to meeting points. Even in such cases, it may be more rational to cooperate with IGOs at each level of the WSIS, which is held with fewer time limits than financial and commercial summits (Klein, 2004).

9 As "a private nonprofit California Corporation created, in response to a summoning by US government officials, to take regulatory actions that [the Department of Commerce] was unable or unwilling to take directly" (Froomkin, 2000a; see also Christou and Simpson, 2008), such an institution logically restricts joint activities to meetings with staff members of the Department of Commerce, and representatives of technical support groups (such as the National Science Foundation and Network Solutions Incorporated [NSI]).

still in the offing; and prominent IGOs such as the ITU, WIPO and, to a lesser extent, the WHO and ISO.

As shown in Figure 9.1, the international ICT order is still centered on ICANN – a situation that assigns heavy responsibilities to its already cross-pressured board members. They can make the unstable internet regime evolve toward more institutionalization, or stay as privatized as was the case at the outset. They may confirm the "decentralized" turn initiated by the US government, or respond to the centralized calls coming from other national governments and firmly relayed by IGO and EU pressure. To this end, they may play with the successive bodies that have been established and that are now used as interface committees between ICANN and its stakeholders, such as the "At-large Membership Committee," the "Governmental Advisory Committee" (GAC) and the three "supporting organizations," which are technically needed to operate the system.[10] It is noteworthy that *this structure has been copied and pasted from the construction of the ITU, WIPO, the WTO and the WMO*. All these bodies, "appointed by the constituencies they represent," "make policy recommendations to the Board" (King, 2004), and they do it independently. Moreover, the GAC, and within it the European Union (the very stakeholders that were evicted from the initial network not because they were *non-American* but due to the fact that, at the time when the system was designed, servers and users were overwhelmingly American), are now back in (GAC, 2004; May, Chen and Wen, 2004; Christou and Simpson, 2007, 2008).

Their comeback may be limited in two ways, however. First, although a majority of the 193 ITU members are increasingly pressing for more leverage on ICANN, they are confronted by a US administration that is determined to keep it national and private. Second, their "Old World, twentieth-century" dedication to promoting the *public* interest, instead of just protecting it from *private* infringements, may not fit the "common good," on which the cyber-community fully agrees. In the meantime, governments must play the game by the existing rules: states operate within the framework of the Californian administration, they do not elect the board of directors and they do not even select candidates; moreover, an opaque "Nominating Committee" outweighs other voting members

[10] These are the Address, Protocol and Domain Name Supporting Organizations.

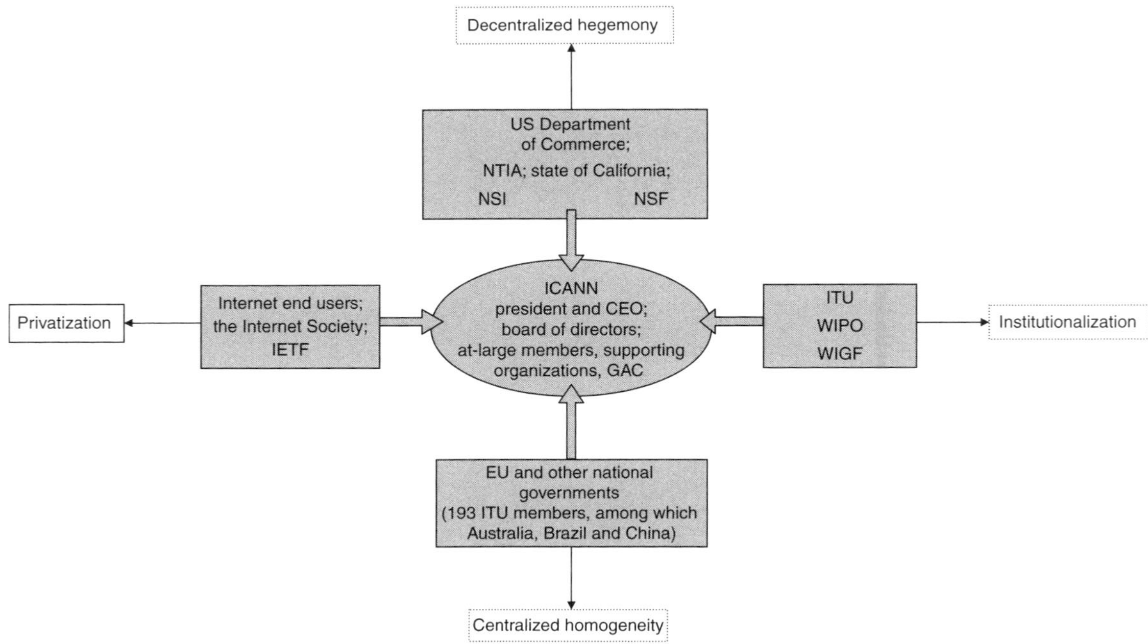

Notes: NTIA = US National Telecommunications and Information Administration; NSF = US National Science Foundation.

Figure 9.1 The international internet regime.

by an eight to seven majority, with a high probability that the support organizations' votes bandwagon.[11]

A couple of strategies are open to ICANN. It may, for example, subcontract to the ITU issues relating to connectivity, while continuing to leave WIPO out of IP address management and logical root access. As a counterpart, ICANN would not address standards and intellectual property issues directly, such as conflicts over property rights between trademarks and domain names,[12] but indirectly, in conveying technical demands to the ITU and keeping full control of the attribution of the top-level domain system. Beyond this reasonable division of labor, ICANN could opt either to stick with its comparative advantage – the monopoly of *technical* guidance – and fulfill its commitments *a minima*, providing full reliability for the root system, or it could accommodate growing *political* concerns about (1) the dissemination of inappropriate materials in sensitive areas and (2) the safety of cyberspace (King, 2004) – an option that would lead to greater centralization.

9.4.2 More centralization?

In ICT, states seem to have delegated part of their sovereignty to NGOs, but this is something of a decoy; they may also have opted for other forms of "substitutability," among which using IGOs as adequate forums to handle sensitive internet issues is the most likely (Drezner, 2004).[13] Global decision-makers have little room for maneuver: there will be no protection of global human and property rights without a permanent, legitimate and universal organization embodying the

[11] The bandwagon effect, closely related to opportunism, is a phenomenon – observed primarily within the fields of microeconomics, political science and behaviourism – that people often do and believe things merely because many other people do and believe the same things. The effect is often called herd instinct, though, strictly speaking, this effect is not a result of herd instinct. The bandwagon effect is the reason for the bandwagon fallacy's success.

[12] As suggested by Sharrock (2001), the issue is to allow "the first to register practice of the DNS to peacefully coexist with the multiple-user structure of the trademark system."

[13] "Great-power options include delegating regime management to non state actors, creating international regimes with strong enforcement capabilities, generating competing regimes to protect material interests, and tolerating the absence of effective cooperation because of divergent state preferences" (Drezner, 2004).

international community's will.[14] The US government may of course resist centralization, as it did once in connection with commerce, when it torpedoed the International Trade Organization at the 1948 Havana conference. Its reluctance to go along with the ITU in spite of the latter institution's credentials in disseminating information indicates a lack of commitment to a world regulation system. Just as the US administration came back powerfully to free trade in 1994 with the creation of the WTO, however, it could sooner or later do the same with the internet. Congressmen may prefer one woe (empowering the ITU and WIPO) to another, such as responding to EU demands, accommodating Chinese claims or letting the European Commission and China each launch its own internet system.

Beyond the WSIS, the European Union, the ITU and WIPO are the main drivers of centralization. They have a common ground in internationalizing new domain names and issuing new generic TLD names. They also share the goal of providing a safer and more reliable environment for governments and national end users (May, Chen and Wen, 2004). As for now, WIPO has provided a *dispute settlement mechanism* (applying the Uniform Domain-name dispute Resolution Policy [UDRP]) and the ITU has preempted any further evolution in *assigning Internet Protocol addresses.*[15] Each initiated a *quasi-treaty* on the internet.[16] The ITU also made a strong bid to *coordinate internet international activities* on behalf of a large coalition, including WIPO, UNESCO, the WTO, ISO, ICANN, the Universal Postal Union (UPU), sector members (private interests) and related NGOs (what has been called "a grand collaboration between all concerned bodies"; Zhao, 2004). In fact, the ITU moved toward retrieving some

[14] For details about the WSIS's objectives and its contribution to advocacy and the opportunity to establish such a new form of internet governance, see Klein (2004).

[15] With advances in next-generation network R&D, its heads are claiming responsibility for having prefigured the SNMP, OSI (domain name system) and HTML protocols.

[16] These are important features of a global governance of the internet, understood by policy-makers as a set of "collective rules, procedures, processes, and related programs [that] includes agreements about standards, policies, rules, and enforcement and dispute resolution mechanisms" (Zhao, 2004). The "treaties" mentioned are the gTLD memorandum of understanding, signed with some solemnity within the ITU precincts in Geneva; and two WIPO treaties covering online intellectual property: on copyrights, and on performances and phonograms (Drezner, 2004).

control over the internet from ICANN, allegedly unable to organize adequate *international coordination* or fix existing *problems of geographic imbalance*.

Although the ITU has a dubious historical record (it concentrated initially on the telegraph that gave birth to the institution, missing the telephone, and then the radio communication opportunities, long before it was sidelined by internet issues) the ITU's credentials for taking charge of internet governance are now more impressive. To switch from a system sponsored by the scientific and educational community to regulation by a telecommunications authority, the ITU can rely on its *"member-driven" culture*, on its long-established *inclusion of the industry* (with its "liberalization" trend), on its *consideration for civil society* (representatives are invited to its "forums") (Zhao, 2004) and on its *multi-positioning*. These moves resonate with a global push toward norm creation.[17] The ITU also managed to have its status legitimized by the Geneva 2003 World Summit on the Information Society.[18]

To sum up, the ITU has made a great comeback on internet issues. It is now in a position to reframe ICANN's former objectives in its own idiomatic and politically correct language. In this venture it is supported by a more discreet WIPO. Whereas the ITU may claim to confine its contribution to development issues, WIPO seems satisfied with the "hard" content of private laws about the domain name system;[19] both will inevitably push toward a global regulatory regime. The ITU itself could end up as the heart of the small group of institutions associated with the delivery of this *new public good*, such as the World Telecommunication Development Conference and the High-Level Summit Organizing Committee.[20] Both organizations

[17] Hans Klein (2004) calls this "timing."

[18] The final declaration of the WSIS states that "[t]he core competence of the International Telecommunication Union (ITU) in the fields of ICTs [. . .] *are of crucial importance* for building the information society" (WSIS, 2003; emphasis added). See also point c2 of the plan of action, enumerating specific goals such as "optimizing connectivity among major information networks" – an obvious assignment for the ITU.

[19] Dirk Lehmkuhl convincingly makes the case for a growing legalization of the sector, due to the "hardness" and binding aspects of private rules, referring to the UDRP as an example in private adjudication, contrasting with the WTO's public system of dispute resolution (Lehmkuhl, 2005, 2007).

[20] The latter is, per se, an instance of organizational imbrication. It is composed of a representative of the UN Secretary-General and the executive heads of almost any and all UN organizations and agencies.

address internet issues in similar terms. They call on NGOs, private interests, civil society and other IGOs to contribute to their grand *development* and *standardization* scheme. This stance, will, in turn enhance their popularity among partners in the Southern Hemisphere, and make a worldwide institutionalization of internet regulation possible.

9.5 Conclusion

A situation that may appear either as a step back toward a dark past or as a true innovation in world politics is actually a *bounded evolution* of global governance models. Suppose that, in not a too far distant future, an international regime of information is established; this will give justice to an often observed but rarely explained fact: the astonishing resilience displayed by IGOs once they have been created (e.g. trade and property), or are on the horizon (the internet), in spite of their having little initial probability of success. History shows that any perturbation of domestic governmental and inter-state activities is eventually conducive to the constitution of a new order. This *iron law* of global institutionalization was made manifest by the rapidly growing inter-institutional order that emerged at the end of the late eighteenth century. IGOs, or the coalitions of the most powerful states that usually hide out within their precincts, know how to find their way in multilateral jungles. Notwithstanding the slow pace of the internationalization of ICT compared to food, health, education, commerce and the environment, it can be predicted that the process will lead to a better and greater regulation. A global and public governance of the world information system seems inevitable in the long run, therefore, despite the unrivalled volatility, privacy and even intimacy of its objects.[21]

[21] Note that this process differs from the federal trend that made the European Union possible: the *spillover* effect first identified in the construction of the European Community may also characterize the decentralized US-sponsored ICT regime at this stage of regime-building, but it will sooner or later face a "glass ceiling" distinguishing *multilateral* action from *supranational* rule. UN agencies and other IGOs are operating within an intergovernmental frame, whereas the European Union (which does the same with its European *Council*, composed of heads of state and heads of government) already has with the European *Commission* the soft equivalent of a federal administration.

Imposing new regulations on major actors in such a context requires negotiating talents; IGO decision-makers are now trained in the art of muddling through as a result of hard cases such as the internet. The more compelled IGOs are (1) to use on any occasion existing governmental channels instead of less formal connections, (2) to give leeway to non-state actors, including for-profit stakeholders, instead of barring them from the definition of the public good by nonprofit-making bodies and (3) to justify their very existence and goals instead of taking it for granted that, once created, very few institutions have ever disappeared in history, the more successful they tend to be. Accordingly, major IGO and NGO players – not to speak of actors that cannot be easily categorized, such as ICANN – have accumulated highly focused knowledge of governance issues. The secret ingredients of their success are known: making room for informality; compartmentalizing the debates; duplicating the decision-making structure; relying on "friends of the chair" or "group coordinators" to fight, if not rally, opponents with the sole help of social pressure; and implementing principles of justice that may accommodate the poorest or less influential actors in the sector. Even management woes in the domestic sphere, such as waste and red tape, organizational slack, bad timing and overlapping mandates, can become instrumental when an attempt is being made to reach a global consensus. Far from limiting their services to a stock exchange of information about states' goals, as assumed in some neoliberal and neo-institutional theories of international relations, international institutions combine the characteristics and functions of both *consensual forums* and *agonistic arenas*. The future information order should borrow from the experience of each.

The diffuse control of ICT is discretely and mechanically progressing in the shadow of standardization. Cognitive approaches and organization studies may be more convincing than mainstream theories in international studies when trying to explain this performance: in ICT, uncontroversial international norms such as "not transforming the standards commons into a basis for overregulating the private market" or "legitimization and maintenance of multistakeholder governance" (Mueller, Mathiason and Klein, 2007) are continually gaining momentum. Here, a "benign neglect" attitude toward technical issues considered as belonging to low politics would automatically benefit private actors and confidential lobbies operating in the information and computer sectors (Graz, 2006). Although very modest in ambition, any technical standardization initiated by private actors and supported by states would look more like "*hegemonization*" than "*homogenization*": in effect, a learning process gives stakeholders the skills and incentives to adjust to the rules made for the implementation of the new norm, whoever is deciding in this matter – either private American operators or the US government acting as a "socializing agent."[22] Those who learn more quickly are supporting the norm, since they have a comparative advantage over newcomers in internalizing it, notwithstanding their initial indifference, if not reluctance, toward the principles incorporated in the norm.

Admittedly, the exact balance between the two ends of the regulation axis (hegemony or homogeneity) may be different in the information realm from what it is in the realms of defense, climate, environment and human rights. This could well be the only difference, however, with these already established networks operating under the umbrella of a paramount intergovernmental institution legally mandated by its member states and founded at the end of a multilateral conference by an international treaty – in other words, an "international regime." Far from being an innovation, the regulation of the internet would in all probability be a mere adaptation of existing patterns.

[22] George Christou and Seamus Simpson (2007) show convincingly that the European Union *accepted* ICANN's governance norms at an early stage and then, for the most part, *shaped* or *adapted* them.

PART III

Self-Regulations, Communities and Private Orders

10 *Online communities and governance mechanisms*

NICOLAS AURAY

10.1 Introduction

Information and communication technologies produce new meeting points through *online communities*, which organize the consumption of information and cultural products by proposing a choice between a wide range of proliferating goods, opinions, critiques, news and commentaries. The proliferation of information communities on the internet is thus linked to the development of a new mode of information retrieval. Unlike the instrumental use of a search engine, which consists of a pre-formatted inquiry, information communities and, more generally, the cultural internet – Web 2.0, participative platforms, folksonomy – support disordered and inquisitive exploration (Auray, 2007). Online communities play a key role here: apart from trimming and altering huge bodies of knowledge, they stimulate a more random discovery of the corpus through mechanisms of suggestion and recommendation, or through the exchange of news, advice and commentaries.

In the configurations of communities studied here, these online corpuses are fed by the aggregation of many isolated contributors from various backgrounds, whose commitments to the group are often weak. This raises the issue of power and organization in these communities: do ICTs transform – and, if so, under what conditions – the community governance process? In other words, how is technology formatting the organization of these places?

The communities studied here are characterized by their huge size, their openness and their processes of collaborative production with explicit rules and detailed manuals. The rules are embedded in technical disciplines, which can be complex and sophisticated. Wikipedia, eBay, Debian and Slashdot are characterized by a chiasm or a structural tension. First, they are based on norms *internalized* by their members. Sometimes they impose sanctions and penalties but most of the time they give "prestige indicators" as rewards to their members, based on peer evaluation depending on the quality of their past contributions: "karma" for Slashdot, "stars" for eBay, "hall of fame" in big forums. These communities are not governed solely by the *internalization* of norms, however; in addition, they are based on the self-organization of collective knowledge production and on *emergent* mechanisms. They make claims of permissiveness, they try not to compel their contributors, by letting them free, and they operate in part without collective intentionality.

This chapter explores the conventions that allow for arranging the collective production. These conventions are explained in more or less collectively defined rules, according to principles relevant to democratic organizations; they are sometimes delegated to automated devices, with limited or uncertain reliability. The chapter therefore analyzes the procedural mechanisms of governance of this kind of electronic community. The first part focuses on the demarcation of borders: how these spaces are protected in the absence of entry barriers and even though they face the onslaught of vandals, spammers, manipulators, cheaters, etc. The answer is twofold: by the fight against underhand vandalism (see section 10.2.1) and the automation of cleaning (section 10.2.2). The second part studies the status of individuals and looks at the devices developed to fix the status of members. They have to ensure that the status reflects the individual's contribution intensity, while maintaining the collective nature of the activity (section 10.3.1), and they have to secure reputations (section 10.3.2). The third part is about conflict pacification by the proceduralization of regulation. One of the issues is the sophistication of the veto (section 10.4.1), but the struggle against conflict focuses on the creation of instances of moderation and mediation committees, rather than on the deployment of a range of sanctions (section 10.4.2).

10.2 The governance of boundaries

Since, in the cultural internet, users want to browse and thereby serendipitously discover content that they would not deliberately have sought,[1] most large online collectives are characterized by the fact that they host opportunistic and occasional contributions. They are open to "weak cooperation" (Aguiton and Cardon, 2007). For instance,

[1] For the centering of online communities on serendipity and the exploratory paradigm, see Auray (2007).

user lists open a frame of intelligibility, which makes the most unexpected or surprising statements relevant. They are open to writing, even to non-subscribers. This strange openness is valued for its epistemic benefits: it makes it possible to construct conditions favorable to discovery. Initiatives taken to restrict this openness are subject to acceptance by a qualified majority. For instance, the fragmentation of lists is a strictly controlled process. On Usenet, the historical model of discussion forums,[2] a breakaway forum has "to have over 80 more YESSES than NOS and over three times more YESSES than NOS" to obtain approval. It is rare for messages to be rejected, according to a procedure adopted by consensus. Usenet uses the "Breidbart index," which calculates the sum of all forums on which the message has been published many times and the square roots of forums on which it has been published, to calculate the threshold over which a user message is banned from a list. This threshold is set by consensus between the members: on the "Big 8" (the eight main moderate scales), a robot rejects a message if this index exceeds twenty over the previous forty-five days. The threshold is reduced to ten in thirty days in the French scale.

Moderation is carefully watched, as the episode of the influential list of debates between "nettime" activists, which established jurisprudence in this respect, attests. In 1997, two years after its creation, following the proliferation of spamming and flaming (hostile and insulting interactions between internet users) and the deterioration of the signal–noise relationship at a level threatening the viability of the list, moderation was introduced. It nevertheless triggered a conspiracy against power-grabbing by moderators. The debate was particularly sensitive around the content of ASCII art and spam art: should they be considered as destructive flooding or as a contribution in the discursive space? The decision was taken to create an additional list, nettime-bold, receiving all the messages that had not yet been moderated. This made it possible to evaluate moderation criteria publicly, and enabled those who so wished to implement their own moderation methods.

Whereas it may seem more effective for the user who asks a question to have to pay a fee, and thus to relieve the advisers, for instance

[2] Usenet, by its hierarchical organization and the cultural weight of a kernel of the system administrators in its governance (the "Usenet dinosaurs"), is slightly different from the other online collectives that I study in this chapter; it was a model for most online collectives, however, because it was the first newsgroup network based on procedural rules and governance mechanisms.

by adding keywords, it is rarely practiced.[3] On the contrary, regular advisers write FAQs to facilitate the integration of new readers. None of the fifty large free software advice exchange projects requires the user making the request to fill in a form or to read the archives before asking a question. Newbies should not have to go through all the archives for an answer before posting a question.

10.2.1 Automatic quality control

When the corpus is read by a large outside public, as in the case of the online encyclopedia Wikipedia, the rule is to authorize writing access to anonymous contributors. The aim is to encourage participation by gratifying newcomers who see that their corrections are immediately taken into account. Despite the risks of vandalism, on the francophone Wikipedia any contributor, even one who is not registered, can write a contribution and even create an article. Only the two largest Wikipedias have started to introduce prior editorial control. Since December 2005 the English-language Wikipedia has been marked by the Seigenthaler affair: a victim of defamation widely reported in the media his complaint that he had been defamed in an article in which an anonymous contributor presented him as directly implicated in the assassination of Robert Kennedy and his brother, although the author did add that nothing had been proved. Even though this kind of vandalism had already taken place previously, in this case it remained online for a very long time without any contributor pointing out this defamatory addition.[4] Since December 2005, on the English-language version of Wikipedia, only registered

[3] In their statistical study, Karim Lakhani and Eric von Hippel (2003) note that, with some 400 questions posted per month between 1999 and 2000, and 1,900 contributors, users of the Apache software help forum were satisfied, no question was turned down and the cognitive charge was left to the information providers. The same applies to Linux user, studied statistically in 2002 (Lanzara and Morner, 2003), with 2,500 questions per month and over 1,000 active participants, and Debian user French, studied statistically from 1997 to 2007 (Dorat *et al.*, 2007), with 700 discussion threads per month and 4,000 active contributors for that period. Lakhani and von Hippel (2003) note that it was with an increase by a factor of 100 only that the Apache design required an amendment.

[4] Considering that he had been insulted, and refused legal action due to US law on the protection of private life, which would have made it difficult to ascertain the identity of clients of internet access providers, he preferred writing on USA Today that “Wikipedia is a flawed and irresponsible research tool” (November 29, 2005).

contributors can now create new articles. Registration is nevertheless limited to the creation of a user name, which can be a pseudonym, and a password. Giving an e-mail address is recommended (if only to recover one's password if one has forgotten it) but not compulsory. On the other hand, there is no need to register in order to correct or complete articles that are already online. Since September 2007 the German Wikipedia makes instantly visible only corrections that have been made by "trustworthy" users. To gain this status of trust, users have to show that they qualify by producing at least thirty corrections in thirty days. Inexperienced users have to wait for validation by a trustworthy editor for their corrections to be taken into account.

Editorial control is limited to a posteriori elimination of reprehensible content and to mutual surveillance. One characteristic of a governance of boundaries characterized by the choice of openness is the presence of automatic tools facilitating the tracking of amendments. Robots used by voluntary correctors verify the presence of offensive words in recent amendments. When they spot an amendment made by an IP, they check the "diff" and compare it to a list of expressions, each of which has a score. If the total exceeds a certain threshold, the robot removes the amendment. Tools scan the origin of the IP addresses used to correct an entry, to identify whether these corrections come from large organizations, which may want to "fiddle" information to suit them. A major governance problem is control of the consequences of the activity of these automated robots. For example, a central rule has been decreed, the "1RR" ("one revert rule"), to "train" the Wikipedia robots so that they do not remove the same IP on the same article twice. The bot can ignore this rule if a human also removes the IP, which creates a "bot – human – bot – human, etc." cycle. These limits embedded in the robots' coding are designed to give the final say to the people using them.

10.2.1.1 Controlling automatic quality control tools

Controlling quality a posteriori is based on tools used to retrieve *more stable* versions from online corpuses. The production and freezing of "stable versions" from a selection of content is therefore based on automatic tools such as annotating robots in Wikipedia, which draw up a list of eligible articles for a stabilized version.[5] In Debian, for

[5] Wikipedia in German, the first to have taken the initiative, produced its own DVD-ROM of over 620,000 articles in November 2007.

example, a software code is automatically transferred from the *unstable* development version to a stable *test* version, if it has been in the archives for over two weeks and if a critically serious bug, causing deadlock, has not been attributed to it during that period. This process can lead to considerable perverse effects by giving a "bonus" to the unpopular packets. The packets that rise most rapidly to the "stable" status correspond not to the best ones but to those that are the least often looked at. As they are not subjected to the sagacity of a large number of "proofreaders," they slip through the net. This problem of the quality cycle is crucial, for quality is precisely the main theme of open-source software.

Thus, in the *design* of these automatic editorial control tools, human control is unavoidable. On Wikipedia, for example, the criteria to cover for labeling these weak corpuses are a subject of debate. It has to be established which algorithm should be used to mix the progress criterion, measured in terms of the robustness of the content with regard to recent amendments, and the criterion of the importance of the data, measured by the number of visits to a page, for example. On Debian, because of the limits of automatic tools, a qualified majority voted for a human procedure to decide on the "stable" version: the "freeze" phase. The members of the collective meet at a time appointed by the project leader, for an intense cycle of tests leading to the "freeze" of the distribution. This cycle is organized as a series of fun, social events called "bug squashing parties" on the IRC charts (Auray, 2004), where a large number of developers synchronize. The choice of elements that will make up the stable version is thus the result of a collective decision.

The impossibility of completely automating the correction work is one of the main bottlenecks. Since 2002 Debian participants have considered the long interval between two stable releases, and the impossibility of controlling the constant increase in the time taken for correction during the test cycle, to be the main problems facing the community. This impression of having reached a critical mass in the project has triggered procedural innovation in the past few years, including the creation of a voluntary quality control group to deal with these issues, and the proliferation of suggestions to restrict the editorial content. Notwithstanding these proposals, however, the problem has persisted. Entrusting it to organizations with paid employees, supported by the online community, can solve the difficulty.

10.2.2 A struggle against underhand vandalism

Unlike collectives based on an existing community of values and intentions, large online collectives are based on weak cooperation characterized by the formation of "opportunistic" links, which do not imply collective intention or a sense of belonging to a "community." The contribution is often casual, largely unintentional, fragile and temporary, and the low level of mutual acquaintance generates risks of vandalism. One type of vandalism that is easy to curb is the provocative kind. It is based on a logic of pranks, such as when an internet user replaces the photo of the pope in Wikipedia by that of Darth Vador. The trickery is temporary and intended more as a joke than to manipulate. On the other hand, the fact that few contributors are acquainted can generate a more harmful kind of vandalism, one that is underhand. This kind is based on the manipulation of information, which is intended to *remain invisible.* Accordingly, online collectives are often infiltrated by real organizations, which manipulate general opinion to run down a rival, or to promote their own products or themselves on the internet. For example, a twenty-five-year-old neurobiology student, Virgil Griffith,[6] developed "informers" to draw up a systematic list of the main manipulations: the discreet falsification of words, changing adjectives, etc. The sources included private firms as well as public authorities (municipalities, states), political organizations and sects.

Underhand vandalism is an intentional falsification of content, which is supposed to be taken seriously and to dupe readers. There is a fine line, however, between strategic manipulation and the contribution of content that enhances general knowledge. In most online communities a writing principle is openness to the members' personal points of view. This is related to the fact that everyone expresses the excellence differently. Even Wikipedia, notwithstanding its encyclopedic principle of "neutrality," defines objectivity in relative terms, as "the sum of relevant points of view on a subject." Contributors are encouraged to introduce a subjective point of view, provided that it is linked to its enunciator and presented impartially. The epistemological grounds for this approach are a subjectivist conception of truth: stabilized scientific facts are presented as statements related to a point

[6] See http://virgil.gr.

of view, whereas controversial theses are cited as relevant to a subject ("What people believe – that's the objective fact," says Jimbo Wales, Wikipedia co-founder and promoter). As it is legitimate to add to the corpus by representing a personal point of view, underhand vandalism is a difficult enemy to combat.

Has it really been proved, moreover, that combating strategic manipulation will enhance the quality of forums? Some models of discussion forums on cultural goods (Dellarocas, 2006) show that an eradication of strategic manipulation could have a globally negative impact on the site by removing incentives to contribute and thus decreasing the amount of information produced.

The governance of online communities is based on two objective criteria to isolate underhand vandalism from controlled partiality, which, in contrast, is welcome. *Unilaterally deleting* contributions with which one disagrees is considered as vandalism, and therefore prohibited. Likewise, the *repeated deletion of content* (such as the Church of Scientology deleting paragraphs criticizing it on Wikipedia) is banned as a "breach of publication" on Wikipedia and is punishable by banishment from the account. The systematic reiteration of a contribution is also considered as underhand vandalism. Other cases are not controlled.

The stakes are high, for underhand vandalism pollutes the corpus and can cause readers to lose interest. In fact, it can result in an insidious "cleansing" of the online community by an activist minority representing a particular point of view. The natural form of underhand vandalism is thus strategic infiltration. Many online collectives have had to deal with it. For example, on Usenet it was necessary to combat the manipulation of discussion forums by sects. A decisive form of control was the setting of rules to define who is eligible to vote on a subject. Since voters' identity is difficult to establish in online collectives, there is a risk of infiltration. For instance, a founding principle of Usenet was that, to vote on the creation of a new discussion forum, anyone interested in the topic could vote, which included people who were *not yet users*. This led to infiltration during the fr.soc.sectes affair on Usenet, between September 1997 and March 1998. The vote for the creation of a discussion topic on sects was held in September 1997 and was marked by the jamming of the ballot boxes. There was massive and organized dissemination of a call to vote "No," from members of the Moon sect. A mass mailing to sympathizers of the sect was intended to encourage them to vote

"No," on the basis of information that was biased, to say the least, and in any case without any relation whatsoever to the original charter of the fr.soc.sectes forum. Some answers to the acknowledgement of receipt of the ballot papers indicated that some of these people did not speak French, and therefore that they were unable to understand the request for voting.[7] The trickery was considered as evident and likely to have changed the result of the vote. Since then Usenet has strictly limited the right to vote on the creation of forums. Only informed participants who fill in a form and thus show that they speak and understand the language and the Usenet rules may now vote.

The principle of openness for the online community's borders is therefore strictly coordinated. This consists of a posteriori cleaning of the content, resembling a system of editorialization (producing stable versions with content selected by automats), and moderate control of strategic manipulations, on the basis of a war on underhand vandalism and hostage-taking by activist minorities.

10.3 The governance of status

Online collectives propose an original articulation between individualism and solidarity. They favor a common good dynamic based on a logic of personal interest, and change members' statuses in accordance with their internal contributions. They highlight the most prestigious statuses by displaying the names of people who excel on a merit list and granting them exclusive rights. Statuses stem directly from internal contributions. The originality of large online self-organized collectives therefore relates to the endogenization of statuses around *profiles*. A pseudonym is the person's name; a profile is the evaluation of that pseudonym on the basis of past transactions.[8]

[7] Online collectives also have to fight against the strategic misuse of voting systems. For instance, during the elections for a project leader, members of Debian had to protect themselves against misappropriation of the "scorings *à la* Condorcet/ Borda" (votes in which all the candidates are arranged by order of preference). Some voters, for example, classified last the candidate who threatened their favorite. The desire to struggle against insincere votes is thus the justification for the change of variant in the Condorcet election, with the replacement of the "single transferable vote" by the "Schwartz sequential dropping."

[8] For example, in *JDN (1211)*, the pseudonym is *JDN* and the profile is *1211*. This means that the person has a score of 1,211 points for the quality of his/her transactions.

There is, nevertheless, an obstacle to enabling these individual scores to emerge. How can contributions be individualized in a space (the one of online communities) based on the collective character of the outputs? An encyclopedic article in Wikipedia, a discussion or a database are based on a sum of complementary individual inputs, and the quality is based on the aggregation of the number plus the individual performance (Surowiecki, 2005). The choice of ranking individuals differs according to the social and relational complexity of the collective knowledge constructed by online collectives. Collectives based on diffuse marks of reputation for individuals can be distinguished from those based on objective scores. The former, like discussion forums, elaborate relationally highly complex technical knowledge, in which individual contributions are entangled in a network of expertise in which it is impossible to detach "discussion threads." The latter, like video platforms, cluster individual content, thus allowing for individuals' evaluation, expressed in the form of cardinal numbers and colored icons.

For example, lists and discussion forums are not simply places for exchanging opinions and advice. They are also places where certain experts build up their authority (Welser *et al.*, 2007) through mechanisms for the selection of partners during discussions. The presence of a core of uncontested experts and the average skills of participants on Debian lists, for example, exert a strong constraint on the production of questions and the selection of those who answer. Their scores nonetheless remain diffuse. The reason why discussion lists are limited to diffuse marks of status is that it is difficult to credit a particular message in a discussion as a "good answer." The result is generally collaborative, and the cognition is distributed, borne by the entire chain. This is illustrated by the relative failure of the "Yahoo Answers!" site,[9] which functions with a system of points and levels. The number of points obtained increases when a contributor has been chosen as the "best answer" in the discussion (though, paradoxically, it also increases for someone who has asked a question for which no best answer has been voted). The points make it possible to access levels that attribute rights. As the answers are collaborative, the "best answer" system has led to misuse of the site, which has deteriorated into a space for recreation, riddles and jokes. Riddles

[9] See http://fr.answers.yahoo.com.

create competition between participants, who are reduced to choosing the funniest answer, so that there is no longer the collaborative aspect. There is a simply a duel between rivals, for the fun of it.

Other online collectives in which individual contributions are easily individualizable associate icons and scores with members. Some of these propose "signs" that enhance visibility. Having a large number of stars on eBay or a good karma on Slashdot means that one's visibility or comments move up in the online community and give one a decisive advantage in terms of reputation. Through this self-amplified mechanism, a bonus of recognition accumulates on those who have already acquired it. The other mechanisms are "ranks," which afford access to different powers. In open-source software projects (such as FreeBSD) or Wikipedia, a minimum number of contributions enable one to be eligible for the rank of "officer" or "administrator," which confers rights on the deletion of accounts or content. The promotion is not always automatic, however;[10] it is subject to an additional vote. In view of the importance of these signs of status for the members, a second level of governance is designed to control the *fairness* of the reputation scale. It focuses in two directions. First, it aims to control the effects of these community members' reflexive knowledge of the calculation algorithms that produce reputation, as this knowledge leads to biases that constantly have to be corrected. Second, this governance aims to control and sanction the effects of reputation on the members' behaviors.

The governing of activity by public evaluation generates problems concerning the *design* of the status scales. The *fairness* of these scales has to be controlled, by avoiding biases and manipulations of their score by individuals (section 10.3.1). At the same time, it is essential to make identities and profiles secure (section 10.3.2). The communities have to be protected from the threat of crooks, who, by usurping profiles, can undermine confidence in the profiles the sites allocate to their members.

[10] Sometimes it may be, though. Since September 2007 the German Wikipedia has given its contributors "indexes of trust." Only the corrections of "trustworthy" contributors are immediately visible. The software indicates the contributions in different colours, according to the author's index of trust, which is based on the author's past contributions; those whose contributions are seldom amended obtain a high index, whereas those whose contributions are amended soon after being posted are given a lower index.

10.3.1 *The effects of reflexive knowledge on the calculation of reputation*

Because they are so important, marks of reputation can easily have undesirable effects in online communities. Members obsessed with the consequences of their behavior on their virtual aura may alter their habits or refuse discussion. Yamauchi *et al.* (2000) show that, in large software development projects, interactional patterns are biased toward action.[11] The tasks performed are not preceded by a declaration of intent. The protective aspect for reputation explains the bias toward action. By not stating their personal engagement in a precise task of the "to-do list," contributors protect their face. "I can get it wrong because I don't tell the others what I'm doing," said a Debian developer in September 2005. Those who have little confidence in their know-how see barriers to their engagement, which would be very strong if they were obliged to state publicly what they were doing.

The main distortions, however, are related to actors' anticipation of the consequences of their evaluations on their own reputation score. Sites for sales between private individuals afford a good example of "bias" related to actors' knowledge of the mechanisms of calculation of reputation. Each member of eBay, for example, has an evaluation profile based on his/her interlocutors' evaluations. Buyers and sellers can mutually assess one another by posting an evaluation for each transaction. It is the buyer who starts, by posting his/her evaluation, and, after the seller has received it, he/she posts his/hers. These evaluations cannot be altered or erased (only comments can be deleted, by common accord). Many buyers therefore prefer not to leave a negative or neutral evaluation when they have had a bad experience, for fear of receiving a negative evaluation by the seller. Negative evaluations out of retaliation have thus become common practice. Consequently, a "kind bias" has appeared (Dellarocas, Fan and Wood, 2004): the

[11] Using transition diagrams based on the coding of language acts in messages of the general discussion forum, Yamauchi *et al.* (2000) show that the probability of transition from "report" to "question" is far greater than that of the opposite transition (of "question" to "report"), which is negligible. Discussions take place after the report on an action, not prior to it. The category with the highest frequency in initiating a thread is "report" (32.3 percent), before "question" (22.6 percent). Moreover, only 14.4 percent of the "reports" lead to a "question" (and thus to a discussion), whereas 28.9 percent have no critical follow-up.

number of negative or neutral evaluations left on the site is smaller than the number of bad experiences signalled.[12] Reflexive knowledge of the calculation of the evaluation leads to bias.

The governance of status aims to correct these effects of reflexivity systematically by constantly adjusting the system so that it corresponds to the acts performed. Since May 2008 eBay has reformed its evaluation system: sellers may no longer leave negative or neutral evaluations of buyers. Certain sites have sophisticated auto-regulatory mechanisms to constantly ensure the convergence of mutual evaluations toward honesty. For instance, the Slashdot news site is based on mutual control of evaluations by members, by means of meta-moderation. If members have their moderation noted as "unfair," then the number of points that they can use for their power of moderation immediately decreases. The system is auto-regulated, insofar as the meta-moderators are recruited among the moderators with the highest scores.

10.3.2 Security of profiles

Sites can turn into hell if pseudonyms are stolen or are publicly slandered without justification. For instance, some celebrities have discovered a "virtual clone" on MySpace, steered by someone else and based on a mixture of truth and falsehood, of information taken from the net and personal pseudo-details that are mostly false. Where does common knowledge end and the usurpation of identity start?[13]

Apart from this threat of usurpation concerning famous people, any individual with a good reputation in an online community is at the mercy of a pseudonym thief attracted by the prestige. This is how "phishing" develops. On eBay, the fact that one is able to have an

[12] As a user of the site notes, "In mid-August I received an email from a seller who didn't follow up. I tried to negotiate but it wasn't possible so I filed a complaint on eBay. I logically posted a negative note on the seller. In retaliation, I assume, the buyer posted a negative note on me! That beats it all! My question is therefore: if a buyer/seller who is a victim of a dishonest buyer/seller can't take the risk of posting a negative note, in case a negative one is posted on them in return, what is evaluation worth?" (forum on the eBay evaluation system, March 5, 2007).

[13] An example is the "false blog" of Jacques Chirac. Likewise, in an article on the misappropriation of a virtual clone of a famous philosopher on the web, Judith Revel wonders what auto-regulatory bodies can be conceived of to avoid people finding themselves with racist or provocative clones (*Libération*, November 8, 2007).

opinion before betting or selling is crucial. This explains the decisive importance of each member's profile, including his/her evaluation history and a score that sums up the trust that can be granted to that person. The score is the product of an evaluation system that enables members to mark and to comment on the buyers and sellers with whom they have carried out transactions. To clear their reputation, certain crooks use a phishing technique: they inundate users with false e-mails, claiming to be the customer service of eBay and asking them to confirm their pseudonym and password because abnormalities have been found in a maintenance operation. Of the thousands of e-mails sent, sometimes a naive user, or one who fears being excluded, provides the requested information. The crook then takes over his/her account and alters the password so that the legitimate owner is dispossessed of it. This false eBay e-mail comes from addresses that cannot be traced, with links that do not remain on the servers – which are often unaware of hosting them.

Online communities are all particularly severe with these usurpers. The sanctions are maximal: "death penalty" on Usenet (i.e. life banishment from the IP address); "permanent disqualification" on Wikipedia (i.e. the IP addresses used by the member are banned from contributing). Legal measures are rare. It is almost impossible, however, for the different sites to ban a person permanently, as they can always reappear with a new address. Only legal action, which implies that charges are laid and that the access providers cooperate, can definitely stop such crooks. Legal identity is badly protected these days, though. In France, pretending to be someone else, by "phishing," is not considered as an offense since, on the internet, usurpation concerns "logical" identities (IP, log-in, e-mail) and not "real" identities, such as surname, first name and address. These logical identities – including the usurping of an e-mail or IP address – are not protected as such. Likewise, the possibility of protecting the profile by virtue of a "property right" is not yet established in practice. To offset this shortcoming, sites use indirect means, invoking fraud through an alteration of the truth likely to cause damage, or public defamation.

10.4 The governance of conflict

Online communities are characterized by regulation, which aims to deal with the maximum number of problems closest to the ground.

Like the struggle against vandalism, the regulation of large cooperative collectives is based on mechanisms of mutual surveillance. Whereas in debates on online cooperation the focus is on participative writing, it is *participative surveillance* that seems specific and new in community sites producing knowledge. Most discussions are maintained at the lowest level. For instance, in discussions on Wikipedia, anyone has the ability to criticize anyone else.[14] It is only when mutual surveillance no longer suffices that additional regulatory procedures are introduced: mediation and sanctions. Following a "warning," mediators are brought into action. A *public* space is then constituted, in which the problematical article is shown to a *third party* that is not a stakeholder in the conflict. The problem is then discussed on a special page examined by voluntary *watchers*. If the authors still differ, in a small minority of cases, a third regulatory body is called on: the arbitration committee, consisting of members elected by peers, to which any contributor may refer a complaint, and which is committed to considering it as admissible and to proposing a sanction.

Conflict governance aims to maximize the possibility of this direct participation and the production of consensus, without it undermining or disrupting the activity of contribution. It functions in two ways. First, the idea is to avoid *paralysis*: how do these advanced communities deal with the highly time-consuming development of a large number of calls to discuss or vote on? How do they cope with the risks of deadlock related to the fact that consensus has to be reached (10.4.1)? The second aim is to avoid the *degeneration* of discussions into fights. It is necessary to counter the constant risk of public argument and controversy deteriorating into *ad hominem* conflict characterized by anger, humiliation and the incapacity of the different partners to respect the standards of public argumentation (10.4.2).

10.4.1 *The struggle against paralysis*

The place granted to participation is subject to the threat of *paralysis*, related to the cost in time of having to put issues to the vote. Because of the asynchronous nature of interactions on the discussion list that frames the meeting, the duration of the vote lasts for several weeks at

[14] The weight of this regulation is relatively weak; on the Anglophone Wikipedia, *only 14 percent of pages have any discussion.*

least – which is a long time.[15] A constant concern of sovereignist online communities is, paradoxically, to ensure that they are not submerged by too many applications to vote on.[16] How do these advanced communities avoid the overconsumption of time? First, they try, as far as possible, to limit the number of votes to a strict minimum. The *vote* must therefore be held only after a discussion has taken place between all the interested participants, over a sufficiently long period (the minimum interval before a call for a vote can be made is two weeks, for example, on Debian). This makes it possible to clarify the debate, to delete the craziest options and to reach consensus. In general, on the most controversial points the discussion is accompanied by "mini-polls," which do not have the value of a final vote but are intended to test the balance of powers. They do not make the decision; they inform members. Virtual participative communities also implement another technique to save time. They submit the votes proposed to a *quorum* (for instance, in Debian the quorum equals 1.5 times the square root of the number of developers, so that, with 800 developers, the quorum is forty-three voters). This quorum is stricter than in the traditional sense, though. The community members vote by classifying all the options by order of preference, according to the Borda method: all the options are compared in pairs, and the blank vote, "None of the above,"[17] is included in the options. The quorum is considered to have been reached when the choice proposed is classified before the choice "None of the above," in a number of votes greater than the quorum. This special quorum therefore controls more than the fact that the *mobilization* of the electoral body is sufficient; it also controls the *determination* of the voters, above a certain threshold. In the classical conception of the quorum, abstention is taken into account; in this sophisticated conception, voters' determination is taken into account.

[15] The duration of the vote on the French ranking of Usenet has a minimum of twenty-one days and a maximum of thirty-one days. On Debian it is two weeks.

[16] As a Debian developer explains, "We want to have as few votes as possible to settle an issue, since each vote requires two weeks to run in order to get the most input. This means that we can't follow a traditional procedural amendment process – each vote has to have all proposed (and seconded) amendments on it, and the procedure has to select from among them" (Buddha Buck, June 11, 2003; Debian vote list, summary of his proposed amendment).

[17] In the discussions, this option is called "*further discussion*" or "*keep talking*."

Finally, virtual communities are vulnerable to deadlock because individuals have the *right to veto*. As a result, the rules have been improved by being made more flexible. These systems are sometimes called systems with a *relative* right to veto, as in the case of Wikipedia,[18] where the veto may be waived in cases of a very strong majority, thus limiting the risks of deadlock. The procedure consists of a first vote during which participants can be for, against or against with a veto. After the vote, the number of "for" votes is counted and compared to the total. If there is no veto, the qualified majority validates the vote (e.g. 70 percent). If there is a veto, a second discussion may follow (depending on the subject) to try to identify other options. The discussion is then followed by a second vote with a higher qualified majority than for the first vote (e.g. 80 percent). If the second vote ends with a veto and 75 percent "for," the "against" prevails. If the second vote ends with a veto and 85 percent "for," the "for" prevails. With this system the veto can be taken into account, but its reversal is nevertheless authorized in the case of a very strong majority, thus limiting the risks of deadlock.

It is interesting that this system was imported from real and long-standing democratic practices. The participant who set it up for Wikipedia, Aurevilly (French Wikipedia, April 9, 2004), noted that

> it's the most common political system when a right to veto is granted to an individual on the basis of collegial deliberation, in order to avoid a single individual definitively blocking the expression of the general will. We sometimes talk of a right to new deliberation instead of the right to veto: the veto can be waived by a new unanimous deliberation of the assembly. This is more or less the system in the US, where the president can veto a law passed by Congress, which can in turn bypass the veto by voting its cancellation with a two-thirds majority. There is also a veto which is so-called relative in terms of duration, such as the one granted to Louis XVI: the veto suspended the deliberation voted for both legislatures.

This is a fine attempt to differentiate between a veto and strong opposition.

Online communities seem to be evolving toward participative mechanisms, but these are characterized by measures to prevent paralysis resuting from an excess of votes and vetoes. Their reflection on the place and function of the vote make them valuable lessons for

[18] The Debian notion of "supermajority" follows the same pattern.

understanding the current mechanisms of consultation, which often shed little light on the moment at which the collective decision is actually *taken*.

10.4.2 The struggle against fighting

Over a certain threshold, discussions in online communities tend to become illegible, and the risk of deterioration increases. There is a saying for this, inspired by Mike Godwin, a pioneer in online communities. Godwin's law is an extension of the *reductio ad Hitlerum*, which is part of the Usenet folklore. In 1990 Godwin declared the following empirical rule: "As a Usenet discussion grows longer, the probability of a comparison involving Nazis or Hitler approaches 1." The longer a discussion, the greater the chances are of just about anything being mentioned. Moreover, a point is reached at which the conversation irreversibly sinks into cacophony and fighting, and the probability of reverting to the initial subject in an impartial tone approaches zero.

This statistical finding can be explained. There are civil forms of expression that have to be used in any electronic discussion: one has to remain impartial, respect one's opponent, maintain a convivial tone and always try to avoid misunderstanding. Electronic conversation, which shortens the interval between the intention and the act (messages can be sent at a click), and leaves lasting traces of all dialogue, makes it difficult to maintain these rules of courtesy in the dialogue and debate.

With regard to governance, the methods employed by communities to avoid deterioration consist of favoring moderation and *mediation* rather than sanctions. As soon as a debate reaches stalemate, a third party who is not a stakeholder in the conflict is automatically brought into the picture, and can thus act as an impartial spectator or even an arbitrator. The idea is to switch from a confined space to a public one, and therefore to urge the protagonists to improve their behavior because they are being watched by a moderator, who may firmly ask them to stop arguing. On Wikipedia, participants in a discussion that becomes bogged down are invited – by means of a warning on a banner on the page – to go to a public page, on which the discussion will be examined by *watchers*. This switch to a public space encourages moderation in discussions. It is accompanied by a reminder, through links, of the rules (policies) that encourage self-discipline. The governance of communities cannot simply decree "policies" framing individual activities, however, and leave it up to members to take the initiative of switching to mediation as the need arises. Two governance mechanisms are essential to limit fighting: the supervision of discussions as soon as precise warning signals appear; and the establishment of referee committees to decide between the contradictory interpretations of the policies.

Online communities cannot simply display a warning banner and leave it up to their members to take the initiative of bringing a controversy into the open. The communities identify objective signals, easily detectable by robots, which warn that a debate is degenerating. The fact that these indicators can easily be traced and thus detected by robots facilitates governance and allows for partial automation. On Wikipedia, for example, which is on the cutting edge in this respect, the crucial sign that will trigger the switching of the debate onto a public page is the existence of a cycle of mutual deletion of contributions. The so-called "three reverts rule" requires that a contributor may not delete contributions of another editor in an article more than three times during a period of twenty-four consecutive hours. The size of the amendment deleted is irrelevant. Any violation of this rule triggers a warning banner and the vigilance of a squad of volunteers who control the dispute. The community sees this rule as an "electric fence," designed to defuse publishing wars as soon as they emerge.

Even when the discussion is placed under the control of public authorities, furthermore, the mere presence of policies is not enough to moderate the dispute. Indeed, one may even consider the wide diversity of policies – forty-two policies and twenty-four guidelines for the Anglophone Wikipedia – to be a source of dissent, because each of these rules is ambiguous and can therefore be interpreted differently according to the context. Moreover, the invoking of contradictory policies encourages power plays between the actors (Kriplean *et al.*, 2007), which is why arbitration committees are set up. For example, on Wikipedia this committee undertakes to receive complaints from contributors who are unable to agree on the interpretation of policies. The referees have to undertake to propose a sanction and to agree between themselves on the adoption of sanctions. If unanimity is not obtained from the outset, they vote three more times, and, if it is still not reached with the fourth vote, they accept a sanction agreed by the majority in the following vote.

The governance of conflict is thus based on a model of three-tiered regulation, one of the most complete versions of which is on Wikipedia. The most formal conflict management mechanism is thus based on the "bottom-up" management of most conflicts, by virtue of procedural rules. When this conciliatory solution proves to be inconclusive, the disputes are referred via partially automated procedures to mediators. When these prove to be incapable of solving the disputes, because of character problems or acrimony, an arbitration committee can decree dissuasive sanctions. The other large online collectives function in much the same way, even though they are not nearly as formalized. The communities producing open-source software are accordingly based on discussions that seek consensus, and, when opinions carry on diverging, they bring in the mediation of technical committees: the Technical Resolution Board (nine people elected by accredited developers) in FreeBSD, and the Technical Committee in Debian (eight members). It is only when an agreement can still not be reached that the subjects are submitted for plenary votes, or proposals to exclude members are formalized and submitted to the decision of the appropriate authorities.

10.5 Conclusion

In the information communities taken as examples in this article, many of which attract a huge number of contributors, the regulatory mechanisms aim to fight not against an under-supply but against an *excess* of participation. The governance is centered on cleaning out the corpus, chasing vandals and organizational "submarines" that want to surf on the site's popularity to defend their own interests. The idea is also to combat redundancy and natural tendencies, when the corpus increases, toward illegibility, a deterioration of quality and a decline into a generalized fight involving many controversies.

The governance methods thus have to respect the principle of openness to outsiders of information communities. They are therefore oriented in three directions. First, the governance of borders is based on the a posteriori quality control of *stable* versions, by systems of selection, within the corpus, and without affecting the way in which it is fed. This ex post selection, based on partial automation as well as on the struggle against underhand vandalism and infiltration by activist minorities, focuses on seeking out surreptitious deletions from the corpus. Second, the governance of status is based on the granting of a high level of symbolic recognition to individual participants. There is an adjustment of the "formats" of this reputation (Thévenot, 2007) to the type of corpus produced by the online collective: the less individualizable the contributions are, the more their marking is diffuse. The governance of status seeks to correct dynamically the biases introduced by the members' reflexive knowledge of the mechanisms for calculating the status score. Third, conflict governance is based on the preference for participative surveillance involving grassroots contributors as much as possible. This participative requirement causes the mechanisms of conflict avoidance to be centered on the struggle against paralysis, involving original mechanisms of quorum by option and relative veto, and on the struggle against fights, involving automated mechanisms of switching toward mediators when conflicts turn sour.

Information communities are thus the emblem of new forms of organization that are highly attentive to individual singularities; they articulate group projects to individual status. Today they find themselves confronted by a growing challenge to their governance methods. Although their success to date has been related to the attribution of symbolic recognition to their members (prestige, renown), will this be enough tomorrow? Might it not be necessary to *remunerate* certain contributors? If so, through which mechanisms? Today, with certain contributors' denunciation of the fact that platforms exploit the content of their voluntary contributions, offers of partial remuneration for contributors by communities are proliferating – such as by Deezer, Bebo.com, etc. What is being lost and what is being gained with this trend? Although it may seem legitimate to remunerate the authors, will this not affect the prevailing modes of governance? Is it necessary to generalize remuneration to cleaning and corrective activities, which are of little value to the ego? Is it legitimate to remunerate contributors who advertise by way of their contributions to information communities? Surely that which made these communities a success should be maintained on the fringes. Virtual communities are *organized reputation systems*, which is part of their vulnerability: they have to endure the price of fame.

11 *Policing exchanges as self-description in internet groups*

MADELEINE AKRICH AND CÉCILE MÉADEL

11.1 The regulation of e-groups

This chapter is devoted to an analysis of the forms of regulation that can be observed in online discussion groups. By regulation, we mean all the actions intended to *define and transform the organization of the activity*: the creation of subscribers' groups, the moderating of interaction, the definition and application of common rules and the management of conflicts. This broad definition of the word "regulation" introduces a shift similar to the one that Foucault's concept of "governmentality" has brought about (Foucault, 1994): there is no prior assumption about the way regulation occurs in practice, nor even about the identity of the participants, insofar as all group members may be involved in these processes.

The issue of regulation is by no means self-evident. Few authors have studied the practices, rules and systems enabling these communities to exist and to last. The reason is probably that, for a long time, the internet was considered by its promoters and by analysts as a space that was free from the constraints of the real world, as a joyful bazaar that lent itself to unbridled exchanges, unexpected encounters and organizational inventiveness, and that had an aversion to hierarchies, to rules and to any form of censorship. Discussion forums sprang from more or less spontaneous initiatives, moreover, based on systems that had few technical constraints as far as their organization was concerned. As the literature has focused primarily on the origins of such systems, it has shed little light on questions of regulation. Online communities, including open forums, closed discussion groups, communities of players, etc., have been extensively explored, but scant attention has been paid to the issue of regulation. It may therefore be trapped in a conceptualization that makes it more or less invisible.

Most early studies considered regulation from the angle of the management of deviant behaviors. These are defined in very general terms, almost independently from the contexts in which they appear, as if the web as such was a single sphere of jurisdiction in which reprehensible actions could univocally be identified and qualified.[1] Researchers have investigated the causes of these forms of delinquency or incivility and therefore have been able to participate in the elaboration of prevention and treatment strategies.

Some have endeavored to identify the profiles of people likely to disrupt interactions, or of groups "at risk" of being the victims of such acts. Mei Alonzo and Milam Aiken (2004), for example, show that, just as occurs in the real world, men are more inclined to adopt disruptive behaviors than women, and that individuals who tend to utter peremptory assertions in interaction or show a taste for sensation-seeking are "good candidates" for this type of activity. Symmetrically, Susan Herring *et al.* (2002) stress the fact that "non-mainstream" groups – such as feminists groups – are more vulnerable when faced with such attacks, because of their wish to be accepting of differences.

Other actors focus on the characteristics peculiar to the medium that could explain the development of these behaviors or fuel potential conflicts. Nancy Baym (1996) has sought to characterize electronic discussion in a communication space, ranging from face-to-face conversation to exchanges in writing. She describes precisely how the specificities of electronic discussion are translated into particular modes of expression, of agreement and of disagreement. Such authors as Virginia Orengo Castellá *et al.* (2000) insist on the more relaxed nature of relationship between interlocutors. They note that less familiarity between interlocutors goes hand in hand with a certain loss of social references, which removes inhibitions. To counter the disinhibiting effects of distant communication, John Davis, Shelly Farnham and Carlos Jensen (2002) propose introducing elements of personalization, such as the use of the voice in communication within the community of online players. Philip Thompsen and Davis Foulger (1996) show that the use of emoticons reduces perceptions of aggressiveness by introducing more subtlety into expression, as non-verbal

[1] The most commonly described of such acts are: *flaming*, which consists in attacking one or more participants in a discussion, by exacerbating irreconcilable points of view or violently criticizing standpoints; and *trolling*, which, unlike flaming, does not specifically attack the content of the discussion, but aims at disorganizing the debate by deliberately introducing irrelevant considerations.

communication does in face-to-face interaction. Judith Donath (2001) examines the possibility of using pictures of the participants' faces in online activities, but also underlines the adverse side to this type of practice, which confines individuals within a characterization in terms of gender, age group, race or social background, and thus profoundly transforms what is at play in these activities.

The second set of studies adopts a very different perspective: rather than positing a homogeneous and well-constituted space, and focusing on the "policing" of individual behaviours and on witch-hunts against the deviants, they study the specific spaces that are known broadly as "online communities," and analyze their modes of governance. The extreme fuzziness of the notion of "online community," concerning both the objects studied and the way they are defined, has been pointed out countless times. Here we simply emphasize that this fuzziness complicates the elaboration of a structured reflection on the issue of regulation, especially since each perspective contains a more or less implicit framing of this subject.

For many authors who, like Jennifer Preece (2000), consider the online community to be a structured space, the problem is quite simple: communities are by definition already "equipped" with norms and a policy, in the sense that they have explicit principles and operating rules.[2] These authors question the circulation of such norms and rules between *online* and *offline* (Hine, Chapter 12), and study the systems and mechanisms – FAQs, Netiquette, screening devices, the emergence of a core group supporting the group leader – through which the norms are made visible to the participants of a virtual group, and operate its management (DuVal Smith, 1999; Josefsson, 2005).

Others question the emergence of norms and even, in some cases, of communities. Rob Kling and Christina Courtright (2003) criticize the nonproblematized use of the notion of community, which appears almost as a natural category. From their point of view, the transformation of a group into a community has to be considered as an accomplishment in itself. The experiences they relate show that a real effort has to be made to build trust as well as to form and lead a group. In this perspective, Baym (1997) and Maria Papadakis (2003) explore

[2] Her definition is explicit and is quoted in many articles: "An online community is a group of people who come together for a purpose online, and who are governed by norms and policies."

the emergence of a culture, common to the participants, based on the use of a specific vocabulary or of particular narrative forms or modes of expression, and the progressive constitution of rituals. This common culture results in the emergence and consolidation of norms that make it possible to set the group's boundaries, to determine who can be admitted and to define acceptable behaviors. A type of continuum emerges between the group activity and its regulation. Hangwoo Lee (2005) highlights the various strategies used in a forum to manage flaming, ranging from denunciation to secession through the sending of poems or excuses, mediation, jokes, manifestations of solidarity, etc. Conflict management is then presented as the almost spontaneous result of the collective activity, without questioning the authority in charge of this policing.[3]

There are, therefore, two contrasting models: on the one hand, regulation appears as the application of rules that already existed in the group, in a movement from the "top" (group leaders) to the "bottom"; on the other, it is conceived of as a continuous collective learning process whose mechanisms remain partly implicit. Very few analysts, such as Gary Burnett and Laurie Bonnici (2003), raise the question of the articulation between the two types of regulation. These authors study what they call "meta-discussions" in two forums, namely debates that explicitly concern acceptable or desirable behaviours, and the group's operating rules. They highlight the importance, in one of the two groups, of reflexive activities that constitute its identity. They nevertheless conclude by reintroducing the separation between implicit norms and rules. Because most of these meta-discussions do not lead to a form of codification, they are considered only as forms of collective learning leading to the constitution of more or less implicit norms. These norms impact on the recruitment of the members and on the form of interaction, and thus on the very identity of the group. As with studies on the construction of norms, these

[3] In other spaces, this interlinking between the list's activity and regulation has been taken very far and systematized through the creation of original socio-technical apparatus. For instance, on the Slashdot.org forum (Lampe and Resnick, 2004), moderation "tickets" are distributed to the participants, which enable them to give a score to certain contributions. The "readers" can then use the final score – which includes other elements, such as the author's renown – as a tool to screen messages. In Debian, a developers' community (Auray, 2007), highly sophisticated voting systems are used to articulate argumentative discussion, deliberation and decision-making.

authors completely overlook the question of explicit modes of regulation (i.e. implying de facto the application of rules by some authority).

11.2 Hypothesis and methods

In this chapter we examine the question of regulation in the light of the above and on the basis of several choices and hypotheses.

First, the groups we are interested in are situated in a specific framework: we study electronic discussion lists that bring together patients/users around health-related issues. These forums have a closed functioning based on explicit membership, and anonymity is rare. These two characteristics ensure a fair degree of stability in the group of subscribers and participants. It seems that each type of "online community" – roughly defined as the interface between a minimal definition of the group's raison d'être and the use of certain media for technical exchange – raises specific problems of regulation. From this point of view, a forum that is constantly open to any internet user cannot operate in the same way as a closed group. Likewise, the problems of regulation for a group of people explicitly united around a project are different from those that emerge in a group of people united by a common "identity" (disease, liking for an activity, occupation, etc.). This position, which is both methodological and analytical, clearly distinguishes our approach from most other studies in this field.

One of the characteristics of the groups we are considering is that they form gradually as new members join, though a small core is at the origin of the group. Interactions are extremely rich and are deployed in a variety of ways; mutual support is, of course, an important component but so are discussions on symptoms of the disease, on treatments and their effects, on research work under way – academic articles circulating in the group – on the media and on the representation they give of the disease, on the socio-economic effects of the pathology or disability, on the political aspects, etc. These are, therefore, (semi-)public arenas (Cefaï, 1996) in which collective problematizations of a shared condition are constituted.

These discussion groups are not based on organizations that existed prior to their creation, such as non-profit associations, even if in certain cases the work of problematization produces certain forms of mobilization; the importation/application of exogenous normative frames is therefore irrelevant. In our opinion, this means that we cannot conceive of these groups as existing apart from their proper activity: the sending and reading of messages. From this point of view, our position is consistent with that of Didier Demazière and François Horn (2007), who consider, in their study of a community constructed for and around SPIP software, that the software and the group constitute each other; in other words, that the modes of organization are configurations of actions and not a matter of structure.

This led us to concentrate on the practices of regulation rather than on the question of norms. This approach has two concrete implications. First, the regulation tools, abundantly described in the literature – Netiquette, moderating tools – are of no interest to us as such. What we are interested in is the way they are mobilized by the actors throughout their activities. Similarly, we do not wish to describe what the common culture of the group consists of. We consider as relevant only those references that the actors make to this supposed culture to support a particular position regarding regulation. Second, it seems essential to consider the different regulatory activities as a whole. This means, on the one hand, considering the activities of the people to whom the particular arrangement of the system has given specific capacities (moderator, owner); these activities are conspicuously absent from the literature on the subject, as if rules in themselves were a sufficient explanation of the regulation issue in its entirety. On the other hand, it means considering the activities led by the people on the list who participate in this formal and informal regulatory work. Here again, this methodological assumption is a noteworthy difference compared to the most common approaches.

Consequently, our study is based on two types of material. The first resulted from extended interviews with ten list managers who have been responsible for several years for one or more constantly active lists (the activity is determined by the number of daily messages) that include a fairly large number of participants (from fifty to several hundred subscribers). The second consisted of an analysis of the activity of the lists themselves through a selection of discussion threads. These were chosen by reconstructing the episodes related by the list managers and, above all, from keywords that seemed relevant to our question: moderator, Netiquette, charter, etc.

First we analyze the way the managers of the lists get involved in the lists' activities; this approach enables us to show the multiplicity of activities that this regulation encompasses. This practical work is often implicit, or even invisible, to subscribers, and this may explain its "academic" invisibility. Then we describe what happens when this regulation becomes visible and when the manager adopts a position of authority. We examine the "enactment" of explicit regulation, the conflicts it may generate and the interpretation that can be made of such conflicts. We show, in particular, that the issue of the group identity is at stake through recurrent debates on these problems within the groups. This is a never-ending issue, given the specific mode of constitution of groups on health-related topics, and the technical and organizational characteristics of the media being used.

11.3 Ordinary regulation

There are a number of existing mechanisms that are supposed to configure use from the outset; a few practical rules that have gradually been established for e-mail are freely applied to discussion lists: the use of smileys, the banning of capitals – a sign of intense anger – the importance of sticking to the subject in the content of the message, and so on. These rules tend to evolve, mainly as a result of technical progress. For instance, setting limits to the "weight" of the message (in bytes), which previously excluded pictures or very long messages, is no longer necessary since the bandwidth has been increased. Ordinary rules of courtesy have been formalized in Netiquette. There is usually a reminder of the rules on the host's home page, which is sometimes also sent to new members. In some cases it is adapted to the particularities of the list or of the actors concerned. Most people agree, however, that these rules of Netiquette are never read either by the subscribers or the hosts of the list.

The technical system provided by the hosts of the lists makes the difference between two positions in the management of a mailing list: the creator-owner, who, alone, holds the power of enforcing the supreme sanction (i.e. the closure of the mailing list); and the moderators, who, like the owner, have access to a few tools. The system automatically refuses messages from non-subscribers. Moreover, it enables the managers (the owner and the moderators) to exercise a control a priori over all the messages before their dissemination (in practice, this possibility has rarely been used), to set up this type of system for a particular person ("fine moderation") and, finally, to expel a subscriber. They may also delete messages from the archives (an a posteriori moderation), although the messages in question remain in the computers of the subscribers who have already received them.

The work done by list managers exceeds by far the sole use of such devices, however, even when they have no specific training. All list managers explain that they have learned the "list regulator's trade" by practicing it, especially during conflicts – which were not always frequent but did tend to recur.[4] There is no transmission from experienced to inexperienced list managers or collective learning (although there are discussion groups at which list managers talk about their experiences and compare notes).

The regulation work they perform has three objectives: (1) constituting, developing and preserving the group; (2) organizing the exchange of messages; and (3) sharing decisions concerning the development of the list.

11.4 Constituting the group, making it exist and protecting it

The moderator's main objective is to set up a group of people who subscribe to the list and keep it alive by sending messages. The process through which a list is created is very simple, and consists very briefly of defining the field, creating the "group" on a list server hoster and waiting for the interaction to happen. It is the server that hosts the list that gives the initial visibility to the project. Some moderators rely on intermediaries, such as physicians specialized in the pathologies concerned, or they signal the creation of their list on open forums. On the list itself, though, the moderator's role is basically limited to a choice: accepting all messages unconditionally or not. Like anyone familiar with forums, the moderator knows that, in these internet spaces, participation is always unequally distributed (Preece, 2004), and a considerable proportion of subscribers will remain "lurkers" – that is, silent observers whose motives are unknown.

In the fields under consideration here, few moderators choose to select members by setting conditions for joining. The most demanding ones simply require new members to fill in a form on which a space is

[4] On the setting of rules to regulate conflicts, see Smith, McLaughlin and Osborne (1998).

left for a "message," the content of which can be as short as "Please register me as a subscriber." Moderators explain that selection criteria might not only put newcomers off but also force them to take a stand when they actually know nothing about the community they are about to join. In the words of one moderator: "I'm very much against having to introduce oneself when one joins. Because when I first went on the internet I used to read for quite a while before talking and I wouldn't have seen any of that if I'd been forced to join."

The absence of formal introductions does not mean, however, that the moderators do nothing to motivate newcomers. Their approach may range from "gentle" encouragement to signalling the person's arrival on the list by a welcoming message. Sometimes the contact is more direct. For instance, a moderator who says he/she "knows everyone" on his/her lists without having met any of them has made contact with them through private e-mails. Another one asks newcomers to phone him/her when they register, so that he/she can ask them about their situation and check that they are indeed concerned. He/she then gives them some information on the disability he/she is dealing with and on good and bad options.

Once the collective has been constituted, the moderators consider themselves responsible for protecting it. Through their intervention or encouragement, they try to avoid anything that could put members off: aggressiveness that could discourage those who feel neutral; complicity between members who know each other too well and make others feel like outsiders; the high "level" of discussions, which could discourage newcomers; etc.

To ensure that the group continues to live and to thrive, moderators sometimes select members and decide on the fate of individuals they consider to be detrimental to the group or to a particular member of the group. This was the experience of one moderator:

> There was a clash not so long ago; I personally sorted it out: a Belgian nurse who came along with her talk on energy, magnetism, obviously controversial subjects, but I'd never have got involved if there hadn't been systematic disparagement of allopathy. You can say what you like, allopathy does help to some extent, so I had to put things straight, and she left; but it could have got out of hand.

Even if they have full, exclusive authority to exclude a member or apply "subtle moderation," however, moderators never consider themselves to be entirely free to make a decision. For example, one moderator, highly upset by what he considered to be a takeover bid on his group, took no measure against the troublemaker but tried instead to "push him to make a mistake so that he discredited himself in the eyes of the group and then had no choice but to exclude himself." In another case, even though the moderator felt that she was authoritarian, she considered that her responsibility to the members of the list as well as to the troublemaker prevented her from clarifying all aspects of the conflict to everyone (here, the fact that the troublemaker, an alcoholic, suffered some psychiatric troubles) and from excluding the agitator too abruptly. She preferred to make sure that he left the list of his own accord.

Finally, for the moderators, managing the group also means being responsible for the words exchanged. They are not always sure about where it can lead them from a legal point of view. Above all, according to them, it compels them to respond to things said on the list, but outside it. As one put it: "Sometimes professionals contact people privately. I receive many messages on the side, privately, with pretty strong reactions, complaints, requests for explanations… Some professionals have left the list, as it became controversial. It frightened them when the discussions are a little heated. Sometimes we're walking on a tightrope." This accepted responsibility is seen by another moderator as a dilemma: should he tell the patients that one of the leading specialists in their rare pathology is on the list, or should he hide it from them to make sure that the interaction does not become constrained but remains spontaneous?

Many decisions taken about the group, in order to constitute it, to maintain it and to preserve it, are thus taken outside the list and out of sight, through the manager's personal intervention. This probably influences the group's composition and the dynamics in the group, but it only very indirectly affects the interaction itself.

11.5 Adapting the interaction

The second main set of tasks described by the moderators is the organization of the e-mail exchange. The aspect that is the least visible but the most restrictive for the moderator consists of, in the words of one of them, "keeping the list alive, animating it – that's quite a job. People don't stay on a list that's not very active. If you don't do all this work the list dies." The moderators apply themselves to encouraging participation, to sending a first answer to triggering others, to giving a link that can feed the discussion, to asking a participant to "say more," etc.

In this way they control the "temperature" of the debates: if it is too calm nothing happens; if it is too heated, the debate turns into a dispute, with the threat of Godwin's law (DuVal Smith, 1999).[5] In the words of one moderator: "It's when things are the most tense that you have the most interesting interactions, that it's rich. When there are conflicts people on the list talk. Otherwise, there are times when not much happens. But some may not like controversy and it could chase them away." In short, according to this moderator, conflict – or flaming, as it is called – seems to be an element that is not only inevitable in electronic communication, as the literature has shown, but is also indispensable to the interests of the interaction.

The literature has focused on the development of flaming in cyberspace – which is said to be facilitated by asynchronous communication, writing in an oral style, anonymity and the possibility of playing with identities (Lee, 2005) – to try to explain the actors' motivations and to analyze their impact on the debate (Orengo Castellá *et al.*, 2000; O'Sullivan and Flanagin, 2001). This leaves unanswered the question of how lists absorb and deal with conflict, and, in particular, the question of the manager's role. The moderators do not actually consider themselves to be better armed than the other members of the list to deal with conflicts, especially since they often consider conflict to be of some value.

Most moderators try to avoid direct calls to order (such as the exceptional "red cards" that they use, which are visible to all). They prefer moderation with time (messages are soon swamped by the mass) or "spontaneous regulation" (since aggressive messages are a "disadvantage," members tend not to answer them). Moderators are sometimes misunderstood and reproached for the absence of authoritarian reaction in a situation of flaming. As one put it: "It's harmful not to react with authority to troublemakers. There are people who feel uncomfortable in these situations and who quit. So, every time, there's some loss."

[5] Godwin's law was formulated in 1990 and states: "As a Usenet discussion grows longer, the probability of a comparison involving Nazis or Hitler approaches 1."

Seemingly approaching certain members "secretly" and giving them "instructions" to participate in the discussion or not is a common practice; as one moderator said, quoting a well-known saying: "Do not feed the troll."

Authoritative arguments are rarely used but can always be mobilized. Usually, after being discussed during a conflict, a rule can be written as a "law" that participants seldom use but it is supposed to provide them with a tool for reasoning and providing answers in situations of conflict. Moderators note that a list's rules in cases of flaming, thus defined, are actually forged and updated during conflicts.

Moderators define a good moderator as someone who knows how to apply the procedures of community life, and especially how to ensure that they *are* applied, and not as someone who just sets the list's policy and draws up guidelines. This can go as far as a position of technical neutrality; in the words of one: "The moderator's role is limited to banning messages that don't concern the list, to getting rid of adverts, and to solving problems of format with the participants." The managers readily acknowledge their refusal to act as overseers, which would give a particular value to their intervention. Some consider that this limits what they want to say and forces them to censor themselves; as another put it: "I'd like to talk about this [organizations' policies] but it's controversial and the others don't want to; I've given my opinion. But I'm sticking to my role as moderator; of course I'd like to intervene but I stop myself. I think that it's not the moderator's role." A good moderator is not someone who gives advice, someone who "preaches"; it's someone who "forces him- or herself to respect others' opinions," to stand back: "I try not to write too much, not to put myself in the position of an unavoidable transit point and the only supplier of information."

This does not mean that the moderators refuse any form of authority. They all say that they have, on rare occasions, encountered situations in which they have had to use their authority to interrupt a discussion and to silence, or even expel, a participant who refused to comply.

What they call "crossing the yellow line" could be, for example, denying that AIDS is a sexually transmitted disease, systematically disparaging allopathy, referring someone to a doctor who is supposed to have a harmful approach, or having a pathologically aggressive behavior: these are "transgressions" affecting the very definition that the list gives itself and what is considered to be its field of competence.

List managers therefore try to calibrate their interventions so that what they say is not systematically considered as being true or fair, and so that reminders of the common rules are clearly heard as such and not as points to be argued about. Seen from their viewpoint, this is not an easy position to hold, because of their proximity to the participants. Their personalized interactions make it necessary to keep a distance if they are to preserve their authority. "I consider it my role to maintain a certain distance, to maintain emotional limits. I always retain my dignity. I want to keep my authority," one moderator commented. She also admitted to "loving them like her children."

11.6 Organizing collectively

Although they have the sole ownership of their list and are therefore the masters of its existence, owners tend to consider its governance as a collective matter. They try to share their authority with others, and are able to dismiss an autocratic type of governance.

Under certain circumstances, moderators consider it legitimate to take decisions alone, in an authoritarian way, such as when they believe they could be legally accountable for the decision, or when the subscribers' safety is in the balance. Besides, in many situations they feel that they have no right to impose their points of view or preferences on the list, as the following comment by one moderator attests it: "Rather than trying to make this list match my expectations (in the name of what would I have the right to?), I prefer to set up a second one in parallel."

In such cases they may seek to share their authority and responsibility, for example by recruiting other managers. These co-moderators may of course lighten their load, but, above all, they enable them to discuss problems pertaining to the management of the list. Spotting and appointing new moderators is a fairly lengthy process, moreover, since the qualities expected, and deemed to be indispensable – consistency, tact, discretion, responsibility, etc. – are not always easy to find.

Some list owners have gone even further, by formalizing a collective regulation, not only to moderate the interactions but also to participate in decisions concerning the definition of the list. We see below, for instance, how a list sets up a management committee. Technical devices – votes, polls – exist and are made available for list managers who would like to involve the entire collective in decision-making, but they are rarely used, even by list managers who want to have "the most democratic functioning possible" (as one expressed it), and they often lead to dead ends. This was the case, for example, of a list manager who "wanted to act democratically" and ran a poll to find out whether the members would agree to split the list in two, depending on the topics. He felt obliged to apply the decision to that list and to maintain its unity but, as he considered it to be harmful, he split his other lists in an authoritarian way, without asking the other subscribers' opinions. Several examples exist of such attempts ending up in decisions based on a procedure that has mobilized only a small percentage of subscribers. List managers who have burnt their fingers this way generally fail to return.

With time, list managers have thus developed rules and routines enabling them more or less to manage the list's activity. These are based on a few general devices, such as Netiquette and the moderation tools made available by list servers. They seem to be peculiar to the moderator's personality, however, and to the specificity of the list as it has gradually come to be defined. Moreover, they are evolving: our descriptions of them must be considered as snapshots taken during the life of a list and of its moderators. A large increase in the number of subscribers and in the rate of participation forces list managers to think about, and sometimes even to alter, the format of their interventions. In the final analysis, important as the regulation of such a list may be, it takes place mainly "underground," since it is largely invisible to the subscribers as the modalities and principles of its action are never clarified.

11.7 Conflicts of regulation: identity and list governance

Can it be said that "adjusted" list regulation functions smoothly and without conflict? There is no straight answer. List members usually interiorize the list's mode of functioning. A form of self-regulation is established, which ensures the fluidity of the interaction – so that all e-mails are answered, for example – and it contains certain members' aggressiveness. There are times, though, when moderators or list owners are prompted to intervene with authority and not simply as members of the list. Although explicit reference to their status is not systematic, use of the imperative and of certain expressions such as "I wish to remind you that" unambiguously marks the enunciator's position. In a significant number of cases, however, this use of authority fails to produce the expected effects, and triggers discussions on its validity instead.

For instance, following a somewhat heated interaction on a list, the moderator may wish to clarify some points, as in this example: "I would just like to remind you that it is important for interaction in the group to remain friendly and respectful. Don't forget to read through your messages before sending them and to change words where necessary if they could seem aggressive to others. We should carry on exchanging our information even if we disagree with one another..."

This apparently moderate message triggered immediate reactions, which brings us to the work by Zizi Papacharissi (2004) on the productive nature of arguments: "Some slightly heated discussions are not necessarily sterile. I think that by maintaining elementary courtesy, everyone has the right to engage in discussions with their own words. On the other hand, it is difficult to be called to order." The message was followed by another, which played down the importance of such behavior and related it to what bound the list members, namely their disease, which made them "grumpy and aggressive."

The "aggressive" charge is reversed here: the small occasional excesses triggered by an impassioned debate are not as difficult to accept as the implicit judgments contained in the intervention of authority. This authority is challenged from the point of view of the principles it refers to; there is no agreement on the tone that is generally appropriate in the discussion nor on the way these principles are translated in the particular context of the list; what may seem aggressive elsewhere is here simply the manifestation of an irritation typical of the disease.

A second example of a more serious incident concerns the challenging of authority. One owner of a list barged into the discussion to announce the expulsion of one of the moderators. This event triggered consternation and anger, as the members of the list felt that nothing had happened that could justify such a sanction. Despite the owner's explanations – according to her, the moderator had had unacceptable behavior on a "neighbouring" list and it was her duty to "protect the group" – the debate carried on. The owner's legitimacy to intervene was called into question because, for months, she had hardly participated at all in the list's discussions. More fundamentally, it was the very idea of regulation from above that the members found unacceptable. Here are two comments:

> I was talking about a self-managed group recently, but I was carried away. I'd forgotten that there was an owner and that we never read. So how does one show that one's the boss? By firing people!

> "Protect the group…"? We're adults, with a free will… I don't like censored writing, because we should have free access to everything written and be free to criticize! Unless otherwise stated!! I don't need people to tell me what to think. That's what democracy is!!

This long and stormy discussion led the owner to explain the legal aspects, especially the necessity for a list to have a legally responsible owner, and to announce the principles, which – in her opinion – justified the decision, she had taken (i.e. equality of all members and tact in moderation).

In defining the list as such, she reproduced a sequence corresponding to a common pattern. Even though the fact of establishing principles of regulation usually means defining the list's identity, which is generally not enough to end the discussion – on the contrary – it does cause its centre of gravity to shift.

Numerous examples like these highlight the largely informal nature of ordinary regulation in lists and the members' ignorance of possible modes of regulation. In the absence of any incident, the group thinks it is self-managed and discovers with stupefaction that, in parallel, there is another functioning resembling enlightened and benevolent despotism. In confrontational situations these two modes of regulation are juxtaposed and create a tension. The question then arises as to what legitimizes the "despot's" authority. As we have seen, the person's suitability for his/her assumed role could be questioned. The challenge often goes as far as the very idea of an authority, though, especially in the absence of an established "code" framing its intervention.

The analysis of arguments exchanged during these conflicts often implicitly indicates two ways in which an authority could be recognized as legitimate.

(1) The first would require partial equivalence between the list and the authority; this implies that the authority can be considered as an expression of the list, which in a sense it personifies; the protagonists then question the tools that enable this

expression and, in particular, allow it to be articulated in an unambiguous statement;

(2) The second would be based on the production of rules adjusted to the particularities of the list. Confrontational situations show that not only the moderators but also all participants in the debate try to mobilize rules or general principles to determine the behavior to be adopted; in these discussions, participants qualify the list's space and then determine the relevant modes of governance.

11.8 How should the list be represented?

The first difficulty is of a practical nature. It occurs when it is necessary to arbitrate a conflict in which agreement cannot be reached on who the arbitrator should be and on what principles the arbitration should be based. The problem quickly arises of defining how the list should be "represented." A question that repeatedly crops up is that of "lurkers," people who join the list and receive messages but never participate themselves. It is raised both as a problem to solve – some see these "voyeurs" as undesirable – and as a challenge to the representation of the list and to its "democratic" functioning.

In a group of people concerned with cancer, a discussion started about a person who had not sent messages for a long time. On this occasion she reappeared: "Expressing myself in front of a room of people, even if it's virtual, really intimidates me." The list's owner reacted with encouragements: "Go on, don't hesitate; you'll see that it's not so bad, and the room is very small. There were fifty of us last time we counted." This message immediately triggered a strong reaction from one of the members, Alain,[6] who described a tension between the list as a group of contributors and the list as a group of members: "When I talk to you, it's friends that I'm writing to. There's no doubt whatsoever about that. I actually think that all the 'real contributors' to the list see things the same way. [. . .] But a quick count in my address book shows that only about twenty (I count twenty-one) of those fifty are active. The others are sitting on the fence of the nudist camp. I fully admit that I accepted the rule of the game in coming here: you can keep your pants on when you join."

[6] The names cited are pseudonyms.

Then he proposed a solution to manage the articulation between the two spaces; it would consist of distinguishing two types of messages: those intended for "friends," who can share personal data, and informative messages intended for the "whole room."

The owner answered by pointing out two facts: the technical impossibility of making the distinction he proposed, and the inoffensiveness of lurkers. She used a general argument on the functioning of lists, moreover, which always contain some nonactive members, who, she noticed, tend to disappear quickly when the moderators are too strict. The discussion was carried on, voices were raised and Alain, along with another member, laid down an ultimatum:

> Either [the owner] excludes all those who don't have the manners to introduce themselves. The list of fifty is made public. We opt for democratic functioning (by that I mean that the ideas that I defend here can be refused). Or else I clear out.

The owner rejected this ultimatum: "In the name of this democracy that some raise like a standard, I can't see what right I have to delete thirty people [from the list] just because two or three would like me to." The two opponents left the list. Then a process of rule production was launched (we elaborate on this below).

This case highlights a recurrent debate on the lists, which reappears during other conflicts: who constitutes the list – all active participants or all the members? What do the moderators or owners guarantee? The constant reference to democracy is significant: the intermediary establishes the potential for everyone to take part to some extent in the debate and decision-making, thereby, from this point of view, promising access to something that resembles a form of participative democracy. To reach a compromise between, on the one hand, self-management, a participative model, and, on the other, an authoritarian model, some members have imagined intermediate systems based on delegation to a small group of loyal members. These initiatives – which might consist merely of the establishment of joint moderation by several members, with discussions on contentious cases – generally emerge when there is a problem or a conflict, and are often proposed by the list's "authorities."

It can be observed, however, that this type of organization simply displaces the target of criticism: its legitimacy is called into question in the same way as the legitimacy of individual managers is.

11.9 Representation and flow: an equation without any solution

Are there other means to overcome the difficulties raised by the unequal participation of members? Is it possible to adopt a democratic functioning principle and to solve conflicts and controversies collectively?

How can one take into account those who never or seldom express themselves, without speaking in their name? Various proposals have been put forward during disputes. The first proposal questions the mechanisms likely to encourage wider participation. Some members partially impute the silence of some to the chattering of others, claiming that it might be difficult for the former to speak when the latter are ever-present, hyperreactive and loquacious. On a list, during a conflict over an e-mail sent to a list member on behalf of the management committee created in an attempt to democratize management, one member said that he wondered how far it was necessary to go to prompt silent members to talk:

> Egalitarianism at all costs doesn't seem to be a solution. By "egalitarianism" I mean the idea that certain people have to talk less, or differently, to allow others to express themselves; a sort of levelling out in the mode and time of expression. For example, does the fact that it is difficult for you to express yourself in an open e-mail in a controversial context oblige me to express myself less or differently, to help you to talk? [. . .] I find that the immense advantage of written, delayed communication is that the person isn't obliged or prohibited from doing anything, except having a minimum of respect for others.

In response to these reservations, another person suggested an opinion poll. This second – recurrent – proposal is supported by the idea that polls and votes are proven tools that, in certain cases, simplify the expression of opinions and cluster them into an operational form, such as the mechanisms of direct democracy, which, while authorizing the expression of the majority, requalify the preliminary debates needed for the efficient functioning of democracy. We noted this above: this option has met with little success – even though servers have integrated it into the set of available tools. The rare attempts to apply it generally end in a low or derisory rate of participation. This does not, however, prevent this option from being regularly mentioned during internal debates on discussion lists. During a debate on a possible change of mail server, a discussion arose on what the specificity of the list was – the server, the owner's role, the number of participants – but no clear conclusion was reached. Then one of the members proposed an opinion poll. He saw this as the most suitable method of consultation, considering the subject of the debate, which could be reduced to a binary choice, and the fact that a variety of arguments had been put forward. The initiator of the discussion excluded this possibility:

> I don't think that that's the issue. It's not a question of adhesion to an idea or a party… It's a matter of a list on which one participates or not. Nobody's asked for a discharge to participate on this list; it's enough to be concerned by our disease… Membership is free, as is unsubscribing, being absent or being present. There's no point in triggering a consultation that'll lead nowhere. No, it's a list instituted by [the owner]; it's nothing if there's no one and it's everything for all those who participate in it or for those who only read it.

This line of argument could be seen as a convenient way of escaping a verdict that failed to meet expectations. The list member nevertheless underlined that all debates on the list regulation come up against the question of what lists actually are. Can they be compared to well-constituted groups, because of the registration procedures, or are they something else? This member was clearly arguing for the second alternative: a list exists only through its manifestations. An important distinction between discussion groups and forums is worth mentioning at this point. Once they have joined the group, most subscribers receive all messages by e-mail. In a sense, they share an experience of communal life, through this comparatively intense flow that attests to the group's vitality. Participation in a forum stems from an individual decision, which has to be made again whenever an opportunity occurs, since it is necessary to go onto the forum's website. The organization of messages is mostly thematic and non-temporal, moreover, and everyone is free to explore his/her own topics of interest. Everyone's experience of a forum is therefore far more individualized than any experience of mailing lists, even if, on certain themes, the lasting engagement of some members can create an effect similar to that of mailing lists. The articulation, observed on these lists, between the question of regulation and that of the list's identity has to be linked to the particular format of the interactions imposed by the medium. A mailing list is a pure performance. Expressing oneself through a message is acting – that is, making "the list" exist. Introducing a vote or opinion poll means performing in another antagonistic way, insofar as this procedure relates to a separation between a clearly constituted group and an object – "the list" – on which the group, a position of exteriority, pronounces itself.

The tension between the two modes of regulation is understandable; the problem of self-management and the use of authority can be solved only by establishing tools of representation. This process flounders on the fact that the list itself is a mechanism of pure representation – that is, without an external referent. In a sense, there is nothing to represent. Discussions on this subject therefore seem to lead to a dead end, and yet they are productive, since representations of the lists are constructed and compared thanks to these discussions.

11.10 How can the rules be adjusted?

When list managers try to modify inappropriate behaviors they rely on a limited corpus of rules to justify their interventions. These general rules are assumed to frame the group functioning. They appear nonetheless to be as questionable as the moderator's legitimacy. This challenging leads to two types of proposals.

First, members ask for an adjustment of the rules concerning a particularity of the list, here mostly related to the patients' status as participants. For example, there was once a disagreement over one of the member's messages proposing screen backgrounds, electronic writing paper and other decorative tools. Some saw this as contradictory to a rule prohibiting advertising. The person argued that she was not selling anything, she simply wanted everyone to benefit from the artistic work that helped her to endure the disease. Other members agreed, considering that her activity was part of the list's normal activities of offering mutual support, which could even be seen as a duty for members. The artist was actually supporting the others by offering a distraction, and the others supported her by giving meaning to her creative activity. Disagreement nevertheless continued on the functions of the list; it was more oriented toward "discussion" on the part of the artist's opponents, and encompassing "support" and "discussion" on the part of the others.

Second, the closing phase in a debate often includes some collective work directed toward the construction of specific rules. After a period of conflict, in which unkind words have been exchanged and when the list seemed to be on the verge of disintegration, some try to learn lessons from the crisis, in order to prevent such an event happening again.

We mentioned above the intense conflict on a list devoted to cancer, between members who considered the list to consist solely of individuals who participated actively and other members, including the owner, who took the contrary point of view and considered a variety of forms of participation as normal. When the two opponents quit, one of the members tried to reformulate the dispute by articulating it to a "functional" definition of the list: "I think I've understood that we haven't all got the same objective: there are those who want to have a relationship and to chat, and who use the list as an ICQ,[7] and the others, who, like me, rather want more factual and informative interaction. In the former case a virtual affect dominates, which, because it is virtual, is wide open to interpretation. In the latter case the rational, 'scientific' approach is protection against excesses."

Fortified by the owner's support, Véronique set about writing a new charter for the list, and based it on this dichotomy between informative interaction, reserved for the list, and affective interaction, supposed to take place via other media. With this objective in view, the charter recommended that participants remain factual and positive, avoid criticism and refrain from responding to abuse. In a sense, the "protestor," Alain, managed to destabilize the former functioning of the list. He asked for the "privatization" of the list and for a shift of focus onto the active participants. The process led to explicit recognition of the list's semi-public status, which implied a reconfiguration of the interaction.

At the same time, this reconfiguration seemed volatile. Very soon things returned to normal, with an inextricable mix of informative and friendly interactions. The production of normative devices, rules, charters and so on cannot therefore be considered as a coherent process tending toward a stricter functioning of the lists, as a form of institutionalization. These devices have varied destinies. When it is a matter of setting up routines – such as the requirement for new members to introduce themselves – they are generally applied. They affect the future of the list, in this case by eliminating all those who do not want to meet the requirement to introduce themselves, even if they

[7] "ICQ" is a homophone of "I seek you," and refers to instant messaging services.

do not determine an univocal identity of the list. When, as the example has shown, they claim to frame behaviors and to set a certain definition of the list, they are rapidly swept away by the very dynamics of the interaction, and become nothing more than witnesses of the conflicts they have endeavored to pacify.

Whether rules are exogenous or endogenous, they are relatively weak devices for controlling how the lists function. What is crucial, however, is that it is in its discussion of the rules that the group ultimately comes to define itself.

11.11 Conclusion

Several conclusions can be drawn from the foregoing. First, it invalidates a representation of regulatory work as being the application of explicit rules, even if they are well defined. This representation is insufficient to account for the accomplishments of individuals who consider themselves to be in charge of the management in discussion groups. Upstream from any confrontational situation, their work is necessary for the life of the group, so that everyone finds his/her place through encouraging interactions and associating enough participants; some kind of collective space can be constituted, along with a feeling of belonging and solidarity. This work remains largely invisible, or at least cannot be seen as a process of regulation in the narrow sense of the term; it implies an authority and an explicit apparatus so that a public assessment of the situation can be made, leading to the application of measures that have been specified in advance. It is nevertheless necessary to facilitate the interactions and keep the list alive. The managers actively demonstrate their concern and continually take care of the list, as they would do for a living organism.

The representation of regulatory work as the application of explicit rules does not account for the management of crises either. Earlier studies described two types of crises: the first is supposedly triggered by an individual considered to be disruptive, and whose behavior is unambiguously qualified as impolite, deviant or even delinquent; the second is said to be produced by disagreements and conflicts between different group members. For the first type of crisis, the solution can be found either in the application of preventive measures aimed at making the participants act responsibly, or in sanctions implemented on the basis of a clear definition of reprehensible behaviors and rules established for punishment. The second type of crisis implies the clarification of the principles and norms underlying the group's functioning.

In the groups we have studied, we found the boundary between these two types of crisis very difficult to define. The qualification of behaviors is almost always an issue in an occurrence that triggers a call for reactions or a reference to supposed behavioral rules. Through this qualification, the group identity is at stake; hence the paradoxical and central role of regulation – here in the narrow sense of the word, namely related to the "policing" of interactions – in the functioning of discussion groups. It is paradoxical because one could say that, basically, there is never really any condition of felicity for this type of regulation; it is often problematical, and its implementation almost invariably leads to new disputes rather than appeasing existing ones. It is central because, through the discussions about its implementation, the identity of the list is at stake. It is a special moment in which, apart from the ceaseless flow of messages deleting one another, a form of reflexivity develops, through which the volatile "we" of the list is embodied, often painfully. This embodiment is always temporary and needs to be renewed, given the labile nature of the lists, which exist only through interactions, without any external referent.

It is important to highlight the extent to which these results have to be related to the particular situations we have studied and placed at the interface between the technical system used by the group and its own raison d'être. Unlike forums, mailing lists create groups technically. Considering how these groups, based on common personal experience with no reference to a collective action program, are constituted, the question of their being a group, in the "social" sense of the term, is constantly raised.

In parallel, the highly particular and paradoxical position of the list managers is clear. The technical system invests them with absolute power: they can exclude members, delete messages and even dissolve the group. At the same time, though, in practice they cannot exert their power, lest they should go against the objectives they had in mind when creating the group.

These spaces thus show a particular form of regulation, with rare and fragile governance tools; a political conception of the organization, involving weak interactions; and powers that cannot be exercised freely without running the risk of killing the collective that has instituted the group. As with the "wild" societies studied by Pierre Clastres (1989), the only instrument of power is the manipulation of speech, which subjects it to constant control by the group. As a result, this power "embodied by its chiefs is not authoritarian, at least not in the sense that the primitive societies would to still have much progress to make to endow themselves with political institutions, but in the sense that they refuse, through a sociological and thus subconscious act, to allow their power to become coercive" (Clastres, 1989). Perhaps electronic lists are inventing their own forms of power, devoid of hierarchical subordination, commanding positions and coercion.

12 *The formation of conventions for internet activities*

CHRISTINE HINE

12.1 Introduction

Much of what the internet has come to be is shaped from the bottom up, by its users, rather than having been dictated from the top down, by its inventors, its vendors and its regulators. In order to address issues of governance adequately, it is necessary to study these clearly articulated but nonetheless highly significant norms of behavior. Although some analyses of internet governance look exclusively at the allocation of addresses and domain names, the issues far exceed this purely technical focus (MacLean, 2004a). The existing governance of the internet is itself an emergent mosaic (Dutton and Peltu, 2007), comprising many different approaches and looking at diverse objects of regulation. In this chapter I focus on the part of the level of governance that William Dutton and Malcolm Peltu (2007) term "user-centric." I look at the ways in which users themselves conceive of appropriate standards of behavior on the internet, and the mechanisms and frames of reference that they deploy to do so.

Ideas about appropriate standards of behavior do not arise through a formulaic consumption of generalized sets of rules, but emerge from highly specific interactions between interpretations of diverse governance regimes and other ways of making sense of online activities. This chapter examines the question of emergent standards of practice, looking at how people develop their own norms of internet use and analyzing the contexts that they draw upon in the course of deciding on appropriate behavior, as individuals and as groups of individuals with specific allegiances. I focus particularly on the emergence of social norms for internet behavior as an ethnographic question. I do not immediately, therefore, discuss how the internet should be the subject of governance and regulation. Instead, I look at some structures of usage that emerge in practice, and the ways in which these involve notions of appropriate use and legitimate controls drawn from diverse sources. The aim is to demonstrate that whether the internet is an appropriate object upon which to focus efforts at governance is far from settled, but that this uncertainty can be a valuable opportunity for stimulating debate.

This chapter introduces some ethnographic accounts of internet use that shed light on the way that conventions for internet activities arise. These accounts are used to demonstrate that the relevant context for the self-regulation of behavior is an emergent phenomenon, not to be assumed in advance on the basis of the features of the medium alone. Section 12.2 introduces the concept of online communities. These social formations develop their own specific norms of behavior within the internet environment, and in some instances the online setting provides the context for standards of behavior to be negotiated that have little obvious connection with offline behavioral norms. For example, Don Slater's (2002) ethnographic work on the online trading of sex pictures shows that what might have been thought an "anything goes" arena was instead thoroughly socially regulated. The online sphere developed its own standards, its own sanctions for dealing with transgressors and, indeed, its own sense of itself as a discrete sphere.

This vision of an online sphere separate in its conventions from offline life pervaded much of the early writing about the internet. Such visions reinforce the perception that there is a separate domain of internet sociality to govern, and that this somehow exceeds or evades other forms of national governance and behavioral regulation. It is clear by now, however, that the notion of a distinct virtual sphere comprised of online communities describes only a small proportion of the everyday experience of internet use. More usually, conventions are transferred from offline contexts, in order to make the online a workable part of an existing communicative ecology (Tacchi, Slater and Hearn, 2003). To illustrate this point, in section 12.3 I turn to some ethnographic studies that have focused on connections across the online/offline boundary. I discuss diverse case studies, including explorations of the use of the internet by transnational communities, and of the use of the internet in Chinese political life. These case studies are used to examine the idea that the relevant framework for understanding the normative structures of internet activities is not necessarily to be found on the internet. Instead, reference is made on a highly variable and emergent basis to different frameworks within which online activities are rendered as appropriate, meaningful and acceptable.

To conclude section 12.3 I describe an ethnographic study I have recently conducted focusing on a scientific discipline's deployment of the internet. In that study I found that the material and virtual cultures of this scientific discipline were thoroughly entwined, and that, although practitioners embraced online communication both for its functionality and its symbolic qualities, they were very concerned to use it in ways that fitted with their existing ethos. In this context, then, the prevailing culture of the discipline largely shaped ideas about the use of the internet, and corresponding efforts were made to develop internet activities that fitted with existing governance structures and values. The very possibility of internet communications provided the occasion for discussions that ranged across the practices and expectations of the discipline, however. The coming of the internet can thus be an opportunity to stimulate wide-ranging discussions about standards and regulation: its perceived novelty is a resource to encourage people to talk about issues they might otherwise take for granted. The concluding section of the chapter then examines the implications of these observations for the ongoing project of internet governance study.

12.2 The internet as a discrete social sphere

There is now an extensive ethnographic literature describing the development of social formations in online settings. Observers of online behavior have argued that complex social structures can emerge on the internet (Jones, 1995). This ability to develop social structure means that it is possible for online contexts to set themselves apart from other contexts, online and offline, and for these new online contexts to develop their own social orthodoxies. In self-defining as communities, and in mutually reinforcing a collective identity, and a set of values and norms of behavior, these online contexts are able to sustain a discrete social sphere. The orthodoxy, which develops in such settings, can be quite distinct from prevalent offline norms, particularly because the internet provides possibilities for like-minded people to come together across geographic and temporal separation.

One of the most influential depictions of online communities has been Baym's (1995, 2000) discussion of an online soap opera discussion group. Baym describes the formation of a community within which very specific understandings of appropriate behavior prevail, including a norm of friendship, a focus on social support and an appreciation of humor. In one sense this community is very closely tied to the offline context, a television soap opera, which it celebrates. Baym (2000) demonstrates, however, that this group also develops a highly specific relationship to the soap opera, and it is this specificity that, she argues, demarcates it as a community of practice in its own right. The online realm of the discussion group is treated by participants as a discrete social sphere, and the appropriate standards of behavior are understood in relation to that discrete sphere. Although there are no overt mechanisms of social control, appropriate behavior is regulated through the collective identification of deviance and the chastising of offenders. This perspective on the online community as a self-contained normative entity has been a particularly influential way of understanding the internet, countering the opposing tendency to think of the internet as socially anarchic.

Another influential early discussion of the emergence of norms of behavior on the internet was provided by the observation of multi-user domains. These online text-based role-playing games allow players to adopt a persona and interact with one another in real time within a fantasy environment described in text. Julian Dibbell (1999) recounts an incident in one MUD that led participants to reflect on the appropriate mechanisms for social control and the potential links between online transgressions and offline structures. The incident that Dibbell describes was a virtual rape, in which one character in the MUD developed a "voodoo doll" program that had the effect of other characters being compelled to carry out his wishes. Those subjected to this program experienced it as a violation, and subsequent community outrage led to the discussion of a range of possible sanctions. The end result for this community was the institution of a system of online voting in order to decide upon appropriate punishments. These punishments were wholly "in-game," generally involving the banning of players who transgressed community expectations.

Looking across online communities, both the norms and the mechanisms through which these norms are identified and enforced vary. Baym's largely female soap opera fans maintained broadly feminine norms of friendship and social support through collective action and the chastisement of offenders. Dibbell's MUD users developed a pseudo-legal structure to enforce behavioral standards that were fairly continuous with, even though separated from, offline standards that protect the integrity of the individual against violation. David Phillips (1996) studied one newsgroup during a period of crisis, and finds that members were drawn to rhetorical strategies for dealing with unacceptable behavior, rather than appealing to structural resources such as the input of employers, network providers or the deployment of offline legal sanctions. Williams (2004), however, describes an online community moving away from "vigilante" modes of regulation toward more structured and formal styles of policing, albeit still confined to online sanctions. Looking at a large sample of online communities using data-mining techniques, Karine Barzilai-Nahon and Seev Neumann (2005) describe the self-regulation of online communities as an efficient alternative to state regulation. Communities with a strong core of members were found to develop their own mechanisms to regulate behavior via the deletion of inappropriate messages, often building on the social capital of long-established members of the group. There is, in fact, an extensive literature focusing on the diverse means that online communities use to regulate themselves and sustain standards of behavior that the majority of those involved will consider acceptable (Wall and Williams, 2007).

The situations described by Baym and Dibbell involve social norms that, althoug enforced online, are fairly recognizable from the offline environment. It is by no means guaranteed, however, that there will be any continuity between online and offline norms. From the observation that online settings can develop as discrete social spheres it follows that orthodoxies can be developed in relation to these specific situations and may not reproduce those that prevail offline. One of the most extreme examples of the situational construction of orthodoxy is the networks that form around otherwise taboo or deviant practices. Turning taboo into the mainstream is facilitated by the ability to speak openly about these issues and create networks within which such talk is sanctioned or celebrated. It has thus been possible for networks to arise in which, for example, self-harm and anorexia, otherwise the target of attempts to treat and control, are celebrated and reinforced by proponents (Tierney, 2006). Alternative orthodoxies therefore can and do arise in opposition to and in separation from the mainstream. It is important to stress that in no way are these separate networks unregulated or free from social norms. To the contrary, there can be rigid and strongly enforced ideas about appropriate behavior. I describe here one example, which shows how highly socially regulated apparently deviant practices can be in online settings.

The example I describe is a piece of ethnographic research conducted by Slater (2002). In this paper he analyzes the trading of sex pictures via IRC channels, arenas in which participants are identified to one another by nicknames, and interactions have a largely ephemeral quality. People take part in a variety of relationships, ranging from the impersonal trading of pictures through to eroticized exchanges. Slater argues that, far from celebrating the ephemeral and virtualized quality of interactions, participants feel the need to develop a form of "ethical sociality," which is brought into being through various "mechanisms of materialization." More specifically, the supply of images is vast, and, given their digital qualities, an image can be shared with another person without it being lost to its original owner. There is thus no scarcity of images. Participants nonetheless develop and enforce scarcity through a variety of social and technical means, including stigmatization of the practice of leeching (downloading excessive amounts of images without reciprocation) and the installation of programs to control the supply of images according to predefined ratios of upload to download. As Slater describes it, life in the "sexpics" scene is dominated by concerns about how to maintain an appropriate social order, and this quest for social order forms a dominant way for participants to understand their experience.

In more traditional senses, the sex pictures scene might be thought of as evading or ignoring regulation. Many of the images that are traded may be in breach of copyright, having been scanned from print publications or downloaded from commercial pornography sites. According to Slater's description, however, this does not mean that it is without regulation altogether. It forms its own sphere of sociality, realized through social norms and technical devices alike, and developing appropriate forms of materialization for the virtual space in which it occurs. As Slater (2002) says in his conclusion:

> [W]hat I have been trying to emphasize is not the marginal or bizarre nature of the IRC sexpics scene, or its disembedded and virtual character. To the contrary what is interesting in this case is the participants' great drive to normalize social life and to make it behave as if it were embedded in a reliable and transmissible normativity.

We could, then, consider this as a case in which internet governance and regulation, or at the very least some strongly policed conventions for use, arise from the bottom up in an internet context as enacted by internet users.

Although the particular upshot of self-regulation is somewhat unusual in the case that Slater describes, the point that virtual communities can self-regulate using a variety of social, legalistic and technical means is much more widely accepted. Online communities can, therefore, be considered as highly regulated in their own terms, although the resulting social structures and norms can vary widely from one another and may or may not mirror those prevailing in offline society. Even though it has been challenging to find practical ways to apply existing national legislative frameworks to the internet, and internet communities have enjoyed relatively high levels of autonomy (Barzilai-Nahon and Neumann, 2005), the internet society that has emerged has been far from "anything goes." Studies of online communities tend to emphasize the bounded nature of virtual communities, however, and the importance of strong ties between at least a core of members in developing and maintaining a sense of a distinctive social locale. This perspective may be somewhat misleading as a representation of the way that many users view the internet, as the next section demonstrates.

12.3 Internet activities as a part of complex cultural dynamics

Although studies of online community self-regulation tend to celebrate the apartness and integrity of the internet, more recently it has been argued that the internet is only rarely experienced as a separate sphere of virtuality, and that often it becomes woven into a set of connections that span online and offline contexts (Miller and Slater, 2000; Wellman and Haythornthwaite, 2002). In the situation that Daniel Miller and Don Slater describe, the use of the internet by Trinidadians assumed a distinctively Trinidadian quality, such that users were able to recognize themselves in the technology and make it their own. It has become increasingly common for ethnographers to see internet activity as woven into everyday life as the "embedded" internet described by Philip Howard (2004). This, then, provides an additional complication when we look at conventions of use and issues of internet governance and regulation. If the internet begins to dissolve as an unproblematically defined object, and if it acquires more complex and less predictable connections with various other contexts, it becomes harder to demarcate it for regulatory purposes.

Medium-based regulation may not, after all, be an approach that sits comfortably with the mundane experience. In this section I delve a little more deeply into this issue, drawing on some recent ethnographic projects.

Nicole Constable (2003) conducted an ethnography of the phenomenon of the "mail order" bride, exploring the experiences of women from China and the Philippines and men from the United States who were seeking foreign marriage partners. Her ethnography combined face-to-face interviews in the United States, China and the Philippines with internet observations focusing on mailing lists and websites on which potential partners interacted. This multi-sited approach enabled Constable to review the complex interactions between conventions in different settings. She describes the multiple allegiances of participants, such that, rather than distinct communities, the various chat rooms, bulletin boards and mailing lists form "an array of social networks and alliances" (Constable, 2003).

Rather than seeing the internet as a self-contained sphere independent of nation states, Constable observes a more complex situation in which "the Internet community both traverses and reinforces state boundaries and definitions of citizenship." The internet becomes a site where relations with nation states and with prevailing gender conventions are both reworked. Exploring participants' experiences in online and offline settings allowed Constable to review the ways in which online activities are structured across diverse sites and are also a part of a wider whole, in which the conventions of any particular online site are suffused with concerns from other domains.

The transnational internet experiences that Constable studied are not an isolated phenomenon. Anastasia Panagakos and Heather Horst (2006) discuss the experience of transnational migrants with the internet, and find a similarly complex picture. They discuss five ethnographic case studies of the use of communications media by transnational migrants, and find that practices are highly variable and influenced by the situations from which migrants originate and in which they find themselves. The internet is not experienced in isolation, but as part of an array of potential media that migrants may be able to use to keep in touch. Usage relates to practical and economic accessibility, and also to perceptions of the abilities of the media concerned to convey emotion and develop intimacy in specific cultural contexts. Panagakos and Horst (2006) stress the importance of contextualizing observations of internet use, and not assuming that the internet automatically provides a transnational sphere that bridges distance.

These studies of transnational internet use therefore stress the ways in which online and offline are mutually interwoven. Online activities become part of a continuum of practice that spans online and offline sites, and the appropriate framework for judging acceptable behavior becomes a live question. In some cases the whole rationale for online activities revolves around an offline context toward which they are directed and upon which they are intended to have an impact. Constable's potential marriage partners may have interacted online to begin with, but many hoped to make relationships that could someday transfer offline. They did participate in online groups that we could refer to as online communities. There were norms of behavior for the various mailing lists and websites that potential marriage partners used. Constable's participants in this sense resembled Slater's online sexpics traders, since each group develops a form of online sociality appropriate to its own goals without drawing upon generalized ideas of what an online forum should or could be. As Constable (2003) says, "On all the lists, men policed and criticized one another openly." Constable's participants have a somewhat different focus, however, in the very strong pertinence that national governance regimes relating to citizenship and international mobility have for their purposes, and much of their online activity was focused toward negotiating these regimes.

The internet activities of Constable's participants were not subject to national governance as such, but, to the extent that some day they hoped to meet up with one another, the potential marriage partners had to pay attention to immigration and citizenship legislation. Their activities oriented to, but posed no challenge to, national governance. Some forms of internet activity can be particularly difficult for formal regimes of governance to address, however, and can be more challenging to the status quo. Guobin Yang (2006) describes such a situation in the case of political activity on the internet in China. He diagnoses a rise in informational politics, which crosses between online and offline. China has both a highly regulated internet and high levels of political activism via the internet. The emergent conventions of internet use by political activists both respond to and challenge official structures of governance. The uses made of the internet by political activists to spread information between people and between digital and conventional mass media, and the specific ways in which this is achieved in "fluid, episodic and emergent" fashion, are particularly resistant to state control. It is partly because the internet networks of political communication are linked into offline networks and yet also spread internationally that they both have an influence on domestic governance and evade its control.

Viewed from this perspective, it appears that the self-regulation of internet activities and the attempts by governments to regulate aspects of behavior in cyberspace both often need to be viewed as contextual phenomena that interweave online and offline frames of reference. The recent ethnographic studies described above find that meaning-making spans online and offline, and that frequently the appropriate standards of behavior are judged by participants and onlookers alike according to frames that are not confined to the online realm. I began this chapter with a focus on emergent conventions for internet usage, suggesting that we need to look not simply at formal regulatory structures but also at the way in which users of the internet work with structures and expectations in practice in order to regulate their own behavior. The relevant structures and expectations may be drawn from diverse contexts in a dynamic and flexible fashion. In the remainder of this section I pursue this perspective, considering the ways in which one group of users has claimed the internet and made it its own and describing the origins of the forms of self-regulation that this group has come to practice in its online activities.

By contrast with the self-regulation of internet-specific social formations such as online communities, a very different form of regulation is created by the interweaving of virtual and material in the creation of sets of communication practices that are crafted to match the concerns of a particular group with a prior offline existence. An example that I have been examining recently is the use of the internet by biologists engaged in the discipline of systematics, responsible for the classification and naming of organisms (Hine, 2007, 2008). Internet use in this discipline can best be understood, I would argue, as part of a complex communication ecology, and as being made meaningful through an existing material culture, set of institutional arrangements and political context. Although how to use the internet is a frequent topic of debate in this field, it would be perverse to talk about regulating or governing the internet as a separate domain from the rest of the discipline's activities. The internet is seen largely as another conduit through which to conduct the discipline's business, and, as such, much of the effort has been directed toward incorporating the internet into the existing structures of governance and self-regulation.

The most obvious aspect of systematics that is subject to governance is nomenclature. Sets of nomenclatural codes specific to each major group of organisms have been in operation since the nineteenth century, to regulate nomenclatural processes. These nomenclatural codes dictate the steps that must be taken to ensure that a name has been validly published, and provide rules for the resolution of conflicts when more than one name has been published for the same group of organisms (while also allowing for differences of classificatory opinion). The nomenclatural codes aim to ensure the stability of names through the principle of priority, which dictates that the earliest published name for a particular taxon will take precedence. Should the same taxon be described subsequently under a different name, that name will be held to be a junior synonym. The starting point for the priority rule varies between groups. For plants, the starting point for priority is *Species Plantarum*, published by Carl Linnaeus in 1753. In the context of the nomenclatural codes, then, the qualities of the internet have been interpreted through the lens of the discipline's orientations toward its past. There is an understandable concern about the durability of a medium that has been around for only a few years. The key focus for the particular form of regulation enacted in nomenclatural codes has been to ensure that modes of publication of new names are sufficiently durable to match up with the eighteenth-century publications that systematists still use.

Although systematists have taken readily to the use of e-mail and websites for much of their routine communication, using the internet for the formal publication of names has taken much longer to become accepted. The revision of the International Code of Zoological Nomenclature published in 2000 opened up the possibility of new names being validly published electronically, including via the internet. Publication was to be considered valid, however, only if five identical copies of the electronic publication were to be made and lodged in five different libraries. The authors of the code were troubled by the possibility that electronic publications might not endure for a long time and also that many forms of electronic publication were amenable to constant updating. Requiring the lodging of identical material copies in libraries was their way to permit the use of a medium that both systematists themselves and their users were increasingly keen to deploy, while retaining the fundamentals of the nomenclatural code intact.

As viewed from the historically sensitized perspective of the nomenclatural codes, then, the problem with the internet was its ephemerality. Rules were introduced to supplement the internet with other more durable media in order to meet the rigorous demands for enduring availability. This is not to say, however, that systematists always think of the internet as an ephemeral medium. In a different context, there are concerns that the medium might also be too real. This specific point refers to the growing practice of making databases of specimens available on the internet. There has been considerable political pressure for systematists to overcome geographic inequalities by making information available electronically. Substantial efforts have been focused on making the catalogues of specimen collections available online, and on developing large-scale publicly available repositories of biodiversity information. One fear that this practice raises relates to the risk of making accessible what should otherwise be confined to expert gaze. The paper sheets on which herbarium specimens are mounted have traditionally been used by experts reviewing the specimens to make their own annotations. The possibility of making all this information available online raises concerns that it might cause additional confusion, especially when annotations included new names not validly published elsewhere. Another concern about the powers of online information relates to the fear that unscrupulous collectors might be able to use specimen records to locate the sites where rare species are growing. The lack of control over audience forms one of the key regulatory fears of systematists, even while placing information online for wide audiences is one of the key political pressures on the field at present.

Yet another way in which internet activities are regulated with an eye to the wider concerns of the discipline relates to the use of online discussion forums. There is a discipline-wide mailing list, which is used as a forum for discussion of topical issues and as a venue for announcements. Throughout my research I drew on this list to keep abreast of the concerns of the discipline. I also conducted online interviews with participants to find out how they viewed its status, and how they felt about the messages they read and the contributions they themselves made. It emerged that many users of this list were quite conscious that this list provided a public forum in which reputations were at stake, and regulated their contributions accordingly. It was felt by many that, despite the easy-going nature of online communication, many of the conventions and the inequalities that prevailed in the discipline at large were also relevant in the online setting. Far from being a discrete social sphere, the mailing list was experienced as a place where the discipline was enacted. The list did have its own norms of behavior, and some sense of its own culture. It was very much viewed as a disciplinary forum continuous with the rest of the discipline, however. There was little formal regulation of list content, but users were highly conscious of the need to self-regulate.

A final sense in which there has been self-regulation of internet usage relates to the institutional perspective. There is a considerable political pressure on systematists to be seen to modernize, and to respond to global concerns with biodiversity conservation by making information accessible in a timely fashion. Individual institutions are held accountable for their use of the internet by funding bodies and governments. In signing the 1992 Convention on Biological Diversity, national governments committed themselves to sharing relevant information with other signatories. As a part of this commitment, national governments have in turn reviewed the activities of the institutions that generate and curate the information. In the United Kingdom, a House of Lords Select Committee on Science and Technology reviewed the state of the discipline in relation to the country's responsibilities under the Convention on Biological Diversity (Select Committee on Science and Technology, 2002). There was considerable discussion of internet activities, focusing explicitly on their practical advantages and on their symbolic qualities in demonstrating the discipline's willingness to modernize. Systematics institutions are consequently conscious that internet activities have a significance that exceeds the online domain. Internet activities do not remain online, but are packaged and re-presented for other audiences as evidence of appropriate kinds of engagement with contemporary concerns.

It is clear, then, that, for the systematics community, the internet is not an autonomous domain but forms an intrinsic part of disciplinary identity and the continuing efforts to maintain the discipline's status and fundability. At the same time, there is continual reference to core concerns, such as the stability of nomenclature and the fear that transfer to the internet might threaten the integrity of established systems. Political pressures to innovate are balanced against concerns to maintain valued aspects of existing forms of regulation. Self-regulation is manifested both at the level of institutions concerned to maintain appropriate kinds of internet activity and at the individual level of systematists concerned to use the internet in ways that enhance rather than damaging reputation.

In the context of the sexpics trading described by Slater (2002), the maintenance of an ethical social order was a constant topic and obsession for those participating. In systematics, the coming of the internet has provided a reflexive opportunity across the discipline, to discuss not only appropriate ways of publishing information but also deeper issues of the responsibilities of the discipline, the political conditions within which it finds itself operating and the nature of its audiences. Discussing what ought to be done in the face of the new medium has become a wide-ranging reflexive opportunity in which many systematists have participated, and all the major systematics institutions have felt obliged to engage. Frames of reference for judging appropriate activities are highly variable, spanning from the conventions of a particular mailing list to the concerns of global politics. Although in some cases the outcomes do fit quite closely with previous structures of regulation, such as the nomenclatural codes, in other instances the emergent practice is less predictable from past experience.

It is not clear in advance, therefore, what qualities any particular community will see in the internet, nor how it will choose to exploit them. The emergent conventions of use draw variably on a range of concerns, including the need to project desirable identities both in the detail of one's use and in being seen to use the technology in appropriate ways. Particular aspects of culture and history may predispose communities toward seeing their own versions of the promise and perils of the internet, and they will also develop highly specific forms of governance to address the situation that they encounter. This perspective aligns with the position on internet governance described by Thomas Malaby (2006). In his introduction to a special issue of *First Monday* focusing on internet governance, he suggests that it needs to be viewed as a process rather than a set of rules, and that this perspective should entail "a recognition that contingency is always a factor for actors as they seek to apply existing practices to new circumstances."

12.4 Conclusion

Studies of online communities suggest that the internet is far from viewed by its users as standing in need of a strong regulatory influence from nation states or international bodies. The distinctive sets of norms and diverse resources for self-regulation that online groups have deployed suggest, rather, that users have been able to develop for themselves such regulatory influences as they need to keep their online experiences fruitful and enjoyable. Although some forms of user-centric (Dutton and Peltu, 2007) governance issues, such as spam or fraud, remain less amenable to community-based self-regulation, the broad issue of unacceptable behavior is one that autonomous online communities have tackled repeatedly. The resources available to online communities to police unacceptable behavior include social means such as chastising or flaming wrongdoers and developing overt codes of conduct, technical responses that delete inappropriate material and exclude offenders, and appeals to offline authorities or legislation. Online self-regulation is mature and often highly effective, though it can be problematic for state governance when the online orthodoxy transgresses offline norms and legal frameworks.

Although online communities may provide a strong case for the self-regulatory capacities of the internet, it is important to be aware, however, that this model encompasses only a small part of the internet experience. Many internet users are not part of such sustained social formations, and their internet use becomes meaningful through its embedding within other aspects of their lives. As described in section 12.3, internet activities can form a part of complex social dynamics, and the model of the autonomous online community can be rather misleading for understanding the ways in which groups with an offline identity or referent self-regulate. The systematists whom I describe participate in some activities that might be described as online communities, and in these contexts they develop norms of behavior that are both specific to that online community and draw upon the wider norms of the discipline. Their efforts to use the internet as a medium for publishing new material are mediated through, on the one hand, the existing rules covering valid publication and, on the other, their understanding of the capacities and challenges posed by the internet. Use of the internet is to some extent regulated through existing frameworks, but the coming of the internet provides an opportunity for examining and reinterpreting those frameworks. It is an issue for debate and, often, controversy just how far, and in what circumstances, aspects of existing practice should transfer to the new domain of the internet.

The examples of ethnographic enquiry that I describe above make clear that the appropriate uses of the internet are not to be read from the technology alone. Nor are they to be read directly from the context of use, if by "context" we mean a particular online forum or offline social group, since the relevance of particular contexts is enacted in the moment and through the social dynamics of use by particular collectives. Socially sanctioned uses emerge dynamically, and this can lead to problems when social sanctioning processes do not come to the same conclusions: parents, for example, may be highly disturbed to find that the child they are attempting to save from self-harming has found a peer group on the internet that celebrates and encourages such actions. Conventions for internet use arise from the bottom up through particular circumstances of use, but the relevance of contexts for determining these conventions is also dynamically defined. Although sometimes the internet may be viewed as a relatively autonomous sphere, as may particular online communities within the internet, in other lights the internet can be seen as an embedded feature of contemporary society and continuous with quite different regulatory frameworks. The internet is both a cultural context in its own right and a cultural artifact (Hine, 2000). It is important, therefore, to consider not just the ways in which regulation arises within internet culture, but to examine also the assumptions about what the internet is and should be that inform our views of how it should be regulated.

Taking this point back to the issue of understanding the self-regulation of internet behavior, it is clear that it is misleading to aggregate "internet behavior" as if it were all one phenomenon, and that we cannot judge in advance which contexts will drive the judgments of users about unacceptable behavior and appropriate internet use. This makes it clear that it may be mistaken to speak of internet governance and regulation as if it were a thing unproblematically set apart from other forms of governance and regulation. In line with recent writings in sociology about technology, we can think of technologies as having a fluid quality (de Laet and Mol, 2000) that makes drawing their identities and boundaries problematic. Framing the issue in this way, it becomes relevant to ask what the object is that we plan to regulate. If, in everyday experience, the internet is not always marked out as a discrete object but is, instead, suffused with and embedded in the diverse concerns of everyday life, it becomes harder to make specific regimes of regulation and governance stick. National regimes of governance are made to adhere in large part through border controls, which ensure that all people know, for most practical purposes, when they are in a particular country and thus which regimes of governance and regulation concern them. Marking out a specific sphere of internet governance and regulation suggests the operation of similar border controls to ensure that everyone knows when he/she comes under that jurisdiction. Ethnographic evidence suggests that marking out the internet as an object of governance and regulation in this way goes against much of the commonplace experience of this technology. The experience of the internet is both more particular, in that each online community may have its own norms, and more diffuse, in that we often do not particularly think of "going on to the internet" when we send an e-mail, check a website or make an online purchase.

This is not to say, however, that the ambiguous nature of the internet and the multiple social formations that it enables and inhabits are to be managed away, or undermine the project of regulation altogether. Ethnographic evidence suggests that individuals and collectives seek to develop an ordering in their internet interactions as in other spheres of their lives. The apparent novelty of the internet, and its separation from more familiar forms of materiality and communication, provide an occasion for reflexive thinking. The systematics community that I studied have discussed how the internet could be used to further their goals in a way that sustained the principles that were important to them. In the process, they found that they were required to specify, often for the first time and in new ways, exactly what it was that they did and what their principles were. New technologies, and, in particular, technologies such as the internet that are viewed as somewhat challenging to the existing social order, provide an opportunity for quite wide-ranging reflection on goals, principles and practices. This reflexive opportunity is, I would suggest, one of the key strengths of the internet as far as regulation and governance are concerned. The interesting opportunity is to use our doubts about what and where the internet is to deepen debates about appropriate ways of ordering social life, and it would be a mistake to attempt to close down on that opportunity too quickly.

There is evidence that the reflexive opportunity offered by the ambiguity of the internet is not confined to discrete groups, such as the systematic community that I described. On the international stage it remains problematic to define exactly what internet governance should be and what the objects are that require to be governed (Hofmann, 2007). Don MacLean (2004a) describes the tendency in some circles to close down on issues of internet governance as relating specifically to the allocation of addresses and domain names. Opposing that tendency, he describes various efforts to open up debate around issues of development and equitable access to the internet in an inclusive information society. These conscious efforts to widen debate and to render the issue one of global politics have made available a space for a reflexive examination of prevailing inequalities. As Ralf Bendrath *et al.* (2007) suggest, the internet is the ultimate symbol of globalization, and it is as such that its coming has offered a chance to examine afresh and debate the role of the nation state and the prevailing inequalities between nations. Jeanette Hofmann (2007) argues that to make a claim about the "problem" of internet governance is also to make a preliminary decision about the institutions and actors that are to be involved. In recent developments she suggests that the debates around internet governance have become a domain for experimenting with ideas about democracy and the nation state. Whether or not there is anything inherent in the internet that has the power to transform the role of the state in social control, the levels of debate that it engenders may in themselves be transformative within global society.

13 The coordination of international civil society and uses of the internet

CHRISTOPHE AGUITON AND DOMINIQUE CARDON

13.1 Introduction

Which organizational solution is appropriate for the international coordination of multiple networks of associations, NGOs, trade unions, think tanks, social movements, etc. known as the "antiglobalization" or "global justice" movement? What kind of governance can a "network of networks" set up to support collective action while preserving the diversity of its components? The global justice movement has answered these questions with an original organizational innovation, the process of World Social Forums, initiated in January 2001. Every year, in Porto Alegre (Brazil), Mumbai, Nairobi and then Belém (Brazil), the WSF brings together thousands of participants in order to discuss and share different agendas of mobilization. Social forums are spaces open to hundreds of debates, seminars and workshops; they are theatres of meetings, confrontations and convergences between actors, incubators of international campaigns and mobilizations; and they are spaces of socialization, training and identity production.

In this chapter, we discuss the history of the changing organization of the WSF since its first incarnation in January 2001. We examine the organizational rules that have been created and the tools that were used in order to govern this heterogeneous coalition. The aim of this case study is thus to examine one of the many possible governance processes for international civil society. Even if there are many differences, the WSF process gives a few insights into possible organizational structures and decision-making-processes for the governance of information society. First, World Social Forums and internet governance institutions are two typical advanced examples of large and international network structures. Second, the resources offered by new technologies are not only tools of communication for the coordination of activists all over the world, they are also conceived as an organizational solution to design new ways of decision-making.

The constellation of WSF actors is exemplary of a large-scale network structure organized, from local to global level, by the coordination of thousands of individuals and groups with heterogeneous properties. This new form of international activism can be seen as a new way of producing a "global civil society," which appears to be largely different from the building of a civil society by international institutions, many of which have promoted different spaces around their activities for civil society organizations. These attempts to represent international civil society remain very controversial. The criteria of representation are unclear, participation in complex and esoteric debates gives the lead to the elite of civil society representatives and the role of the broader civil society in the decision-making remains very weak. These problems have been raised by many observers of civil society participation during the process of the World Summit on the Information Society.

In a very different way, the process of social forums creates an autonomous space in which the actors of the "global civil society" can interact without needing the legitimacy given by participation in international institutions processes. It builds a representation of the "global civil society" by the voluntary mobilization of various and multiple networks, but it does not claim to represent it. With no ambiguity, the "Charter of Porto Alegre,"[1] which has acquired a quasi-constitutional value in the "antiglobalization" world, ensures that "[t]he World Social Forum brings together and interlinks only organizations and movements of civil society from all the countries in the world, but it does not intend to be a body representing world civil society" (article 5). The global justice movement exists in the form of networks, and the movement itself exemplifies many features of the transformation of activism in recent years. Instead of hierarchical mass organizations led by delegates, these new movements/coalitions are built by the coordination of small groups that refuse delegation processes, specialize their objectives and prefer direct and symbolic action to representative politics. Even though there is a strong heterogeneity inside the global justice movement, central actors and leading figures are representative of this new form of activism; they are more flexible, more individualistic and more oriented toward international

[1] The World Social Forum Charter of Principles is available online at www.forumsocialmundial.org.br/main.php?id_menu=4&cd_language=2.

struggles. The governance system of WSF appears, in this way, as a good example of the new organizational form of large and internationally networked movements/coalitions.

In this chapter we focus on the governance of social forums, but this governance could probably not have been achieved without the preceding decade of encounters between movements and NGOs, during the forums organized around the United Nations summits or in the campaigns for debt cancellation and the Tobin tax, or mobilizations against the WTO, the World Bank, the IMF and the G8. Those encounters created a sort of informal network of people sharing the same concerns. All these networks of people with weak but regular relations often reached a sort of common agreement in their concerns, based not on formal discussions and bargaining but something more like a "background noise." For example, during the January 2001 WSF the "background noise" was a generalized anti-neoliberal sentiment, but specifically targeting the WTO and the international financial institutions (IFIs). During the 2002 WSF, however, which took place after September 11, 2001, the prevailing mood was against neoliberalism, but also against war and fundamentalism, and by 2003 the war on Iraq was the main preoccupation. This observation has also been described in other fields. For example, Anne-Marie Slaughter (2004) describes processes in the legal arena by which informal processes in the international arena generate similar domestic norms, as well as common practices and ethics.

In addition, the development of international networks of debate and mobilization, which has accelerated since the demonstrations against the WTO ministerial conference in Seattle in 1999, is particularly fertile ground for the emergence of innovative uses of communication tools, as well as a locus of original innovation. The people engaged in this "movement of movements" make extensive use of information and communication technologies and constitute a demand for advanced distance cooperation tools: open and cooperative online publication, content-sharing between sites, discussion lists with decision-making procedures, videoconference, tools for recording and synthesizing debates, etc. These needs are closely linked to the coordination constraints weighing on the actors. The use of communication tools is, furthermore, directly subjected to the cultural and political constraints specific to this type of network organization. A movement that claims to create a large public space in which the transparency of decision-making is guaranteed, that refuses the delegation of power to a specialized center, that establishes direct communication between its members and with the outside and that promotes linguistic diversity and a plurality of opinions has to incorporate these principles into the communication systems that it opts for. In the same way as for all the recent international campaigns and mobilizations, such as campaigns on debt and trade, the European march against unemployment or the Zapatista "intergalactic" encounters, ICTs were indispensable for organizing the WSF. Mailing lists and websites were used after the first WSF in 2001, but, at this stage, without real impact on the consensus-building process: the Brazilian organizing committee, in the case of the WSF, or the European Assembly, in the case of the European Social Forum (ESF), were the framework for organizing the forums and resolving conflicts and difficulties. Three elements gave more importance to the technical tools.

First, there was the radicalization of the "horizontality" in the social forum process: in 2005 the decision was made to build the whole programme from the bottom up. The necessity for collaborative tools became obvious, but a contradiction appeared between an internet based on people and the WSF process, based on movements and organizations. Online horizontal networks face two risks: reproducing hierarchical processes by allowing only "one" representative per movement or organization, or having to resolve endless miscomprehension if all members of movements are allowed to be part of the online networks. The first version of the website built for the ESF and the WSF tried to resolve this contradiction, but with a process that was too complex, and the social forums are still searching for the best way to resolve this problem.

Translation and respect for linguistic diversity were the tools of the second technological wave in the social forum process. Since the 2002 European Social Forum in Florence, an international network of volunteer interpreters, known as "Babels," have offered interpretation during the workshops and seminars, with the clear political objective of guaranteeing linguistic diversity and allowing grassroots movements to be part of such international gatherings. In parallel to Babels' involvement to the social forum processes, there were different attempts to develop technical tools to avoid the increasing costs of the interpretation equipment and to expand the number of languages available in the social forum rooms. All these attempts faced difficulties, but they were the starting point for a more general evolution of the conditions in which the social forums had to be organized. To give priority to local production and to cooperatives, to use only free software applications, to respect the environment and have a "waste-free" forum and to give priority to volunteer involvement and the solidarity/cooperative economy instead of commercial services became one of the challenges for the social forums as they tried to bridge the old contradiction between those who want to change the world through actions aimed at states and the global system and those who want to change the world through the transformation of practices and day-to-day life.

The third technological experience was developed for the organization of the "Global day of action," on January 26, 2008. This year, instead of a classical WSF, a day of action was proposed that would allow all movements and organizations to organize debates, demonstrations, symbolic actions, etc. This decentralized action required coordination between movements and a way to visualize the actions. A website was set up, with the particularity to be based on a world map on which every coalition, movement or organization could register and show its own actions. This tool gave worldwide visibility to all movements, including those in regions where the social forum process was quite weak, such as Siberia. This was a new way of expressing the horizontality of the process and to give a representation of the movement without any kind of delegation or hierarchy.

13.2 Network coordination principles

How can one build a collective actor identified by a stable public identity, organizational duration and strategic intentionality while preserving the basically heterogeneous and plural structure of its components? In order to explore the various configurations taken by the organization of social forums, we use a small analytical model in considering that they have to define common projects (represented by "P") respecting specific horizontal constraints (represented by "C"). To explain the dynamic of changes in the organizational process of the WSF, we assume that two different projects are co-present in the objectives of organizers: (P1) producing a common space; and (P2) enhancing the emergence of

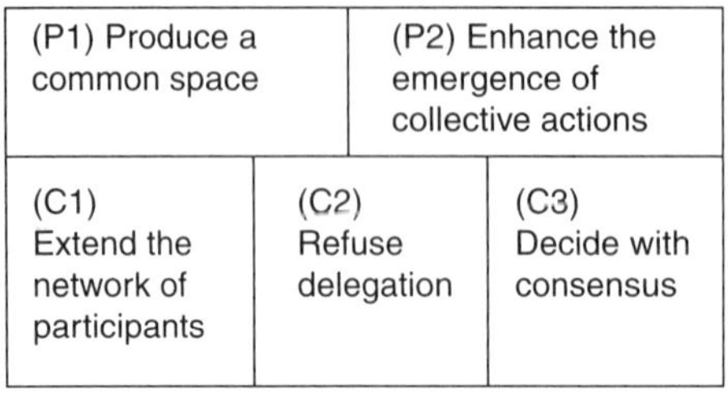

Figure 13.1 Projects and constraints for the organization of social forums.

collective actions. We also assume that they have to satisfy three constraints of horizontality: the extension of the network toward new actors (C1), the prohibition of delegation mechanisms (C2) and the adoption of consensus for all decision-making processes (C3). See Figure 13.1.[2]

Organizational choices made by organizers of the social forums have to respect these three constraints in order to avoid criticisms that they are not respecting the "Charter of Porto Alegre" and the principles of networks. Most of the time these three constraints are closely interlinked in the discourse of forum participants and critics. This abstract model can help us explain the dynamic transformation of the organizational structures of the World Social Forum, however. The first feature that can be highlighted with this model is the indisputably dual nature of the WSF project. The prime objective of social forums is indeed to produce a common and plural space of encounter between heterogeneous actors that have multiple, and sometimes contradictory, political agendas (P1). From this point of view, social forums constitute a framework open to the articulation of actors with different points of view. The socializing vocation of forums is the main feature here, and plurality is a central concern. Another objective is present in the building of the WSF, however, which is to define a place in which the strategy of collective mobilization can emerge (P2). From this point of view, social forums are places devoted to the building of new international mobilization.

These two objectives present in the building of the WSF – a space expressing diversity and a space for campaign-building – have created multiple tensions between actors. The WSF thus appears as the result of a compromise between the "strategic" tendencies of the global justice movement, which insists on the need for a collective coordination of

[2] For a more detailed explanation of this analytical model, see Aguiton and Cardon (2005).

mobilizations (P2), and the "pluralist" tendencies, which insist on diversity of vision and the socializing vocation of the forums (P1). Internal debates between these two representations of the aim of social forums have structured the transformation of how these forums are organized ever since their beginning. Actors often oppose the forum as a *space* (P1) and the forum as a *movement* (P2) (see Collective work, 2003). These two organizational projects do not present a great degree of originality in the repertory of international coordination structures, however. The aim of the first project (P1) is to give birth to a large international conference, while the second project (P2) tries to dress in new clothes the old idea of the international coalition of workers, socialists, anarchists or unionists (Löwy, 2004). This opposition between reformist and radical politics nevertheless remains too traditional and does not capture the specific effect of network structures on activist strategies. This is the reason why we need to consider these two projects with regard to the rules of self-limitation that those promoting the social forums have applied to themselves.

13.3 Three horizontal constraints

Achieving this double project meant respecting the network structure of the antiglobalization coordination movement. Three constraints of horizontality governing the organizational principles of the WSF have been enshrined in the "Charter of Porto Alegre." The first constraint (C1) is respect for the principle of diversity. Activists express their own diversity in various texts and internal declarations. In so doing, they claim an open forum in which everyone can participate, and are very conscious of the necessity of constantly extending the networks to new actors. The Charter of Principles states (article 1):

> The World Social Forum is an open meeting place for reflective thinking, democratic debate of ideas, formulation of proposals, free exchange of experiences and interlinking for effective action, by groups and movements of civil society that are opposed to neoliberalism and to domination of the world by capital and any form of imperialism, and are committed to building a planetary society directed towards fruitful relationships among Humankind and between it and the Earth.

World Social Forums claim to be an open space with no strong criteria in terms of selecting participants. The charter does not exclude anybody apartt from political parties and organizations that use or advocate violence.[3] It promises to preserve the diversity of the various interests, to support the internationalization of networks, to preserve the ideological disparity among actors and to maintain equality between "big" and "small" actors. Left-wing Marxist organizations, Christian associations, academics, professional NGOs, etc. are linked together in the forum coordination structure. It is easy to see why a network organization was chosen as the best solution for preserving diversity without promoting a central leadership.

The desire to expand the network and to respect the principle of diversity had an unexpected consequence: the creation of a large number of parallel forums, or even counter-forums, taking place during official forums. Some of these were set up by movements and organizations that are part of the official forums but that want to keep a certain level of autonomy and to have some visibility, such as the farmers from Via Campesina or the movements of unemployed and marginalized people. Other parallel forums have been organized by institutions that support the social forums but without having the "right" to be part of the official forums: a forum of Members of Parliament, a forum of local authorities, and so on. Finally, there are the counter-forums organized to express viewpoints other than the official forums: a more positive approach to political parties and armed struggle was expressed by the Mumbai Resistance 2004, and autonomous spaces were set up to reject the presence of mayors and political institutions in Paris in 2003 and in London in 2004. Despite the small distortions to the Charter of Principles and the possible ideological differences with the official forums, the "off" forums run parallel to the "on" increase in the importance and the impact of the WSF in the public spaces and the worldwide debates about neoliberal globalization.

The second horizontal constraint (C2) is the most visible and the most discussed. The founders of the WSF decided that the forum

[3] "The World Social Forum will always be a forum open to pluralism and to the diversity of activities and ways of engaging of the organizations and movements that decide to participate in it, as well as the diversity of genders, ethnicities, cultures, generations and physical capacities, providing they abide by this Charter of Principles. Neither party representations nor military organizations shall participate in the Forum. Government leaders and members of legislatures who accept the commitments of this Charter may be invited to participate in a personal capacity" (article 9).

should have no centre, and forbade anyone or any organization to speak in the name of the WSF. This prohibition has been expressed in article 6 of the "Charter of Porto Alegre":

> The meetings of the World Social Forum do not deliberate on behalf of the World Social Forum as a body. No-one, therefore, will be authorized, on behalf of any of the editions of the Forum, to express positions claiming to be those of all its participants. The participants in the Forum shall not be called on to take decisions as a body, whether by vote or acclamation, on declarations or proposals for action that would commit all, or the majority, of them and that propose to be taken as establishing positions of the Forum as a body. It thus does not constitute a locus of power to be disputed by the participants in its meetings, nor does it intend to constitute the only option for interrelation and action by the organizations and movements that participate in it.

This clause of self-limitation characterizes the essential properties of network organization. Nothing can be said or done in the name of the whole network. There is no centre place to struggle for. Actors can speak only in their own name or in the name of their organization. World Social Forums do not have a decision-making center, they do not have a spokesperson and they do not sign any text or declaration. Actors can do no more than express their ideological and strategic diversity. This constraint does generate many tensions inside the movement, however. For many organizations, participating in the social forum is a way to build a common agenda of actions and mobilizations, and for this reason they have set up the Assembly of Social Movements inside the forums, which has generated much controversy.

The third horizontal constraint (C3) emerges from the tension between the project of creating a common space while preserving the openness and diversity of the movement. The only decision-making process that is allowed in this context is consensus. It appears at the outset as the only possible decision-making procedure to coordinate the organizations of various sizes, functions, internal organizations, and social and geographical origins. No criteria can be defined to differentiate the diversity of organizational forms and sizes. Each organization, whatever its structure, past, size, social object or political position (within the limits of the Charter of Principles), has potentially the same weight in the WSF decision process. Consensus does not mean unanimity, however. It identifies refusal more than adhesion. The participants must continue the discussion until they agree on one compromise and resolve, or limit, the opposition. Consensus-building appears to be a very peculiar political process in which the use of time, bargaining and negotiation are central features. It also creates a specific culture of discussion that is less oppositional and more subtle than debates in a majority context.

Consensus in itself is not a new technique for making decisions. Philippe Urfalino (2007) quotes several of the studies to show that it was used in most of the tribal systems and farming communities. The main reason why consensus was used in these societies is that they had to face problems that affected them in a similar way, even if their living conditions were slightly different. Facing a drought or an invasion, it is reasonable to believe that one solution might be the best, and that it might be possible to reach this conclusion by a long discussion with people who have perhaps experienced the same situation (for example, the Council of Ancients, set up in France under the Directory in the late eighteenth century) deciding by consensus. Clearly, the consensus we are talking about in this chapter is very different. It is a consensus between very heterogeneous bodies – heterogeneous in terms of their size, their topic, their form of organization, their cultural background, etc. In both cases, consensus is not unanimity. Urfalino explains that a consensus does not require the agreement of all, but the assent of the reluctant. The "modern" consensus is more a veto right rather than a positive implication, and the weight of the veto is related to the "power" of those who use it. Instead of being a way of finding the best solution to resolve a problem, the consensus in this kind of arena is very often a package deal.

After experiencing multiple organizational forms, the organizers of the WSF decided for self-organization in preference to centrality. In the following section, we illustrate the different organizational choices that have been made in different periods of the social forum's history. We briefly distinguish a chronology of three different organizational structures: (1) the hierarchical governance of the historical founders; (2) the Assembly of Social Movements; and, lastly, (3) a self-organized process for decision-making. The evolutionary trajectory from each of these different organizational models to the next was driven by an upsurge of criticism as to the way forums are organized and led. In the next section, we explain the choice of self-organization by the proprieties of network structures (autonomy, diversity, heterogeneity and decentralization). We examine the changing role of the

International Council (IC) and the structure of the WSF's coordination between 2001 and 2005. One of the most important changes is the transformation of the scheduling of forum activities. The program of WSF is no longer defined by the International Council but by the participants using a self-organized declaration system on the internet. The role of the International Council is becoming mainly procedural. It serves to encourage coordination between actors, to organize the keeping of records of the events that occurred during forums and to design coordination tools for the participants.

13.4 Co-optation and assembly models

The organizational structure of the WSF has undergone many radical changes in five years. In a trial and error process, actors have experimented with different institutional solutions. In this section, we briefly describe two institutional structures that were chosen in the early years of the WSF and the ESF in order to decide the organization and the schedule of social forums. These two organizational forms received much criticism, however, because they did not accord with the main constraints of network organization. This is the reason why the transformation of WSF structure, which we discuss in the next section, was decided for the fifth meeting of the WSF, in January 2005.

13.4.1 The model of co-optation

The first institutional model that was chosen by the promoters of the WSF is a closed structure of governance whose recruitment is carried out by co-optation. The initiative for establishing the World Social Forum was taken by a small network of actors. Initiated by Oded Grajew, coordinator of a Brazilian association of small companies (CIVES), and Francisco Whitaker, executive secretary of the Justice and Peace Commission of the Brazilian episcopate (CBJP), after a discussion with Bernard Cassen, president of the Association for the Taxation of financial Transactions for the Aid of Citizens (ATTAC) and director of the French newspaper *Le Monde Diplomatique*, the first idea for the WSF belonged to a few individuals linked by long-standing personal relationships (Cassen, 2003). The first governing body of the WSF, the Brazilian Organization Committee (BOC), which was set up in Porto Alegre in January 2001, gathered together eight organizations. Six of them were "small" but influential NGOs (ABONG, IBASE, CJG, ATTAC-Brazil, CBJP and CIVES), the other two were mass organizations: the trade union CUT (Central Ùnica Trabalhadores) and the movement of landless peasants (MST – Movimento Trabalhadores rurais sem Terra). The BOC organized the first WSF and appeared as the hierarchical center of the event. The founders deliberately refused to widen their representativeness by internationalizing the composition of their group (Cassen, 2003). They assumed responsibility for all decisions, defined the architecture of the event, selected the issues for debates and invited the speakers.

World Social Forums can be compared to a huge conference attended, in 2004, by some 100,000 people around forty-eight plenary sessions and over 1,200 self-organized seminars and workshops. In this context, public speaking is governed by a number of constraints. In order to be open to all the possibilities of expression, a three-level architecture has been defined, with plenary meetings (twenty-eight, for example, in 2002), seminars (100) and workshops (700), all concentrated into four days. In the first period of the WSF, the programs for plenary sessions and seminars were decided by the BOC. Conversely, in a bottom-up process, workshops were self-organized activities suggested by one or more organizations – a choice that is never disputed provided the participants adhere to the "Charter of Porto Alegre." The organization of debates is also markedly different in the plenary sessions and in seminar/workshop sessions (Agrikoliansky and Cardon, 2005). The plenary sessions reproduce the form of the meeting or the academic conference: eight speakers address large rooms containing several thousand people, under the authority of a chair. On the other hand, seminars and workshops assemble a smaller number of participants in small rooms and are open to a large variety of speech situations: free discussions with the room, participative exercises, reflexive seminars, etc. During the first three meetings of the WSF, which mixed centralized programming and self-organized proposals, the first process focused all the attention onto the organizers. It benefited from the majority of the resources available at each forum (rooms, translation, communication), and, consequently, the plenary session themes were considered as the choice of WSF organizers.

Criticism regarding the control exerted by the co-opted network of the founders arose very quickly, however. The hierarchical domination of the BOC was denounced because it clashed with the constraint of openness (C1). Some denounced its "occult," opaque and abstract power, characterized by selective preferences, coalitions of actors reserving key resources for themselves (speaking time and visibility in particular), the personalization of central figures, etc. These complaints underlined the lack of legitimacy of the core Brazilian founders, all of whom were men, white, relatively old and intellectual (N. Klein, 2002). This form of central governance appeared inappropriate in part because it did not fit with the claim to be changing the culture of politics in WSF. An interview with Susan George, a young Argentinean activist, underlines this contradiction: "To have a 'secretariat' of a network is the opposite of having a network. This could lead to struggles for power, struggles which could end up destroying the existing networks. Instead, the Forum should offer economic and technical support for the network to actually happen rather than try to centralise or give the network a voice or a space, a location" (Adamovsky and George, 2004).

In order to democratize the governing of the WSF, an International Council was created in June 2001 after the first forum. Even if it allowed an internationalization of the organizing center of the forum and a real widening of the movements represented, its composition was the result of co-optation. Gradually, the IC has acquired the legitimacy to behave as the main decision-making structure of the WSF. In February 2003 it included 113 organizations, and by 2011 this number had risen to 162. The progressive opening of the IC to new members has contributed to a democratization of the government of the WSF, but it has not brought any resolution to the problem of its extremely elitist character. Small organizations encounter difficulties integrating into the IC if they do not have strong links with the historical founders. Heikki Patomäki and Teivo Teivanen's (2004) estimates, that around 120 people are influential in the IC, and that 1,000 to 2,000 people take part in the collective discussions but do not have a real influence on the decisions, remain by and large valid today.

The first round of WSF meetings have also been criticized with a second line of argument, linked to the second constraint of horizontality (C2). The issue was not the closing of the organizational center but the prohibition from speaking on behalf of the World Social Forum. During social forums the Assembly of Social Movements, which is one event among others, benefits from a high profile because it gathers together some central actors of the global justice movement. Participants in this assembly sign a declaration at the end of their meetings called the "Declaration of the Assembly of Social Movements." Sometimes, however, this declaration has been treated by some journalists and interpreters of the WSF as though it were "the declaration of the WSF." This interpretation has created a lot of tension between actors of the movement in confronting the two original projects of social forums: (P1) versus (P2). Defenders of the concept of the forum as a *space* strongly denounce the idea that the forum could appear as a *movement*. "If we do transform the Forum into a Movement," writes Chico Whitaker (2004), "we will be – without any help at all from those we are fighting against – throwing away a powerful instrument of struggle that we have been able to create by drawing on the most important instrument of struggle that we have been able to create by drawing on the most recent political discovery, of the power of open, free, horizontal structures." This debate, opposing plurality to collective mobilization, has been profoundly changed by the subsequent evolution in the structure of the WSF.

13.4.2 *The assembly model*

From the start the organization of the European Social Forum has been very different from that of the WSF. The government of the ESF belongs to a large and open assembly, the European Preparatory Assembly (EPA), in which every European organization can participate. This large and democratic open structure has created a very specific mode of coordination and discussion for the actors of the movement. In this way, the EAP generalizes and extends the system of coordination set up by the International Council, by ensuring greater accessibility and by widening the scope and the perimeter of participation in social forum processes. Decisions are made there by the consensus of those present, which, at least theoretically, gives an equal voice to each participant and generates debates that are often long and exhaustive. Setting up an assembly in a network universe sometimes appears difficult and contradictory, however. On average, the EAP gathers between 200 and 250 organizations, from the Catholic charity Caritas to the French Communist trade union, the CGT (Confédération Générale du Travail), the Human Rights League and any kind of local group or collective such as Babels, the network of voluntary translators and interpreters. In this context, it can be very difficult to form a consensus even if this decision-making process constrains the actors to endorse cooperative attitudes. Many procedural techniques of discussion are used during debates, and this style of discussion appears to many actors as a kind of "bureaucratic participation" (Callinicos, 2004).

Respecting the third constraint of horizontality, achieving consensus (C3), raises many new difficulties. Observations carried out during the preparation of the ESF held in Paris – Saint Denis (2003) showed how the construction of the program had exhausted the time and the energy of the actors: competition between organizations to impose their theme, seminar titles being extended in order to satisfy everyone, the "tyranny" of small actors imposing their agenda, complex quota systems to ensure the representation of various nationalities, etc. Building the program absorbed the energies of the organizers. The complexity of entering into this network style of collective discussion gave the impression of a bureaucratization of the participative process. This organizational form has been regarded as a "participative bureaucracy" as a result of the conflict between the logic of representation and the need for a consensual and open coordination between movements.

To understand how this "participative bureaucracy" arose, we need to understand how the ESF is organized. Two key structures ensure the management of the European Social Forum process: the European Preparatory Assembly, in charge of the program, the methodology and the main orientations of the process, with three sessions a year; and the National Organisational Committee, in charge of the practical organization of the forum. Both are open but, in practice, they are animated by a relatively small group of organizations. The national committees have a different composition depending on the country where the forum takes place, but usually they have a core group of fewer than ten organizations. The EPA is larger, but strong influence is exerted by the organizations that are able to follow all the sessions, plus the subcommittees, in particular the Program Commission. Most of these organizations come from the countries that have the largest participation in the World and European Social Forums: Italy, France and, to a lesser extent, Greece and Belgium. New participants in the ESF process can therefore have the impression of facing a "participative bureaucracy," for three main reasons: the constraints resulting from honoring the requirement for consensus in an open space; the weight of the historically core group of organizations, in particular from France and Italy; and the complexity of the "negotiations" between the EPA and the national committees, which have to deal with their own national realities.

13.5 The agglutination process

During a meeting in Perugia in April 2004, the International Council of the WSF decided to address the critics of the verticality of the plenary sessions and radically change the organizational form of the fifth WSF (held at Porto Alegre between January 26 and 30, 2005). The model of organization developed by the IC members gave up on the principle of selection "by the top" of the themes and speakers for the plenary meetings, these being purely and simply removed, and delegated the entire scheduling of forum activities to the participants. In doing this, the IC relinquished its decision-making power in terms of the definition of the issues of the forum. Thus it profoundly modified the legitimacy of the organizational center of the WSF and the role of the International Council.

Going by the name of "agglutination process," a methodology of expression and aggregation in several phases for proposals of activities for the forum was initiated. Even if many alternative solutions have been organized for those who do not have access to the network, the internet is the main actor in this new process. In May and June 2004 an internet questionnaire was addressed to the 4,000 or so organizations that had already taken part in social forums, in order to collect the issues that seemed of priority to them, those on which they wished to intervene and the types of mobilization in which they were engaged or wished to engage. From a lexicographical analysis of the 1,800 answers obtained during this consultation, eleven "grounds" ("Common goods," "Economic sovereignty," "Human rights and dignity," etc.) were defined by the Methodology Commission of the IC. From July to October 2004 2,557 proposals of activity (seminar, workshop, dialogue table, etc.) were recorded by the organizations on the WSF's website. Each organization declared to which "ground" it chose to be "agglutinated" and if it agreed to join or merge with other proposals. The information-processing system offered lists of discussions and mapping tools to facilitate possible cooperation and the agglutination of proposals.[4] Organizations proposing events could decide: (1) to organize their event alone; (2) "to agglutinate" with a similar proposal; (3) to dialogue with another event by sending a representative to another seminar; (4) to organize a sequence of events in order to build a collective dynamic (seminar of discussion > meeting of proposal of alternatives > convergence toward a platform of mobilization); or, finally, (5) to take part in the daily meetings of each "agglutination" every evening between 6 p.m. and 8 p.m. This agglutination process aimed to facilitate interlinking between actors and to encourage the building of collective mobilization.

The spirit of the process of agglutination combined the claims for open participation and the mistrust of delegation and centralization that characterize the new culture of politics emerging in the antiglobalization movement. Using a blend of fluidity and tools available on the internet, it maximizes the constraint of horizontality to which the building of the social forum must conform to reduce criticism. Self-organized processes facilitate the extension of the network of actors and intensify their links while enhancing articulation between participants. At the same time it contributes to the proceduralization of the governance of forums. The main role of the International Council, the organizing center of the WSF, has been redefined in this new self-organization model, and it consists of the facilitation of dialogue and the keeping of records of the debates and events. Substantive discussions are relatively rare in IC meetings, at which debates are mainly practical, on topics such as the location of the next forum, procedures for opening up to new members, relations with the other continental, national or local forums, the organization of the annual event, etc. With the new organizational model, the IC must privilege its functions of animation over strategy. It must help to "help the network work" by providing a reflexive function for the various actors, by giving visibility to the points of convergence between actors and by constituting an organizational memory (Dedeurwaerde, 2004). It is precisely in this direction that the recent initiatives taken by the organizers of the European and World Social Forums are directed.

[4] The website proposing a dynamic cartography of the networks of agglutinations is www.portoalegre2005.info.

13.6 Conclusion

The experience of the World Social Forum shows not only the extension of horizontality and the evolutionary path to a procedural role for the decision-making bodies but also the relative instability of this kind of governance, which is related to the necessary tension between the construction of a common space and the development of collective action. In this chapter we have seen how this tension was used, through the constraints of enlargement, an absence of delegation and insisting on consensus, in connection with the decision-making process. The mobilization of arguments criticizing the different kinds of decision-making structures has maintained this tension, however. In recent years, when the fields of common action at the world level have been less clear than they were in the period between Seattle in 1999 and the campaign against the invasion of Iraq in 2003, the risk has been that the social forums would simply become open spaces and lose their mobilization capacities. The animators of the forums have mobilized their imagination in order to maintain the "mobilization spirit" and the positive tension between open space and mobilization.

For the 2009 World Social Forum, held in Belém, in the Amazon region of Brazil, it was decided to reorganize the agenda. The first day was reserved to pan-Amazonian issues, under the responsibility of the movements coming form the broad Amazon region. The second and third days were devoted to all the self-organized seminars and workshops, and on the fourth and final days "convergence assemblies" took place, on specific themes, in order to help the different groups and movements to set up an agenda of action for the future. Twenty-four such assemblies were organized, on topics such as women, climate change, social justice, the sciences and democracy. This new organizational setting gathered the two opposite conceptions of the forum as a common space and as a mobilization tool. No one was obliged to join a specific assembly, and, if the divergences between movements were too great to organize a common meeting, provision was made for two – or more – parallel assemblies to be held. In practice, this happened only once. The process was seen as a success, and the same kind of agenda was set up for the 2011 World Social Forum, which was held in Dakar, Senegal.

If we enlarge this approach, we can say that this instability is consistent with the growth of the "governance by project mode," which is well known in management circles (Boltanski and Chiapello, 2006), in this phase of globalization, as opposed to relying on more stable and long-term programs. The project mode fits badly with the requirement for stability for international frames that are supposed to last for a long period of time, which translates into a need for clear rules and formal legitimacy. The strength of the social forums is their capacity to renew their shape and reform themselves perpetually, as Boaventura de Sousa Santos (2008) has noted in his studies on the WSF. The inclusiveness of both social forums and internet governance bodies and their capacity to modify their structures readily is appropriate for the speed of transformations in their related areas and the short time span of project mode. They could provide good examples for other fields of action that are involved in the same kind of perpetual redefinition process.

PART IV

The Changing Nature of the Law: Coding, Contracting and Ruling

14 DRM at the intersection of copyright law and technology: a case study for regulation

SÉVERINE DUSOLLIER

14.1 Introduction

Digital rights management systems, based on cryptography or other technical means, have been developed in recent years to address the thorny issue of protecting and managing copyright in an electronic environment. DRM systems are now embedded in DVDs, in some musical CDs and in the online distribution of music, news, films and images. They aim to control the use of the work, for example by preventing access thereto by unauthorized persons, by preventing the making of a copy thereof, by allowing only the uses that have been paid for or by imposing the viewing or listening of the work on a specific device or in a determined region.

As soon as new technology has been invented that can enhance the effective exercise of copyright, the fear has arisen that a similar technology might be used to defeat the technical protection. The WIPO treaties of 1996[1] have thus enacted legal protection for the technical protection, and they have been followed by similar pieces of legislation in many countries, such as the United States[2] and the European Union.[3] The relevant pieces of legislation in these states, known as anti-circumvention provisions, prohibit the act of circumvention itself in connection with the DRM systems and the so-called

Research for this chapter was finished in 2006. As a result, it does not include information or sources after that date.

[1] WIPO Copyright Treaty, December 20, 1996, article 11, and WIPO Performances and Phonograms Treaty, December 20, 1996, article 18.

[2] Digital Millennium Copyright Act, Pub. L. no. 105–304, 112 Stat. 2860 (October 28, 1998).

[3] Directive 2001/29/EC of the European Parliament and of the Council of May 22, 2001, on the harmonization of certain aspects of copyright and related rights in the information society, *Official Journal of the European Communities*, June 22, 2001, L 167: 10–19.

preparatory activities (i.e. any act of distribution or manufacture of devices enabling or facilitating the circumvention). Section 14.2 of this chapter briefly explains the new copyright framework resulting from the development of DRM technologies and their protection by the anti-circumvention provisions.

These provisions constitute the most interesting battlefield between the traditional vision of copyright law and regulation by technology. DRM, as a technology, has noteworthy effects on copyright regulation. As is described in section 14.3, DRM systems, when applied to limiting access to controlling the use of some works, act as a technical norm regulating the use of an intellectual object, in a similar manner to the aims of copyright legal norms. The normative effect of DRM technologies is rather different from the normative effect of copyright law, however, both in terms of content and in terms of nature. I then proceed to address these differences and qualify the affirmation that, as far as DRM systems and anti-circumvention laws are concerned, "code is law" (Lessig, 1999b).

On the other hand, DRM technologies tend to dictate the very design of copyright law to lawmakers. Section 14.4 explains how the scope of copyright is no longer decided according to what its proper scope should be but according to what the technology can do. The definition of the technical devices protected against circumvention systematically refers not to the exclusive rights of the copyright owner but to what the copyright owner is able to protect through technology. This brand new scope for copyright protection is not even restricted by any limitations, exceptions or fair use provisions. The legitimacy, under copyright law, of making a private copy, a parody, a criticism, an educational use or a research use does not matter as soon as a technical mechanism is able to inhibit such use or copy of the work. Any use of a work therefore enters, through the legal prohibition of the circumvention of a DRM system, into the arena of control granted to copyright holders.

Consequently, the ambiguous relationship between DRM and copyright is a particularly interesting case study for regulation. DRM systems can be both a new norm, parallel to that of copyright law, regulating access to and the use of copyrighted works, and the source for the copyright regulation itself. Technology is a complement that does not completely achieve the wholeness of copyright law, but it could also be a substitute, likely to make copyright law completely irrelevant. This chapter aims to describe this twofold action of the technology into copyright norms, and concludes that there is an urgent need for copyright law to resume its proper role.[4]

14.2 Copyright protected and managed by technology

The digital age has undoubtedly given rise to new threats to copyright protection. Technology can also be seen, however, as providing new tools and means for protecting copyrighted works in the digital environment. Technological solutions and aids have been devised very rapidly by the copyright industry. "The answer to the machine is in the machine," predicted Charles Clark in the mid-1990s (Clark, 1996). To repair the legal fence that copyright used to provide for protecting works, a fence that began to collapse under the assaults of the digital world, rights owners considered erecting a stronger and more effective technical fence.

Nowadays the technical protection of copyright is no longer a prediction or a dream, and many copyrighted works are distributed in a protected format: musical CDs used to embed anti-copy mechanisms, DVDs contain a complex technical protection that prevents copying or playing on unauthorized devices or that ensure a geographical distribution of the films, and e-books cannot be copied, modified or used in certain ways. The legal online provision of music or films is aided by intricate functionalities that inhibit some uses, such as redistribution of the work in peer-to-peer networks, the transmission of protected content outside a specifically defined user domain or the making of multiple copies. There are many other examples of the irruption of technological measures into the diffusion of copyrighted works, products and services, from music to films, from e-books to software.

Some technological measures aim to manage the licensing of usage rights and the provision of works in accordance with such usage rules: they are called digital rights management technologies. Such systems identify and describe the intellectual property rights pertaining to digital content and technically apply and enforce any usage restrictions decided by the rights holders as to such content. The success of the DRM terminology resulted in its use to name all technology

[4] This chapter is taken in part from the thesis I have published about the consequences of the DRM protection of copyrighted works for the copyright regime and principles (Dusollier, 2005).

protecting copyright content, from access control mechanisms, which manage a user's access to works, to anti-copy technologies, which implement a prohibition or limitation on the copying of content. In this chapter, the term "DRM" is used to cover any technological measure that intervenes in the protection of a copyrighted work, either by prohibiting some acts of use or by automatically enforcing and managing the usage rules related to such work. I also refer to technological measures, which is the terminology used by anti-circumvention provisions.

Along with the development of DRM systems to protect copyright, copyright holders have asked for the legal protection of such technical aids and barriers. Technology can be defeated by other technology, as was proven by the early hacking of the DVD protection system and of many other DRM systems. Laws have been enacted to prohibit tampering with the technological measures protecting copyrighted works at the international and national levels. Such legal provisions prohibit the circumvention of the technical protection and the making of or distribution of devices that help or facilitate such circumvention. As I have written elsewhere (Dusollier, 1999), the aim of such legal recourse is to "electrify" the technical fence now surrounding and blocking access to copyrighted works. Building such a fence around works was not considered sufficient, and the fence builders (which is what copyright owners have become) begged for pain to be inflicted on those who still dared to cross the barrier.

The first international legislation that provides such protection was the WIPO treaties of 1996 on copyright and related rights, which require the states that ratify them to

> provide adequate legal protection and effective legal remedies against the circumvention of effective technological measures that are used by authors in connection with the exercise of their rights under this Treaty or the Berne Convention and that restrict acts, in respect of their works, which are not authorized by the authors concerned or permitted by law.

This mandate for the adequate protection of copyright-protecting technological measures has been complied with by the United States, in the form of its Digital Millennium Copyright Act of 1998, and by the European Union, in a directive on copyright and related rights in the information society of 2001 (the "Copyright Directive"). This directive has now been implemented in all EU member states.

Roughly described, anti-circumvention provisions make it illegal to circumvent a technological measure protecting copyright or to make or traffic in tools or devices that could help or facilitate circumvention. In both legal texts, a tool or device is deemed to be illegal when it is promoted, advertised or marketed for the purpose of circumvention, or has only a limited commercially significant purpose or use other than to circumvent or is primarily designed, produced, adapted or performed for the purpose of enabling or facilitating the circumvention of any effective technological measures. The manufacture, import, distribution, sale, rental, advertisement for sale or rental, or possession for commercial purposes of such unlawful means is prohibited.

In the United States, the technological measures to be protected against circumvention are of two kinds. On the one hand, it is prohibited to circumvent or to traffic in devices that aim to circumvent technological measures that effectively control access to copyrighted works. On the other hand, as far as technology measures that effectively protect a right of the copyright owner (i.e. the right to copy, to display, to perform, to distribute or to communicate the work) are concerned, only the distribution of circumvention devices is deemed to be unlawful. In the European Union, the technological measures to be protected by such new provisions are broadly defined as "any technology, device or component that, in the normal course of its operation, is designed to prevent or restrict acts, in respect of works or other subject-matter, which are not authorized by the right-holder of any copyright or any right related to copyright" (article 6(3) of the Copyright Directive).

The issues raised by those anti-circumvention provisions are many. The main effect of the use of technology in the protection of copyright and the further intervention of the law to protect this technical aid is to multiply the layers of monopoly enveloping the copyrighted work. Henceforth a piece of music or an audiovisual work is subject to three cumulative layers of protection. The first – and traditional – one is its protection by the law of copyright or related rights, which grants to the author a defined power to control the use of his/her work. Second, the work can be protected by a technology that inhibits some uses thereof. This second layer of protection is, moreover, doubled by the law, through the anti-circumvention provisions, which forbid neutralizing or tampering with the technological protection. "Law – technology – law" has become the three-tiered protection scheme that can be applied to literary and artistic works. This threefold monopoly sets up new regulations into copyright, which I address now.

14.3 The regulation of copyright by technology

The reservation brought forward by the recourse to technology sets up a new kind of control over access to and the use of copyrighted works. The new layer of protection granted by DRM technology to copyrighted works such as music, films, documents and e-books has all the features of a regulative norm. It prevents users from carrying out some acts accessing and using works, thereby acting as a "code" regulating the enjoyment of artistic and literary works (section 14.3.1). This regulation by technology is not neutral, however, and brings about new norms applying to the enjoyment of artistic works (14.3.2). In addition, a technical norm of this type differs subtly from the copyright legal norm itself, and such differences imply considering the regulative power of the technology as somewhat relative and incomplete, albeit more extensive in some ways (14.3.3).

14.3.1 The regulative nature of the technological measure and the anti-circumvention provisions

Through the joint efforts of the three forces, the copyright owner enjoys a broader monopoly over the work: his/her exclusive rights are completed by the factual control granted by the technical aid and by the new remedies provided by the anti-circumvention provisions. Jean-Marc Mousseron and Michel Vivant (1989) have analyzed the different modes of control that one can have over an immaterial good. They call such control a "reservation," and draw a distinction between two major modes of reservation. First, reservation by a secret, or intellectual reservation, enables the intangible thing to be kept unknown by impeding or limiting its divulgation; second, economic reservation, or reservation by the market, divulges the work or invention while retaining some control over it, namely through the grant of an intellectual property right or of remedies sanctioning some behavior (as in the case of unfair competition practices). The history of IP has been one of the gradual granting of new legal reservations over the immaterial assets that promoted the divulgation and diffusion of intellectual works and products on the market, such as copyright or patent.

The reservation resulting from combining the DRM and anti-circumvention provisions is a hybrid mixture of intellectual reservation (since technological measures can reduce access to works) and economic reservation (since technological measures will control the diffusion of works in the market), of factual and legal modes of economic reservation. Technological control can either make impossible or reduce access to or use of the work, or can monitor and manage such acts of use. In the first case, the reservation over the work is evident: the user cannot benefit from some use of the work. For instance, someone acquiring a protected DVD cannot make a copy thereof, whatever its purpose. In the second case, the user will be able to use the work, but such usage will be controlled and might be in return for payment, which is another type of economic reservation. An example is the FairPlay DRM enshrined in iTunes pieces of music delivered by Apple, wherein the number of copies and transfer to some types of equipment is limited and controlled.

In some ways, the different sorts of reservation that a technological measure can impose as to digital content remind us of the distinction drawn by Gilles Deleuze (1990) between technologies of discipline and technologies of control. Technologies of discipline constrain, lock up and prevent while technologies of control authorize but in a regime of probation. Deleuze says that regulation enforced by the first types of technology is a sort of mould, while that enforced by the second types operates as a modulation. DRM technologies are closer to a modulation mechanism of regulation, since they determine and adjust the extent of the use of the work allowed according to the user, to the license he/she entered into or to the remuneration he/she paid. They do not block access to the work but make it subject to the disciplinary conditions as decided by the right holder. When the right owners decide to provide digital content with some defined usage rules (e.g. including a number of copies, a number of allowed viewings, etc.) this usage becomes the norm for the recipients and users of such content, even though the usage they are entitled to enjoy from such works under the law might be broader and less restricted.

In this sense, we can say, with Lessig (1999b) or, before him, Joel Reidenberg (1998), that the code is law; in other words, that the digital code put in place by DRM systems acts as regulation, thereby modifying our cultural and social behavior as to copyrighted works.

14.3.2 The false neutrality of DRM

The image of the copyright monopoly over works, as reflected in the successive mirrors of the technical protection and anti-circumvention provisions, has shifted, sensibly, to one of broader control over access to and use of the works. In the technological measures and the anti-circumvention provisions, copyright is not portrayed alike but has been distorted, to a worrisome extent.

Initially, copyright is about entitling the author to control the public exploitation of his/her works and to decide in what ways the works will be made available to the public. For that purpose, copyright grants the author the right to authorize the making of copies of his/her work (the right of reproduction) and the right to authorize the diffusion of his/her work to the public (which can encompass, depending on the country, rights of public communication, of display, of performance, of distribution).[5]

The "public" element of such rights is crucial. The core of the copyright monopoly is the public diffusion of the work, either directly by acts of communication or indirectly by the making of copies that can be distributed or perceived by the public. What copyright covers is the making available of the work to the public; it is not the reception or enjoyment of the work by an individual member of that public. This "publicity" of the copyright monopoly is rooted in the history and justifications of literary and artistic property (Dusollier, 2005).

In a digital world in which intermediaries have disappeared and the copyright owners have started to distribute their works directly to the public, resorting to technological measures enables them to control both sides of the transmission: from the making available to the reception of or the getting access to works. This is the very purpose of many DRM technologies that are available today. Access controls manage the end user's access to digital content, DRM systems monitor and enforce the usage of the work by the end user, sometimes preventing further distribution of the work to another public or impinging the making of a copy thereof, sometimes controlling mere acts of use that do not imply a copy or a public transmission of the work.

[5] In most countries, the author also enjoys a moral right, the objective of which is to protect his/her personality enshrined in the work through the rights of paternity (or attribution, to use less sexist terminology), of divulgation and of integrity.

The technological protection of copyright thus makes access to and the enjoyment, use and consumption of works enter the sphere of the monopoly exercised by the copyright holders. This extension of the copyright area of control is not simply allowed by a technical and factual action but is also secured by the law through the anti-circumvention provisions.

In the United States, the case law applying the DMCA has construed the notion of the technological measures that are protected against circumvention so as, basically, to include any technology under the sun.[6] If, by using the work, one is in one way or another faced with the operation of a technological function, even without noticing it, that technological measure is, under this case law, a technological measure controlling access to the work. The mere existence of a technical aid or control makes it a technology protected against circumvention! The right holder, by using a technology to prevent any act of access to or use of the work, therefore automatically gains the further protection of such a technical barrier by the anti-circumvention law.

It is the same in the European Union, where the technological measure to be protected is defined as "any technology, device or component that, in the normal course of its operation, is designed to prevent or restrict acts. . .which are not authorized by the right owner of any copyright or any right related to copyright as provided for by law."[7] A DRM system will consequently be protected against circumvention as soon as it protects an "act. . .not authorized by the right owner." One could not dream of a better tautology: obviously, since the right holder has decided to protect technically an act of use related to his/her work, it means that he/she was willing not to authorize such an act. Any DRM system or anti-copying device is then addressed by such a legal remedy, and the protection of the copyright law, by its anti-circumvention element, extends to any act of use of the work.

In a way, it could be said that the normative action of the DRM system and of the legal protection thereof, under the pretence of

[6] See, for example, *Universal City Studios, Inc., et al.* v. *Shawn C. Reimerdes et al.*, 111 F. Supp. 2d 294 (SDNY 2000) *conf'd*, 273 F.3d 429 (2d Cir. 2001); *United States of America* v. *Elcom Ltd. & Dmitry Sklyarov*, 203 F. Supp. 2d 1111 (ND Cal. 2002); *Lexmark Int'l* v. *Static Control Components, Inc.*, 2003 US Dist. LEXIS 3734 (ED Ky. 2003); and *321 Studios* v. *Metro Goldwyn Mayer Studios, Inc., et al.*, no. C 02–1955 SI (ND Cal. 2004).

[7] Article 6 § 3 of the "Copyright Directive."

simply enforcing the rights of copyright owners, have assumed a broader duty. DRM technologies sometimes only replicate the rights granted by copyright (when they impede the copy covered by the reproduction right conferred by copyright law), sometimes they colonize new territories in the land of free uses of works (when they submit the number of viewings to a graduated fee). Either they reinforce the copyright prerogatives or they create new reservations over the work. The technical tool can thus act as a *representative* of the copyright, as it technically conveys the rights of the author, by preventing the reproduction, communication or modification of the work. It can also go beyond that mere representative function, however, and act as a *mediator*, in the sense that the technology can shift the object of those rights or build up some new relations to the work, by constraining the access thereto or by determining the conditions for its reception and enjoyment (this distinction is borrowed from Bruno Latour, 1993). In the first case, the technology is the means of the copyright enforcement; in the latter case, it is both the means and the end of an extended protection of the work.

14.3.3 The nature and scope of the technical regulation of copyright

It is worthwhile to note that such a normative effect of the technical regulation over works differs, in nature and scope, from that of copyright law. Technological measures embedded into copyrighted works might have, to some extent, more pervasive power in inducing and constraining a defined behavior as to the access to and use of works (section 14.3.3.1). This normative power is, equally, less than the traditional copyright norm, however, as far as the object of the norm (14.3.3.2) and the operation of the norm (14.3.3.3) are concerned.

14.3.3.1 The normative effect of the technological measure: an a priori reservation

A key difference between any regulation by law and regulation by a technical act lies in the self-execution of the technical response to the norm infringement. This is particularly true with DRM in the copyright field.

The technical means imposes itself on any user of the technically protected work. Its force rests upon intrinsic and immediate elements of the technological measure, which operate prior to any copyright infringement. The technical norm prevents de facto a de jure infringement; it acts before the infringement of the legal norm of copyright could even take place. To that purpose, the technology is an ex ante remedy (i.e. a remedy that intervenes before the unlawful act that would justify the sanction). In a way, the technology replaces morality, which resides in the hope that the user will not infringe the copyright. Unlike morality, however, compliance with the law is ensured by technology securely and with no hesitation.

This differs from the legal norm, which applies ex post remedies that have to be asked in front of a court, thus resting on elements exterior to the infringed legal norm itself. As Lessig (1999b) says, "The constraints of architecture are self-executing in a way that the constraints of law, norms, and the market are not. This feature of architecture – self-execution – is extremely important for understanding its role in regulation."

This self-executing norm makes enforcement of the technological norm rather different from enforcement of the law. Both norms integrate the idea of "force," which is beautifully conveyed in the English terms *enforcement*, *enforceability* and *to enforce the law* (Derrida, 1994), or in the French expression *force de loi*. This principle of the "law in-force" is fundamental to the legal norm. The regulation enabled by the law finds its force in the very limits of the law itself, and solely within such limits. The "enforcement" of the law that leads to remedies and sanctions draws its legitimacy from the law that is infringed, even though such remedies and sanctions have recourse to institutions and means that are parallel and external to the infringed legal rule and that intervene after the infringement. Conversely, the force embedded in the DRM system, or in other technical means of copyright enforcement, lies in the technology itself.

This gives the technical norm a greater effect on access to and the use of copyrighted works. The user is to some extent forced to comply with the technological dictate, without being able to argue the legitimacy of that copyright enforcement in justice.

14.3.3.2 The object of the DRM regulation: the embodiment of the work

The constraint enabled by the DRM system on the copyrighted work is somewhat less than what copyright law achieves, however. Indeed, the monopoly that the technological measures grant to the copyright holders is rather limited. As a mere factual constraint, the technical barrier cannot enshrine the artistic work in its entirety, as an intangible and immaterial object. Technological locks, such as DRM systems, encapsulate only a tangible copy of the copyrighted work, its embodiment in a physical entity.

This copy can be a tangible medium, such as a disk, a tape, a piece of paper, a CD or a DVD, or it can be a stream of bits that conveys either the transmission of the work through digital networks or its storage in a hard disk or server. It is through such copies of the work, whether a tangible object or an intangible vector that enables its transmission, that the exploitation and commercialization of the work take place. As an example, the technical protection of a DVD does not constrain the use of the film, which might be viewed in other formats, but, rather, the use of the film as embodied in that specific copy in the DVD. As to DRM systems, their architecture usually comprises a repository of works that delivers and simultaneously secures a copy of the work requested by the user. The making of a copy to be provided to the user is thus concomitant to the affixing of a technical protection. As "commodification is linked to the embodiment in a physical object" (Radin, 2002), the technological protection of copyrighted works aims to secure the digital exploitation of works through their commoditized forms, thus, in turn, increasing the commodification of works.

The work itself resists any physical or technical appropriation, thereby making the technical reservation incomplete. The work might exist in an unprotected format. Even though some recent works can be distributed only in technically protected copies, they are only ersatz substitutes for the work itself. Copyright governs the intellectual work, the discourse or expression that remains the same in the ubiquity and diversity of the material objects that embody it. Each of these material embodiments does not know the same uniqueness in such ubiquity (Bergé, 2002; Benabou, 2005). The artistic or literary work still exists beyond its embodiments. A piece of music, for instance, even though it has been distributed publicly in technically protected format, has an ubiquitous and autonomous existence. It can be sung, performed, fixed, reproduced and communicated to the public. Equally, a literary work can be read or rewritten without the need for that copy to result from the material object. This is less true for other types of works, such as films, pictures or software, that are more strongly dependent on the media in which they are embodied. For these works, their reproduction will probably require going back to the media that might be technically protected.

As a conclusion, it is not the work as an intangible and diverse thing but the work in its multiple materiality that forms the object of the technical reservation, the work as a commodity, a good or a service. This does not mean that the technical measure has no effect on the work itself, which exists also through its material embodiments. Access to the work depends on the number of material embodiments. Even though the pieces of Shakespeare are distributed as e-books that are technically protected against reproduction or free access, it is not very difficult to enjoy such works without any technical constraint. It will be the same with the *Mona Lisa*, whose reproduction could be displayed at the Louvre Museum with an anti-copy mechanism, but many copies of the famous painting can be found elsewhere. In contrast, should a film be distributed only in a technically locked-up DVD, access to its viewing, besides access to theatres that could screen it, will be possible only on the conditions laid down by the right owners in the technical features of the DVD. In that sense, one can say that technological measures produce scarcity in some cultural sectors.

14.3.3.3 The operation of the DRM regulation: a catalogue of technical acts

The rights granted by copyright reserve some acts of use of the work that are synthetically defined. For example, the right of reproduction is defined so as to cover any act of copy of a work, whatever the way or technology of reproduction might be. The manual copy, the printing, the scanning, the filming, the adaptation, the caching of a work are all acts that will trigger the exclusive right of reproduction. The definition of "reproduction" or "communication to the public" is neutral, in the sense that it is not linked with any specific technology.

Conversely, what a technical measure can do to protect a work against undue reproduction will always be defined in an analytical way. No technical tool will be able to prevent all acts of reproduction that could be covered by the copyright law, but it will pursue a specific function by inhibiting one precise act of copy (e.g. the printing, the burning of a CD or DVD, the making of a digital copy on one's hard disk, or any other act of use, such as access to one copy, the verification of the compliance of the player with the technically defined format of the work, and so on). This specific and restricted function of technical protection could be compared to what Latour has called the "script of the device" (Latour, 1993; Akrich, 2006): a program of action that has been defined by the right holder and determines the design of the DRM system.

The DRM system therefore does not achieve the same type of control over the work as copyright law does. It is not, as some say, the machine translation of the rights of the copyright owners, but only the exercise and application of the will of the copyright owners as to one or some copies of the work and as to a defined act of use carried out in a defined context.

In other words, the technical reservation of the work is not as complete as its legal reservation. Even though DRM implies an immediate and proactive enforcement of its usage rules, it will be as extended as the copyright law in the work only by compiling each technical constraint on each embodiment and copy of the work. The sum of all technological measures on each copy of the work could never constrain all potential users of the work, however.

14.3.4 Copyright law designed by the technology

The technical protection of copyright does not only have a normative effect by itself; it also induces the very design of the regulation by copyright law. Indeed, many features of copyright regulation have been dictated, in recent years, by the technological norm. This technological mandate in copyright law is particularly evident as far as DRM systems are concerned. Anti-circumvention laws are strongly dependent on what technology *can* do and not on what technology *should* do according to social and legal norms.

First, no lawmaker has ever prohibited or limited the use of a technological measure when the latter infringes the boundaries of copyright. DRM technologies can be used to monitor and manage the use of public domain material. Anti-circumvention laws will not bring any remedies against the person who bypasses a technological measure affixed to non-copyrighted content, however, or who sells means to circumvent such a technological measure. The constraint on the public domain element nevertheless remains, or, one should rather say, the constraint on one embodiment of a public domain element impedes the free use of that particular embodiment. DRM technologies can also inhibit acts of use that could have a social value. For instance, e-books give the right holder the ability to prevent the display of the text in large print, as normally enabled by the system to favor visually impaired people. Lawmakers have never reflected on the social consequences of such a technical regulation, which is left solely to the decision of the copyright industry.

Second, as we have seen earlier, the scope of the anti-circumvention provisions is defined largely by the scope of the technological measures. On the one hand, the definition of the technological measures to be protected against circumvention systematically refers not to the exclusive rights of the copyright owner but to what the copyright owner is able to protect through technology. US case law has protected any technological measure affixed to the work, since such a relationship between the technology and the intellectual work technically meant that, to get access to the work, one would necessarily pass through the technical gate, and hence unlawfully circumvent it, if no due authorization had been given. The European definition of the technological measures in the anti-circumvention provisions refers to the technical protection of any act unauthorized by the copyright owner. I have already said that such a definition makes any technical fence a protected technological measure as soon as its very presence indicates that the constrained act of use is not permitted by the right owner. For comparison, the WIPO treaties of 1996 that are the source of the anti-circumvention provisions deal with "technological measures that are used by authors *in connection with the exercise of their rights* and that restrict acts which are not authorized by the authors concerned or *permitted by law*" (emphases added). Here the link between the scope of the copyright law and the scope of the legal protection of technological measures is direct. The WIPO treaties do not entitle the copyright owners to gain further protection through anti-circumvention provisions.

The same is true for copyright exceptions and limitations or fair use. Most countries know some limitations to the copyright monopoly when other social or cultural values are at stake, for instance for education, libraries, handicapped people, parody, quotation, criticism or review. What happens to such copyright exceptions when a technological measure can prevent any act of reproduction, whatever its purpose? Can a person be liable for circumvention activities when he/she tampers with a technical lock only to benefit from an exception afforded by the law or when he/she distributes circumvention devices with the sole purpose of helping users to benefit from such exceptions? This is undoubtedly the trickiest issue of the anti-circumvention provisions (Dusollier, 2005).

Although the WIPO treaties paid attention to safeguarding the copyright exceptions within the anti-circumvention provisions, by laying down that technologies that inhibit acts permitted by the law will not be protected against circumvention, the US and EU provisions did not. Both the DMCA and the EU Copyright Directive state that the technological measure prevails over the exercise of fair use or exceptions to copyright. Such exceptions excuse neither an act of circumvention nor an act of trafficking in circumvention devices. Armed with technological measures and anti-circumvention laws, the right holder is now entitled to prevent the users from making a fair use of copyrighted works.

This clearly results from the EU Copyright Directive and from the US DMCA. Both texts provide for some safeguarding of exceptions, but these are rather limited and insufficient. The US legislation lays down only a list of very restricted and ill-founded exceptions to the circumvention prohibition[8] and entrusts an administrative body with evaluating the "adverse effect on fair use" that the application of the anti-circumvention provision might have.[9] The EU directive requires member states to find solutions so as to enable the legitimate user of a work to benefit from some exceptions, notwithstanding the presence of a technological measure that constrains the normally free use.[10] This solution is limited to some exceptions, however, and for the most part leaves room for the intervention of the copyright holders themselves. Indeed, the solution is based on voluntary intervention on the part of the right holders. Such intervention, as the text of the directive implies, could be found in contracts with the user or in modification of the very design of the technology. One can think of putting in place technological measures that permit the making of one copy or of one low-quality copy. In Germany, scientific publishers have entered into an agreement with libraries to supply them, provided some conditions

[8] 17 USC § 1201(d) to (j). [9] 17 USC § 1201(a)(C).
[10] Article 6 § 4 of the "Copyright Directive."

are met, with versions of electronic publications that are not technically protected, so as to enable them to make preservations and archiving copies thereof.

If copyright owners propose anything to address these exceptions, lawmakers are no longer obliged to rule on the matter. The logic of such solution is at best rather dubious: it entitles copyright owners to employ any technical constraint on the work, but, in order to reassure users, it encourages the former to let users benefit from some freedoms, leaving the search for an appropriate balance to the copyright owners themselves and thus, once again, to fully deploy technical methods. The regulation by law is curiously absent from such an architecture.

Furthermore, this solution does not apply, according to the EU directive, "to works or other subject-matter made available to the public on agreed contractual terms in such a way that members of the public may access them from a place and at a time individually chosen by them."[11] The wording of this provision plainly refers to the definition of the right to make works available to the public,[12] as laid down in article 3 of the directive. It would mean that any on-demand service will not have to comply with the obligation to safeguard the exceptions and could be completely locked up. The vagueness of the wording could nevertheless jeopardize all the good intentions of European lawmakers. Making works on the internet available on demand could become the prevalent business model for the distribution of works. The requirement that such services have to be delivered on contractual terms does not matter much given the ease with which a click-wrap license can be embedded in digital products. Some scholars have expressed concerns that this paragraph could comprise the entire internet and make void any obligation for preserving some exceptions. The uncertainty of the business models that will prevail on the internet in the future could definitely prove them right. It also shows the preference that European lawmakers are showing to

[11] Article 6 § 4 of the "Copyright Directive."

[12] Article 3 of the "Copyright Directive" states that "Member States shall provide authors with the exclusive right to authorize or prohibit any communication to the public of their works, by wire or wireless means, including the making available to the public of their works in such a way that members of the public may access them from a place and at a time individually chosen by them."

copyright owners by letting them exclude exceptions altogether by distributing their works under the terms of a contract.

Copyright owners are thus granted some legitimacy in controlling, through technology, acts of use traditionally exempted by copyright law. Here also, what technology can do becomes what the extent of copyright should be. One section of the preamble in the European directive is very clear in this respect. It says that "[private copy] should not inhibit the use of technological measures or their enforcement against circumvention."[13] In other terms, the European legal text validates the technological definition of what should remain free private copy or not. Another principle of the directive leans in the same direction. The text says that the levies that are traditionally applied to blank tapes and copying devices to compensate for private copy exception should take into account the application of the technological measures preventing such private copying from taking place. This so-called "phasing out" means that, as soon as the anti-copy measures are put in place, no levy should be paid on copying equipment or blank tapes or CDs. Here again, the regime of a private copy exception in connection with fair remuneration gives way to a regime of technical prohibition of private copies. The private copy exception will nevertheless survive in many countries, but in an ambiguous situation. As to technically protected works, users will no longer enjoy the right to a copy that is granted to them by law, while, for works that are not technically protected, authors will not benefit from fair remuneration in compensation for the private copies that will still be made. The legal regime that used to embed a fair balance between the two interests has given the floor to a regime defined only by technical capacity.

One should also bear in mind that, for all copyright exceptions that are not listed in the "safeguarding" regime of the European directive, the technical regulation can be as complete as the copyright owners decide.

That technical colonization of uses that were recognized as uncopyrightable by the law can be explained by some law and economics discourse that tends to consider copyright exceptions and fair use as nothing but market failures. In such a view, copyright exceptions are not key elements in the copyright architecture that are justified by

[13] Preamble, section 39.

social and philosophical motives, but are simple areas without control that the copyright owner is doomed to tolerate for want of a way to exercise his/her rights fully. Technological measures are deemed to give back to copyright owners the control they have lost over the uses that were previously tolerated as exceptions. Such an argument is rather circular: there is a market failure, in that the market alone cannot achieve a better solution for the allocation of resources. As far as copyright exceptions are concerned, the law has already intervened to cure the existing market failure, by allocating to the users some uses of copyrighted content (e.g. because the social benefit of leaving such uses beyond the reach of copyright was considered stronger than the benefit of allowing the copyright owners to control them). There would be a market failure only if the law had entitled the copyright owner to exercise his/her rights and if the market did not enable such an exercise. Therefore, the rhetoric about the original market failure that technology could suddenly solve, thereby restoring full copyright control (whereas copyright control has never been – and never should be – complete), does nothing but create that market failure. That perverse reasoning makes it easy to claim afterwards that the exception is not justified anymore since the market failure has disappeared! In other words, in order to prove that the copyright holder should be entitled to exert technical control over some uses that have been allocated by law to the user, the argument in favor of the technological measures states that such control is already and in fiction enjoyed by the copyright owner.

14.4 Conclusion: restore the law in copyright regulation

In conclusion, it is certainly true to say that, in the United States and the European Union, technological capacity now dictates the legal scope of copyright protection.

Regulation by law has been determined on the sole basis of what the technology can achieve, without any due consideration of what the proper scope of the monopoly over works should be. The social and public justifications for permitting some uses of copyrighted works stand aside to let the technology deploy its full capacity. Technological measures are becoming substitutes for copyright even though they are still broadly advertised as mere complements to it. The WIPO treaties addressed only DRM systems preventing uses covered by copyright, and gave immunity to copyright exceptions and limitations. Conversely, the EU and US anti-circumvention provisions address any use that technology can encapsulate, and consider exceptions and fair use as nothing but failures of the copyright body that technology can heal.

This phenomenon has been dubbed *private ordering* by some American scholars (Cohen, 1998; Samuelson, 2002). Elkin-Koren has defined this notion as the fact that "the rule-making process regarding the use of information is privatized, and the legal power to define the boundaries of public access to information is delegated to private parties" (Elkin-Koren, 2001). By resorting to technological measures to enforcing their rights, copyright owners unilaterally decide what the extent of their monopoly and what their reservation over their works should be and what the benefits of the users should look like.

Regulating the simple use of works, or access to works, by technological measures and anti-circumvention laws enables the distribution of the works to any individual to be regulated. From exploitation of the work, its diffusion to the public as a whole, the copyright has shifted to control of the business model, aided by technology, of the distribution of copyrighted works to individuals.

This move has distorted the copyright law to an extent that we are only beginning to experience and understand. The technology that helped achieve it was both the pretext and the means to accomplish this shift in copyright.

How we should address this replacement of the foundations and principles of copyright by rules imposed by the mere technical fact is one of the key questions in the field of copyright today. Failing to give an adequate and balanced answer to it would be tantamount to stealing copyright from the public and giving it to industry. The public is becoming more and more contemptuous of copyright. It leads to an increasing tendency to infringe copyright. Paul Goldstein (1997) has said that one great virtue of copyright is its balance, "one that weighs authors' interests against the need for public access. This balance has withstood, and been shaped by, the test of time and, however incompletely, has won civil obedience through the reasonableness of its command."

By putting technology on the throne of copyright in order to achieve a more fine-grained control of the use of the work by individuals, this can only engender greater civil disobedience. Technology as a tool to help copyright in the digital age would then finally be the end of copyright.

Thwarting this development should rest on a proper understanding of the very nature of technology and the way it interacts with law. By its very nature, technology is prosthetic: it creates a shortfall and substitute for that failure rather that completing it. For instance, the typewriter was specifically invented to enable the blind to write, to access mechanical writing. Ultimately used by everybody, the typewriter changed the way we write and communicate. When using such a machine, one has to unlearn the vision of touch and appropriate a sort of blindness (Preciado, 2000). Technology was created to remedy a deficiency but, in order to operate fully, it itself created a similar deficiency. The use of technology in copyright is similar. It is a solution to the lack of an effective protection of copyright. In order to deploy its full operation and power, however, it has to create an absence of copyright, or at least a dissimulation of copyright behind the dictate of technology. Restoring the law in copyright, going back to its source principles, is the only solution for keeping an acceptable balance in intellectual property and using technology as an adequate tool and aid. The application of a technology-aided paradigm of copyright is about managing the relationship between technology and copyright law, not about replacing one by another.

To this end, the extraordinary potential of DRM systems both to constrain the use of works and to influence lawmakers needs to be curbed. This could be achieved by different and complementary legal actions. First, lawmakers should not be reluctant to control what technology can achieve, and could, in some cases, regulate technical operations, or even prohibit the technology from constraining some uses of works. The anti-circumvention legal provisions should also define the technological measures to be protected by reference to the exercise of exclusive rights of copyright or to the use of technology in the framework of the copyright exercise; it should, however, clearly limit technical prerogatives. Finally, the law has to find an effective and balanced solution for safeguarding the benefit of all copyright exceptions. The key social role and value of the limitations that lawmakers have imposed on copyright and on copyright owners should be stressed and reaffirmed.

It is a matter for regret that this is not the path that present-day copyright lawmakers have decided to follow.

15 Governing access to user-generated content: the changing nature of private ordering in digital networks

NIVA ELKIN-KOREN

15.1 Introduction

Copyright law, which governs the use of creative works, is undoubtedly one of the legal regimes most susceptible to digital technology. The ease of copying and distributing works through digital networks makes it increasingly difficult for copyright owners to enforce their rights, established by *public ordering*. At the same time, however, digital networks have opened up new opportunities for governing cultural works through *private ordering*. Content providers can contract directly with the masses of end users connected via digital networks. They can also technically control the use of works, long after their distribution to the public, by employing technological protection measures (TPMs).

Public ordering and private ordering are two fundamentally different approaches to governance. Public ordering refers to rule-making processes, which are designed by the state and its apparatus. Its norms reflect the outcome of collective action mechanisms, which are formulated and applied from the top down by public institutions. Private ordering, by contrast, concerns bottom-up processes, whereby each party voluntarily chooses to undertake the norms that will govern its behavior. This definition captures the fundamental justifications for the enforcement of norms created by private ordering: their self-imposition by the parties is considered morally justifiable and economically efficient. One question addressed by this chapter is whether this description holds for private ordering when applied to licenses that govern access to creative works.

Private ordering is applied within a legal system and enforced by law enforcement mechanisms. The notion of private ordering sometimes refers to extralegal systems in which rules are followed without any legal obligation. This chapter addresses private ordering as it refers to the origin of norms, however – namely to decentralized processes by which norms are formulated, when enforcement is achieved through the legal system. Contracts are a typical example. Contract law defines when a mutual undertaking by the parties constitutes a legally enforceable contract, offering remedies against those who breach their contractual obligations. Similarly, anti-circumvention regimes in the United States (the Digital Millennium Copyright Act) and in the European Union (the Copyright Directive, article 6) provide technological measures with some immunity against circumvention.

Private ordering is playing an ever greater role in governing the terms of access to creative works. Right holders often use end-user license agreements (EULAs) to expand the scope of the protection provided under copyright law, by limiting the rights of users under legal doctrines such as "fair use" and "first sale." At the same time, private ordering has also been employed in recent years by open-access initiatives, to promote access to creative works and facilitate interaction and the exchange and sharing of creative materials.

The dominance of private ordering destabilizes copyright law on two levels: institutional and normative. On the institutional level, the shift to private ordering blurs the distinction between property and contracts. As further explained below, this is due to the pervasive nature of licensing in digital format, and to the legal policies that hold such contracts enforceable against third parties. Once terms of access, established by a contract, govern each and every access to a work, they have the same impact as property rules. These self-help mechanisms for governing information challenge the norms designed through collective action (copyright) and require reconsideration of the type of desirable government intervention. Questions arise as to whether the state should enforce privately created norms when they are inconsistent with copyright, and what the justification is for enforcing such terms in the first place.

At the normative level, digital networks introduce new modes for the production and distribution of creative works (Benkler, 2006). The Web 2.0 brings the individual to the forefront of the creative process, with users independently generating and distributing their content, using different licensing strategies. Governing access to user-generated content (UGC) by private ordering raises a whole set of issues related to licensing through platforms, the interdependence of users and platforms, and the licensing by many to many. The changing creative landscape of the Web 2.0 expands the ethos of creativity, supplanting the proprietary exclusivity-based discourse with a new set of values: sharing, participation and collaboration. Even so, some private ordering strategies may reinforce proprietary notions, even unintentionally.

This chapter analyzes the rise of private ordering as a dominant strategy for governing creative works in the digital environment. It explores the changing nature of private ordering in the Web 2.0 environment, in which it is used for governing UGC. Section 15.2 describes the rise of private ordering in the digital environment. Section 15.3 scrutinizes the arguments of proponents and opponents of private ordering to govern access to creative works. Section 15.4 describes the use of private ordering to govern access to UGC, analyzing the different nature of private ordering in this environment and the special consideration it raises. Section 15.5 examines whether the ascendancy of UGC gives rise to different considerations related to private ordering for governing access to creative works.

15.2 The rise of private ordering in digital networks

Digital technology has given rise to new mechanisms for governing the use of creative works. Creative works, once a non-excludable public good, for which exclusivity was established only by intellectual property rights, are increasingly subject to terms of access drafted by content providers. Prior to the digital era contractual arrangements were prohibitively expensive for governing copyrighted materials. Most of the content produced by the content industry during the twentieth century was distributed in physical copies. Millions of copies produced by book publishers and the recording industry were distributed to anonymous buyers through intermediaries and retail stores. It was simply unfeasible for publishers to identify each and every purchaser of their copies and to make a bargain with each. Having no direct contractual relationship with potential consumers of their works, publishers had to rely on copyright laws to secure their rights in copyrighted materials.

Digital networks made it much easier to contract. Direct communication between owners and users allows copyright holders to identify potential users and to conclude a bargain. Owners may further establish a long-term relationship with users, offering renewable licenses and monitoring the performance of contractual obligations. Contract formation is also easier. Owners can make access to informational products contingent upon acceptance of the terms of a license. Downloaders of content made available online are required to agree to the terms of use before gaining access. Digital copies may also be distributed with a license attached, which is prompted during installation of the digital copy (a "clickwrap" license) or simply pops up on the screen before the music plays or the video clip runs (a "browsewrap" license).

EULAs were used early on by software providers to define the scope of protection for software, at a time when it was still unclear whether software is entitled to any intellectual property protection. When copyright laws worldwide were expanded to cover computer programs, and in some jurisdictions software was even granted patent protection, licenses were used for acquiring additional legal protection. Restrictions on the use of software include provisions limiting the right of consumers to resell the purchased copies of a computer program (often secured under first-sale doctrine) and the right to reverse-engineer the program (often secured under fair use). In some cases EULAs were employed to limit the use of informational goods that were not otherwise protected under copyright law, such as a database of phone numbers.[1]

Digital networks further facilitate self-help measures that were not effectively available for governing information in an analogue environment. Technological protection measures enable information vendors to distribute creative works subject to terms codified by the code itself. Content providers can set the terms of access in the digital package that wraps the content, so the terms literally become part of the product – that is, the copy of the work purchased by the consumer. TPMs can be designed to enforce copyright as defined by legislation, but also to expand the scope of protection by disabling uses that are explicitly exempted under copyright law. For instance, a computer program or a copy-protected DVD may simply disable the creation of unauthorized copies. Any authorized use would require entering an access code. Some protection measures place control over access to the digital content, or prevent copying and distribution without authorization (Bomsel and Geffroy, 2005). Other measures simply monitor

[1] See *ProCD Inc.*, 86 F. 3d 1447.

the user's interaction with the content and report back to the content owner. Protection measures may be installed on copies of informational materials distributed to the public (such as MP3 files or DVDs), or may be implemented through the platforms that provide access to content, such as a website, a media player or social media platforms.

Private ordering has also been employed in recent years by open-access initiatives to facilitate access to creative materials. There is no strict definition of open access, or open content, and the term is often used to describe a wide range of activities with different strategies, goals and ideological commitments. Some initiatives focus on availability, promoting free and unrestricted access to all kinds of content, such as open-access journals (e.g. BioMed, Public Library of Science) and courseware (e.g. the Massachusetts Institute of Technology's OpenCourseWare project). Other initiatives emphasize freedom: to use copyrighted materials, and especially to modify, remix and tinker with preexisting materials. The conviction shared by many open-content initiatives is that the online environment facilitates new ways of sharing and collaborating in the production of creative works, and that copyright law in its current scope creates an obstacle to exercising these new opportunities (Lessig, 2001; Litman, 2004; Benkler, 2006).

The pioneering attempt to secure freedom in software through a matrix of licenses was the innovative General Public License, designed by the Free Software Foundation (FSF) in the late 1980s. FSF licenses endorse four freedoms related to computer programs: to run the program, to study it, to modify it and to share or redistribute the original program and any modified versions thereof. The Free Software Foundation, founded by Richard Stallman, manages the GPL, which aims to secure free software principles. The GPL is a *copyleft* license, which has a viral effect: it applies automatically to any new copy of the software and any derivative program that is based on the original one. Subsequent creators are therefore bound by the terms of access defined by the license, and must strictly apply them to any subsequent work they create using the original free software. The Open Source Initiative, launched in 1998, adopted a more liberal strategy, defining the key elements that have to be met for a license to qualify as an open-source license. Consequently over 100 different open-source licenses are estimated to be available today.

The colossal success of the free software movement was followed by successful licensing initiatives for other creative works, such as

Creative Commons, as well as licenses for scientific building blocks, such as BiOS. Creative Commons offers a user-friendly licensing scheme that applies to copyrighted materials of all types. The licensing platform allows authors to generate licenses of their choice. As further discussed below, the licensing scheme is modular, and licensors can therefore mix and match predefined provisions requiring attribution (the Attribution [A] license), banning commercial use (Non-Commercial [NC]), prohibiting the preparation of any derivative work (NoDerivs [ND]) or stipulating that any subsequent derivative work will be subject to the same terms as the original (ShareAlike [SA]). While Creative Commons' Attribution license is the least restrictive on access, permitting any use as long as credit has been given, the Attribution-NonCommercial-NoDerivs license is probably the most restrictive Creative Commons license. The license permits the copying of the work as is, bans any alteration or transformation that builds upon the work and excludes any commercial use. Creative Commons' automatic licensing platform simplifies the licensing process and is intended to help end users to identify works easily that are authorized for use. The license is accessible in a legally enforceable format, but is also accessible in comprehensible language, intended for potential users, and in machine code, so that works subject to more permissible terms can be located automatically by search tools.

The different goals of private ordering, and the different ways in which these strategies are employed, should not hide the fact that it has become a dominant source of the norms that govern access to creative works. Should we welcome this development? Can private ordering produce optimal terms of access for creative materials? Are these norms better than terms of access determined by public laws? Should licenses and TPMs take priority over norms created through public ordering, or should private ordering be subject to copyright law? The next section addresses some of these questions.

15.3 Information governance under scrutiny

The governance of creative works through private ordering was a highly controversial issue from the start, and has remained so for over a decade (Elkin-Koren, 1997, 1998; Cohen, 1998; Lemley, 1999; Guibault, 2002; Easterbrook, 2005). Advocates of private ordering believe that using it for governing access to creative works is superior to public ordering. In essence, they argue that private ordering is more efficient than copyright law because the bargaining parties are often better informed. Therefore private ordering, rather than rules designed by central governments, will better serve the parties' interests and better promote overall public welfare. Essentially, proponents of private ordering make the following claims: first, that governments cannot determine the optimal terms of access to creative works; and, second, that information markets are capable of generating the most efficient terms (Bell, 1998; Dam, 1999; Easterbrook, 1996; Hardy, 1996; Merges, 1997; O'Rourke, 1997).

Underlying this approach is a deep distrust of governmental rule-making processes. To private ordering advocates, governments are wanting in the ability to address the needs of owners and users of copyrighted materials. They are unable to determine the requirements of different owners and users of creative works, and lack reliable means to ascertain the appropriate level of protection that should be assigned to each work (Easterbrook, 1996; Merges, 1997). The risk of error escalates when rapidly changing technologies require flexibility and constant adjustment to ever-changing needs (Hardy, 1994).

Advocates of private ordering further assume that market processes are better suited for governing the terms of access to creative works. From a market perspective, EULAs are perceived as an integral part of the product. Just as a computer program can be priced by its features, it could also be priced on the basis of the scope of permissible uses provided by the license. A licensee's consent to purchase a restricting license at a lower price is no different from his/her consent to purchase a computer subject to a one-year (rather than a three-year) warranty at a lower price. The contract-as-product view becomes even more powerful when TPMs are employed, and the terms of the use and the creative work are both represented in the same digital format (Radin, 2006).

If the licensee is willing to pay a higher price for less restrictive licenses, the market will provide for it (Easterbrook, 1996: 211). Essentially, private ordering advocates believe that terms that govern the use of creative works are shaped by market forces, in the same way that the quality and price of goods are determined through free competition. Individual users express their preferences for particular terms of use through their purchasing choices, and content providers satisfy the demand by adjusting the license restrictions and price.

Finally, private ordering advocates argue that it may enhance efficiency by facilitating price discrimination (Meurer, 1997; Fisher, 2004). Rather than distributing information at a fixed price, subject to copyright restrictions alone, providers can tailor different packages for particular consumers, selling limited rights at a lower price. Users will pay for precisely the type of use they wish to acquire. Users who want to make special use of the copyrighted materials will pay a higher price for expanded authorizations. Users who make only basic use will be charged a small fee for a limited license.

Opponents of private ordering disagree with this description of the market for licenses. They challenge the proposition that private ordering will lead to greater efficiency in governing access to creative works. Many scholars, including me, warned against the widespread enforcement of EULAs and mass licenses for copyrighted materials (Elkin-Koren, 1998; Cohen, 1998; Lemley, 2006; Radin, 2006). Below is a brief summary of some of the counterclaims.

15.3.1 Is this a contract?

The main critique raised by opponents of private ordering is that unilateral licenses and TPMs are not really contracts, and therefore should not be perceived as reflecting the consent of end users of creative works (Cohen, 1998). For contracts to be efficient, they must reflect the voluntary consent of all parties involved. This is often absent in mass-license transactions, however. Users cannot be considered to have agreed to the terms of use if they are not adequately informed of the contract terms and do not properly understand them. One cannot seriously talk about a license-as-product when the terms of use are often nontransparent, and are hardly ever read by anyone. This is especially true for TPMs, for which restrictions on use are embodied in the program, and therefore are nontransparent at the time of the bargain.

The idea that the license is the product, and the terms of use are simply part of the creative work, is unsound. Terms of use for creative works are not as transparent as price. Even people able and willing to read the terms of use are hard-pressed to determine accurately the impact of these terms on their utility. Apart from incomprehensible legal drafting, this is also because of the abstract nature of copyright restrictions and the legal definitions of intangible uses. The legal description of acts covered by the license is often unintuitive and controversial. For instance, browsing would not be often conceived as reproduction, and saving a file in the Shared Documents library would be commonly understood as public distribution or public performance. It is often difficult, furthermore, to determine ex ante what type of usage one would wish to make of creative works. Creative uses are likely to be more spontaneous and to emerge through engagement in reading, listening or otherwise experiencing a work. Consumers' purchase decisions are therefore unlikely to be based on specific terms of use. They are more likely to treat the license as a general name for an authorization to use the information.

EULAs, which are unilateral statements drafted by right holders, are often enforced nonetheless, even in the absence of assent by end users. Courts have held online contracts enforceable based on very minimal evidence of assent.[2] For instance, shrinkwrap licenses were enforced even when the licensee became aware of the terms only after the computer program had been purchased.[3] Similarly, browsewrap licenses were held enforceable even when the license provisions were simply posted online stating that the mere use of the product or website constituted acceptance of the terms of the license.[4]

This outcome reflects a general approach by courts to electronic contracting, thinning the requirement of consent. Courts expect a fairly minimal demonstration of assent in treating unilaterally drafted licenses as a binding contract (Lemley, 2006). As eloquently described by Margaret Radin (2006: 1231):

> The idea of voluntary willingness first decayed into consent, then into assent, then into a mere possibility or opportunity for assent, then merely fictional assent, then to mere efficient rearrangement of entitlements without any consent or assent.

In respect of licensing works protected by copyright, moreover, the enforceability of licenses might get even stronger. It is often suggested that these online contracts are in fact a *property license*, which is not a contract. It is a unilateral legal action, through which a property owner can exercise his/her rights and define the scope of the authorized use. The binding force of a property license does not derive from

[2] See *ProCD Inc.*, 86 F. 3d 1447. [3] See *ProCD Inc.*, 86 F. 3d 1447.
[4] See *Register.com, Inc.*, 356 F. 3d 393; but see also *Specht*, 306 F. 3d 17.

exercising autonomous will and therefore it does not require consent by the user. The binding force of the licenses stems from the property rules, in this case copyright law. Copyright law empowers owners to exclude others from making certain uses of the work, and a license is necessary to permit what the law otherwise prohibits. Such permission to use the work could be conditional and might be subject to various restrictions. In this view of EULAs as property licenses, the burden of proof rests on the user, who must show that the use was properly authorized by the right holder.

15.3.2 Blurring distinctions: private/public, contracts/property

Typically, rights and duties created by contracts are rights in personam – that is, they bind only the parties to any given contract. Contracts create rights against parties who have undertaken an obligation by consenting to the terms of the agreement. Holding parties legally obliged to keep their promises is considered morally justifiable (Fried, 2006) and efficient. Presumably, the parties are best positioned to ascertain the cost and benefits associated with their choices. From an economic standpoint, therefore, a contract is considered efficient only if it reflects the free will of consenting parties. This is why contracts typically do not impose duties on third parties who have not voluntarily agreed to their terms.

Treating EULAs as contracts, even in the absence of any meaningful consent, or viewing EULAs as property licenses, which allow enforcement against every conceivable user, might carry serious consequences for access to copyrighted materials. First, when the mere use of copyrighted materials is seen as constituting consent to a legally binding contract, access to works is automatically governed by unilaterally defined terms of access. These provisions, drafted by private parties, acquire general applicability and become effective against all, not just the parties who have undertaken them voluntarily. The distinction between private and public ordering collapses.

Second, enforcing standard licenses against parties who did not undertake the terms of use blurs the distinction between property and contracts. Copyrights differ from contractual obligations, in that the right and the corresponding duties they impose on third parties "run with the asset" (Hansman and Kraakman, 2002). Copyright law defines the initial entitlements, while contract law governs their transfer; copyright law creates rights against the world (in rem), whereas contracts apply only to their parties (in personam). A legal policy that treats contractual restrictions as enforceable against third parties gives rise to contracts that run with the asset.

Third, when copyright owners can enforce use restrictions against third parties, beyond the bundle of rights defined by the property rule, they are able unilaterally to constitute new types of property. Property rules reflect an exclusion strategy for regulating the use of resources: they restrict access rather than specify the permissible or prohibited uses of any particular resource. They automatically inflict a standard bundle of duties on all persons in society to avoid a use, unless authorized by the owner. When the legal duties defined by the license become enforceable against all subsequent users, all users must bear the burden of learning the content of each and every license term in order to avoid violation. This is why typically the law does not enforce contracts that run with the asset, and claims against third parties are normally denied. Thomas Merrill and Henry Smith (2001) explain that the objection to new forms of rights in rem is aimed at reducing information costs. Property rights, they argue, communicate a standard bundle of rights related to an asset, thereby reducing the transaction costs involved in determining the type of rights and obligations that are associated with that asset. When we allow content providers to create property-like rights (rights of exclusion, which are automatically imposed against everyone who uses the resource) we substantially increase the information cost of potential users. These are the costs incurred by third parties (i.e. non-owners) who seek to avoid copyright infringement (Long, 2004). End users of creative works who simply seek to avoid inadvertent interference with copyright will be required to investigate which restriction of the many applicable licenses applies to their respective use. These costs of avoidance may, undesirably, increase barriers on access to creative works (Elkin-Koren, 2005).

15.3.3 Markets cannot be trusted to secure optimal access to creative works

Skeptics of private ordering argue that it is unlikely that market mechanisms will secure efficient access to creative works, on account of market failures. The market for creative works is likely to suffer from information asymmetries. Producers of creative works enjoy a systematic information advantage over end users. The former can better assess the risks and benefits associated with any provision and can better understand the impact of any given term on the potential exploitation of the work. Since they execute a large number of similar transactions over time, they have sufficient incentive to collect information about the legal implications of each provision and the validity of the different terms included in the license. Such information asymmetries should make us more skeptical about the outcome of free bargaining for formulating terms of access to creative works.

A major problem with private ordering for governing access to creative works is externalities. Not everyone affected by the rights and duties created by the license are represented in the transactions pertaining to their interests. Assuming that the terms of use are agreed by the licensor and licensee, the most they can reflect is the preferences of users to pay less for limited rights or to pay more for expanded privileges. The terms may reflect the immediate value that users place on any given transaction, but they will fail to reflect the public utility and the benefits to society as a whole. For instance, a EULA restriction on reverse-engineering may affect not only the purchaser of the computer program but also the public at large, which would be denied compatible programs that may foster innovation and lower the price. A schoolteacher may be reluctant to purchase a license to use a certain documentary film even though it might be socially beneficial if he/she made the work available to his/her elementary school students.

The terms of access often carry positive or negative externalities for others. Access to creative works is necessary to foster further innovation, creativity and progress, because creative works are ingredients used in generating subsequent works. Access to cultural goods cultivates the workforce for further creation: it educates; it stimulates our minds; it expands our understanding of the world around us; it provides inspiration and facilitates creativity and innovation. Wide and indiscriminate access to creative works is therefore necessary in order to make it possible for subsequent authors to make further creations (Elkin-Koren, 2007). Indiscriminate access to creative works is also essential for widespread participation in the creation of culture. Such participation does not necessarily involve actively generating new works. It may also take the form of engaging with creative works, and constructing meaning that arises from the way it is represented through our reading novels, listening to music and making actual use of cultural artifacts in our everyday lives (du Gay *et al.*, 1997).

The social utility encompassed in the use of creative works may not be accurately reflected through individuals' purchase choices in market exchanges. These considerations make people generally more skeptical of the ability of market mechanisms and private ordering to regulate the use of information efficiently (Elkin-Koren, 1997).

15.4 Governing access to user-generated content

We have seen that digital technology has fostered greater reliance on private ordering as a way of governing access to creative materials. Digital networks are changing the creative environment in ways exceeding governance, however. One of the most fundamental changes is the introduction of new modes of production and distribution for creative works. The lower cost of coordinating creative efforts and distributing materials to a large audience enables individuals to play a bigger role in generating and distributing new content. The twentieth century featured mass-produced content provided by media conglomerates and large publishing houses, but the online environment gives rise to individual creators. UGC flourishes: bloggers post news and analysis; independent musicians distribute their music through MySpace; amateur photographers post their photos on Flickr, or distribute their homemade videos on YouTube. Digital networks put the user at the forefront of creative processes, enabling individuals to participate and collaborate actively in the production and distribution of creative works.

Works in digital format can easily be remixed and incorporate pre-existing materials, or merge into collaborative creative enterprises. Building on prior works may require a costly process of determining which uses are permissible, however, and possibly negotiating a license to use the work. Avoiding a copyright infringement becomes a major challenge for amateur creators, and the risk of liability erects new barriers to creative and collaborative activities in the UGC environment.

One of the current legal challenges is to secure the interests of participants in this creative environment. For this purpose, we need a better understanding of the parameters that affect access to creative materials in this context, and the ways in which terms of access are designed.

Does the ascendancy of UGC give rise to different considerations related to private ordering for governing access? The objections to private ordering governing access to creative works presumed an environment in which standard licenses were designed by the content industry to govern mass-produced content in a unified and often restrictive manner. Would the same concerns equally apply to the new creative landscape of UGC? This environment is characterized by the following features: content produced by users is facilitated by platforms; the relationship between users and platforms is multi-layered; users are both consumers of services and producers of content; and content is subject to a variety of licensing strategies. The following sections discuss each of these features.

15.4.1 Licensing platforms

A report recently published by the OECD identifies the special role reserved for platforms in the UGC environment (OECD, 2007). UGC is often made available through commercial platforms on which users generate and distribute their own content while simultaneously consuming content and services provided by the facility. Social media platforms allow users to share opinions, pictures, movies and music. Other platforms make possible collaboration in producing new creative works, such as computer programs (e.g. Linux) or encyclopedias (e.g. Wikipedia). Platforms coordinate and facilitate access to UGC via search engines (e.g. Google, Yahoo!), distribution platforms (e.g. YouTube, Flickr), social networks (e.g. MySpace, Facebook) and virtual worlds (e.g. Second Life). Platforms thus promote collaboration and interaction among individual users by providing a combination of different functions. These may range from the basics, hosting the content and enabling access, which are services provided by standard online intermediaries, to social/community functions, such as rating, social networking and virtual identity.

Even though users are the producers of the content, they do not usually draft the licenses that govern it. Ownership in the content, and the rights of others to reproduce, modify and distribute it ("terms of access"), are often defined by the platforms that facilitate the content, or by ready-made licensing schemes provided by third parties.

Social media platforms govern UGC by standard terms of access designed by the platform. The terms of use in major social media platforms show little diversity (based on a comparison of MySpace, Facebook, Linkedin, YouTube, Flickr and Second Life carried out in November 2007). All terms of use are available "as is," and reserve the right of the platform to change the terms at any point. In most cases the agreement is entered simply by the act of using the site. Under most terms of use the user remains the owner of the content uploaded by him/her. By posting the content on the social media site, however, the user authorizes the platform to use, modify, publicly perform, publicly display, reproduce and distribute such content through the site. The license is worldwide, nonexclusive, fully paid and royalty-free, and permits sublicensing. Some licenses terminate when the user removes the content from the sites, while others are perpetual and irrevocable (e.g. LinkedIn, Second Life). YouTube's license terminates after a "commercially reasonable time."

Some licenses define only the terms of access vis-à-vis the platform, authorizing the platform freely to use content that was made available through its services. In other cases, terms of access will secure the rights of other users to use the content without any restrictions. The license posted by Second Life, for example, automatically grants users the right to use, reproduce, distribute, display and perform content displayed on the platform. The right of subsequent users freely to use prior works is particularly important for collaborative enterprises such as Wikipedia.

In some cases, users may select how they wish to license their work to others. Flickr, for instance, allows users to make their photos available by simply posting a copyright notice ("All rights reserved") or subscribing to a Creative Commons license of their choice. It is interesting that the vast majority of users on Flickr selected the most restrictive Creative Commons license. A random count shows that, although the most liberal license was used by 7.5 million users, the most restrictive license was used by over 22 million.[5]

Independent licensing schemes ("norm generators"), such as Creative Commons or free software licenses, allow user-creators to apply ready-made terms of access to their works. These licenses are available for authors who wish to release their creative works under particular terms of use. The significance of these independent schemes increases as users seek more mobility and freedom to transfer their content from

[5] See Flickr: www.flickr.com/creativecommons (accessed April 15, 2008).

one platform to another. The advantages of independent licensing schemes grow greater as content aggregators turn into an increasingly important point of access to content. In such a distribution structure, terms of use are attached by the generator of the content, while access is facilitated by the aggregators.

15.4.2 The dual nature of platforms

The terms of access of mass-produced content are often drafted unilaterally by multinational corporations and enforced against uninformed consumers. Terms of access in EULAs were therefore relatively restrictive, limiting the freedom of consumers to make full use of their purchased copies. One would expect content producers to respond to consumers' preferences, but often these were not reflected in the EULA provisions, since markets rarely developed any special demand for particular terms of access because of several market failures.

In the UGC environment, terms of access are drafted by platforms, reflecting the dual nature of social media platforms as commodities of their owners and communities of their users. Platform–user relationships are multilevel and more complex than vendor–consumer relationships. Many online services are provided free of charge. Users do not pay with their money but invest other types of consideration: their free labor, their social connections, their engagement in online discussions, their personal data and their privacy.

In their capacity as producers of content and generators of economic value, users are more likely to care about how their intellectual property rights are being used. Users are more likely to be informed and motivated to negotiate the terms of access to creative works in social media platforms. They will generally seek more say in determining the terms of access to their own works and the works of others. At the same time, users might be more vulnerable, and suffer various disadvantages vis-à-vis the platform.

Social media platforms facilitate a community, not merely a market for users. For end users, a platform is not simply a means for distributing information and facilitating the sale of goods; it also functions as a community. End users may have a vested interest in social media platforms. They are invested in their profiles, creative efforts, social connections, and the social status and reputation they have earned. Quitting the social media platform might be costly. When data and content created on a platform cannot be easily transferred, nor the community of users easily reproduced, users might not have an exit option, so they might not be in a position to demand particular terms.

From the platforms' perspective, users are perceived as one of the company's assets. The community of users is a commodity that increases the market value of the enterprise. Social media platforms generate profits by maintaining an engaged community of creative participants. The platform's economic value derives from the network of users, who create value. Users generate original content or editorial functions; they provide eyeball to advertisers and produce data for marketers. In fact, there is no value in the platform other than the users who actively engage in it. To a large extent, platforms may find themselves at the mercy of their users, especially if users have decided collectively to play by different rules.

Recent examples suggest that end users actually care about the terms of use, and in some cases have been successful in exerting pressure on providers to modify what they believed were unreasonable terms. For instance, the website Fark.com revised its copyright terms after public outrage following a story on BoingBoing. The original terms provided that every submission by users "carry with it an implied assignment of the entire copyright interest in the submission." Terms of service by other hosting services such as Yahoo! (early in 1999) and MySpace were revised in response to complaints by end users. These examples are consistent with eBay's sellers' boycott following eBay's announcement of a new fee structure. Another story relates to Digg, a social aggregator using the editorial functions performed by its users. Digg faced a community revolt following its decision to remove an HD-DVD decryption post after receiving a "Cease and desist" letter from the owner of the IP. The community of users protested about Digg's editorial intervention, and its front page was rife with HD-DVD decryption posts. Finally, Kevin Rose, Digg's founder, posted a public apology promising to avoid in the future such interventions as taking materials down.

These stories demonstrate that, even though terms of access might be drafted by the platforms, they are not determined unilaterally in the same way as EULAs are. They reflect the complexity of new social media. Users of platforms are more engaged in setting the terms, and platform owners must be more attentive to users' preferences, since they are more dependent on the community's vitality.

15.4.3 The dual role of users: a user-producer

Users of social media platforms play a dual role: they generate original content, which is made available by the platform, and at the same time they use content originated by the platform and by other users. When terms of access are designed by amateur users, should we expect them to opt for fewer restrictions on the use of their works?

Creative activities of users are often carried without the expectation of remuneration, and content is often distributed on a not-for-profit basis. In many cases users' motivation is nonmonetary, and reflects a wide range of human needs and interests: self-expression, affiliation and connecting with others, or acquiring prestige and self-esteem. Amateurs' content often involves lower investments, and those engaged in creative activities simply do it for pleasure. UGC is therefore less dependent on a business model that secures a financial return for each creative investment, like mass-produced content in the past.

One may further presume that, since end users act concurrently as producers and consumers of creative works, they are more likely to take into account, on the whole, all the significant interests involved. The claim is that this dual role may enable owners to reach the terms of access reflected through public ordering. This may constitute a social contract intended to reflect our shared understanding of the optimal access to creative works, regardless of our immediate vested interest in any particular rule.

General rules adopted by society through collective action mechanisms are, arguably, more distant from the temporary interests of particular parties. Public rule-making processes allow a choice to be made behind a Rawlsian "veil of ignorance." That, of course, is if we momentarily put aside the deficiencies of governments, especially those identified by public choice theory.

Are users in a UGC environment more likely to exercise their rights in ways that facilitate more access to creative works? Are they more likely to act in a socially informed manner when selecting the terms of access that would apply to their works?

Several anecdotes suggest that this may not always be the case. The story of Danica Radovanovic's blog highlights the commercial pressures and the confusion among Creative Commons licensors over the purpose of the license. Radovanovic runs a blog called "Belgrade and beyond," hosted by WordPress.com. Radovanovic's blog was subject to a CC/BY/ND license.[6] She changed it to a CC-BY-ND-NC license. She was upset to discover that her blog was being mirrored by a Chinese user, who used Google AdSense to generate profits from ads. Radovanovic notified the blog hosting service, and also sent a notice to Google ADSense service regarding the alleged infringement. Within a few days she managed to block the Chinese mirroring site (which apparently also made Wikipedia available in China).

Radovanovic's story reflects the evolving interests and commercial pressures in the UGC environment. She didn't want to lose income generated through Google AdSense, and also wanted to stop what she saw as unjust, preventing the mirroring site from benefiting from her own efforts. In the absence of any commitment to values of access in the licensing scheme, she enforced her license to block access. The story also shows how commercial interests of users could take priority – and are likely to push for further restrictions.

Another lawsuit brought by the celebrity Adam Curry against a Dutch magazine[7] demonstrates how a Creative Commons license can be used to gain control over the use of a picture, and restrict its dissemination and use. The *Weekend Magazine* published photos of Curry's daughter without his permission. The photos were posted by Curry himself on Flickr and were marked "for public use." A sidebar titled "Additional information" was linked to Creative Commons' logo. Another click linked to the Creative Commons Attribution-NonCommercial-ShareAlike license. The license allowed free use of the photos for noncommercial purposes as long as credit was granted. Curry argued that the use of his photograph violated his privacy – a claim that the court dismissed. Curry further argued that the publication by the magazine violated the license and infringed his copyright. The court held that the republication of the photos by the magazine was commercial and therefore violated the terms of the Creative Commons license. The license, the court held, was enforceable, and automatically applied to the use, even when the user had not explicitly agreed to its terms and was not even aware of it. The court's

[6] "BY" means that the user of the license should "attribute the work in the manner specified by the author or licensor"; see http://creativecommons.org/licenses/by/3.0. This is not an acronym, then, but a kind of code that refer to licensing conditions.

[7] *Curry* v. *Audax*, Rechtbank Amsterdam, Docket no. 334492/KG 06–176 SR, 3/9/06 District Court of Amsterdam, March 9, 2006.

view was that the defendant should have diligently investigated the applicable terms, and conducted a thorough and precise examination before publishing photos from the internet. In case of doubt, the court held, the defendant should have requested authorization from the copyright holder.

Curry used his copyright to protect the privacy of his daughter (even though he himself posted her pictures on the web). Others may wish to use copyright for other purposes, not necessarily consistent with free and open access. One example concerns Canadian photographer David Wise, who threatened to sue Betty Hinton, a Canadian politician who used his photograph in her campaign. The picture was downloaded from Flickr and was subject to the Creative Commons Attribution-ShareAlike license. The photographer said that he would not have allowed the use of the photograph for the campaign since he disagreed with the campaign's political views.

These anecdotes reflect the power that comes with copyrights – that is, control over creative works and the way they are used. The stories further reflect the wide range of interests that this type of control over the use of works may serve. Commercial interests, as in the case of Radovanovic, are probably the most pressing. Commercial pressures are, in fact, likely to increase as the UGC environment matures and new business models evolve, allowing users to benefit from their labor. Even for Radovanovic, though, it was not just about money. It was also about justice, the wish to prevent others from benefiting from the fruits of her creation. Protecting privacy, political convictions, moral beliefs and personal reputation can also impel right holders to limit access to their creative works. They may do so even if they themselves wish to access and freely use other people's works, and generally support a rule that provides more liberal access to and use of creative materials. Even in the UGC environment, therefore, leaving the terms of access up to the right holders might not guarantee efficient access to creative works.

15.4.4 Different licensing strategies: standardization and modularity

The UGC environment is a many-to-many licensing environment. Every user is empowered to determine the terms of access to his/her own content, which results in an explosion of terms. Licensing platforms can bring some level of uniformity, which, as explained below, might be crucial for securing access to creative works.

The Creative Commons and FSF licensing schemes reflect two different licensing strategies, and it is therefore interesting to compare the two. Creative Commons' strategy is modular and allows each author to choose his/her own selection of standard terms. The FSF's strategy, by contrast, offers a standard license that applies as is to every piece of software created under the license.

Although the General Public License subscribes to a rather rigid set of principles, Creative Commons' strategy endorses *choice*. The platform allows owners to select their own combination of terms. The only standard provision that applies automatically to all licenses requires credit to the original author (Attribution). The other provisions are modular and allow a mix-and-match approach: NonCommercial, which prohibits any commercial use of the work; NonDerivs, which prohibits the transformation, alteration and creation of any derivatives based on the original work; and ShareAlike, which requires that all subsequent works based on the original work be subject to the same terms as the original work. Several other licenses are simply tailored for specific needs, such as the developing-countries license, or sampling. I call this modular strategy a *strategy of choice*.

Standard terms and modular terms represent two different strategies for governing access. While modularity offers flexibility and promises easier adaptation to changing circumstances, standard terms establish a more rigid regime.

Elsewhere (Elkin-Koren, 2006), I have argued that the modular licensing strategy of Creative Commons, which seeks to promote access to creative works, may be self-defeating and may introduce new barriers to access. There are, basically, two reasons for this: the diversity of licenses and the unintended consequences of endorsing choice by authors.

The first point is that the strategy of choice creates a diversity of licenses, and makes it more difficult for users to build on each other's work. A diversity of licenses is confusing. Creative Commons sought to replace the "no-entry" copyright regime, which requires a license prior to each and every use, with a "license inside" regime. Once potential users recognize the Creative Commons icon (CC) they can safely assume that they are free to copy and redistribute the work, even though it is copyrighted. To be effective, however, the Creative

Commons icon must be distinctive. It has to communicate a clear message to the general public regarding permissible uses. The strategy of choice weakens the distinct meaning of the icon. The icon does not tell us much about which uses of the work are authorized. One still has to investigate the type of license it is. Does it prohibit the preparation of derivative works? Does it allow commercial use? Is it a share-alike license?

A diversity of licenses may further reduce interoperability among different licenses and make it difficult to integrate them into new creative works. Such integration and remixing of preexisting works is an essential part of creativity, especially in the digital environment. The modularity of license terms creates a diversity of licenses, which inevitably leads to conflicting terms. If an artist wants to create a derivative work using a picture that is subject to a NonCommercial-ShareAlike license and another picture that is Attribution-ShareAlike, he/she may find out that he/she simply cannot do so. Attribution-ShareAlike would require subsequent works to be distributed without any further restrictions and NonCommercial-ShareAlike would limit permissible use to noncommercial uses only. In other words, the modularity of provisions facilitated by Creative Commons may create barriers to access, in terms of the higher transaction costs involved in figuring out the different licenses and having to resolve conflicting license terms.

The licensing strategy may also carry a normative message. Licensing platforms may serve as a gigantic educational system. If a licensing platform enables authors to select restrictions of their choice, without setting any limits, the dominant message it communicates is the sovereignty of authors. When a licensing platform includes mandatory provisions that reflect a definition of freedom in information, it endorses values of sharing, collaboration and exchange in creative processes. Authors who employ a Creative Commons licensing scheme therefore receive a normative message not much different from that assumed by the proprietary model: authors are entitled to govern their works as they please; they are free to exclude some uses; everything we create can be licensed; and, in fact, a license is necessary for each and every use.

The user-friendly toolkit for licensing copyright makes the sovereignty of authors over their creative works more pervasive. Creative Commons brought copyright into the desktops of individual writers, bloggers, amateurs, posters on Flickr and YouTube and subscribers to social networks. The ability to exercise copyright, once the sole territory of commercial publishers, is now available to individual users. These newcomers to the copyright realm had always had copyright, but they rarely used it. Many users were probably unaware of their rights, and never bothered to assert them. Licensing was either too complicated or too expensive. By making the licensing available to all, licensing platforms strengthen the hold of copyright in the UGC environment.

To summarize, the use of private ordering by end users to govern UGC may not necessarily promote access to creative works. In a many-to-many licensing environment, in which every user can design his/her own license, licenses might create barriers to access. Authorizing access to creative works should be straightforward. Every restriction on access imposes a burden on each and every user: the need to study the scope of restriction to avoid an infringement. The cost of this will increase as the terms of access become more diversified. To guarantee access to creative works, terms of access must be standardized. A variety of restrictions means extra cost. Paradoxically, private ordering strategies, which facilitate less choice by authors, are the most useful for facilitating access.

15.5 Conclusion

Critics of private ordering as the dominant mechanism for governing access to creative works are skeptical about the idea that market mechanisms can adequately secure access to creative works. This skepticism derives from a fundamental disbelief in the existence of a market for different access terms, and the view that what right holders call "contracts" are simply unilateral provisions that are held to be enforceable against third parties. In the absence of meaningful consent there is no reason to assume that these arrangements are efficient. Skepticism regarding a market mechanism for governing access to creative works also assumes that access to informational goods involves externalities and therefore may call for central intervention. Overall, skeptics of private ordering to govern access reject the view of "contract-as-product." Consumers' choice to acquire content, they argue, should not be viewed as acceptance of the terms and conditions that define the scope of permissible use.

This notion of contract-as-product is further challenged by user-generated content. The contract-as-product approach presumes that mass copies of creative works are produced and distributed by the content industry, just as with any other commodity. Content in the UGC environment, by contrast, is produced by individual users who interact and collaborate via social media platforms. These differences between mass-produced content and UGC may entail different considerations in governing access to creative works.

First, as the analysis shows, access to UGC is often governed by the facilitating platform. Users control the means for producing and distributing content, but coordination is facilitated by platforms. Users who produce the content do not have the legal power to determine the terms of access. In some cases, users may not even own the content they produce. Individual creators might have interests and stakes different from those of the platform. This is not to suggest that regulation by platforms would necessarily produce more restrictive terms. For instance, platforms that use UGC to draw attention and increase traffic to their facilities may have an incentive to minimize the control exercised by each user/producer over the content he/she has produced. In other cases, however, individual users may have greater incentive than a platform to share content freely, on a variety of platforms, on a noncommercial basis.

Second, users in the UGC environment have multiple roles. Vis-à-vis the platforms, users consume some services, and in return produce some content. At the same time, they are consuming content produced by others. The dual role of users as both consumers and producers challenges the view that consuming UGC is simply a bargain between platforms and users/consumers for the purchase of products or services. One cannot seriously argue that consumers of UGC express their preferences for particular terms of use through their purchasing choices. The fact that users "pay" for access with free labor, social connections and personal data makes users in the UGC environment far more vulnerable than consumers of commodities. The notion of a "bargain," which is central to the contract-as-product view, may not fully capture the complexity of processes taking place in online UGC communities.

Third, the UGC environment blurs more traditional distinctions between commercial and noncommercial. Platforms facilitate communities of users, but, at the same time, this virtual community is also a commodity for platform owners. Platforms are often commercial entities, which turn the content and social interactions produced by end users into a market commodity. A similar duality characterizes participating users. The shift from the mass-market production and distribution of content to UGC creates commercial pressures on individual users, who now become an independent unit of production. Conflicting desires to share and control content may come into play. The interdependence of platforms and users make individual users and platforms both vulnerable in novel ways that require further study.

Fourth, social media platforms facilitate new forms of collective action. Individuals in the UGC environment are acting collectively, for instance, when they post their homemade videos on YouTube and rate the videos posted by others. Action by individual users in the UGC environment is not "collective" in the classical sense. It is not an act of collective governance that generates norms of general applicability. Individuals' actions are coordinated rather than bounded by a single set of formal rules expressing their choices at any given moment. Theirs is not exactly a group action either, since it does not entail the long-term commitment of community affiliation. People may go in and out of social networks, and may engage in ad hoc collaboration with others. The content they produce endures nonetheless. Governing the rights and duties regarding access to such content is therefore a long-term undertaking. Collective action in this context is not a market transaction either. Participating users are not paid for their actions, and they make no purchasing choices. The nature of such coordination and self-management is yet to be explored.

On a conceptual level, the emerging environment may require us to be more cautious in applying our traditional notions of consumers and to examine our presumptions about legal doctrines such as contracts of adhesion. The discourse of disparities of power may have to make way for a more egalitarian view of partnership, in which platform owners and users may have to collaborate to attain the optimal terms of use that will maximize the interests of all.

We need to develop a framework that will help us conceptualize a social activity that is a commercial asset, a market commodity and, at the same time, a community. That social media platforms also constitute communities of users loosens somewhat the strict economic view of this phenomenon. For the platform, the terms of access must serve a commercial interest, maximizing the economic value of the online activities. For users, however, the terms of access may have to guarantee more than just economic viability. Their vested interests are more profound. Content produced in social media platforms may reflect a user's personality and identity. It may reflect a joint effort, a community asset, which goes beyond the sum of the different parcels of ownership of each contributor. The relationship of each user to such content may reflect a sense of belonging and a long-term commitment to a community of peers. Issues related to sovereignty, autonomy and liberty may come into play.

16 The effects of electronic commerce technologies on business contracting behaviors

BRUNO DEFFAINS AND JANE K. WINN

16.1 Introduction

Contract law provides a framework within which relationships can be established and administered for the mutual benefit of the parties; electronic commerce (e-commerce) provides tools for reducing the costs of establishing and administering these relationships. When traditional contract law doctrines are applied to electronic commerce, however, the result may be uncertainty, the costs of which may offset any efficiency gains from technological innovation. In order to prevent the application of traditional contract law doctrine from impeding the use of new technologies, some changes may be needed. Precisely what changes are needed is not always clear, however, so the reform of contract law to accommodate technological innovation has been the subject of some controversy in recent decades. This chapter considers some major challenges to contract doctrine created by the use of e-commerce and the range of regulatory responses that different national and regional authorities have adopted, and assesses the practical impact they have had on technological innovation in the governance of markets.

In some situations, conventional legal reasoning and traditional contract law are completely adequate to resolve issues related to electronic contracts. For example, in an early US case, *Howley* v. *Whipple*,[1] the court found that a telegram could meet a requirement that a contract be in writing, noting "it makes no difference whether the operator writes the offer or acceptance with a steel pen an inch long attached to an ordinary penholder, or whether the pen is a copper wire a thousand miles long. In either case, the thought is communicated to the

[1] See 48 NH 487 (1869).

paper by the use of a finger…" In other situations, however, established contract law may not provide an adequate framework. In such cases, parties interested in adopting e-commerce technologies can be expected to lobby for law reforms and other institutional changes.

The emergence in the 1980s of electronic data interchange (EDI) technology to support "just-in-time" manufacturing processes was perceived as causing disruptive changes in business behavior, because, unlike telex or fax technology, it became possible for the first time to form contracts with nothing more than machine-to-machine communications. Managers who wished to adopt innovative e-commerce technologies were worried that, if lawyers and judges applied anachronistic legal concepts to new business practices, then the use of EDI technology might deprive them of all recourse to the courts. Such concerns triggered law reform projects around the world designed to remove irrational impediments to the growth of e-commerce. One of the most significant efforts was spearheaded by the United Nations Commission on International Trade Law (UNCITRAL). The 1996 UNCITRAL Model Law on Electronic Commerce (EC Model Law) was initially designed merely to remove obstacles to the use of EDI, but later it was expanded to cover all forms of e-commerce, including internet commerce. At the heart of the EC Model Law are the principles that old and new methods of forming contracts should be treated as functionally equivalent in contract law, and that contract law reforms should be "technology-neutral" (i.e. not used to promote specific e-commerce technologies). The EC Model Law influenced law reform efforts around the world, in developed and developing countries alike. The spread of business-to-business (B2B) e-commerce technologies made possible in part by these law reform efforts has been a major factor fueling the growth of the supply chains and global markets that integrate buyers and suppliers around the world.

In recent years the volume of e-commerce appears to be continuing to grow, though the rate of adoption by businesses of e-commerce technologies is not easy to determine. Several years ago the US Census Bureau began estimating the volume of e-commerce transactions within selected market segments in the US economy, and these statistics provide a rough measure of the degree of acceptance of e-commerce technologies by US businesses. Based on statistics for 2004, the Census Bureau estimated that B2B e-commerce accounts for more than 90 percent of all e-commerce transactions, and that e-commerce accounts for nearly $1 trillion or 24 percent of all transactions in the manufacturing sector and over $800 billion or 17 percent of all merchant wholesale transactions (US Census Bureau, 2006). Although business-to-consumer (B2C) internet commerce has attracted more attention in the mass media, e-commerce accounts for only 2 percent of retail transactions.

Law reforms based on the EC Model Law appear to have satisfied the most broadly based business demands to remove legal obstacles to the use of e-commerce technologies. It appears to be the case that sophisticated businesses in developed market economies now believe that they are unlikely to face any arbitrary or irrational obstacles to enforcing contracts formed using new technologies, as evidenced by the lack of any ongoing controversy surrounding their use of e-commerce technology to form contracts. Although the regulation of e-commerce in producer markets has been less politically controversial than the regulation of e-commerce in consumer markets, major innovations in contract law have nevertheless occurred as a result of the growing adoption of B2B e-commerce. The most significant innovation has been the growth of technical standards as a form of commercial law in global markets. In markets in which B2B e-commerce is well established, technical standards and standard-developing organizations play a role at least as important as national contract laws in regulating e-commerce between businesses. As a result, in producer markets, the most important e-commerce regulatory challenge may be finding and implementing the optimal standards infrastructure, while, in end user markets, the challenge remains finding and implementing the optimal legal infrastructure.

Although some sophisticated businesses began forming electronic contracts using EDI technology on a routine basis in the 1980s, in consumer markets electronic contracts did not become a major issue until a decade later, when the internet was finally opened to commercial activity. Beginning in the 1990s there have been many major national and regional efforts to overhaul consumer protection laws to address the new challenges of consumer internet commerce. With regard to law reforms targeting technology end users rather than producers, regulatory strategies adopted in the European Union and in the United States have diverged significantly. The United States has favored a "hands-off" approach, letting market forces play a significant role in defining consumers' rights in internet markets as well as the appropriate form of security for internet transactions. In contrast, the European Union has tried to use regulation to establish minimum levels of both consumer protection and transaction security. E-commerce adoption rates in both business and consumer markets appear to be higher in the United States than in the European Union, but it is unclear whether the differences in regulatory strategies are a major cause of this disparity, or simply another reflection of important cultural and institutional differences between the two systems. For example, US enthusiasm for e-commerce and for "deregulation" in recent decades may reflect a higher tolerance for allocating economic risks to individuals rather than collective entities in American society compared to most European societies (Whybrow, 2005).

16.2 Governance framework

Regulators within developed economies have been remarkably consistent in their efforts to promote e-commerce, because it offers the promise of reduced information asymmetries and lower transaction costs within their national markets, and opportunities for businesses and consumers to participate in markets that were previously inaccessible (Clinton and Gore, 1997; EC, 2005). This consensus with regard to the social value of e-commerce does not necessarily extend to regulatory strategies to achieve it, however. Strategies for regulating e-commerce include: private law doctrines, such as contract law combined with market competition and minimal government intervention; direct government intervention, in the form of legislation to encourage interoperability by promoting the adoption of specific standards; direct government intervention to prohibit or mandate particular contract terms; and the de facto or de jure delegation of regulatory authority to intermediaries such as standard-developing organizations. Policies adopted to promote e-commerce have been remarkably consistent with other national policies regarding economic activity: the United States has favored a more market-oriented approach that strives to keep government intervention in markets within narrow limits, while many European countries have relied more heavily on non-market forms of coordination, including direct government intervention, to achieve goals that would be perceived as social rather than economic in the United States. Political economists have used the labels "liberal market economy" (LME) to describe the US approach and "coordinated market economy" (CME) to describe the European approach (Hall and Soskice, 2001).

Differences between LME and CME approaches to the regulation of e-commerce are clearest in consumer (or end user) markets, rather than in producer markets now dominated by supply chains. In consumer/end user markets, the United States and the European Union have taken different approaches to the regulation of consumer internet markets, and the regulation of the security of internet contracts. The United States has left its existing consumer protection laws substantially unchanged, allowing a process of "creeping deregulation through statutory obsolescence" with regard to some activities in consumer internet markets. It has also adopted a "hands-off" approach with regard to the security of internet contracts, allowing market competition to determine the appropriate level of security. By contrast, the European Union has updated consumer protection laws at the EU level in an effort to ensure that consumers enjoy no fewer protections in internet commerce than in traditional commerce, and has expanded the scope of consumer protection in all markets by requiring the application of unfair contract terms law throughout the internal market. It has also tried to harmonize the regulation of electronic signatures as a technology to increase the security of internet contracts – an effort that has so far met with a deplorable lack of success.

With regard to the regulation of B2B e-commerce, an important difference between the United States (as the leading LME) and most other countries (including European CMEs) is in the organization of standard-developing institutions (Tate, 2001). Decentralized control over markets under US federalism and a cultural preference for "bottom-up" (i.e. market-driven, private-sector-controlled) standardization efforts has produced fragmented, decentralized standard-developing processes in the United States. In contrast, standard-setting processes within most other countries tend to be centralized in a single organization. In the European Union, the work of "national standards bodies" in different member states is now often coordinated at the EU level by the work of the European standards organizations.[2] These institutional differences in approaches to standard-developing often

[2] These are CEN (European Committee for Standardization [Comité Européen de Normalisation]), CENELEC (European Committee for Electrotechnical Standardization [Comité Européen de Normalisation Electrotechnique]) and ETSI (European Telecommunications Standards Institute).

matter a great deal with regard to competition to set information and communication technology standards in global markets (Winn, 2006). With regard to the markets for B2B e-commerce standards, however, the impact of such regulatory competition in recent years has often been relatively muted compared with the ICT standards competition in other markets, such as mobile telephony. This may be partly atttributable to the fact that B2B e-commerce technologies now bring only incremental instead of radical innovation to the business processes of the firms that adopt them.

At first glance, US dominance in many markets for e-commerce products and services would seem to suggest that the "light regulation" approach favored by LMEs such as the United States provides a better governance structure to promote e-commerce than does the more traditional regulatory approach favored by CMEs in Europe. More careful analysis reveals that this conclusion may not be warranted, however. LME governance models tend to subordinate the public regulation of economic activity carried out by government agencies to private initiatives within market institutions, but, in the absence of actual competition, this deference to private control may lead to market failure rather than greater productivity. The divergent approaches taken in recent years by US antitrust and EU competition regulators with regard to the operation of de facto ICT standards controlled by Microsoft illustrate this point. Although US regulators seem willing to treat almost any market outcome as the result of market competition, EU regulators appear more concerned with potential abuses of monopoly power that may result when strong network effects drive convergence around ICT standards controlled by private parties.

Industrial organization models show that, if markets are not competitive or at least contestable, dominant players may provide users with too low a level of services. Indeed, digital industries are known for the "winner takes all" type of competition. This is also a recognized characteristic of competition between standards. Recent experience in markets affected by e-commerce technologies shows that new entrants can compete by implementing new "concepts" in internet-based services and that the possibility of such innovation creates an ongoing threat to the positions of established providers of e-commerce products and services. This potential for new competitors to emerge suddenly helps explain why large e-commerce players often have the right incentives to continue to deliver high-quality products and services. In addition, traditional commerce remains a permanent competitor for e-commerce players. If actual competition or the threat of innovation giving rise to new competitors is not present, however, then government enforcement of competition law may be a key variable in the optimal governance structure for e-commerce regulated more by ICT standards than by contract law.

16.3 Business-to-consumer electronic contracts

By the late 1990s the explosive growth in popularity of the World Wide Web among relatively unsophisticated consumer computer users led to the growth of large-scale B2C internet businesses, and unprecedented numbers of consumers engaging directly in cross-border trade – a practice that had formerly been limited almost exclusively to businesses. As might be expected, reactions from regulators in the United States and the European Union to the growth of domestic and international B2C markets diverged markedly. EU regulators have been expanding their oversight of consumer markets, and expanding the role of administrative agencies in enforcement, at precisely the time that US contract law has turned away from public regulatory models. The growing gap in contract law doctrine with regard to consumer transactions appears to be yet another example of diverging long-term trends in political culture and economic regulation on either side of the Atlantic (Löfstedt *et al.*, 2001). The United States was very active in enacting consumer protection laws during the 1960s and 1970s while there was relatively little activity in this area in Europe. The trends reversed during the 1980s, when the United States embraced more market-oriented approaches that require individuals to bear more risk in consumer transactions while the European Union embarked on a sweeping program of legislation to protect consumers from many of those risks.

The United States adopted a "light regulation" strategy based on deference to merchant-drafted standard form contracts and judicial precedent rather than new legislation, whereas the European Union opted to enact new laws to ensure parity between internet and traditional markets with regard to consumer rights. The European Union followed up major consumer law reforms such as the 1993 "Unfair Contract Terms Directive" with a broad package of law reforms designed to make B2C markets as safe for consumers as traditional "bricks and mortar" retail markets. The efforts of EU regulators to build confidence in B2C e-commerce do not appear to be having much effect, however, while the failure of US regulators to intervene in B2C markets with new regulations does not appear to have diminished the enthusiasm of US consumers for internet commerce. US internet businesses have successfully leveraged their market position in the United States to expand in Europe, taking the higher level of regulation in their stride, while EU internet businesses have yet to have much impact on the US market. It is unclear what impact the more restrictive legal environment for EU internet retailers is having on their success in global markets, but they certainly do not appear to be profiting from a "race to the top" (Porter, 1990).

Political scientists and economists distinguish between "economic regulation," aimed at supporting competition in markets, and "social regulation," aimed at protecting health and safety. Consumer protection laws are now treated as a form of economic regulation in the United States; government intervention is treated as appropriate only when it is clear that competition is not doing an adequate job of meeting consumer needs (Epstein, 2006). EU lawmakers appear to be skeptical that mere economic regulation will provide enough support for online consumer markets in Europe. The European Commission has repeatedly emphasized the idea that online commerce is unlikely to grow in popularity in the European Union unless consumer confidence can be enhanced, and the most obvious means to achieve that end is greater regulation of B2C transactions to protect consumers (EU Council and EC, 2000). The European Union has proceeded on multiple fronts in its efforts to make internet commerce safe for consumers, including strong data protection legislation, which is clearly considered a form of social regulation in the European Union (Kuner, 2003), and legislation governing the terms of "distance contracts," in addition to legislation limiting the enforcement of "unfair contract terms" in any consumer transaction, online or offline. These law reforms have in effect turned EU consumer contract law into another form of social regulation.[3]

[3] For example, within the European Commission, consumer protection matters are handled by the Directorate General for Health and Consumers, which also oversees health and food safety regulations, while, in the US federal government, they are often handled by the Federal Trade Commission, which also has jurisdiction over antitrust law enforcement.

Many elements of EU consumer protection policy do appear to be motivated simply by a desire to level the playing field among consumers to ensure that social rather than economic policy objectives are met (Howells and Weatherill, 2005). By mandating a high minimum level of protection, EU online consumer contract law forces all merchants to internalize high compliance costs and constrains the range of possible innovation in marketing channels. By contrast, US online consumer contract law sets a much lower mandatory minimum level of protection (Winn, 2005), which appears to have opened the door to more rapid growth and greater innovation in online retail marketing, although, of course, many of these innovations ultimately fail (German, 2005). If the US approach has allowed more of the costs associated with innovation to be borne by disgruntled individual consumers than the EU approach would permit, then it would not be the first time that changes in the interpretation of American contract law have had the effect of subsidizing the growth of new markets (Horwitz, 1977).

Laws governing consumer contracts generally and internet contracts in particular diverge in the United States and the European Union in large part because the "Unfair Contract Terms Directive"[4] (which regulates form contracts offered by merchants to consumers whether online or offline), the "Distance Selling Directive"[5] (which regulates transactions between remote merchants and consumers, whether by means of television, telemarketing, internet or other electronic communications medium) and the "Electronic Commerce Directive"[6] (which promotes transparency and accountability in online commerce) have had a significant impact on B2C transactions.[7] Unlike the statutory

[4] Council directive 93/13/EEC of April 5, 1993, on unfair terms in consumer contracts; see *Official Journal of the European Communities*, April 21, 1993, L 95: 29–34.

[5] Council directive 97/7/EEC of May 20, 1997, on the protection of consumers in respect of distance contracts; see *Official Journal of the European Communities*, June 4, 1997, L 144: 19–27.

[6] Council directive 00/31/EC of June 8, 2000, on certain legal aspects of information society services, in particular electronic commerce, in the internal market; see *Official Journal of the European Communities*, July 17, 2000, L 178: 1–16.

[7] As a general rule, EU directives do not affect the rights and obligations of individuals until the directive has been transposed into national law. This chapter focuses on the provisions of the relevant directives as indicative of the law of individual member states.

framework established by the "Unfair Contract Terms Directive," US contract law protects consumers from predatory merchant practices with the weaker equitable doctrine of "unconscionability." Although this doctrine may target the same kind of unfair commercial practices as unfair contract terms law, its application is much less predictable, because of the wide variations in judicial precedents applying the doctrine. As a result, most – although not all – US courts reviewing internet consumer contract terms do not hesitate to enforce terms that would be invalidated as unfair contract terms in any EU country (Winn and Webber, 2006).

US companies competing in B2C markets, including Amazon, Google, Yahoo!, eBay and Microsoft, have managed to develop powerful brands and achieve significant market share, not only in the US market but in most European markets. At a minimum, this suggests that the EU commitment to raising the level of protection offered to European consumers throughout the internal market has not precipitated a "race to the top" that fuels the growth of globally competitive EU internet companies (Porter, 1990). The competitiveness of US internet companies in global markets may be due in part to the fact that the challenges of global markets are equivalent to those they face in intensely competitive US retail markets. Another possible explanation is that, since the crash of the dot.com bubble in 2001, there has been a substantial "flight to quality" among US consumers, which has favored the growth of a handful of dominant internet merchants such as Amazon or eBay in the place of the teeming anarchy of the B2C internet markets of the late 1990s. If this is the case, then the relatively lax US regulation of B2C internet markets may, paradoxically, create an opportunity for some internet merchants to distinguish themselves on the basis of their commitment to providing more than the minimum level of service required by law. Internet retailer Amazon, like the mail order retailer Lands End, built brand recognition by voluntarily providing US consumers with an unconditional money-back guarantee of satisfaction, which is an even higher level of protection than that mandated by EU consumer protection law. In contrast, any European merchant hoping to challenge Amazon in EU internet markets cannot try to build brand recognition by guaranteeing consumers' satisfaction with its offerings because such a policy is mandatory, not optional, under EU consumer protection laws. The US laissez-faire approach to regulating internet consumer markets may therefore, ironically, have fueled the growth of national "champions" in global markets while the EU approach of setting high mandatory minimum levels of protection so as to build consumer confidence in the internet market may, inadvertently, have slowed the growth of local companies.

16.4 Security of electronic contracts

One of the most fundamental problems that has to be solved in order to make the switch from traditional commerce to e-commerce is finding a way to ascertain the identity of a transacting party communicating within a network of computers. Authenticating computer users poses serious, but not insurmountable, business and technological challenges. Before the internet made the use of open, insecure networks for commerce commonplace, the problem of authentication was normally solved with a combination of business processes and technologies that established a closed network of computers. Examples of successful, well-established e-commerce systems that operate in global markets using closed networks of information systems include bank wholesale funds transfer networks, electronic data interchange trading partner relationships that use value-added networks, airline computer reservation systems, credit card systems, automated clearing houses and automated teller machine electronic funds transfer systems. Participation in each of these systems is limited either by government regulation and licensing systems or by an individual enrollment process that has significant screening functions and, in some cases, an existing network participant to act as guarantor before a new entrant is accepted. In such a closed system, the process of formalizing security policies, defining roles, establishing access controls and taking the other steps required to deploy an effective system for authenticating users may be difficult and expensive, but not impossible.

When internet commerce first became possible in the mid-1990s there was widespread agreement about the need for new forms of strong authentication technologies that could be used efficiently in this new environment. Given the consensus that the lack of security inherent in internet communications created an acute need for new forms of strong authentication that would be widely adopted and broadly interoperable, it is not surprising that regulators in many countries believed that law reforms could promote internet commerce by eliminating competition between authentication standards. Josh Lerner and Jean Tirole (2006) have noted that owners of intellectual property or mere sponsors of an idea (e.g. authors, security issuers, sponsors of standards) often need to persuade potential buyers or adopters of the worth of their property or idea. To accomplish this, they often resort to more or less independent certifiers. Many reformers thought they could help establish a system of such certifiers through regulation.

Developers of "digital signature" technologies promoted the idea that "public key infrastructures" maintained by "certificate authorities" would make reliable, effective authentication widely available. Although some regulators might have thought that simply requiring the use of such technology would have been the most appropriate law reform, the law reform model that ultimately won out was more indirect: parties seeking the enforcement of contracts signed with digital signatures would enjoy an evidentiary presumption that the signature was valid, which would simplify the process of enforcing the contract in court. Although the first round of law reforms to promote this technology used the term "digital signature" to describe it, this was roundly criticized as being too "technology-specific," so subsequent law reform efforts used the term "electronic signature" and described it in what were intended to be more technology-neutral terms. A decade of experience of trying to implement these laws has shown, however, that there is only one type of technology that meets the requirements of the legislation: the technology formerly known as "digital signatures."

Once again, CMEs and LMEs adopted very different regulatory strategies for dealing with the challenges of internet commerce security. CMEs tried to provide a centralized, coordinated solution, while LMEs deferred to market demand. Although electronic signature laws have proved to be popular in civil law jurisdictions, including many leading CMEs, whose legal professions include notaries and whose commercial laws place a heavy emphasis on signature formalities in traditional commerce, common law jurisdictions without exception resisted enacting them. Commercial law under the common law tradition is, in practice, quite flexible with regard to requirements of form, often treating them as questions of proof at trial rather than mandatory elements of transactions. Commercial lawyers practicing in common law jurisdictions also had confidence that case law would develop to guide courts and transacting parties with regard to how parties to e-commerce transactions should be authenticated.

Immediately after the "Electronic Signature Directive" was issued in 1999 the European Commission took the further step of convening the European Electronic Signature Standardization Initiative, which published a comprehensive suite of standards to promote the adoption of interoperable electronic signature applications in the European Union. In 2003 the Commission sponsored a study of the impact that electronic signatures were having on European markets, and discovered that it was negligible outside the context of "e-government" applications for which member state or local governments required businesses to use them in order to gain access to necessary government services. Although there was no evidence that private parties were using electronic signatures to form contracts, this might merely reflect a slow initial adoption rate as the implementing standards had only recently been issued. A few years later, however, the evidence that the strategy to create certifiers through law reform was a failure was less ambiguous. A study by the Commission in 2006 conceded that the market adoption of electronic signatures had not developed as expected. The Commission study identified as possible factors contributing to this failure the complexity of the technology and the reluctance of certification service providers to act as "trusted third parties" out of liability concerns.

Common law jurisdictions such as the United States, Canada, Australia and New Zealand (which are also leading LMEs) that resisted calls for such legislation have left it to the market to decide what authentication technology was appropriate for internet commerce, and what standards would guarantee interoperability. In the ensuing unregulated competition between technology vendors, many compelling technical solutions have been brought to market, but none has been able to gain a decisive market share. As a result, the default for retail internet transactions in the United States remains user ID and password logons even though the security problems associated with such systems are very well known. This appears to be a clear instance of the problem frequently encountered in markets in which interoperability is essential to maintain the operation of networks, namely that migration from one standard to another can be very difficult. Demand among businesses and consumers for reliable, interoperable authentication technologies continues to grow, however. The vulnerability of internet e-commerce has attracted the attention of organized crime, which now operates on a global basis and routinely evades national law enforcement efforts, resulting in rising levels of identity theft and financial account fraud in the United States and other jurisdictions where internet commerce has gained in popularity.

Competition between developers of authentication technology in the United States has led to the development of new "identity management" standards. Developers of different identity management standards may soon be engaged in a "standards war" to decide which among the competing standards will achieve widespread adoption. The Liberty Alliance is a consortium started by Silicon Valley technology companies, including Sun Microsystems, Oracle and Hewlett-Packard, that now includes such diverse organizations as General Motors, France Télécom, Nokia, NTT DoCoMo, American Express and MasterCard. The Liberty Alliance's original mission was to develop a comprehensive suite of ICT standards to permit two business enterprises to create a "federated identity system" that permits the sharing of trustworthy credentials across organization boundaries.

Not to be left behind, Microsoft and IBM organized the Web Service Interoperability Organization (WS-I), which developed a competing comprehensive suite of ICT standards for strong authentication. This effort has been joined by other leading technology companies, including Hewlett-Packard, Intel, Oracle and SAP AG, among others. Microsoft also announced the development of a "user-centric" identity management system together with its new Vista operating system. This identity management system – CardSpace – is designed to serve as a platform from which authentication systems developed by Microsoft or its competitors can be accessed. The open-source community has also developed standards for a very "lightweight" form of identity management – OpenID 1.0 – which provides weak authentication for social commerce, such as blogs and social networking sites. OpenID is not currently adapted for use in conventional commercial transactions, although the developer community supporting the project has announced its intention to produce OpenID 2.0, which should be suitable for commerce. It is too soon to declare whether any of these competing standardization efforts will achieve widespread adoption in the United States, let alone in global ICT markets, but early indications are that at least one of them might.

With regard to the Lerner and Tirole forum-shopping analysis, the credibility of the Liberty Alliance as a certifier of strong authentication technology comes from its broad base of support among many global technology companies. The governance challenges facing such a broadly based participatory organization may undermine its credibility, however. The credibility of the WS-I is based on the market power of Microsoft and IBM, its leaders and strongest members; the ability to leverage significant market power and simpler governance structure may confer a form of de facto rather than de jure credibility in the minds of some end users. Microsoft's credibility as a certifier of authentication technologies was undermined by the failure of Passport, one of its early efforts in this area, but that credibility may be restored if the identity management system embedded in its new Windows Vista operating system achieves widespread popularity. The credibility of the OpenID standards developers is based on the enormous popularity of social commerce, especially among technologically sophisticated young people around the world. In the case of digital signatures, it appears that the sponsors of a less attractive technology chose a certifier that lacks both competence and credibility, with the result that end users disregard the technology and the certification.

This situation can be analyzed in general as a coordination game, or in particular as a "battle of the sexes" game (Mattli and Büthe, 2003). A simple coordination game would require two players to both choose the same of two possible strategies in order to receive a higher payoff. In the more complicated "battle of the sexes" variation, one player is the husband who wants to go to a sporting event while the other player is the wife who wants to go to the opera. The husband does not like opera and the wife does not like sport, but they each prefer to be in the other's company to attending an event alone. In the context of end users trying to agree on a technology for strong authentication, the end users will maximize their payoffs by agreeing on a single authentication standard, even though some prefer the Liberty Alliance standards and others prefer Microsoft standards. Adoption of either standard would result in a Nash equilibrium. Once a critical mass of end users has agreed which standard to adopt, it would become the market standard and, as a result of network externalities, would be expected to achieve near-universal adoption. Up until now, however, there has been no consensus among end users with regard to a standard for strong authentication, and adoption rates for strong authentication technologies have been low as a result. The risks associated with a change in technology standards and uncertainty over the sharing of costs and benefits among trading partners have impeded the adoption of strong authentication technologies, even though it is clearly in the best interest of end users to find a common solution.

16.5 Business-to-business electronic contracts

The use of e-commerce between businesses is one of many factors that have contributed to the transformation of business contracting in recent decades. This transformation is in part a response to the globalization of markets, resulting in the organization of production and distribution into global networks known as supply chains. For enterprises struggling to adapt to these new conditions, the use of e-commerce is a necessary but not sufficient condition of success. When successfully implemented, e-commerce technologies allow enterprises to reduce waste and inefficiency in production and distribution radically by increasing the coordination between trading partners to a degree that was formerly possible only with vertical integration. Migrating management systems from traditional administrative processes to those using e-commerce is a difficult and dangerous task, in part because of the complexity of the business information systems required and the lack of standardization among business enterprises.

Standards play an indispensable role in the administration of supply chains, because of the large volumes of information that have to be exchanged between separate enterprises. In the absence of standards, the administrative overheads associated with translating to and from incompatible data formats can be substantial (Gibb and Damodaran, 2002). Modifications to business information systems to permit the high-volume exchange of data between trading partners are required on an ongoing basis as each enterprise's system is upgraded. The wide variety of information flows and the diversity of customer–supplier interactions make the standards infrastructure very complex, resulting in a large absolute number of standards. For example, the RosettaNet consortium has identified more than 100 separate business processes for which standard protocols, called partner interface processes, are necessary within the electronics sector.

Firms within an industry can put needed standards infrastructures in place to support integration efforts in several ways, and each approach has implications for the efficiency and completeness of the resulting systems. If the industry is dominated by a single firm, usually an original equipment manufacturer (OEM), that firm can create standards and impose them on the rest of the industry. AT&T took this role in telecommunications during the era of regulation and developed and implemented most of the standards used within that sector. In the case of personal computer operating systems, Microsoft's dominance has allowed it to set standards that hardware and software firms alike are obligated to support. In an alternative scenario in imperfectly competitive markets, each large OEM can develop its own standards and insist that its suppliers comply to enjoy continued business. This has long been the practice in the US automotive sector, in which the "Big Three" (General Motors, Ford and Daimler-Chrysler) have routinely imposed their unique standards on direct suppliers. Potentially, many or all of the firms in an industry can work together to create a mutually beneficial infrastructure for integration, either by forming a consortium through an industry trade or technical association, or with the help of one or more standards development organizations. Even so, it is difficult to manage power and influence issues within consortia and other voluntary organizations, and success in creating efficient standards is not assured. In addition, any incomplete representation of entire industries linked through supply chains within these groups means that important suppliers and customers may be left out of the process.

From the standpoint of economic theory, this approach to standardization is likely to lead to inadequate standards infrastructures for at least two reasons. The first arises from the public goods nature of these standards, which inevitably leads to a free-rider problem and resultant under-provision of the good. The second reason is coordination failure, in which asymmetric incentives lead participants to pursue investments that are suboptimal for the industry as a whole. This problem appears particularly acute in the case of ICT (Brousseau, 1994). Coordination failures arise from asymmetries in incentives between market participants, either among competitors or among levels in a supply chain. In the competitive case, firms acting in their self-interest may invest in standards or other forms of human capital that are not optimal for the industry as a whole. This is especially critical in imperfectly competitive markets, in which strategic interaction is important. As an example, the separate and incompatible systems created by the automotive OEMs for the exchange of technical data are a direct result of the focus on private optima among the oligopolistic Big Three. A second type of failure may occur between customers and suppliers along the supply chain, especially if the size and technical capabilities of the partners are quite different. Small firms in the lower tiers may have an interest in improving their information infrastructure but may lack the financial resources or technical capability to make it happen. Their incentives to invest are further reduced if they believe that any cost advantages they obtain from increased efficiency will be quickly competed away through lower prices. The larger firms might more easily take on the burden of developing improved information systems. If, however, most of the initial benefits will accrue to their suppliers, these firms and OEM corporations may conclude that their investment might not pay out over their required time horizon (Deffains and Demougin, 2006).[8]

From a theoretical perspective, the problem of a supplier selling through multiple competing retailers has received significant attention. The literature on this problem has focused on the design of coordination schemes, such as contractual arrangements between the parties that allow the decentralized supply chain to perform as well as a centralized one. Frank Mathewson and Ralph Winter (1984) show that, when the supplier has all the bargaining power, the joint profit of the supply chain is maximized in equilibrium (see also Segal, 1999). In contrast, Fernando Bernstein and Leslie Marx (2006) demonstrate that, when retailers have the bargaining power, the supply chain profit is not maximized. In addition, they show that some retailers may be excluded from trade with the supplier. In other words, the maximization of the joint profit implies an advantage for the supplier.

Other than the "media-neutral" reforms to contract law described earlier, there have been no changes in the law applicable to B2B contracts in either the United States or the European Union. Unlike consumer contract law, in which large variations are found between the laws of different countries, the general principles of contract law

[8] This is the classical "hold-up" problem.

applicable to transactions between businesses are often substantially similar.[9] Furthermore, even though the move from traditional markets and vertically integrated firms, on the one hand, to supply chain hybrids, on the other, has been little short of revolutionary in many markets, conventional contract law doctrines in both the United States and the European Union appear to be adequate to accommodate major changes in the character of B2B contracts. The terms of contracts between businesses are presumed to reflect competitive forces and the self-interest of the parties to a greater degree than contracts between merchants and consumers, and general contract law doctrines are presumed to be adequate to permit the parties to respond to competition and express their self-interest (Schwartz and Scott, 2003). Empirical research into whether traditional principles of contract law work equally well in supply chains or traditional markets is not easy to conduct, however. One recent study of supply chain contracts in the US automobile industry suggests that even global multinationals may be less rational in their contract negotiations than economic theory would suggest (Ben-Shahar and White, 2006).

Unlike B2C transactions, in which the terms and conditions are generally posted by merchants on the internet for all the world to see, and about which there has been a large volume of litigation in the United States resulting in a significant number of reported judicial decisions, the terms of B2B contracts generally remain confidential and appear to be rarely if ever litigated, even in the United States. Given that trillions of dollars worth of contracts have been formed using e-commerce technologies over the last twenty years, it is likely that the dearth of judicial decisions resolving disputes arising out of B2B contracts formed using IT reflects a lower rate of litigation for these contracts than contracts formed by traditional means. Assuming that B2B contracts formed by means of e-commerce do indeed give rise to fewer litigated disputes, then the lower litigation rates may be at least partly attributable to the greater accuracy of sophisticated electronic contracting systems. Human error in preparing orders or confirmations may be eliminated before performance begins, reducing

[9] "Similar" is not the same as "identical," however; the desire of businesses engaged in cross-border trade to reduce the costs associated with such differences as do exist have helped produce the UNCITRAL Convention on the International Sale of Goods and the UNIDROIT (international Institute for the Unification of Private Law) Principles of International Commercial Contracts.

the number of disputes about what the actual terms of contracts are. Although the greater accuracy of B2B electronic contracting systems clearly provides part of the explanation for what appears to be a lower rate of litigation, it seems unlikely that it is a complete explanation.

A more complete explanation may require examination of the business behavior of firms that have achieved competitive advantages by increasing their use of information technology in their relationships with customers and suppliers. Early analysis of the impact of increased use of ICT among business contracting parties provided the "electronic markets hypothesis" (EMH): that, as ICT reduces coordination costs between firms, market-based forms of economic activity will grow in importance (Malone, Yates and Benjamin, 1987). According to this hypothesis, the immediate connection between a buyer and a supplier increases cooperation and efficiency between firms. The success of worldwide retail chain Wal-Mart has frequently been attributed to the EDI system installed among its pool of suppliers. The ubiquity of the internet, moreover, allows more companies to operate on a common platform without heavy investment in closed-information networks such as EDI. The more those companies conduct trades online, the more profitable internet-based supply chain management will become (Garicano and Kaplan, 2001).

The EMH assumed that the reductions in transaction costs enabled by new communication technology would fuel the growth of decentralized market systems at the expense of either cooperative or hierarchical systems. Major sources of transaction costs identified in the EMH included coordination costs, the complexity of product descriptions and asset specificity, and it was assumed that new communication technologies could reduce all these costs (Brousseau, 2002). If one of the primary determinants of asset specificity is the unequal diffusion of knowledge, then the growth of the internet would indeed lead to a reduction in asset specificity, and so favor the growth of markets (Park and Yun, 2004). Although the use of the internet and other ICTs may reduce coordination costs and diminish the problem of complexity in connection with product descriptions, there is no evidence that it is having any impact on the degree of asset specificity generally.

The relationship between investment in ICT and reducing coordination costs may not be as simple as the authors of the EMH assumed, furthermore. A recent study of investment in supply chain technologies showed that, although investments in technology to improve the efficiency of supply chains normally increases the efficiency of the firms making the investment, a significant number of companies that invested heavily in supply chain technologies were actually less efficient after their investment than beforehand (Kanakamedala, Srivatsan and Ramsdell, 2003). In light of the shortcomings of the EMH, others have suggested a "move-to-the-middle" hypothesis (MMH), arguing that greater use of ICTs will fuel the growth of supply chains as a new form of hybrid economic organization between market and hierarchies (Clemons, Reddi and Row, 1993; Park and Yun, 2004).

Economic theory predicts that hybrids will emerge whenever they offer lower transaction costs than either markets or firms (Williamson, 1996). ICT-enabled supply chains allow trading partners to enjoy some of the stability and continuity associated with firms, while maintaining the sharp incentives provided by markets. Under the conditions of unregulated competition that prevail in global markets, the combination of continuity with accountability permits manufacturers to compete profitably. Under the MMH perspective, the choice of governance mechanism is dependent on the costs of coordination and the transaction risk associated with the coordination. Normally, decreases in coordination costs would cause increases in transaction risk. By contrast, under the MMH perspective, ICT would create a unique environment in which both coordination costs and related transaction risk could be reduced simultaneously, and therefore two highly coordinated, interdependent firms would be a dominating governance mechanism in supply chain management. The success of such a governance mechanism, however, may depend on the degree to which standards are successfully developed for the exchange of information among trading partners joined together in supply chains.

16.6 Conclusion

The spread of e-commerce within market institutions has created pressure for legal institutions to adapt to technological innovation. Early reforms carried out in the 1980s and 1990s to remove irrational impediments to the adoption of e-commerce technologies enjoyed widespread success. As a result, the sophisticated businesses that were early e-commerce adopters are no longer demanding any law reforms.

For B2B commerce, attention has shifted to the development of ICT standards as a form of e-commerce regulation and as part of the process of optimizing supply chain operations. By contrast, the regulation of e-commerce in consumer markets has been the subject of intense political controversy and diverging regulatory strategies in LMEs and CMEs.

With regard to B2C commerce, the United States has adopted a strategy of incremental deregulation through statutory obsolescence. A considerable body of judicial decisions upholding standard form contracts that would be unenforceable in the European Union allows merchants engaged in internet commerce to decide unilaterally what rights American consumers should have. Intense competition in US retail markets may have blunted some of the impact of such judicial deference to merchant contract-drafting, however. EU regulators have tried to respond to the greater cautiousness of European consumers by establishing high mandatory minimum levels of online consumer protection throughout the internal market. This strategy does not yet appear to have triggered a "race to the top" that would support the growth of strong European global B2C market players that can compete with US giants such as Amazon or eBay, nor to have overcome the persistent fragmentation into national markets that still hinders the growth of the internal market in many sectors of the EU economy.

The fascination of lawyers and legislators with the notion of electronic signatures appears to have short-circuited the normal process of discovering the requirements of business and consumers for authentication standards and technologies. As a result, even though the system of certificate authorities established according to electronic signature laws remains underdeveloped, the use of electronic signatures in commercial transactions appears to be even more underdeveloped. The US market-led effort to develop authentication technologies and promote standards for interoperability has not yet succeeded, but, as these efforts more closely track actual user requirements, they seem more likely to succeed in the future.

In both the United States and the European Union, B2B merchants have organized themselves into supply chains with their trading partners, which appear to operate with little or no government intervention once technology-neutral laws removing irrational impediments to the use of electronic contracts have been enacted. The ability of sophisticated B2B contracting parties to resolve their disputes outside courts suggests that the parties involved in supply chains rely even less on formal public legal institutions than parties to conventional commercial transactions. Unlike the first two examples of electronic commerce governance, significant differences in US and EU approaches to the governance of supply chains and B2B electronic contracts are much more difficult to detect. The governance of successful B2B supply chains probably owes more to market competition and the successful development of standards than to law reform.

Conclusion

17 Internet governance: old issues, new framings, uncertain implications

ERIC BROUSSEAU AND MERYEM MARZOUKI

17.1 Internet governance: the "What?", "Why?", "How?", "Who?" and "Where?"

In the opinion of many actors and commentators, the subject of internet governance tastes like an old wine in a new bottle – to the extent that some consider, for instance, network neutrality to be more a matter of co-regulation than of internet governance (Marsden, 2010). This experience of déjà vu occurs infrequently when we are dealing with network infrastructure and protocols; it is widespread, however, when – as throughout this book – we address the regulation of content (Frydman, 2004; Marzouki, 2008a; Mopas, 2009). Even after granting that the internet is the target and not the means of the governance process,[1] actually delimiting the full scope and complexity of internet governance remains a work in progress – as attested by the efforts to define its contours as an academic research field (DeNardis, 2010a, 2010b).

Despite its broad definition by the Working Group on Internet Governance (WGIG, 2005) mandated during the World Summit on the Information Society, the field remains amorphous. Even the meaning of the term "internet governance" varies according to the background and objectives of those who invoke it. The result is many ambiguities and misunderstandings in defining the field and the issues at stake. The differences pertain to all dimensions of internet governance, as summarized in the following list.

The "What?" – narrow or broad object? A first set of ambiguities arises with the definition of what, exactly, should be governed. Some would restrict the field to the management of critical internet resources, meaning infrastructure and protocols or, at the

[1] In this sense, internet governance is a process that differs from e-government in both nature and objectives.

least, domain names (Mueller, 2002; Paré, 2003; DeNardis, 2009). Others view internet governance as embracing any and all types of regulation – including that of content and behavior – provided only that the object of regulation is somehow related to electronic communications (Benedek, Bauer and Kettemann, 2008).

The "Why?" – particular or general interest? It is widely agreed that internet governance decisions affect – directly or indirectly, explicitly or implicitly – all current and future end users, which includes individuals, private companies and organizations, and public institutions. A second set of ambiguities, however, is related to the intentions and objectives of internet governance policies that stem from different visions of the network. Some view the internet as a commons: it conveys services of general interest and thus should be governed as a public good and with a focus on human rights and democracy (Jørgensen, 2006). Others see the internet as a terrain for technical innovation and economic globalization, which leads to requirements (driven by market economics) concerning the liberalization of services and fair competition. This perspective underlies an analysis of how power configurations use diplomacy and negotiation to shape the internet (Singh, 2008) and how it is affected by global information and communication technology policies (Cowhey and Aronson, 2009).

The "How?" – infrastructure, protocol, application or content layer? A third set of ambiguities regards the level at which internet governance applies. Of course, different layers entail different agents defining and implementing such governance policies. Some argue that the core of internet governance issues lies in the definition, operation and political economy of the network infrastructure and protocols (DeNardis, 2009). Others concentrate on the role of gatekeepers at application and content levels when defining the means and rules of access to information and communication (Deibert *et al.*, 2010).

The "Who?" – public or private policy? A fourth set of ambiguities concerns the question of which sectors should be in charge of the internet governance process. A report from the International Institute for Sustainable Development (IISD, a Canada-based policy research institute) argues that it is inappropriate to consider issues that "fall primarily in other public policy arenas" as internet governance issues; instead, it suggests calling them "internet public policy" issues (Souter *et al.*, 2010). This claim fails to capture many of the areas touched by internet governance, however, or the diversity of the stakeholders shaping the process. It also fails to acknowledge that the internet is, for the most part, a privately ordered space and therefore one that must be able to take for granted a pluralistic policing environment (Stenning, 2009).

The "Where?" – global, regional, national or local level? A fifth set of ambiguities arises when an attempt is made to establish the political settings in which internet governance policies should be discussed, adopted and implemented. The global and interconnected nature of the internet obviously plays a major role in this discussion. Building on the theories of networked governance and cooperative production by peers, some argue that transnational institutions and forms of internet governance are more appropriate than sovereign modes. This perspective eventually leads one to argue in favor of the denationalization of internet governance as an alternative to the nation states model (Mueller, 2010). Without following the libertarian path, others analyze the different intergovernmental institutions and specialized agencies that have been set up to deal with public policies in the sector (Drake and Wilson, 2008). Regardless of the institution or forum addressing the question of internet governance, any analysis needs to treat the legitimacy, transparency, accountability and inclusiveness of that governance (Weber, 2009).

In the end, the extensive range of the "What?", "Why?", "How?", "Who?" and "Where?" concerns results in a wide set of interrelated issues. The internet governance pie, whether unified or divided, certainly looks even more delectable given the possible combinations of ingredients and their influence.

When a global private organization such as the Internet Corporation for Assigned Names and Numbers decides that domain name policy should be subordinated to the principles of intellectual property rights (Komaitis, 2010), it performs internet governance as defined in a narrow sense, acting under the influence of some particular interests. When a national public entity such as a government adopts and enforces a piece of legislation criminalizing the dissemination of child pornography on the internet, it performs (at the content layer) internet governance in a broad sense, acting on behalf of the general interest. In between these two extreme and sharply demarcated examples are a nearly infinite set of intricate issues affecting internet governance, and thus many areas of individual and collective life. The lack of consensus – with regard not only to the specifics but also to the scope of what should be done – may seem surprising when one considers that more than ten years have elapsed since the United Nations decided to hold a World Summit on the Information Society and six years since it actually did so. The current situation reflects the drawn-out process of devising a political construct, however.

This process has been characterized by strong controversies, and it is unquestionably far from complete. In section 17.2 we explain how the scope of internet governance has been widened from mere technical governance to encompass a broader understanding. This process has contributed to widening the diversity and number of involved stakeholders, at the cost of the capture of decision-making processes by those able to master the technicality and the diversity of the discussions and the implementation of solutions. In section 17.3 we examine the major trends evident in the ongoing debates over internet governance, thereby demonstrating how this kind of book can contribute to better solutions. We conclude the chapter by resituating the internet governance issue in the more general framework of global governance.

17.2 Internet governance as a political construct in progress

The notion of internet governance did not emerge in a vacuum. To the contrary, it is largely rooted in long-standing (though still evolving) public policy discussions. Internet governance is much more than a public policy issue, however, in the light of four characteristics that capture the essence of the internet: (i) the interconnection is global; (ii) its management is distributed; (iii) historically, it has been privately coordinated and operated; and (iv) it is intended for the exchange of information and the sharing of capabilities. Other networks, including telecommunication networks, may share one or more of these characteristics, but none exhibits all of them at the same time. This fact bestows a unique nature on the internet governance process.

17.2.1 From a narrow technical object to a broad political issue

The earliest references to internet governance as a tentative political construct date back to 1998, when two international conferences explicitly named the concept.

The International Telecommunication Union's 1998 plenipotentiary conference in Minneapolis adopted resolution 73,[2] which instructed its secretary-general to place the question of a world summit dedicated to "the information society" on the agenda of the United Nations. That same year a conference held by the Internet Society (INET '98) and one by the Computer Professionals for Social Responsibility (CPSR '98) both put internet governance on the global political agenda[3] – at least, the agendas of the technical community and civil society. Although the concept of internet governance was still unknown to policy-makers and business corporations, it had already been recognized and framed by the technical community and civil society groups dealing with information and communication issues.

It is not surprising, then, that the latter two groups – later identified, at the WSIS and, even more clearly, at the Internet Governance Forum, as "stakeholders" – played a major role in the political construction of the concept. This occurred even though INET and the CPSR had different views on the "Why?", "How?" and "Where?", and especially on the "What?" and "Who?". This difference of perspective and vision has persisted from the early days (in 1998) right up to the fifth annual IGF meeting in 2010. In short: the technical community's approach to internet governance assumes a circumscribed area within which decisions are made by self-regulated technical institutions whose objectives are to "protect the core Internet principles and values,"[4]

[2] All the cited UN, ITU and WSIS documents are available at www.itu.int/wsis; IGF documents are available at www.intgovforum.org.

[3] The INET conference series has been organized since 1992 by the Internet Society (ISOC). The CPSR is a global civil society organization that was originally founded by US computer scientists in 1981; it has incubated a number of projects that have led to the formation of some renowned organizations and conferences, such as the Electronic Privacy Information Center (EPIC) and the Computers, Freedom and Privacy (CFP) conference series. Information and documents on the INET '98 and CPSR '98 conferences are available online at www.isoc.org/inet98 and http://cpsr.org/prevsite/onenet, respectively.

[4] It is interesting that a new "dynamic coalition on core Internet values" was formed at the 2010 IGF meeting. Its launching workshop description includes

whereas the civil society approach incorporates a much broader scope affecting all fields and necessarily involving the entire range of social actors according to commonly defined rules.

This broad conception of internet governance by actors in civil society has evolved, however, in successive WSIS and IGF proceedings, as a function of the involved civil society groups. The CPSR '98 conference featured a keynote speech by Lawrence Lessig as a preview of his *Code and Other Laws of Cyberspace* (Lessig, 1999b), and it held discussions on such topics as "Public interest in the age of the behemoth," "Panic over privacy: a case study in regulation," "Universal access: a global perspective" and "Convergence and the internet's future: avoiding the tragedy of the commons." Even though more than a decade has now passed since then, some of these topics remain sufficiently visionary and provocative that they should remain on future IGF agendas.

When the civil society Internet Governance Caucus (IGC) first discussed its terms of reference in 2003, however, the first draft stated that the group was formed to deal with the "Internet resource and its allocation governance issues [and] especially the governance structure itself as its starting point."[5] Although the IGC was willing to address multistakeholder participation in internet governance structures, it sought to restrict that participation to internet technical resource management structures and, in particular and primarily, to ICANN. The IGC accordingly restricted itself to a narrow definition of the internet governance concept. At that time, other issues were handled by the numerous other thematic caucuses formed by civil society at the WSIS.

the following statement: "The Internet model is open, transparent, and collaborative and relies on processes and products that are local, bottom-up, and accessible to users around the world. These principles and values are threatened when policy makers propose to regulate and control the Internet, with inadequate understanding of the core values." The full text is available online at http://igf.wgig.org/cms/dynamiccoalitions/90-dc-meetings-2009/481-dynamic-coalition-on-core-internet-values.

[5] This comes from the first message sent to the IGC mailing list by the then caucus coordinator, on April 1, 2003. Mailing list archives are available at http://lists.cpsr.org/lists/arc/governance. The IGC is a loose coalition of civil society organizations and individuals formed during the WSIS at the same time that other civil society thematic caucuses were created. After the WSIS resumed and the Internet Governance Forum was created as a follow-up process, the IGC became the de facto unique representative of civil society at large. More details are available from the IGC website: www.igcaucus.org.

Discussions among government representatives have witnessed the same evolution with regard to a narrow versus broad understanding of internet governance. As documented in the literature (Raboy, Landry and Shtern, 2010), by the end of the WSIS's first phase, the conference held in Geneva in December 2003 and the preparatory meetings leading up to it, the battle over internet governance was focused on the internationalization of domain names and other critical matters of internet resource management policy. At this point there were almost irreconcilable positions of unilateralism (the US government, through its contract with ICANN) and multilateralism (the governments that were members of the UN system through their membership of the ITU). The long and heated, almost epic, discussions ended diplomatically with the creation of the Working Group on Internet Governance, which was charged with the task of defining internet governance and the policy issues surrounding it.[6] Paragraph 50 of the WSIS Geneva Declaration of Principles explicitly calls for the creation of this working group. Although the WGIG's name includes *governance*, it is only *management* of the internet that is mentioned in the declaration's two immediately preceding paragraphs. Paragraph 48 highlights the need for an equitable distribution of the internet's resources, for its stable and secure performance and for multilingualism to be taken into account. Paragraph 49 lists all the actors that need to take part in this process – namely, the four recognized WSIS stakeholders. These stakeholders acknowledged that technical and public policy issues were both at stake, but that it remained their intention solely to *manage* the internet and its critical resources.

It was only after the wider definition espoused by the WGIG report – and after the formation of the IGF as one of the WSIS follow-up forums – that the understanding of internet governance broadened. The WGIG defined an extensive set of issues encompassed by internet governance, ranging from the "administration of the root zone files and system" to "capacity building" and "meaningful participation in global policy development," as well as a whole set of human rights and consumer rights issues directly at stake in the governance of information and communication processes. From the civil society perspective, then, the IGC had widened its scope according to this

[6] An account of WGIG history, composition and outcomes is available from the WGIG website: www.wgig.org/index.html.

broad definition of internet governance and, accordingly, expanded its membership to include civil society participants that had previously been involved in other thematic caucuses. From the government perspective, the WGIG report was welcome, but the fundamental issue of control over critical internet resources – which was viewed as a matter of state sovereignty – remained unresolved even by the end of the WSIS's second phase, the conference held in Tunis in November 2005 and the preparatory meetings leading up to it. Arguments over this issue led to full-on opposition between the unilateral and multilateral visions that lasted up until the convening of the Tunis conference.

The confrontation was provisionally resolved by the following two simultaneous decisions. The first was to convene the IGF as a post-WSIS "new forum for a multi-stakeholder policy dialogue," as set forth by the mandate in paragraph 72 of the "Tunis agenda." The other was to initiate a process of "enhanced cooperation," as defined in paragraph 69, "to enable governments, on an equal footing, to carry out their roles and responsibilities, in international public policy issues pertaining to the Internet, but not in the day-to-day technical and operational matters, that do not impact on international public policy issues."

This split decision was the WSIS's "answer" to both dilemmas – unilateral versus multilateral and technical versus political – of internet governance.

17.2.2 From NWICO to WSIS: revisiting an old conflict

Whether defined in a narrow or a broad sense, internet governance emerged as one of the leading issues of the WSIS's second phase, mainly as a result of civil society action.

The evolution of the WSIS was so unexpected, indeed, that many commentators identified two paradoxes about the summit (Raboy and Landry, 2006). The first paradox concerns the World Summit's organization by the ITU instead of by UNESCO, which was considered a more appropriate agency to take the lead on information and communication issues. The second paradox is the choice of Tunisia as the venue for the WSIS's second phase. Many considered it an intolerable affront to hold a summit on information and communication in a country whose citizens were notably muzzled at that time. Both alleged paradoxes proceed mainly from erroneous analysis, however: they ignore the historical antecedents of the WSIS. In fact, the choices of the ITU and Tunis are linked. The idea of a high-level international meeting aimed at "reducing the digital divide" was, in fact, proposed by Tunisia at the ITU's 1998 plenipotentiary conference, which adopted this principle.

The original proposal was fully coherent, since the meeting's purpose was to discuss and find solutions to the global issues of deploying and financing the infrastructure for digital networks and, in particular, the problem of international interconnection costs and of interconnection agreements between intercontinental network operators (Abramson, 2005; Badasyan and Chakrabarti, 2005). In line with a concept of the "digital divide" that was limited to infrastructure issues and with a technocentric vision of the "information society," therefore, these choices were not devoid of rationality. The ITU was an appropriate UN agency because it had declared itself (in its 1998 resolution) to be "conscious of the emergence of the concept of the information society in which telecommunications play a central role." For similar reasons, Tunisia was a developing country no less legitimate than any other as a venue for this summit (Jørgensen and Marzouki, 2005) – provided one sticks to a technical vision of the information society, as the ITU apprehended it (Ksibi, 2006).

The idea turned from an ITU-level meeting for addressing operational objectives, however, into a much more ambitious proposal for a World Summit on the Information Society, adopted by the UN General Assembly in December 2001. At about the same time, in fact, the United Nations adopted its declaration concerning the Millennium Development Goals (MDGs); these goals established a series of objectives covering a wide spectrum of areas that included peace efforts and strengthening of the UN as well as human rights, democracy and good governance.[7] Via this "Millennium Declaration," member states had already committed themselves to "ensure that the benefits of new technologies, especially information and communication technologies are available to all." Although the concept of an "information society" was not mentioned, its main elements – an "emancipatory" vision of technical progress and an instrumental vision of the "information society" – were emphasized. It should be noted, though, that the

[7] More detailed information on the UN Millennium Declaration and the Millennium Development Goals is available at www.un.org/millenniumgoals.

reference to "new technologies" was actually made only as a means of achieving the declaration's goal of "development and poverty eradication."[8]

The WSIS nevertheless frequently referred to the "Millennium Declaration" and the MDGs in their entirety. In 2002, for example, the Marrakech ITU plenipotentiary conference identified as one of the WSIS's goals the need to achieve the Millennium Development Goals. During the subsequent WSIS process, these goals have often been recalled by all stakeholders as key WSIS issues, motivations, decisions and actions. The four official WSIS documents[9] thus mention the MDGs in great detail but always with an eye toward promoting a "brave new digital world" (Leuprecht, 2005). The WSIS's civil society declarations of 2003 and 2005 also channeled the MDGs, but from a less technocentric perspective.

This unexpected extension of the original scope of the conference – in particular, by reference to the entirety of the MDGs – introduced to the WSIS the very ambiguities conveyed by the notion of "information society." It was no surprise therefore that, during its first phase, the WSIS experienced the revival of a thirty-year-old conflict that had originally arisen during discussions at UNESCO during the Cold War on the New World Information and Communication Order (NWICO).

Since that time, the central question of regulating information exchanges and communication had remained unresolved, even as it became more crucial with the explosion of technologies and the development of a global economy – factors that gave the question an even more complex dimension. On the one hand, the post-9/11 "war on terrorism" questioned, even in Western democracies, the necessity of complying with principles of human rights and the rule of law.

[8] The Eighth Millennium Goal is to develop "a global partnership for development" by (among other things) "co-operation with the private sector, mak[ing] available [to all] the benefits of new technologies, especially information and communications." The indicators defined by the United Nations to assess progress toward this goal were simply two classical, "per 100 population" ITU indicators: (i) the number of telephone lines and cellular subscribers; and (ii) the number of personal computers and internet users.

[9] These are the Geneva Declaration of Principles and the Geneva Plan of Action of 2003 and the Tunis Commitment and the Tunis Agenda for the Information Society of 2005.

It highlighted also the crucial nature of the so-called "information war." On the other hand, the means of communication were no longer "concentrated in a handful of countries" (a circumstance decried by the Non-Aligned Movement in 1976), because the political and economic landscapes had been dramatically transformed by the emergence of new economies and the strengthening of formerly weak nation states. In a world with the internet, furthermore, governments are not the sole gatekeepers. The control of global communication infrastructure and hence of information flows has become distributed among many de facto regulators.

The same lines of conflict as during NWICO discussions now therefore appeared between promoters of development and those primarily attached to the establishment/preservation of fundamental liberties, and the same old arguments were rehashed (Hamelink, 2005). Veterans of the MacBride Round Tables,[10] including members of the Communication Rights in the Information Society (CRIS) campaign, were thus opposed to media groups and associations promoting freedom of expression. The former brandished a "right to communicate," which was eventually reframed as "communication rights" (Jørgensen and Marzouki, 2005; O'siochrú and Alegre, 2005); the latter promulgated a "free flow of information" doctrine (Koven, 2003). The protagonists remained the same at the governmental level as well, as if there had been no historical, political, economic or technological evolution in three decades. This conflict, which had already proved sterile during NWICO times (Mattelart, 2000), was once again unproductive, preventing the WSIS from making any attempt to discuss and rebalance the unequal terms of exchange in the information and communication sector.

17.2.3 Governing an information society without defining its polity

The World Summit on the Information Society failed to resolve the very questions that had led to its convening – that is, managing the network infrastructure and financing. Here again, an explanation can be drawn from the participation of civil society.

[10] More information on NWICO actors and the MacBride Round Tables are available on this resource's website: www.nwico-wsis.net.

The second phase of the WSIS took a different shape from the first, as there was a major change in the typology of civil society participants (Marzouki, 2008b). Some groups (e.g. key members of the CRIS campaign) moved away, seeing little hope within this framework of advancing their specific objectives, which focused on the right to communicate. They chose instead to concentrate their efforts on issues germane to their concerns and capacity of action. Toward this end, these groups switched to the UNESCO arena; here discussions were ongoing in anticipation of adopting the Convention on the Protection and Promotion of the Diversity of Cultural Expressions.[11] The publicity surrounding the Geneva summit had raised the interest of organizations active in sectors as diverse as the Millennium Development Goals themselves and carrying the same instrumental perspective of the information society as the one advocated in the WSIS definition. It also led to increased involvement by individual participants. In particular, academics and consultants joined the WSIS on the basis of their specific interest in internet governance. This was especially true for many members of the technical community and for political scientists. The trend is most notably attested to by the composition of the Working Group on Internet Governance and by the related intense publication activity during this period under the auspices of international organizations (MacLean, 2004b; Drake, 2005; Stauffacher and Kleinwächter, 2005).

During the WSIS's first phase the diversity of civil society actors and of their interests and claims did not prevent them from reaching a consensus on some sectoral issues, mainly through a juxtaposition of specific and nonantagonistic claims against the positions of governments and of the private sector. Points of conflict soon emerged among civil society actors over three main issues, however: multistakeholder partnership and internet governance (McLaughlin and Pickard, 2005), human rights (Marzouki and Jørgensen, 2005) and the financing of infrastructure (Peyer, 2005). Clearly, these issues are less related to stakeholders' identities than to political choices.

The WSIS second phase had fewer conflicts in terms of substance but also fewer asserted positions. The dullness of the 2005 Civil

[11] More information on this convention, which was adopted in 2005, is available on the UNESCO website: www.unesco.org/new/en/unesco/themes/2005-convention.

Society Declaration is indicative of changes in the type of civil society involvement from one summit phase to the other. This dynamic can be explained by three factors, which are related to the three contentious issues that arose during the first phase of the WSIS.

First, many non-governmental organizations involved in the defense of human rights focused, during the Tunis conference, on the bad record of the host country regarding freedom of information and communication. Observation missions, meetings and the organization of other public events were accordingly at the core of NGO activity during this second phase. Tunisia's bad reputation even hijacked the PrepCom proceedings of the preparatory committee meetings.[12]

Second (and this is the main explanation), internet governance and multistakeholder partnership were the focus of an ad hoc working group: the WGIG. Discussion of these issues, which was actually confined to this restricted arena during the WSIS's second phase, led to the creation of the global Internet Governance Forum. The IGF was thus established under the auspices of the United Nations by the "Tunis agenda" and "Plan of action"; indeed, it was mandated to meet regularly in order to implement internet governance according to the principles, processes and procedures defined by that agenda. Hence the IGF has been, since 2006, an annual international meeting that serves only as a discursive space to facilitate a "global conversation." In particular, the IGF does not allow itself to make any decision or offer any recommendation; it thereby ensures its own survival, which is constantly threatened by the power game between states (Malcolm, 2008). For instance, China and the Group of 77[13] threatened not to renew the IGF's five-year mandate in 2010.[14]

[12] This was especially true with the Hammamet preparatory committee meeting in June 2004, as reported by the WSIS Civil Society Human Rights Caucus; see www.iris.sgdg.org/actions/smsi/hr-wsis/tunis.html.

[13] The Group of 77 at the United Nations, also known as the Non-Aligned Movement, is a loose coalition of developing nations, designed to promote its members' collective economic interests and create an enhanced joint negotiating capacity in the United Nations. There were seventy-seven founding members of the organization, but the organization has since expanded to 131 member countries. The group was founded on June 15, 1964, by the Joint Declaration of the Seventy-Seven Countries, issued at the United Nations Conference on Trade and Development (UNCTAD).

[14] See, for example, transcripts of IGF sessions at www.intgovforum.org.

Third, the financing of infrastructure was the topic of a different ad hoc working group, whose final report raises more questions than it answers and has seen no follow-up. A global Digital Solidarity Fund (DSF) had been created at the end of the Geneva phase, and it was formally approved at the conclusion of the Tunis phase. In acting mainly as a patronage tool, however, the DSF amounts to little more than a private foundation. It can therefore hardly be seen as a substitute for policies that aim to develop internet infrastructure and access. It mainly supports projects based on information and communication technologies.[15] To date, the DSF has failed to promote effectively its principle of a "1% digital solidarity tax" as a source of financing. This "tax" would consist of successful tenders in public projects related to ICTs *donating* to the DSF 1 percent of the transaction value, a fee meant to be deducted from their profit margin. Although some local authorities have signed up, this mechanism is struggling to find a critical mass of support, and still has to convince doubters of its relevance in political terms and, especially, in legal terms (Weber and Menoud, 2008).

Given these developments, the WSIS ended without resolving two of the main issues that this UN world summit had sought to address: the financing and governance of the Internet. Even though an "information society" has been enshrined by the United Nations, therefore, the concept lacks definition not only of its organization fundamentals but also of its conditions of access and participation in this "society" and the articulation of powers that govern it.

17.2.4 From organized civil society actors to policy entrepreneurs

The sidelining of organized civil society actors has been another consequence of these developments at the WSIS. This is most probably a long-term trend, as it has been reinforced in the post-WSIS framework of the IGF since 2006.

It is common knowledge that the WSIS proceedings included neither trade unions nor antiglobalization social movements nor most of the NGOs that traditionally structure civil society participation in major intergovernmental conferences and world summits; what is puzzling is

[15] This is evident from the DSF website: www.dsf-fsn.org.

why these excluded groups showed so little interest in the WSIS (Marzouki, 2008b). This lack of understanding of the WSIS political stakes was complemented by blindness about the transformations that might have resulted in terms of how the civil society representation was organized.

The post-WSIS phase has, moreover, witnessed the sidelining of most organized civil society players, especially those that formed coalitions and caucuses during the WSIS. This shelving – to which, it seems, most of them consented – led to participation by only a handful of civil society organizations, rather than large coalitions, and to most individuals acting on their own. This generalization applies, at least, to the dominant shape of the civil society Internet Governance Caucus, which became the forum for gathering and representing civil society in the post-WSIS phase. This trend was strengthened with the Internet Governance Forum, which was created by the WSIS as a follow-up to the WGIG.

The WGIG had proposed a definition of internet governance that reflected a much wider perspective than managing the system for domain names. Indeed, this definition refers to the "development and application by Governments, the private sector and civil society, in their respective roles, of shared principles, norms, rules, decision-making procedures, and programs that shape the evolution and use of the Internet." Thus are included not only the governance of the critical resources needed to ensure the network's proper functioning but also the governance of its uses. This definition also speaks to multistakeholder governance and not to political regulation by governments alone.

Greater involvement on the part of actors other than governments – most notably of civil society organs – in the management of world affairs is, naturally, a welcome development. Such multistakeholder governance does raise some democratic issues, however. When coupled with a trend to deal with any and all internet-related public policy issues, it might result in an arena immune to the rule of law. The risk is that such governance arrangements need not comply with international protections for human rights (since only governments are bound by these standards), and thereby dilute the responsibilities of states and their accountability to citizens. In one of its own reports, the WGIG (2005) highlights that it "comprised 40 members from Governments, private sector and civil society, who all participated on an equal footing and in their personal capacity." The WGIG limited its task to identifying different, even contradictory, approaches to internet governance without deciding in favor of any of them. The IGF's having reproduced the WGIG modus operandi in itself raises democratic concerns, however, since the latter's mandate extends to "discuss public policy issues related to key elements of Internet governance."

The WGIG definition of internet governance, as adopted by the WSIS in 2005, refers to the same general object as do widely agreed definitions of governance. One definition is as follows: "Governance is a term that applies to the exercise of power in a variety of institutional contexts, the object of which is to direct, control and regulate activities *in the interests of people as citizens, voters and workers*" (Robinson, 1996; emphasis added). Another puts it this way: "Governance may be defined as a process of coordinating actors, social groups and institutions, in order to achieve collectively defined and discussed objectives. Governance refers then to the set of institutions, networks, guidelines, regulations, norms, political and social usages, as well as public and private actors *contributing to the stability of a society and polity, to its orientation, to the capacity to conduct affairs, to provide services and to ensure its legitimacy*" (Boussaguet, Jacquot and Ravinet, 2004; translation by authors, emphasis added). Fundamental components are missing in the WGIG definition, however – namely the governance objectives and the governed polity. In other words, the definition of internet governance, as established since the WSIS and supported through five years of the IGF process, remains instrumental only: although it covers the "What?" and the "How?" and, to some extent, the "Where?" of internet governance, it is sorely deficient in addressing the "Why?" and "Who?" components.

Civil society actors, from the WSIS to the WGIG to the IGF, have played a major role in defining internet governance as a political construct, and the viability of this concept is evidenced by the high degree of interest it has raised in the academic literature. This literature typically analyzes civil society participation in terms of NGOs and other civil society *organizations* (Cammaerts and Carpentier, 2005; Raboy and Landry, 2006) or in terms of *individuals* (Lakel and Massit-Follea, 2007; Pavan and Diani, 2008; Cammaerts, 2010), but researchers have not analyzed the evolution of participation from collective to individual civil societies. We have shown that detailing this evolution sheds light on the political consequences of the progressive delegitimization and/or disqualification of organized social actors. Indeed, doing so illuminates how the various civil society stakeholders understood and built expertise, in matters of internet governance, that reflected their visions and interests and the game they played. Some empirical analyses have shown that the establishment of the IGF, its advisory committees and its rules of procedure have reinforced the participation and influence of various "experts" (academics and consultants) to the detriment of NGOs, trade unions and social movements (Raboy, Landry and Shtern, 2010). So-called policy entrepreneurs (Kingdon, 1995) thus found their window of opportunity in the context of a weakened role for the state (Marzouki, 2008b).

17.2.5 The uncertain implications of a new governance territory

The transformation by which civil society perceived and presented itself as one of the three internet stakeholders (with governments and the private sector as the other two) should also be analyzed through the prism of an *individual*-centric vision of society, as theorized by Georg Hegel building on the Scottish Enlightenment philosophers. The Gramscian perspective, which identifies "civil society" as an organized and autonomous sphere independent from the market and the state, may indeed no longer be relevant in light of the concept's actual evolution.

In fact, "communication rights" were at the heart of heated debates during the WSIS's first phase (2002–3), most notably on account of the involvement of organized civil society actors (CRIS campaign members, civil society human rights caucus members, media caucus members) with strong and diverging viewpoints on how those rights should be defined. Research linked to the WSIS's second phase (2003–5) shows – and research subsequent to the establishment of the IGF confirms – that there has been a regression in prominence of the concerns related to socio-economic and development or *collective* rights. Evidently, consensus can be reached only on *individual* rights such as freedom of expression and privacy. These developments are obviously in line with declines in traditional forms of representative democracy and with the crisis faced by nation states in the context of globalization.

These transformations could pave the way to new global governance, if not a new world order, and some see this as an opportunity to reduce further the role of governments (Mueller, 2010). In any case, the evolution of civil society strongly affects our definition and understanding of human rights, democracy and the rule of law. In such an unstable transition period – while the state's role is being reconfigured from that of the "welfare state" to the "regulatory state," or even, as advocated at the national level by new public management philosophy and practices, to simply the "steering state" (Bezes, 2009) – governance developments could lead to uncertain implications, especially in the digital "territory" characterized by a high diversity of powerful gatekeepers and de facto regulators. The inconclusive nature of the debates in many arenas, and especially within the IGF, should be contrasted, moreover, with the operational pragmatism of those instances in which de facto governance principles were implemented – often behind the veil of simple technical regulation, as is well illustrated by ICANN. Internet governance is, indeed, developing.

17.3 Deterritorialization and reterritorialization of the internet

The current institutional framework is characterized by inconsistencies, overlapping domains, missing links and, most of all, a constant evolution. Internet governance is de facto operating and framing the process of that evolution nonetheless. Three main issues dominate today's debates: the risk of fragmentation, the network's degree of openness and the protection of data. We review each of these issues in turn.

17.3.1 A threat of rampant fragmentation, beyond democratic and legal control

It has been pointed out in several chapters that the digital world's imaging of the actual one is increasingly characterized by the notion of *heterarchy.* All kinds of gatekeepers (technical intermediaries, community leaders, public agencies, service providers, etc.) emerge and tend to impose restrictions on use of the network by systematizing the control of information exchanges and access to services. The threat is clear: the internet could rapidly split into a set of interconnected information networks controlled by commercial and governmental gatekeepers. The price of this development would be a decrease in the global integration of the networks and an attendant massive loss of information and positive network externalities – regardless of the extent to which it protected citizens'/users' freedom and privacy.

The present fuzziness in the process of building a satisfactory global governance framework favors this path of evolution. Indeed, governments and commercial interests have made loud calls for "pragmatic" solutions to a set of particular issues (including criminal activities, property right infringement, threats to security, the protection of trade secrets, etc.). Even the protection of citizens' fundamental liberties could lead to a call for the building of digital fences. Note that control of access, procedures of identification and the filtering of content have already been combined, so that internet and mobile service providers can manage access to services on an individual basis. The logic is both economical and political. On the one hand, most commercial service providers are interested in technologies that will enable them to implement digital tolls while preventing leaks or a misappropriation of information services. On the other hand, public authorities have an interest – which can be enhanced by public opinion – in fighting what they consider to be abuses and criminal uses of the internet. The result is either development of public control capabilities or pressures on providers of information and internet services. This dynamic explains the persistent trend of fragmentation, whereby the end-to-end character of the information infrastructure is markedly declining.

Whether or not the public and private attempts to control internet use prove successful is actually a secondary issue. In any case, it is the generalization of these measures that leads to a decrease in global connectivity and to an increase in the complexity (and costs) of using the information infrastructure. Such a trend leads to diminished capabilities of sharing information and knowledge but reinforces the status quo of market and political powers. Since uncertainty might well hinder innovation and investments, moreover, the true "conservative" dimension of these movements needs to be emphasized. Whether led by governments or corporations, their goal is to restore the past order. Governments seek to recover their sovereignty and ability to regulate access to and exchanges of information. Corporations seek to enshrine their past business models, as illustrated by entertainment industries preventing free access to content; these industries would rather implement pay-per-view or subscription-based systems than consider alternative business models that could still remunerate creation but also increase creative diversity. In both cases, the full economic and social potential of digital technologies is not explored because, in part, most of the discourse is concerned with fending off perceived threats to survival.

Two phenomena must be mentioned as having a large impact on the evolution of digital matters. First is the relatively recent trend of international governance based on voluntary adhesion to nonmandatory norms. Because consensus is hard to achieve between stakeholders, and especially (owing to divergent national interests) between governments, new norms tend to be developed on a voluntary basis within forums. In accordance with the procedures of ICANN and related organizations, these norms are elaborated cooperatively among industries, high-profile governments and the most active stakeholders. An example is the Anti-Counterfeiting Trade Agreement (ACTA), initiated in 2008 and formally launched in 2010, which seeks to establish international standards for the enforcement of intellectual property rights. This agreement would establish a new, *international* legal framework, which countries could join on a voluntary basis, and its own governing body that would not be subordinate to any existing institutions. The aim is to standardize and coordinate enforcement policies and to develop, when needed, more adequate national capabilities. Clearly, this effort is a response to what the most developed countries view as a fundamental threat: the huge numbers of counterfeit goods and ever-increasing instances of copyright infringement. The scope of ACTA includes counterfeit goods, generic drugs and copyright infringement on the internet. The plan is to organize an agreement among some OECD countries and then to convince emerging economies that they should sign on (Yu, forthcoming).

The other trend is the "mission creep" evidenced by those agencies or international agreements that succeed in addressing an issue. Their promoters are then often tempted to extend the scope of their initial mission on the basis of the legitimacy and capabilities accumulated during an initial phase that addressed a legitimately agreed-upon issue. The strong desire to expunge criminal activities could easily, for instance, be used to justify the implementation of oversight capabilities with respect to all exchanges of content; clearly, this would increase the likelihood of infringing on freedom of expression and privacy rights. It is also well known that, once created, organizations tend to expand their activity beyond their initial goals – if for no other reason than because members and various stakeholders have an interest in the organization's continued existence. That ISPs developed hotlines for reporting child pornography is an example of mission creep. In fact, many of them are now relied upon to encourage the exposure of extended lists of abuses.

Both trends make it clear that the development of new regulations, often under the shadow of governments, tends to escape the control of democratic and legal institutions. Most often it is a question of sophisticated implementation technologies discussed by closed groups of high-level bureaucrats, engineers and public and private decision-makers, whose compliance with democratic and legal norms is difficult to assess. Pragmatism often requires quick decisions, furthermore, even though international agreements tend to create (sometimes unfortunate) irreversibilities. Ex post demands for conformity are weak and probably hopeless given that actual technical implementation results in de facto adoption and thus stimulates imitation of the existing (albeit imperfect) solutions. The fait accompli therefore tends to be a central characteristic of this trend toward fragmentation.

This is why pockets of resistance persist. Cryptographic resources and peer-to-peer networks are mobilized by groups of activists to reduce the likelihood of external control. A good illustration of such a "technological" defense is the Tor project, whose aims include hindering identification elements when a user accesses the internet and disseminating exchanges of information in order to circumvent surveillance efforts.[16] A parallel course is taken by human rights activists who attempt to identify potential threats and to influence the process of norm-making: by involving themselves in international discussions (in particular, those of the IGF); by lobbying ministries, regulators and parliamentary members at the national and regional levels; and/or by suing governments and corporations responsible for implemented solutions that infringe citizens' essential rights.

Beyond these losses in terms of the global information infrastructure's potential, the current trend of fragmentation could also lead to a major political reordering. In this case we could lose the potential for innovative principles of collective regulation, and the resulting order

[16] More information on the Tor project is available at www.torproject.org.

could well lead to a regression in which the hierarchy of norms is weakened at all levels and replaced by the coexistence of unarticulated norms and in which democratic control over their elaboration and implementation is more difficult. Such control has never been universal but was the dominant paradigm in most developed countries after World War II. The end point of this trend line would be consistent with what some specialists in international relations refer to as "new medievalism" (Bull, 1977; Spruyt, 1994; Friedrichs, 2001).

17.3.2 Neutrality in managing access and flows

To a large extent, the fragmentation debate overlaps with the one over "net neutrality." We should continue to differentiate between the two issues, however, because they do not concern the exact same questions and dynamics. The fragmentation debate clearly involves network content and the control of information flows, whereas the NN debate is related to the fundamental dialectic of network management and is therefore more concerned with the actual data flow. On the one hand, the internet relies on the renowned "end-to-end" principle whereby the network's role is to serve as passive intermediary among active terminals. Under this principle, all content, sites, platforms and users are considered equal in terms of how the network and its communications are managed. The end-to-end principle is the very source of the network's flexibility, because (i) it favors interconnection among heterogeneous networks and (ii) it enables the sustained implementation of innovation in services by connecting new equipment and software to the network. On the other hand, the quality of the service cannot be guaranteed without the technical management of flows when congestion occurs. Remedies may be based on queues but also on rerouting, discrimination between flows and even the incomplete transmission of certain packets. The ISPs have limited capacity and the volume of data transported on the internet is skyrocketing, so telecommunication operators and access providers increasingly employ traffic management software to streamline their networks, prevent congestion and promote value-added services. The latter generally require the management of priorities within the network to ensure that bandwidth-demanding flows are delivered on time and to guarantee the integrity and security of access and of information exchanges.

The network neutrality debate therefore has two dimensions. The first is that of discrimination between flows, and it raises mainly techno-economic issues related to the nature of competition within the network. The key issue is whether an ISP should be allowed to discriminate between other service providers on the basis of commercial preferences and payment. This debate echoes the one that developed in the 1980s about the neutrality of so-called "common carriers." Then and now the central questions are *who* should pay for the development of the infrastructure and, if bandwidth is scarce, *on what basis* access should be provided. The question of payment pits the information service providers (especially those of the Web 2.0) against ISPs and "backbone" providers. The latter would like to charge the information service providers for the increased traffic that they generate. In response, the former argue that their information services are what allow ISPs to market and sell high-speed access to the final users and thereby generate revenue for financing the infrastructure. The question of access pits ISPs against the most advanced and intensive users. Indeed, ISPs could easily solve their capacity constraints by downgrading the quality of service to targeted uses or users. They could also employ this capability to throttle certain flows while promoting their own services (examples include online telephony, music and video) or those of their allies. More broadly, network management practices tend to favor (centralized) servers and information service providers whereas strict neutrality with respect to bandwidth demand would favor (dispersed) end users and peer-to-peer practices. For one mode to prevail would mean unfair discrimination, however – between either users or service providers, with possible abuse of a dominant position in the latter case.

The second dimension of the NN debate is that of content-filtering, which raises issues related to freedom and fundamental rights. The key issue here is whether an ISP should be allowed to perform "deep packet inspection" and possibly block targeted traffic (Daly, 2010; Bendrath and Mueller, 2010). On the one hand, this might be justified in terms of service quality, which improves if the ISP can block junk mail, defuse viruses and block cyber-attacks. On the other hand, these capacities could be used to repel certain norms (and thus to advance others), legal and moral alike. The point is that, once they can filter content, ISPs (and, more generally, information service providers) might well be pressured to block content disliked by some authority

Purpose \ Object of filtering	Data flows	Content
Quality of service	Optimization of bandwidth use (especially when synchronization is needed)	Assurance of quality, reliability, and security
Use of the network	Discrimination between alternative services and providers	Control to block access and to block the exchange of targeted contents

Figure 17.1 Objects and purposes of content-filtering by ISPs.

or organized group. Most agree that legal authorities can legitimately rely on ISPs to help enforce certain legal norms, as in cases of transmitted child pornography or other criminal activity. Few would support a government hindering the ability of opponents to access and exchange information, however, a religious group's attempt to impose its moral norms or the blocking by economic interests of access to information about their operations.

With the matrix shown in Figure 17.1 we attempt to clarify matters by distinguishing the two separate "levels" of the debate that are often conflated in public discourse and the media. Although filtering and discrimination might well be justified in the service of technically optimizing the infrastructure's capabilities while maintaining its fundamental neutrality, the same techniques can bias the competition between information service providers toward those allied with the ISPs and also lead to the exercise of political power without any guarantee of legitimacy.

The position of the various stakeholders is often complex in these debates. For instance, ISPs would probably prefer to be allowed to discriminate between flows, because doing so would allow them to charge information service providers for the traffic they initiate. They would likely also be pleased to promote their own services and those of their allies, moreover. At the same time, ISPs are strongly disinclined to filter content, not only because it would be costly to implement but also because it could make them liable for violations of intellectual property rights or of any other public regulation. Citizens are probably most concerned about their use of the internet being controlled by an ISP, although they would value any operations performed by the ISP to enhance the quality of the service. Political authorities and interest groups would naturally value the ability to filter content toward the end of promoting compliance with their various norms. Economic interests – except for those (e.g. the major entertainment industries) that would ally with ISPs – would much prefer that ISPs *not* be able to discriminate between data flows. It should be clear that a strict application of the NN principle promotes a "political" vision of the network as an essential resource that should be available, without restriction, to everyone; in this view, the question of how to finance the development of the infrastructure is less important. The NN vision thus contrasts with a more techno-economic view, which admits that traffic management is required given a limited infrastructure that must necessarily be optimized.

In different countries, the debate on how to deal with the NN issue has resulted in sensibly different regulatory frameworks for internet traffic management practices (ITMPs). More important, though, is the fact that existing frameworks are still evolving, and hence ISPs may face alternative regulations later on – whether they are distributing services on the basis of a cable, telephone or Hertzian network. As pointed out by John Stevenson and Andrew Clement (2010), the prevailing practice in developed countries is to limit ITMPs as much as possible and to relieve network congestion by encouraging the development of infrastructure. When they are allowed, ITMPs should be transparent to users. The reason is that such practices might be problematic: from a technical point of view, because they might hinder innovation, and from a social perspective, given their potential negative political and economic consequences. Broadly speaking, ITMPs have no supportive constituency but are seldom forbidden outright. The countries that allow operators to employ ITMPs typically rely on competition between network providers to control possible drifts in behavior.

It is worth mentioning that, at the international level, the NN debate is echoed by the question of asymmetrical peering agreements between the North and the South. Because most of the bandwidth and information resources originate in the most developed countries, access to the global information infrastructure by ISPs located in developing countries (and especially in the least developed countries) is priced at a very high level. In short, Southern users want to be connected more than Northern providers want to connect them. This imbalance is reflected in the high cost of internet access for Southern users, who also suffer from a poor quality of service because the South's infrastructure has not been (and, perhaps, cannot be) fully developed. The persistence of asymmetry in peering agreements is one of the factors hindering the establishment of an advanced information infrastructure in developing countries, and it reinforces the digital divide between North and South.

17.3.3 Privacy and identity

One of the characteristics of the Web 2.0 is its new approach to the relationship between individuals and collectives. On the one hand, as illustrated by online social networks, individuals voluntarily share private information with others on a relatively wide scale. In so doing, they have shifted the traditional boundaries between private and public life, staking out an ever larger space of hybridization between the two. On the other hand, as illustrated by P2P networks and cloud computing,[17] individuals also opt for systems that enable them to share computing capabilities and information resources on an automated and relatively anonymous basis. Such behavior blurs the traditional frontier of property rights: they no longer provide the ability to control what uses are made of one's personal data and property or to discriminate between those seeking access to confidential or proprietary information.

These divergent evolutionary paths – which mainly reflect the behavior of individuals (who do not always anticipate the consequences for their own privacy, rights and security) – have a parallel in those advocated by governments and corporations. The desire to reestablish sovereignty over network activities or (respectively) to secure business models leads to the development of technologies that aim to identify and track individual activities. In neither case is the intent to act systematically and purposefully against citizens. Because they are responsible for the general interest and welfare, however, it

[17] In the case of cloud computing, it is most often the information systems manager who decides whether or not to opt in; with P2P the decision to opt in (or out) remains that of the final users. Once the decision to opt in has been made, however, in neither case can users control how their data and resources are used by third parties, because the automated systems that manage the sharing are complex and opaque.

is legitimate for governments to seek to fight crime, to avoid fiscal and other anticivic evasion and to ensure the security of citizens and of essential collective infrastructures. Firms also act legitimately when they seek to preserve the collective investment of all stakeholders by preventing leaks of industrial and trade secrets or to secure remuneration for the services they provide. (We remark also that the customized management of information about consumers/users could be of value to all concerned parties.) These considerations have led to the development and deployment of myriad technologies (e.g. video surveillance, the tracking of card and phone use, geolocalization, control of access, radio frequency identification) along with expert systems able to merge and manage the data resulting from these systems.

The increased use of electronic chips in all kinds of devices, the expansion of network uses into all domains of life and the generalization of the ability of information-processing devices to communicate – in short, the pervasiveness of computing – inevitably leads to the systematic tracking of individuals in most aspects of their lives, however. For this reason, questions about the status of personal data have become more central. We can identify two opposed visions on this score. The first is that personal data (and privacy in general) should simply be considered as a *property* right. Individuals are accordingly free to transfer pieces of their private information in exchange for various benefits. This vision is promoted by those interests that believe that private information is the fuel of future information services in particular and, more generally, of a society featuring highly customized services. The second viewpoint is that privacy should be considered as a *fundamental* right, because it is the root of individual and collective protection against all forms of tyranny. In this view, the potential negative externalities of releasing information on individuals would justify strong public intervention and regulation to prevent overly customized tracking by any organization, public or private. This perspective also accounts for – and, in the absence of public oversight, calls for – activists to provide the means to circumvent tracking technologies.

One of the individual (and sometimes collective) responses to such threats to privacy consists of managing one's "identities"; here avatars are the most sophisticated way of proceeding. Pseudonyms, holding multiple cards and devising "built" identities are all meant to subvert attempts to track, profile and/or control. These tools enable individuals to live parallel lives in response to the standardization imposed by, and the intrusive possibilities laid open by, modern societies. The resulting complex issue stems from the decreasing confidence that system users have in their ability to identify others accurately. In the end, you are never quite sure who (whether individuals or organizations) you are exchanging information with, having business with or meeting online. Obvious issues of individual and collective security follow from this lack of confidence. In response, some organizations – in particular, governments and transnational corporations – might well develop unacceptably intrusive technologies to verify identities, which would constitute a major threat to freedom and individual security *unless* the type of "checks and balances" mechanisms operative in Western democracies for the last century and a half were guaranteed. Such a guarantee would be difficult to provide, however, given that most states are not democratic, that systems of an international scale are built by actors with widely differing interests and capabilities, that "solutions" can be (surreptitiously) embedded in the technology itself and that there is a high risk of the network being captured – or at least dominated – by some governments and private providers of security, technology or information services. Clearly, then, the challenge is to build governance frameworks that balance the need for security with individual freedom and rights. This is a context in which innovation (and therefore openness) is needed and in which all stakeholder types should be encouraged to promote solutions whose adoption would appeal to many in the absence of collectively devised solutions.

17.4 Conclusion: the (re)building of national and international orders

As illustrated by the points we have made with regard to the management of access, flows and identity, most of the stakes involved in the governance of the internet (and of the information society) cannot be disconnected from overarching questions about national and international government. Indeed, the fundamental issue is how individual and collective action can be regulated in an arena without frontiers – that is, without strong national borders but with strong interconnections between the various domains of public life and private industry that rely on the digital management of information.

The problem is that a laissez-faire approach, aside from possibly leading to discriminatory and suboptimal solutions, is also plainly unrealistic: many high-level actors can propose pragmatic solutions, which can be endorsed by many other actors (and also by individuals) because all actors have a fundamental need for (minimal) order and security. For this reason, a handful of powerful states may be able to establish minimal coalitions for proposing and imposing new institutional frameworks together with technical solutions implemented by such central players as the major domain names registries, search engines and Web 2.0 service providers. As pointed out in this book, the dynamics at play in the various interweaved domains are multiple and complex, and, overall, the game is open-ended.

The most obvious point is that many jurisdictional competences must be (re)delimited, sometimes via the creation of new jurisdictions. It is not entirely clear whether an integrated system of governance can be built or whether, to the contrary, the only solution is to build a polycentric system based on mutual tolerance for heterogeneous practices (with regard to filtering, network neutrality, trading, etc.). The integration option would inevitably start with the reshaping of ICANN, which would become a (quasi-)intergovernmental agency if the Governmental Advisory Committee gradually took it over – as called for by the Group of 77. The second, polycentric, option could be implemented as an evolving arrangement among some national governments (those of the G-20, or even only those of the G-8), a few major information technology players, and organizations such as ICANN that have developed their own organizational logic and capabilities and already represent some compromise within the technical community.

This latter scenario, the more probable of the two, would develop in a context in which some issues – namely, sovereignty, security and conflict – are increasingly viewed as central while such values as fundamental rights, democracy and the rule of law are viewed as unrealistic constraints in the light of the pragmatic requirement to implement solutions rapidly. Efforts to establish international regulations arise, moreover, in a context in which the defense of diversity may well lead to a generalized and self-defeating relativism. In connection with the control or filtering of content, for instance, human rights are increasingly opposed to notions such as sovereignty and cultural identity. After all, free speech tends to be contested by all kind of actors that are willing to claim defamation (against religions, employers, etc.). These trends are naturally of concern – especially for established democracies, since authoritarian regimes are not expected to tolerate (much less provide for) free speech. Unlike the liberal states built in the nineteenth and twentieth centuries, emerging orders are not necessarily anchored in the philosophy of the Enlightenment.

One force behind the evolution of internet governance is the enlargement of the debate beyond the technical management of the network to include the institutionalization of the information society. The resulting scope, technicality and complexity of the debate means that only a small number of actors are able to manage it, even as the number of stakeholders has progressively increased. As a consequence, the essential debates tend to be "captured" by a few, and minimal coalitions are able to make and implement far-reaching decisions. Reorganizing the debate is therefore probably the best way to direct the process of building internet governance down a promising path. In particular, the appropriate level of governance (together with related issues) should be determined more precisely, so that an improved federal system can be constructed on the basis of having identified those governance levels, the principles of subsidiarity and the interdependences between issues. A precise mapping of the scope of alternative public goods and the most apposite way to provide them – the issue of *aggregation technologies*[18] – would make it easier to establish not only the roles of communities, governments, independent agencies, international organizations, and so forth but also the best way to coordinate them. It would certainly be a major contribution if the academic community could pin down what is known about these issues. This contribution is necessary if we are to organize a more consistent system of authorities within a network that enables evolution *and* checks and balances – two characteristics that are much needed in any context of sustained learning and innovation.

[18] This term refers to how individual contributions to the collective good determine the quality of the good available for consumption (Hirschleifer, 1983; Cornes and Sandler, 1984). For summation goods, each unit contributed to the public good adds an identical and cumulative amount to the overall level of the good available for consumption. For example, any reduction in the emission of greenhouse gases corresponds to the aggregate (summed) cutbacks of the polluter countries. Other important types of aggregation technologies are: weakest-link public goods, for which the smallest contribution fixes the quantity of the public good for the entire group (for example, pest diffusion); best-shot public goods, for which the overall level of the public good equals the largest single individual provision level (e.g. finding a cure for a disease); and weighted-sum public goods, for which different contributions can have different impacts (as in the cleanup of polluted sites).

References

Abbate, J. (1999), *Inventing the Internet*. Cambridge, MA: MIT Press.

Abramson, B. D. (2005), "Internet connectivity in LDCs," paper presented at the international workshop on "African research and education," Geneva, September 27; available at http://event-africa-networking.web.cern.ch/event-africa-networking/cdrom.html.

Adamovsky, E., and George, S. (2004), "What is the point of Porto Alegre? Activists from two generations in dialogue with openDemocracy," in Sen, J., Anand, A., Escobar, A., and Waterman, P. (eds.), *World Social Forum: Challenging Empires*, 130–5. New Delhi: Viveka Foundation.

Agrikoliansky, E., and Cardon, D. (2005), "Un programme en débats: forums, formes et formats," in Agrikoliansky, E., and Sommier, I. (eds.), *Radiographie du mouvement altermondisliste: Le deuxième forum social européen*, 45–74. Paris: La Dispute.

Aguiton, C., and Cardon, D. (2005), "Le Forum et le réseau: une analyse des modes de gouvernement des forums sociaux," paper presented at the symposium "Cultures et pratiques participatives: une perspective comparative," Paris, January 21.

(2007), "The strength of weak cooperation: an attempt to understand the meaning of Web2.0," *Communications and Strategies*, **65** (1), 51–65.

Ahlert, C., Marsden, C., and Yung, C. (2004), "How 'liberty' disappeared from cyberspace: the mystery shopper tests internet content self-regulation," RootSecure.com, www.rootsecure.net/content/downloads/pdf/liberty_disappeared_from_cyberspace.pdf.

Akrich, M. (1992a), "The description of technical objects," in Bijker, W., and Law, J. (eds.), *Shaping Technology/Building Society: Studies in Sociotechnical Change*, 205–24. Cambridge, MA: MIT Press.

(1992b), "Beyond social construction of technology: the shaping of people and things in the innovation process," in Dierkes, M., and Hoffmann, U. (eds.), *New Technology at the Outset: Social Forces in the Shaping of Technological Innovations*, 173–90. Frankfurt: Campus Verlag.

(2006), "La description des objets techniques," in Akrich, M., Callon, M., and Latour, B. (eds.), *Sociologie de la traduction: Textes fondateurs*, 159–78. Paris: Presses de l'Ecole des Mines.

Akrich, M., and Méadel, C. (2007), "De l'interaction à l'engagement: les collectifs électroniques, nouveaux militants dans le champ de la santé," *Hermès*, **47**, 145–54.

Alger, C. F. (1988), "Perceiving, analysing and coping with the local–global nexus," *International Social Science Journal*, **40**, 321–40.

Alonzo, M., and Aiken, M. (2004), "Flaming in electronic communication," *Decision Support Systems*, **36** (3), 205–13.

Amin, A., and Roberts, J. (2008), "Knowing in action: beyond communities of practice," *Research Policy*, **37** (2), 353–69.

Anderson, B. (2006), *Imagined Communities: Reflections on the Origin and Spread of Nationalism*, rev. edn. London: Verso.

Antonova, S. (2008), *Powerscape of Internet Governance: How Was Global Multistakeholderism Invented in ICANN?* Saarbrücken: VDM Verlag.

Aoki, M. (2001), *Toward a Comparative Institutional Analysis*. Cambridge, MA: MIT Press.

Armstrong, M., Cowan, S., and Vickers, J. (1994), *Regulatory Reform, Economic Analysis and British Experience*. Cambridge, MA: MIT Press.

Arthur, W. B. (1989), "Competing technologies, increasing returns, and lock-in by historical events," *Economic Journal*, **99** (1), 116–31.

Auray, N. (2004), "La régulation de la connaissance: arbitrage sur la taille et gestion aux frontières dans la communauté Debian," *Revue d'économie politique*, **113**, 74–99.

(2005), "Le sens du juste dans un noyau d'experts: Debian et le puritanisme civique," in Proulx, S., Massit-Folléa, F., and Conein, B. (eds.), *Internet, une utopie limitée: Nouvelles regulations, nouvelles solidarités*, 71–95. Quebec City: Presses de l'Université Laval.

(2007), "Folksonomy: a new way to serendipity," *Communications and Strategies*, **65** (1), 67–91.

Auray, N., Poudat, C., and Pons, P. (2007), "Democratizing scientific vulgarization: the balance between cooperation and conflict in French Wikipedia," *Observatorio*, **1** (3), 185–99.

Awerbuch, S., Crew, M., and Kleindorfer, P. (2000), "Transmission: enabler of wholesale competition," in Crew, M. (ed.), *Expanding Competition in Regulated Industries*, 23–40. Boston: Kluwer Academic.

Badasyan, N., and Chakrabarti, S. (2005), "A simple game theoretic analysis of peering and transit contracting among internet access providers," paper presented at the 33rd research conference on "Communication, information and internet policy," Arlington, VA, September 25; available at http://web.si.umich.edu/tprc/papers/2005/486/Badasyan_Chakrabarti_ transit.pdf.

Baldwin, C. Y. (2008), "Where do transactions come from? Modularity, transactions, and the boundaries of firms," *Industrial and Corporate Change*, **17** (1), 155–95.

Baldwin, C. Y., and Clark, K. B. (2000), *Design Rules*, vol. I, *The Power of Modularity*. Cambridge, MA: MIT Press.

Barlow, J. P. (1995), "Is there a there in cyberspace?" *Utne Reader*, **68** (March/April), 50–6.

(1996), "A declaration of the independance of cyberspace," Davos, Switzerland, https://projects.eff.org/~barlow/Declaration-Final.html.

Barzel, Y. (1989), *Economic Analysis of Property Rights*. Cambridge University Press.

Barzilai-Nahon, K., and Neumann, S. (2005), "Bounded in cyberspace: an empirical model of self-regulation in virtual communities," paper presented at the 38th annual Hawaii international conference on system sciences. Waikoloa, HI, January 6.

Baym, N. K. (1995), "The emergence of community in computer-mediated communication," in Jones, S. G. (ed.), *Cybersociety: Computer-Mediated Communication and Community*, 138–63. Thousand Oaks, CA: Sage.

(1996), "Agreements and disagreements in a computer-mediated discussion," *Research on Language and Social Interaction*, **29** (4), 315–45.

(1997), "Interpreting soap operas and creating community: inside an electronic fan culture," in Kiesler, S. (ed.), *Culture of the Internet*, 103–20. Mahwah, NJ: Lawrence Erlbaum Associates.

(2000), *Tune In, Log On: Soaps, Fandom and Online Community*. Thousand Oaks, CA: Sage.

Beau, F. (ed.) (2007), *Culture d'Univers: Jeux en réseau, mondes virtuels, le nouvel âge de la société numérique*. Paris: FYP Editions.

Beck, U. (1986), *Risikogesellschaft: Auf dem Weg in eine andere Moderne*. Frankfurt: Suhrkamp Verlag.

(1992), *Risk Society: Towards a New Modernity*. Thousand Oaks, CA: Sage.

Bell, T. W. (1998), "Fair use vs. fared use: the impact of automated rights management on copyright's fair use doctrine," *North Carolina Law Review*, **76** (2), 557–619.

Ben-Shahar, O., and White, J. J. (2006), "Boilerplate and economic power in auto manufacturing contracts," *Michigan Law Review*, **104** (5), 953–82.

Benabou, V.-L. (2005), "Pourquoi une œuvre de l'esprit est immatérielle," *Revue Lamy Droit de l'immatériel*, **1**, 53–8.

Bendrath, R., Hofmann, J., Leib, V., Mayer, P., and Zürn, M. (2007), "Governing the internet: the quest for legitimate and effective rules," in Hurrelmann, A., Leibfried, S., Martens, K., and Mayer, P. (eds.), *Transforming the Golden-Age Nation State*, 130–51. Basingstoke: Palgrave.

Bendrath, R., and Mueller, M. (2010), "The end of the net as we know it? Deep packet inspection and internet governance," paper presented at the 108th annual meeting of the American Political Science Association, Washington, DC, September 2; available at http://ssrn.com/abstract=1653259.

Benedek, W., Bauer, V., and Kettemann, M. C. (eds.) (2008), *Internet Governance and the Information Society: Global Perspectives and European Dimensions*. Utrecht: Eleven International.

Benkler, Y. (2006), *The Wealth of Networks: How Social Production Transforms Markets and Freedom*. New Haven, CT: Yale University Press.

Bergé, J.-S. (2002), "Entre autres droits, la propriété intellectuelle," *Propriétés Intellectuelles*, **2002** (4), 9–14.

Berman, P. S. (2002), "The globalization of jurisdiction," *University of Pennsylvania Law Review*, **151** (2), 311–546.

Berns, T., Docquir, P.-F., Frydman, B., Hennebel, L., and Lewkowicz, G. (2007), *Responsabilités des entreprises et corégulation*. Brussels: Bruylant.

Bernstein, F., and Marx, L. M. (2006), "Reservation profit levels and the division of supply chain profit," working paper, Duke University, Durham, NC; available at http://faculty.fuqua.duke.edu/~fernando/bio/Bernstein-Marx.pdf.

Bezes, P. (2009), *Réinventer l'Etat: Les réformes de l'administration française (1962–2008)*. Paris: Presses Universitaires de France.

Birnhack, M. D., and Elkin-Koren, N. (2003), "The invisible handshake: the re-emergence of the state in the digital environment," *Virginia Journal of Law and Technology*, **8** (2), article 6, www.vjolt.net/vol8/issue2/v8i2_a06-Birnhack-Elkin-Koren.pdf.

Blumenthal, M. S., and Clark, D. D. (2001), "Rethinking the design of the internet: the end-to-end arguments vs. the brave new world," *ACM Transactions on Internet Technology*, **1** (1), 70–109.

Boltanski, L., and Chiapello, E. (2006), *The New Spirit of Capitalism*. London: Verso Books.

Bomsel, O., and Geffroy, A.-G. (2005), "Economic analysis of DRMs roll-out over the internet," Ecole des Mines de Paris; available at www.cerna.ensmp.fr/Documents/OB-AGG-EtudeDRM.pdf.

Bonaccorsi, A., Giannangeli, S., and Rossi, C. (2006), "Adaptive entry strategies under competing standards: hybrid business models in the open source software industry," *Management Science*, **52** (7), 1085–98.

Bonner, D. (2006), "Checking the executive? Detention without trial, control orders, due process and human rights," *European Public Law*, **12** (1), 45–71.

Bourdieu, P. (1980), *Questions de sociologie*. Paris: Editions de Minuit.

Boussaguet, L., Jacquot, S., and Ravinet, P. (eds.) (2004), *Dictionnaire des politiques publiques*. Paris: Presses de Sciences Po.

Boyd, D. (2002), "Faceted id/entity: managing representation in a digital world," master's thesis, Massachusetts Institute of Technology, Cambridge, MA.

Boyle, J. (1997a), "A politics of intellectual property: environmentalism for the net?" *Duke Law Journal*, **47** (1), 87–116.

(1997b), "Foucault in cyberspace: surveillance, sovereignty, and hard-wired censors," *University of Cincinnati Law Review*, **66** (1), 177–205.

Brady, G. L. (2003), "International governance of the internet: an economic analysis," *Economic Affairs*, **23** (2), 40–4.

Brock, G. (1994), *A Telecommunications Policy for the Information Age*. Cambridge, MA: Harvard University Press.

Brousseau, E. (1993), *L'économie des contrats: Technologies de l'information et coordination interentreprises*. Paris: Presses Universitaires de France.

(1994), "EDI and inter-firm relationships: toward a standardization of coordination processes?" *Information, Economics and Policy*, **6** (3/4), 319–47.

(2002), "The governance of transactions by commercial intermediaries: an analysis of the re-engineering of intermediation by electronic commerce," *International Journal of the Economics of Business*, **9** (3), 353–74.

(2004), "Property rights on the internet: is a specific institutional frame needed?" *Economics of Innovation and New Technology*, **13** (5), 489–507.

(2007), "Multi-level governance of the digital space: does a 'second rank' institutional framework exist?" in Brousseau, E., and Curien, N. (eds.), *Internet and Digital Economics: Principles, Methods and Applications*, 617–48. Cambridge University Press.

Brousseau, E., and Curien, N. (2007), *Internet and Digital Economics: Theories and Applications*. Cambridge University Press.

Brousseau, E, Dedeurwaerdere, T., Jouvet, P. A., and Willinger, M. (forthcoming), *Global Environmental Commons: Analytical and Political Challenges in Building Governance Mechanisms*. Oxford University Press.

Brousseau, E., and Rallet, A. (1999), *Technologies de l'information: Organisation et performances économiques*. Paris: Commissariat Général du Plan.

Brousseau, E., and Raynaud, E. (2009), "Centralizing/decentralizing governance: what are the trade-offs?" working paper. EconomiX, University of Paris Ouest.

(2011), "'Climbing the hierarchical ladders of rules': a life-cycle theory of institutional evolution," *Journal of Economic Behavior and Organization*, **79** (1/2), 65–79.

Brousseau, E., and Saussier, S. (2009), "Contracting with government," in Nickerson, J. A., and Silverman, B. S. (eds.), *The Economic Institutions of Strategy*, 487–521. Bingley, UK: Emerald Group.

Brousseau, E., Schemeil, Y., and Sgard, J. (2010), "Constitution, states and development," *Journal of Comparative Economics*, **38** (3), 253–66.

Brown, I., and Marsden, C. (2007), "Co-regulating internet security: the London Action Plan," Oxford Internet Institute; available at www.oii.ox.ac.uk/research/GigaNet_IanBrown_LondonActionPlan.pdf.

Brunekreft, G., Neuhoff, K., and Newbery, D. (2005), "Electricity transmission: an overview of the current debate," *Utilities Policy*, **13** (2), 73–93.

Buchner, B. K., Carraro, C., and Ellerman, D. (2006), "The allocation of European Union allowances: lessons, unifying themes and general principles," Working Paper no. 108.06. Fondazione Eni Enrico Mattei, Milan.

Bull, H. (1977), *The Anarchical Society: A Study of Order in World Politics*. London: Macmillan.

Bull, H. P. (1979), "Datenschutz contra Amtshilfe: von der 'Einheit der Staatsgewalt' zur 'informationellen Gewaltenteilung,'" *Die öffentliche Verwaltung*, **32** (3), 689–701.

Burkert, H. (2000), "Privacy – data protection: a German/European perspective," in Enge, C., and Keller, K. H. (eds.), *Governance of Global Networks in the Light of Differing Local Values*, 43–70. Baden-Baden: Nomos.

Burnett, G., and Bonnici, L. (2003), "Beyond the FAQ: explicit and implicit norms in Usenet newsgroups," *Library and Information Science Research*, **25** (3), 333–51.

Callick, R. (2006), "China throws net over blogs," *The Australian*, December 14, World, 13.

Callinicos, A. (2004), "The future of the anti-capitalist movement," in Dee, H. (ed.), *Anti-Capitalism: Where Now?*, 96–119. London: Bookmarks.

Callon, M., Lascoumes, P., and Barthe, Y. (2009), *Acting in an Uncertain World: An Essay on Technical Democracy* (trans. Burchell, G.). Cambridge, MA: MIT Press [first edition in French; Paris: Seuil, 2001].

Callon, M., Law, J., and Rip, A. (eds.) (1986), *Mapping the Dynamics of Science and Technology: Sociology of Science in the Real World*. London: Macmillan.

Cameron, P. D. (ed.) (2005), *Legal Aspects of EU Energy Regulation: Implementing the New Directives on Electricity and Gas across Europe*. Oxford University Press.

Cammaerts, B. (2010), "Power dynamics in multi-stakeholder policy processes and intra-civil society networking," in Mansell, R. E., and Raboy, M. (eds.), *The Handbook of Global Media and Communication Policy*, 129–46. Oxford: Blackwell.

Cammaerts, B., and Carpentier, N. (2005), "The unbearable lightness of full participation in a global context: WSIS and civil society participation," in Servaes, J., and Carpentier, N. (eds.), *Towards a Sustainable Information Society: Deconstructing WSIS*, 17–49. Bristol: Intellect.

Cassen, B. (2003), *Tout a commencé à Porto Alegre... Mille forums sociaux!* Paris: Mille et Une Nuits.

Castells, M. (2001), *The Internet Galaxy: Reflections on the Internet, Business, and Society*. Oxford University Press.

Cefaï, D. (1996), "La construction des problèmes publics: définition de situation dans les arènes publiques," *Réseaux*, **75**, 43–66.

Chadwick, A. (2006), *Internet Politics: States, Citizens, and New Communication Technologies*. Oxford University Press.

Chao, H.-P., Oren, S., and Wilson, R. (2008), "Reevaluation of vertical integration and unbundling in restructured electricity markets," in Sioshansi, F. P. (ed.), *Competititve Electricity Markets. Design, Implementation, Performance*, 27–64. Amsterdam: Elsevier.

Chen, C. (2004), "United States and European Union approaches to internet jurisdiction and their impact on e-commerce," *University of Pennsylvania Law Review*, **25** (1), 423–54.

Cheung, A. S. Y. (2006), "The business of governance: China's legislation on content regulation in cyberspace," *New York University Journal of International Law and Politics*, **38** (1), 1–37.

Chevallier, J. (2003), *L'Etat de droit*, 4th edn. Paris: Monchrestien.

Christensen, T., and Lægreid, P. (2006), "Agencification and regulatory reforms," in Christensen, T., and Lægreid, P. (eds.), *Autonomy and Regulation: Coping with Agencies in the Modern State*, 8–52. Cheltenham: Edward Elgar.

Christou, G., and Simpson, S. (2007), "Gaining a stake in global internet governance: the EU, ICANN, and strategic norm manipulation," *European Journal of Communication*, **22** (2), 147–64.

(2008), "International policy implementation through gate keeping: the Internet Corporation for Assigned Names and Numbers," in Jutta, J., Verbeek, B., and Reinalda, B. (eds.), *International Organizations and Implementation: Enforcers, Managers, Authorities?*, 75–87. London: Routledge.

Clark, C. (1996), "The answer to the machine is in the machine," in Hugenholtz, P. B. (ed.), *The Future of Copyright in a Digital Environment*, 139–46. The Hague: Kluwer Law International.

Clarke, R. V. (1997), *Situational Crime Prevention: Successful Case Studies*. New York: Harrow and Heston.

Clastres, P. (1989), *Society against the State: Essays in Political Anthropology*. New York: Zone Books.

Clemons, E. K., Reddi, S. P., and Row, M. C. (1993), "The impact of information technology on the organization of economic activity: the 'move to the middle' hypothesis," *Journal of Management Information Systems*, **10** (1), 9–36.

Clinton, W. J., and Gore, A. Jr. (1997), "The framework for global electronic commerce," White House, Washington, DC; available at http://clinton4.nara.gov/WH/New/Commerce.

Coase, R. H. (1960), "The problem of social cost," *Journal of Law and Economics*, **3** (1), 1–40.

Cohen, J. E. (1998), "Copyright and the jurisprudence of self-help," *Berkeley Technology Law Journal*, **13** (13), 1089–143.

Cohendet, P., and Amin, A. (2004), *Architectures of Knowledge: Firms, Capabilities and Communities*. Oxford University Press.

Coleman, S., and Blumler, J. G. (2008), *The Internet and Democratic Citizenship: Theory, Practice and Policy*. Cambridge University Press.

Collective work (2003), *Où va le mouvement altermondialisation? ...et Autres questions pour comprendre son histoire, ses débats, ses stratégies, ses divergences*. Paris: La Découverte.

Comba, V., and Vignocchi, M. (2005), "Scholarly communication and open access: research communities and their publishing patterns," paper presented at the conference "Open access: the option for the future?" Oslo, August 13; available at http://hdl.handle.net/10760/7276.

Constable, N. (2003), *Romance on a Global Stage: Pen Pals, Virtual Ethnography and "Mail Order" Marriages*. Berkeley: University of California Press.

Cooter, R. D. (1994), "Structural adjudication and the new law merchant: a model of decentralized law," *International Review of Law and Economics*, **14** (2), 215–31.

Cornes, R., and Sandler, T. (1984), "Easy riders, joint production, and public goods," *Economic Journal*, **94** (3), 580–98.

Cowhey, P. F., and Aronson, J. D. (2009), *Transforming Global Information and Communication Markets: The Political Economy of Innovation*. Cambridge, MA: MIT Press.

Cowhey, P. F., and Mueller, M. (2009), "Delegation, networks, and internet governance," in Kahler, M. (ed.), *Networked Politics: Agency, Power and Governance*, 173–93. Ithaca, NY: Cornell University Press.

Cox, R. W., and Jacobson, H. K. (1974), *The Anatomy of Influence: Decision Making in International Organization*. New Haven, CT: Yale University Press.

Crozier, M., and Thoenig, J.-C. (1976), "The regulation of complex organized systems," *Administrative Science Quarterly*, **21** (4), 547–70.

Crumley, C. (1995), "Heterarchy and the analysis of complex societies," *Archeological Papers of the American Anthropological Association*, **7** (1), 1–5.

Cullen, R., and Choy, D. W. (2005), "China's media: the impact of the internet," *San Diego International Law Journal*, **6** (May), 323–40.

Curien, N., and Moreau, F. (2007), "The convergence between content and access: internalizing the market complementarity," *Review of Network Economics*, **6** (2), article 5.

Daly, A. (2010), "The legality of deep packet inspection," paper presented at the 1st interdisciplinary workshop on communications policy and regulation "Communications and competition law and policy: challenges of the new decade," Glasgow, June 17; available at http://ssrn.com/abstract=1628024.

Dam, K. W. (1999), "Self-help in the digital jungle," *Journal of Legal Studies*, **28** (2), 393–412.

David, P. A. (1985), "Clio and the economics of QWERTY," *American Economic Review*, **75** (2), 332–7.

Davis, J. P., Farnham, S., and Jensen, C. (2002), "Decreasing online 'bad' behavior," in Terveen, L. G., and Wixon, D. R. (eds.), *Extended Abstracts of the 2002 Conference on Human Factors in Computing Systems*, 718–19. New York: ACM Press.

De Laet, M., and Mol, A. (2000), "The Zimbabwe bush pump: mechanics of a fluid technology," *Social Studies of Science*, **30** (2), 225–64.

De Sousa Santos, B. (2008), *The World Social Forum and the Global Left, Politics and Society*, **36** (2), 247–70.

Dedeurwaerde, T. (2004), "The contribution of network governance to sustainable development: with box study one sustainability assessment impact," draft paper, Catholic University of Leuven.

(2005), "From bioprospecting to reflexive governance," *Ecological Economics*, **53** (4), 473–91.

Deffains, B., and Demougin, D. (2006), "Governance: who controls matters," *Zeitschrift für betriebswirtschaftliche Forschung* [*Magazine for Marketing and Management*], 2006 (special issue), S1–S20.

Deibert, R. J. (2009), "The geopolitics of internet control: censorship, sovereignty and cyberspace," in Chadwick, A., and Howard, P. N. (eds.), *Routledge Handbook of Internet Politics*, 323–36. New York: Routledge.

Deibert, R. J., Palfrey, J. G., Rohozinski, R., and Zittrain, J. (eds.) (2008), *Access Denied: The Practice and Policy of Global Internet Filtering*. Cambridge, MA: MIT Press.

(eds.) (2010), *Access Controlled: The Shaping of Power, Rights, and Rule in Cyberspace*. Cambridge, MA: MIT Press.

Delamotte, E., Lamarche, T., and Prince, B. (2006), "Communautés et nouveaux modes de (télé)communications," *Terminal*, **97/98** (1), 7–17.

Deleuze, G. (1990), *Post-scriptum sur les sociétés de contrôle: Pourparlers – 1972–1990*. Paris: Editions de Minuit.

Dellarocas, C. (2006), "Strategic manipulations of internet opinion forums: implications for consumers and firms," *Management Science*, **52** (10), 1577–93.

Dellarocas, C., Fan, M., and Wood, C. A. (2004), "Self-interest, reciprocity, and participation in online reputation systems," Paper no. 4500-04. Sloan School of Management, Massachusetts Institute of Technology, Cambridge, MA; available at http://ssrn.com/abstract+585402.

Demazière, D., and Horn, F. (2007), "The functioning of a free software community: entanglement of three regulation modes – control, autonomous and distributed," *Science Studies*, **20** (2), 34–54.

DeNardis, L. (2009), *Protocol Politics: The Globalization of Internet Governance*. Cambridge, MA: MIT Press.

(2010a), "The privatization of internet governance," paper presented at the 5th annual Global Internet Governance Academic Network (GigaNet) symposium, Vilnius, September 13; available at http://giganet.org/page/2010-annual-symposium.

(2010b), "The emerging field of internet governance," working paper, Yale Law School, New Haven, CT; available at http://ssrn.com/abstract=1678343.

Derrida, J. (1994), *Force de loi*. Paris: Editions Galilée.

Dibbell, J. (1999), *My Tiny Life: Crime and Passion in the Virtual World*. New York: Henry Holt.

Donath, J. (2001), "Mediated faces," in Beynon, M., Nehaniv, C. L., and Dautenhahn, K. (eds.), *Cognitive Technology: Instruments of Mind, 4th International Conference, CT 2001, Warwick, UK, August 6–9, 2001, Proceedings*, 373–90. New York: Springer.

Dorat, R., Conein, B., Latapy, M., and Auray, N. (2007), "Multi-level analysis of an interaction network between individuals in a mailing-list," *Annals of Telecommunications*, **62** (1), 3–4.

Drake, W. J. (ed.) (2005), *Reforming Internet Governance: Perspectives from the UN Working Group on Internet Governance*. New York: United Nations Publications.

Drake, W. J., and Wilson, E. J. III (eds.) (2008), *Governing Global Electronic Networks: International Perspectives on Policy and Power.* Cambridge, MA: MIT Press.

Drezner, D. W. (2004), "The global governance of the internet: bringing the state back in," *Political Science Quaterly*, **119** (3), 477–98.

Du Gay, P., Hall, S., Janes, L., Mackay, H., and Negus, K. (1997), *Doing Cultural Studies: The Story of the Sony Walkman.* Thousand Oaks, CA: Sage.

Dusollier, S. (1999), "Electrifying the fence: the legal protection of technological measures for protecting copyright," *European Intellectual Property Review*, **21** (6), 285–97.

(2005), *Droit d'auteur et protection des œuvres dans l'univers numérique: Droits et exceptions à la lumière des dispositifs de verrouillage des œuvres.* Brussels: Larcier.

Dutton, W. H., and Peltu, M. (2007), "The emergent internet governance mosaic: connecting the pieces," *Information Polity*, **12** (1/2), 63–81.

DuVal Smith, A. (1999), "Problems of conflict management in virtual communities," in Kollock, P., and Smith, M. (eds.), *Communities in Cyberspace*, 134–63. London: Routledge.

Easterbrook, F. H. (1996), "Cyberspace and the law of the horse," *University of Chicago Legal Forum*, **1996**, 207–16.

(2005), "Contract and copyright," *Houston Law Review*, **42** (4), 953–73.

Eberlein, B. (2005), "Regulation by cooperation: the 'third way' in making rules for the internal market," in Cameron, P. D. (ed.), *Legal Aspects of EU Energy Regulation*, 59–88. Oxford University Press.

EC (2001), *European Governance: A White Paper*, COM(2001)0428 final. Brussels: EC; available at http://eur-lex.europa.eu/LexUriServ/site/en/com/2001/com2001_0428en01.pdf.

(2003), *First Report on the Application of Directive 2000/31/EC of the European Parliament and of the Council of 8 June 2000 on Certain Legal Aspects of Information Society Services, in particular Electronic Commerce, in the Internal Market (Directive on Electronic Commerce)*, COM(2003)702 final. Brussels: EC.

(2004), *Commission Decision of 24.03.2004 relating to a Proceeding under Article 82 of the EC Treaty (Case COMP/C-3/37.792 Microsoft)*, COM(2004)900 final. Brussels: EC.

(2005), *i2010: A European Information Society for Growth and Employment*, COM(2005)229 final. Brussels: EC.

(2007a), *Inquiry pursuant to Article 17 of Regulation (EC) no. 1/2003 into the European Gas and Electricity Sectors (Final Report)*, COM (2006)851 final. Brussels: EC.

(2007b), *Towards a European Charter on the Rights of Energy Consumers*, COM(2007)386 final. Brussels: EC.

Ehrenmann, A., and Smeers, Y. (2005), "Inefficiencies in European congestion management proposals," *Utilities Policy*, **13** (2), 135–52.

Eisenstein, E. (1979), *The Printing Press as an Agent of Change: Communications and Cultural Transformations in Early-Modern Europe*. Cambridge University Press.

Elias, N. (1990 [1939]), *La Dynamique de l'Occident*. Paris: Presses Pocket.

Elkin-Koren, N. (1997), "Copyright policy and the limit of freedom of contract," *Berkeley Technology Law Journal*, **12** (1), 93–113.

(1998), "Copyrights in cyberspace: rights without law," *Chicago–Kent Law Review*, **73** (4), 1155–202.

(2001), "A public-regarding approach to contracting over copyrights," in Dreyfuss, R. C., Zimmerman, D. L., and First, H. (eds.), *Expanding the Boundaries of Intellectual Property*, 191–222. Oxford University Press.

(2005), "What contracts can't do: the limits of private ordering in facilitating a creative commons," *Fordham Law Review*, **74** (2), 375–422.

(2006), "Exploring creative commons: a skeptical view of a worthy pursuit," in Guibault, L., and Hugenholtz, P. B. (eds.), *The Future of the Public Domain: Identifying the Commons in Information Law*, 325–45. The Hague: Kluwer Law International.

(2007), "Making room for consumers under the DMCA," *Berkeley Technology Law Journal*, **22** (3), 1119–55.

Epstein, R. A. (2006), "Contract, not regulation: UCITA [Uniform Computer Information Transactions Act] and high-tech consumers meet their consumer protection critics," in Winn, J. K. (ed.), *Consumer Protection in the Age of the "Information Economy,"* 205–40. Aldershot, UK: Ashgate.

EU Council and EC (2000), *eEurope 2002 Action Plan: An Information Society for All*. Brussels: EC.

Farrell, J., and Saloner, G. (1986), "Installed base and compatibility: innovation, product preannouncements, and predation," *American Economic Review*, **76** (5), 940–55.

Feindt, P. (2012), "Reflexive governance and multi-level decision-making in agricultural policy: conceptual reflections and empirical evidence," in Brousseau, E., Dedeurwaerdere, T., and Siebenhüner, B. (eds.), *Reflexive Governance for Global Public Goods*. Cambridge, MA: MIT Press.

Fernback, J. (2007), "Beyond the diluted community concept: a symbolic interactionist perspective on online social relations," *New Media Society*, **9** (1), 49–69.

Firer-Blaess, S. (2007), "Wikipedia: hiérarchie et démocratie," Homo Numericus, October 11, http://homo-numericus.net/spip.php?article276.

Fisher, W. W. (2004), *Promises to Keep: Technology, Law and the Future of Entertainment*. Palo Alto, CA: Stanford University Press.

Flichy, P. (2001), *L'imaginaire d'Internet*. Paris: Editions la Découverte.

Foray, D. (2004), *The Economics of Knowledge*. Cambridge, MA: MIT Press.

Foucault, M. (1994), *Dits et écrits*, vol. IV. Paris: Gallimard.

Fried, C. (2006), *Contract as Promise: A Theory of Contractual Obligation*. Cambridge, MA: Harvard University Press.

Friedrichs, J. (2001), "The meaning of new medievalism," *European Journal of International Relations*, 7 (4), 475–502.

Froomkin, A. M. (2000a), "Semi-private international rulemaking: lessons learned from the WIPO domain name process," in Marsden, C. T. (ed.), *Regulating the Global Information Society*, 211–36. London: Routledge.

(2000b), "Wrong turn in cyberspace: using ICANN to route around the APA and the constitution," *Duke Law Journal*, **50** (1), 17–186.

Froomkin, A. M., and Lemley, M. A. (2003), "ICANN and antitrust," *University of Illinois Law Review*, **2003** (1), 1–76.

Frydman, B. (1997), "Quel droit pour l'internet?" in *Internet sous le Regard du Droit: Actes du Colloque du 30 octobre 1997*, 279–316. Brussels: Editions du Jeune Barreau de Bruxelles.

(2004), "Coregulation: a possible legal model for global governance," in de Schutter, B., and Pas, J. (eds.), *About Globalisation: Views on the Trajectory of Mondialisation*, 227–42. Brussels: VUB Press.

Frydman, B., and Rorive, I. (2002a), "Fighting Nazi and anti-Semitic material on the internet: the Yahoo! case and its global implications," paper presented at the conference "Hate and terrorist speech on the internet: the global implications of the Yahoo! ruling in France," New York, February 11; available at www.philodroit.be/IMG/pdf/yahoo.pdf.

(2002b), "Regulating internet content through intermediaries in Europe and the USA," *Zeitschrift für Rechtssoziologie*, 23 (1), 41–59.

Gac (2004), "Operating principles as amended," GAC, Marina del Ray, California; available at gac.icann.org/system/files/GAC_Operating_Principles_1.pdf.

Garicano, L., and Kaplan, S. N. (2001), "The effects of business-to-business e-commerce on transaction costs," *Journal of Industrial Economics*, **49** (4), 463–85.

Gasser, U. (ed.) (2002), *Perspektiven des Informationsrechts* [*Perspectives on Information Law*]. Baden-Baden: Nomos.

(2004), *Information Quality Regulation: Foundations, Perspectives and Applications*. Baden-Baden: Nomos.

Gay, J. (ed.) (2002), *Free Software, Free Society: Selected Essays of Richard M. Stallman*. Boston: GNU Press.

Gehring, V. V. (2002), "Do hackers provide a public service?" *Philosophy and Public Policy Quarterly*, **22** (1), 21–7.

Geist, M. (2002a), "Fair.com? An examination of the allegations of systemic unfairness in the ICANN UDRP," *Brooklyn Journal of International Law*, **27** (3), 903–38; available at http://aix1.uottawa.ca/~geist/geistudrp.pdf.

(2002b), "Fundamentally Fair.com? An update on bias allegations and the ICANN UDRP," University of Ottawa; available at http://aix1.uottawa.ca/~geist/fairupdate.pdf.

Gensollen, M. (2006), "La culture entre économie et écologie: l'exemple des communautés en ligne," in Greffe, X. (ed.), *Création et diversité au miroir des industries culturelles*. Paris: Documentation Française.

German, K. (2005), "Top 10 dot-com flops," CNet.com, August 5, www.cnet.com/1990–11136_1–6278387–1.html.

Geroski, P. A. (2000), "Models of technology diffusion," *Research Policy*, **29** (4/5), 603–25.

Gibb, B., and Damodaran, S. (2002), *ebXML: Concepts and Application*. Indianapolis: John Wiley.

Gibson, W. (2000), *Neuromancer*. New York: Ace Books.

Gilbert, R. J. (1995), "Networks, standards, and the use of market dominance: Microsoft," in Kwoka, J. E., and White, L. J. (eds.), *The Antitrust Revolution: The Role of Economics*, 2nd edn., 409–30. Oxford University Press.

Gilbert, R., and Newbery, D. (2007), "Electricity merger policy in the shadow of regulation," Energy Policy and Economics Working Paper no. 019. University of California, Berkeley.

Glachant, J.-M., Dubois, U., and Perez, Y. (2008), "Deregulating with no regulator: is the German electricity transmission regime institutionally correct?" *Energy Policy*, **36** (5), 1600–10.

Glachant, J.-M., and Pignon, V. (2005), "Nordic congestion's arrangement as a model for Europe? Physical constraints vs. economic incentives," *Utilities Policy*, **13** (2), 153–62.

Godard, O. (2012), "Managing global risks through 'proportionate' precaution: collective preferences and state sovereignty in the balance," in Brousseau, E., Dedeurwaerdere, T., and Siebenhüner, B. (eds.), *Reflexive Governance for Global Public Goods*. Cambridge, MA: MIT Press.

Goldberg, V. (1976), "Regulation and administered contracts," *Bell Journal of Economics*, **7** (2), 426–52.

Goldsmith, J. L. (1998), "Against cyberanarchy," *University of Chicago Law Review*, **65** (4), 1199–250.

Goldstein, P. (1997), "Copyright and its substitutes," *Wisconsin Law Review*, **1997** (5), 865–71.

González-Díaz, M., and Vázquez, L. (2008), "Make- or buy-decisions: a new institutional economics approach," in Brousseau, E., and Glachant, J.-M. (eds.), *New Institutional Economics: A Guidebook*, 255–71. Cambridge University Press.

Graham, C. (2006), "The politics of necessity: electricity and water in Great Britain," *Journal of Consumer Policy*, **29** (4), 435–48.

Graz, J.-C. (2006), "International standardisation and corporate democracy," in Giesen, K. G., and van der Pijl, K. (eds.), *Global Norms in the Twenty-First Century*, 118–33. Newcastle: Cambridge Scholars Press.

Green, R. (2003), "Cost recovery and the efficient development of the grid," in Lévêque, F. (ed.), *Transport Pricing of Electricity Networks*, 137–53. Boston: Kluwer.

Guash, J. L. (2004), *Granting and Renegotiating Infrastructure Concessions: Doing It Right*. Washington, DC: World Bank.

Guash, J. L., Laffont, J.-J., and Straub, S. (2003), "Renegotiation of concession contracts in Latin America," Policy Research Working Paper no. 3011. World Bank, Washington, DC; available at http://papers.ssrn.com/abstract_ id=340580.

Guibault, L. (2002), *Copyright Limitations and Contracts: An Analysis of the Contractual Overridability of Limitations on Copyright*. The Hague: Kluwer Law International.

Gunningham, N. (forthcoming), "Regulatory reform and reflexive regulation: beyond command and control," in Brousseau, E., Dedeurwaerdere, T., and Siebenhüner, B. (eds.), *Reflexive Governance for Global Public Goods*. Cambridge, MA: MIT Press.

Habermas, J. (1996), *Between Facts and Norms: Contributions to a Discourse Theory of Law and Democracy*, 2nd edn. Cambridge, MA: MIT Press.

(2001), *The Postnational Constellation: Political Essays* (trans. Pensky, M.). Cambridge, MA: MIT Press.

Hahn, R. W., Litan, R. E., and Singer, H. J. (2007), "The economics of 'wireless net neutrality,'" Working Paper no. RP 07-10, AEI-Brookings Joint Center, Washington, DC.

Halewood, M., and Nnadozie, K. (2008), "Giving priority to the commons: the International Treaty on Plant Genetic Resources for Food and Agriculture," in Tansey, G., and Rajotte, T. (eds.), *The Future Control of Food: A Guide to International Negotiations and Rules on Intellectual Property, Biodiversity and Food Security*, 115–40. London: Earthscan.

Hall, P. A., and Soskice, D. (2001), "An introduction to varieties of capitalism," in Hall, P. A., and Soskice, D. (eds.), *Varieties of Capitalism: The Institutional Foundations of Comparative Advantage*, 1–68. Oxford University Press.

Hamelink, C. J. (2005), "Human rights implication of WSIS," *Revue québécoise de droit international*, **18** (1), 27–40.

Hans-Bredow-Institut (2006), *Final Report: Study on Co-Regulation Measures in the Media Sector.* Hamburg: Hans-Bredow-Institut; available at http://ec.europa.eu/avpolicy/docs/library/studies/coregul/final_rep_en.pdf.

Hansmann, H., and Kraakman, R. H. (2002), "Property, contract, and verification: the numerus clausus problem and the divisibility of rights," *Journal of Legal Studies*, **31** (S2), 373–420.

Hardy, T. I. (1994), "The proper legal regime for 'cyberspace,'" *University of Pittsburgh Law Review*, **55** (4), 993–1055.

(1996), "Property (and copyright) in cyberspace," *University of Chicago Legal Forum*, **1996**, 217–60.

Hauben, M., and Hauben, R. (1997), *Netizens: On the History and Impact of Usenet and the Internet.* Los Alamitos, CA: IEEE Computer Society Press.

Hedley, S. (2006), *The Law of Electronic Commerce and the Internet in the UK and Ireland.* London: Routledge Cavendish.

Heffernan, J. (2006), "An American in Beijing: an attorney's ethical considerations abroad with a client doing business with a repressive government," *Georgetown Journal of Legal Ethics*, **19** (3), 721–31.

Heller, N. (2002), "'Customizable privacy': a new approach to international regulation of the internet," *Journal of Public and International Affairs*, **13** (Spring), 63–81.

Helm, D. T. (2004), *Energy, the State and the Market: British Energy Policy since 1979.* Oxford University Press.

Hennebel, L., and Lewkowicz, G. (2007), "Corégulation et responsabilité sociale des entreprises," in Berns, T., Docquir, P.-F., Frydman, B., Hennebel, L., and Lewkowicz, G. (eds.), *Responsabilités des entreprises et corégulation*, 147–226. Brussels: Bruylant.

Herrera, G. (2006), *Technology and International Transformation: The Railroad, the Atom Bomb, and the Politics of Technological Change.* Albany, NY: SUNY Press.

Herring, S., Job-Sluder, K., Scheckler, R., and Barab, S. (2002), "Searching for safety online: managing 'trolling' in a feminist forum," *Information Society*, **18** (5), 371–84.

Hindman, M. S. (2008), *The Myth of Digital Democracy.* Princeton University Press.

Hine, C. (2000), *Virtual Ethnography*. Thousand Oaks, CA: Sage.
(2007), "Connective ethnography for the exploration of e-science," *Journal of Computer Mediated Communication*, **12** (2), 618–34.
(2008), *Systematics as Cyberscience: Computers, Change, and Continuity in Science*. Cambridge, MA: MIT Press.
Hirschleifer, J. (1983), "From weakest-link to best-shot: the voluntary provision of public goods," *Public Choice*, **41** (3), 371–86.
Hirsh, R. (1991), "Regulation and technology in the electric utility industry: a historical analysis of interdependance and change," in High, J. (ed.), *Regulation: Economic Theory and History*, 147–77. Ann Arbor: University of Michigan Press.
Hofmann, J. (2007), "Internet governance: a regulative idea in flux," in Kumar, R., and Bandamutha, J. (eds.), *Internet Governance: An Introduction*, 74–108. Hyderabad: ICFAI University Press.
Hogan, W. (2002), "Electricity market restructuring: reforms of reforms," *Journal of Regulatory Economics*, **21** (1), 103–32.
Horwitz, M. J. (1977), *The Transformation of American Law, 1760–1860*. Cambridge, MA: Harvard University Press.
Hosein, I., Tsiavos, P., and Whitley, E. A. (2003), "Regulating architecture and architectures of regulation: contributions from information systems," *International Review of Law, Computers and Technology*, **17** (1), 85–97.
Howard, P. N. (2004), "Embedded media: who we know, what we know, and society online," in Howard, P. N., and Jones, S. G. (eds.), *Society Online: The Internet in Context*, 1–27. Thousand Oaks, CA: Sage.
Howells, G., and Weatherill, S. (2005), *Consumer Protection Law*, 2nd edn. Aldershot, UK: Ashgate.
Hunold, C., and Dryzek, J. (2005), "Green political strategy and the state: combining political theory and comparative history," in Barry, J., and Eckersley, R. (eds.), *The State and the Global Ecological Crisis*, 75–95. Cambridge, MA: MIT Press.
Hunter, D. (2003), "Cyberspace as place, and the tragedy of the digital anticommons," *California Law Review*, **91** (2), 439–521.
Iannacci, F. (2005), "Coordination processes in open source software development: the Linux case study," *Emergence: Complexity and Organization*, 7 (2), 21–31.
IGF (2008), *Programme, Agenda and Format of the Hyderabad Meeting*. New York: United Nations; available at www.intgovforum.org/hyderabad_prog/ProgrammePaper.05.06.2008.pdf.
IGP (2006), "Comments of the Internet Governance Project: the continued transition of the technical coordination and management of the internet domain name and addressing system," Docket no. 060519136–6136–01.

IGP, Syracuse, NY; available at www.internetgovernance.org/pdf/ntiacomments-igp-final.pdf.

INACH (2006), *Annual Report 2005*. Amsterdam: INACH; available at www.inach.net/content/INACH-annual-report-2005.pdf (accessed April 7, 2007).

Isbister, P. M. (2004), "Current developments: developments in the executive branch," *Georgetown Immigration Law Journal*, **18** (4), 595–7.

IUCN (1980), *World Conservation Strategy: Living Resource Conservation for Sustainable Development*. Gland, Switzerland: IUCN.

Jessop, B. (1998), "The rise of governance and the risks of failure: the case of economic development," *International Social Science Journal*, **155** (1), 29–45.

(2003), "Governance and metagovernance: on reflexivity, requisite variety, and requisite irony," in Bang, H. P. (ed.), *Governance as Social and Political Communication*, 101–16. Manchester University Press.

Jones, S. G. (1995), "Understanding community in the digital age," in Jones, S. G. (ed.), *Cybersociety: Computer-Mediated Communication and Community*, 10–35. Thousand Oaks, CA: Sage.

Jørgensen, R. F. (ed.) (2006), *Human Rights in the Global Information Society*. Cambridge, MA: MIT Press.

Jørgensen, R. F., and Marzouki, M. (2005), "Human rights: the missing link," in Drossou, O., and Jensen, H. (eds.), *Visions in Process II: The World Summit on the Information Society, Geneva 2003 – Tunis 2005*, 17–23. Berlin: Heinrich Böll Foundation.

Josefsson, U. (2005), "Coping with illness online: the case of patients' online communities," *The Information Society*, **21** (2), 143–53.

Joskow, P. L. (2002), "Electricity sector restructuring and competition: a transaction cost perspective," in Brousseau, E., and Glachant, J.-M. (eds.), *The Economics of Contracts: Theories and Applications*, 503–30. Cambridge University Press.

(2006), "Patterns of transmission investment," in Lévêque, F. (ed.), *Competitive Electricity Markets and Sustainability*, 131–86. Cheltenham: Edward Elgar.

Joskow, P. L., and Tirole, J. (2005), "Merchant transmission investment," *Journal of Industrial Economics*, **53** (2), 233–64.

Kanakamedala, K., Srivatsan, V., and Ramsdell, G. (2003), "Getting supply chain software right," *McKinsey Quarterly*, **2003** (1), 78–85.

Katsh, E. (2006), "Online dispute resolution: some implications for the emergence of law in cyberspace," *Lex Electronica*, **10** (3), article 8, www.lex-electronica.org/articles/v10–3/katsh.pdf.

Katyal, N. K. (2006), "Internal separation of powers: checking today's most dangerous branch from within," *Yale Law Journal*, **115** (9), 2314–49.

Katz, M. L., and Shapiro, C. (1985), "Network externalities, competition, and compatibility," *American Economic Review*, **75** (3), 424–40.

Kaul, I., and Mendoza, R. U. (2003), "Advancing the concept of public goods," in Kaul, I., Conceição, P., Le Goulven, K., and Mendoza, R. U. (eds.), *Providing Global Public Goods: Managing Globalization*, 78–111. New York: United Nations.

Keohane, R. O. (2001), "Governance in a partially globalized world: presidential address, American Political Science Association, 2000," *American Political Science Review*, **95** (1), 1–13.

Kerr, I. R., and Gilbert, D. (2004), "The role of ISPs in the investigation of cybercrime," in Mendina, T., and Brtiz, J. (eds.), *Information Ethics in an Electronic Age: Current Issues in Africa and the World*, 163–72. Jefferson, NC: McFarland Press.

Kesan, J. P., and Gallo, A. A. (2006), "Why are the United States and the European Union failing to regulate the internet efficiently? Going beyond the bottom-up and top-down alternatives," *European Journal of Law and Economics*, **21** (3), 237–66.

King, I. (2004), "Internationalizing internet governance: does ICANN have a role to play?" *Information and Communication Technologies Law*, **1** (3), 243–58.

Kingdon, J. W. (1995), *Agendas, Alternatives, and Public Policies*, 2nd edn. New York: HarperCollins.

Klaus, G., and Buhr, M. (1974), *Philosophisches Wörterbuch*, 10th edn. Leipzig: VEB Bibliographisches Institut.

Klein, H. (2002), "ICANN et la gouvernance d'internet," in Massit-Folléa, F., and Delmas, R. (eds.), *La gouvernance d'internet*, 93–129. Paris: Hermès Sciences.

(2004), "Understanding WSIS: an institutional analysis of the UN World Summit on the Information Society," *Information Technologies and International Development*, **1** (3/4), 3–13.

Klein, N. (2002), "Democratizing the movement: when activists gathered at the first World Social Forum, no single agenda could contain the diversity," in Klein, N., *Fences and Windows: Dispatches from the Front Lines of the Globalization Debate*, 193–207. Toronto: Knopf Canada.

Kling, R., and Courtright, C. (2003), "Group behavior and learning in electronic forums: a sociotechnical approach," *The Information Society*, **19** (3), 221–35.

Kollock, P., and Smith, M. (eds.) (1999), *Communities in Cyberspace*. New York: Routledge.

Komaitis, K. (2010), *The Current State of Domain Name Regulation: Domain Names as Second-Class Citizens in a Mark-Dominated World*. London: Routledge.

Kooiman, J. (1993), "Social-political governance: introduction," in Kooiman, J. (ed.), *Modern Governance: New Government–Society Relations*, 1–6. Thousand Oaks, CA: Sage.

(2003), *Governing as Governance*. Thousand Oaks, CA: Sage.

Kotok, A. (2001), "Can XML help write the law?" XML.com, May 9, www.xml.com/pub/a/2001/05/09/legalxml.html.

Koven, R. (2003), "A new opening for press controllers," in Karlekar, K. D. (ed.), *Freedom of the Press 2003: A Global Survey of Media Independence*, 31–9. Lanham, MD: Rowman & Littlefield.

Kraemer, K. L., Dedrick, J., Melville, N. P., and Zhu, K. (eds.) (2006), *Global E-Commerce: Impacts of National Environment and Policy*. Cambridge University Press.

Kranich, N. (2004), "The information commons: a public policy report," Brennan Center for Justice, NYU School of Law, New York; www.fepproject.org/policyreports/InformationCommons.pdf.

Krehbiel, K. (1991), *Information and Legislative Organization*. Ann Arbor: University of Michigan Press.

Kreimer, S. F. (2006), "Censorship by proxy: the First Amendment, internet intermediaries, and the problem of the weakest link," *University of Pennsylvania Law Review*, **155** (1), 11–101.

Kriplean, T., Beschastnikh, I., McDonald, D. W., and Golder, S. A. (2007), "Community, consensus, coercion, control: CS*W or how policy mediates mass participation," paper presented at the international conference "Supporting group work," Sanibel Island, FL, November 6; available at http://portal.acm.org/citation.cfm?id=1316648.

Kropp, S., and Lauth, H.-J. (2007), "Zur Aktualität der Gewaltenteilung: Überlegungen zu einem bleibenden Thema," in Kropp, S., and Lauth, H.-J. (eds.), *Gewaltenteilung und Demokratie: Konzepte und Probleme der "horizontal accountability" im interregionalen Vergleich*, 7–27. Baden-Baden: Nomos.

Ksibi, A. (2006), "Statistical indicators on reading and literacy for the information society versus the ITU's technicist indices," in Flaten, T. K. (ed.), *Management, Marketing and Promotion of Library Services Based on Statistics, Analyses and Evaluation*, 342–56. Munich: KG Saur.

Kuner, C. (2003), *European Data Privacy Law and Online Business*. Oxford University Press.

Kwoka, J. E., and White, L. J. (eds.) (2004), *The Antitrust Revolution: The Role of Economics*, 4th edn. Oxford University Press.

Lacharite, J. (2002), "Electronic decentralisation in China: a critical analysis of internet filtering policies in the People's Republic of China," *Australian Journal of Political Science*, **37** (2), 333–41.

Laffont, J.-J., and Tirole, J. (1991), "The politics of government decision making: a theory of regulatory capture," *Quarterly Journal of Economics*, **106** (4), 1089–127.

(1993), *A Theory of Incentives in Procurement and Regulation*. Cambridge, MA: MIT Press.

(1996), "Creating competition through interconnection: theory and practice," *Journal of Regulatory Economics*, **10** (3), 227–56.

(2000), *Competition in Telecommunications*. Cambridge, MA: MIT Press.

Lakel, A., and Massit-Folléa, F. (2007), "Société civile et gouvernance de l'internet au Sommet mondial sur la Société de l'Information: la construction d'une légitimité ambiguë," *Hermès*, **47** (1), 41–63.

Lakhani, K., and von Hippel, E. (2003), "How open source software works: 'free' user-to-user assistance," *Research Policy*, **32** (6), 923–43.

Lampe, C., and Resnick, P. (2004), "Slash(dot) and burn: distributed moderation in a large online conversation space," in Dykstra-Erickson, E., and Tscheligi, M. (eds.), *Proceedings of ACM CHI 2004 Conference on Human Factors in Computing Systems*, 543–50. New York: ACM Press.

Langlois, R. N. (2002), "Modularity in technology and organizations," *Journal of Economic Behavior and Organization*, **49** (1), 19–37.

Lanzara, G. F., and Morner, M. (2003), "The knowledge ecology of open-source software projects," paper presented at the 19th European Group of Organizational Studies colloquium, Copenhagen, July 3.

Lascoumes, P., and Le Galès, P. (2007), "Introduction: understanding public policy through its instruments. From the nature of instruments to the sociology of public policy instrumentation," *Governance*, **20** (1), 1–21.

Lastowka, G., and Hunter, D. (2004), "The laws of the virtual worlds," *California Law Schwitter Review*, **92** (1), 1–75.

Latour, B. (1993), *La Clef de Berlin et autres leçons d'un amateur de sciences*. Paris: La Découverte.

Layman, E. A., and Caldwell, M. E. (1963), "Modern logic and judicial decision making: a sketch of one view," *Law and Contemporary Problems. Jurimetrics*, **28** (1), 213–70.

Léautier, T. O., and Thelen, V. (2009), "Optimal expansion of the power transmission grid: why not?" *Journal of Regulatory Economics*, **36** (2), 127–53.

Lee, C.-C. (2003), "The global and the national of the Chinese media: discourse, market, technology, and ideology," in Lee, C.-C. (ed.), *Chinese Media, Global Contexts*, 1–31. London: Routledge.

Lee, H. (2005), "Behavorial strategies for dealing with flaming in an online forum," *Sociological Quarterly*, **46** (2), 385–403.

Lee, J. (2002), "Trying to elude the Google grasp," *New York Times*, July 25, E1.

Lehmkuhl, D. (2005), "How private governance arrangements may produce binding outcomes," *International Journal of Civil Society Law*, **3** (4), 34–55.

(2007), "Between transnational take-off and national landing: jurisdictional dynamics in the domain name area," in Dunn, M., Krishna-Hensel, S. F., and Maue, V. (eds.), *The Resurgence of the State: Trends and Processes in Cyberspace*, 85–110. Aldershot, UK: Ashgate.

Lemley, M. A. (1998), "The law and economics of internet norms," *Chicago–Kent Law Review*, **73** (4), 1257–94.

(1999), "Beyond preemption: the law and policy of intellectual property licensing," *California Law Review*, **87** (1), 111–72.

(2006), "Terms of use," *Minnesota Law Review*, **91** (2), 459–83.

Lemley, M. A., and Lessig, L. (2001), "The end of end-to-end: preserving the architecture of the internet in the broadband era." *UCLA Law Review*, **48** (4), 925–72.

Lemos, R. (2007), "Techno brega," paper presented at the 2nd "Access to knowledge" conference, New Haven, CT, April 29.

Lenhart, A., and Fox, S. (2000), "Downloading free music: internet music lovers don't think it's stealing," Pew Research Center, Washington, DC.

Lenoble, J., and Maesschalck, M. (2003), *Toward a Theory of Governance: The Action of Norms*. The Hague: Kluwer Law International.

(2007), "Reflexive governance: some clarifications and an extension and deepening of the fourth (genetic) approach," REFGOV Working Paper no. SGI-TNU-2, Catholic University of Louvain; available at http://refgov.cpdr.ucl.ac.be/?go=download&type=pub&code.

Lerner, J., and Tirole, J. (2002), "Some simple economics of open source," *Journal of Industrial Economics*, **50** (2), 197–234.

(2006), "A model of forum shopping," *American Economic Review*, **96** (4), 1091–113.

Lessig, L. (1999a), "The code is the law," *The Industry Standard*, April 9.

(1999b), *Code and Other Laws of Cyberspace*. New York: Basic Books.

(2001), *The Future of Ideas: The Fate of the Commons in a Connected World*. New York: Vintage Books.

(2004), *Free Culture: How Big Media Uses Technology and the Law to Lock Down Culture and Control Creativity*. New York: Penguin Books.

Leuprecht, P. (2005), "Brave new digital world? Reflections on the World Summit on the Information Society," *Revue québécoise de droit international*, **18** (1), 41–56.

Levine, M. E., and Forrence, J. L. (1990), "Regulatory capture, public interest, and the public agenda: toward a synthesis," *Journal of Law, Economics, and Organization*, **6** (2), 167–98.

Levinson, D. J., and Pildes, R. H. (2006), "Separation of parties, not powers," *Harvard Law Review*, **119** (8), 2311–85.

Lewin, T. (2001), "Children's computer use grows, but gaps persist, study says," *New York Times*, January 22, A11.

Libecap, G. (2002), "A transactions-cost approach to the analysis of property rights," in Brousseau, E., and Glachant, J.-M. (eds.), *The Economics of Contracts: Theories and Applications*, 140–56. Cambridge University Press.

Lichtman, D., and Posner, E. (2004), "Holding internet service providers accountable," in Parisi, F., Polsby, D. D., and Cohen, L. R. (eds.), *Supreme Court Economic Review*, vol. XIV, 221–60. University of Chicago Press.

Liebowitz, S. J., and Margolis, S. E. (1994), "Network externality: an uncommon tragedy," *Journal of Economic Perspectives*, **8** (2), 133–50.

Lievens, E., Dumortier, J., and Ryan, P. S. (2006), "The co-protection of minors in new media: a European approach to co-regulation," *Journal of Juvenile Law and Policy*, **10** (1), 97–151.

Litman, J. (2004), "Sharing and stealing," *Hastings Communications and Entertainment Law Journal*, **23** (1), 1–48.

Littlechild, S. (2006), "Foreword: the market versus regulation," in Sioshansi, F. P., and Pfaffenberger, W. (eds.), *Electricity Market Reform: An International Perspective*, xvii–xxix. Amsterdam: Elsevier.

Liu, J. (1999), "Legitimacy and authority in internet coordination: a domain name case study," *Indiana Law Journal*, **74** (2), 587–626.

Löfstedt, R. E., Vogel, D., Renn, O., Slater, D., and Rogers, M. D. (2001), "The changing character of regulation: a comparison of Europe and the United States," *Risk Analysis*, **21** (4), 399–416.

Long, C. (2004), "Information costs in patent and copyright," *Virginia Law Review*, **90** (2), 465–549.

Losowsky, A. (2004), "Online: a 21st-century protest," *Guardian*, March 25, Life, 21.

Louafi, S. (2007), "Epistemic communities and international governance of biological diversity: a reinterpretation of the role of IUCN," in Thoyer, S., and Martimort-Asso, B. (eds.), *Participation for Sustainability in Trade*, 111–20. Aldershot, UK: Ashgate.

Löwy, M., (2004), "Towards a New International?" in Sen, J., Anand, A., Escobar, A., and Waterman, P. (eds.), *World Social Forum: Challenging Empires*, 19–24. New Delhi: Viveka Foundation.

Malaby, T. M. (2006), "Introduction: contingency and control online," *First Monday*, **11** (9), article 2, http://firstmonday.org/htbin/cgiwrap/bin/ojs/index.php/fm/article/view/1606/1521.

Malcolm, J. (2008), *Multi-Stakeholder Governance and the Internet Governance Forum*. Wembley: Terminus Press.

Malone, T. W., Yates, J., and Benjamin, R. L. (1987), "Electronic markets and electronic hierarchies," *Communications of the ACM*, **30** (6), 484–97.

Manekshaw, C. S. J. (2005), "Liability of ISPS: immunity from liability under the Digital Millennium Copyright Act and the Communications Decency Act," *Computer Law Review and Technology Journal*, **10** (1), 101–33.

Marsden, C. T. (2010), *Net Neutrality: Towards a Co-Regulatory Solution*. London: Bloomsbury Academic.

Marzouki, M. (2006), "The 'guarantee-rights' for the realization of the rule of law," in Rikke, F. J. (ed.), *Human Rights in the Global Information Society*, 197–218. Cambridge, MA: MIT Press.

(2007), "Identity control, activity control: from trust to suspicion," *Annals of Telecommunications*, **62** (11/12), 1207–22.

(2008a), "European internet policies between regulation and governance: issues with content regulation," in Benedek, W., Bauer, V., and Kettemann, M. C. (eds.), *Internet Governance and the Information Society. Global Perspectives and European Dimensions*, 127–40. Utrecht: Eleven International.

(2008b), "Ambiguïtés de la société de l'information et ambivalences de la société civile: le révélateur SMSI," in George, E., and Granjon, F. (eds.), *Critiques de la société de l'information*, 69–87. Paris: L'Harmattan.

Marzouki, M., and Jørgensen, R. F. (2005), "A human rights assessment of the World Summit on the Information Society," *Information Technologies and International Development*, **1** (3/4), 86–8.

Marzouki, M., and Méadel, C. (2006), "Internet co-regulation as public action instrument: deliberative democracy or organization of powers?" in Bratosin, S., and Bertelli, D. (eds.), *Participative Democracy in Europe*, 27–33. Toulouse: LERASS.

Massit-Folléa, F. (2002), "De la régulation à la gouvernance d'internet: quel rôle pour les usagers-citoyens?" *Les cahiers du numérique*, **3** (2), 239–63.

Mathewson, G. F., and Winter, R. A. (1984), "An economic theory of vertical restraints," *RAND Journal of Economics*, **15** (1), 27–38.

Mathiason, J. (2008), *Internet Governance: The New Frontier of Global Institutions*. London: Routledge.

Mattelart, A. (2000), *Histoire de l'utopie planétaire: De la cité prophétique à la société globale*. Paris: La Découverte.

Mattli, W., and Büthe, T. (2003), "Setting international standards: technological rationality or primacy of power?" *World Politics*, **56** (1), 1–52.

May, B. E., Chen, J.-C. V., and Wen, K.-W. (2004), "The differences of regulatory models and internet regulation in the European Union and the United States," *Information and Communication Technology Law*, **13** (3), 259–72.

Mayer-Schönberger, V., and Lazer, D. (eds.) (2007), *Governance and Information Technology: From Electronic Government to Information Government*. Cambridge, MA: MIT Press.

Mayntz, R. (1998), "New challenges to governance theory," Jean Monnet Chair Paper no. 98/50. European University Institute, Florence.

(2003), "From government to governance: political steering in modern societies," paper presented at the "Summer academy on integrated product policy," Würzburg, September 7.

McCarthy, J. T. (1996), *McCarthy on Trademarks and Unfair Competition*, 4th edn. St Paul, MN: West Group.

(2000), *McCarthy on Trademarks and Unfair Competition: Supplement*. St Paul, MN: West Group.

McCubbins, M. D., Noll, R. G., and Weingast, B. R. (1987), "Administrative procedures as instruments of political control," *Journal of Law, Economics, and Organization*, **3** (2), 243–77.

McCulloch, W. (1945), "A heterarchy of values determined by the topology of nervous nets," *Bulletin of Mathematical Biophysics*, **7** (4), 89–93.

McGeary, A. (2001), "China's great balancing act: maximizing the internet's benefits while limiting its detriments," *International Lawyer*, **35** (1), 219–30.

McLaughlin, L., and Pickard, V. (2005), "What is bottom-up about global internet governance?" *Global Media and Communications*, **1** (3), 357–73.

MacLean, D. (2004a), "Herding Schrödinger's cats: some conceptual tools for thinking about internet governance," paper presented at ITU workshop on internet governance, Geneva, February 26.

(ed.) (2004b), *Internet Governance: A Grand Collaboration*. New York: United Nations Publications.

Méadel C. (2006), "Le marché eBay: qualification croisée des biens et des personnes," *Hermès*, **44**, 79–84.

Merges, R. P. (1997), "The end of friction? Property rights and contract in the 'Newtonian' world of on-line commerce," *Berkeley Law Journal*, **12** (1), 115–36.

(2004), "A new dynamism in the public domain," *University of Chicago Law Review*, **71** (4), 183–203.

Merrill, T. W., and Smith, H. E. (2001), "The property/contract interface," *Columbia Law Review*, **101** (4), 773–852.

Meurer, J. M. (1997), "Price discrimination, personal use and piracy: copyright protection of digital works," *Buffalo Law Review*, **45** (3), 845–98.

Mifsud Bonnici, J. P. (2008), *Self-Regulation in Cyberspace*. The Hague: TMC Asser Press.

Miller, D., and Slater, D. (2000), *The Internet: An Ethnographic Approach*. Oxford: Berg.

Mol, A. P. J. (2006), "The environmental state and informational governance," *Nature and Culture*, **1** (1), 36–62.

Montero, E., Demoulin, M., and Lazaro, C. (2004), "La Loi du 11 mars 2003 sur les services de la société de l'information," *Journal des Tribunaux*, **6125**, 81–95.

Montesquieu (Baron de), de Secondat, C.-L. (1941 [1748]), *De l'Esprit des lois*. Paris: Garnier; available at http://dx.doi.org/doi:10.1522/cla.moc.del1 [English: (1914), *The Spirit of Laws* (trans. Nugent, T., rev. Prichard, J. V.). London: G. Bell & Sons; available at www.constitution.org/cm/sol.txt].

Mopas, M. S. (2009), "Imagining the internet and making it governable: Canadian law and regulation," Ph.D. dissertation, University of Toronto; available at www.synergiescanada.org/browse/theses/otu/17802.

Mousseron, J.-M., and Vivant, M. (1989), "Les mécanismes de réservation et leur dialectique: le 'terrain' occupé par le droit," *Semaine Juridique, Cahiers de Droit de l'Entreprise*, **1** (1), 2–4.

Mueller, M. L. (1994), "On the frontier of deregulation: New Zealand telecommunications and the problem of interconnecting competing networks," Policy Study no. 177. Reason Foundation, Los Angeles; available at http://reason.org/files/0e43f6e967f9d02710fb40b905b8d5a1.pdf.

(2002), *Ruling the Root: Internet Governance and the Taming of Cyberspace*. Cambridge, MA: MIT Press.

(2010), *Networks and States: The Global Politics of Internet Governance*. Cambridge, MA: MIT Press.

Mueller, M. L., Mathiason, J., and Klein, H. (2007), "The internet and global governance: principles and norms of a new regime," *Global Governance*, **13** (2), 237–54.

Mydans, S. (2007), "Monks are silenced, and for now, internet is, too," *New York Times*, October 4, 1; available at www.nytimes.com/2007/10/04/world/asia/04info.html?ex=1349236800&en=26850407b42e0592&ei=5124&partner=permalink&exprod=permalink.

Nagel, S. S. (1990), "Literature on computer software and legal decision making," *Law Library Journal*, **82** (3), 749–60.

Nas, S. (2004), "The Multatuli Project: ISP notice and take down," paper presented at the 4th international system administration and network engineering conference, Amsterdam, October 1; available at www.bof.nl/docs/researchpaperSANE.pdf (accessed April 7, 2007).

New York Times (2008), "US imposes more sanctions to press Myanmar's rulers," *New York Times*, February 6, 5; available at www.nytimes.com/2008/02/06/world/asia/06myanmar.html?scp=50&sq=burma&st=nyt (accessed April 21, 2008).

Newbery, D. M. (2000), *Privatization Restructuring, and Regulation of Network Utilities*. Cambridge, MA: MIT Press.

Newbold, J. (2003), "Aiding the enemy: imposing liability on US corporations selling China internet tools to restrict human rights," *Journal of Law, Technology and Policy*, **2003** (2), 503–29.

Nguyen, X. (2004), "Collateralizing privacy," *Tulane Law Review*, **78** (3), 553–604.

Nip, J. Y. M. (2004), "The relationship between online and offline communities: the case of the queer sisters," *Media, Culture and Society*, **26** (3), 409–28.

Noam, E. M. (2001), *Interconnecting the Network of Networks*. Cambridge, MA: MIT Press.

(1994), "Beyond liberalization II: the impending doom of common carriage," *Telecommunications Policy*, **18** (6), 435–52.

Noll, R. G. (1999), *The Economics and Politics of the Slowdown in Regulatory Reform*. Washington, DC: American Enterprise Institute.

Norris, P. (ed.) (1999), *Critical Citizens: Global Support for Democratic Government*. New York: Oxford University Press.

North, D. C. (1990), *Institutions, Institutional Change and Economic Performance*. Cambridge University Press.

(1995), "The new institutional economics and Third World development," in Harris, J., Hunter, J., and Lewis, C. M. (eds.), The *New Institutional Economics and Third World Development*, 17–26. London: Routledge.

(2005), *Understanding the Process of Economic Change*. Princeton University Press.

O'Rourke, M. A. (1997), "Copyright preemption after the ProCD case: a market-based approach," *Berkeley Technology Law Journal*, **12** (1), 53–91.

Ó'Siochrú, S., and Alegre, A. (2005), "Communication rights," in Ambrosi, A., Pimienta, D., and Peugeot, V. (eds.), *Word Matters: Multicultural Perspectives on Information Societies*, 49–72. Caen: C&F Editions.

O'Sullivan, P. B., and Flanagin, A. J. (2001), "Reconceptualizing 'flaming' and other problematic messages," *New Media and Society*, **5** (1), 69–93.

OECD (2007), *Participative Web: User-Created Content.* Paris: OECD; available at www.oecd.org/dataoecd/57/14/38393115.pdf (accessed October 24, 2007).

Ogus, A. (2000), "Self-regulation," in Bouckaert, B., and De Geest, G. (eds.), *Encyclopedia of Law and Economics*, vol. V, *The Economics of Crime and Litigation*, 587–602. Cheltenham: Edward Elgar; available at http://encyclo.findlaw.com/9400book.pdf.

Orengo Castellá, V., Zornoza Abad, A. M., Prieto Alonso F., and Peiró Silla, J. M. (2000), "The influence of familiarity among group members, group atmosphere and assertiveness on uninhibited behavior through three different communication media," *Computers in Human Behavior*, **16** (2), 141–59.

Ostrom, E. (1990), *Governing the Commons: The Evolution of Institutions for Collective Action.* Cambridge University Press.

(1998), "A behavioral approach to the rational choice theory of collective action: presidential address," *American Political Science Review*, **92** (1), 1–22.

Padovani, C., and Pavan, E. (2009), "Information networks, internet governance and innovation in world politics," in Amoretti, F. (ed.), *Electronic Constitution: Social, Cultural, and Political Implications*, 154–73. Hershey, PA: IGI Global.

Palfrey, J. G., and Rogoyski, R. (2006), "The move to the middle: the enduring threat of 'harmful' speech to the end-to-end principle," *Washington University Journal of Law and Policy*, **21** (1), 31–66.

Palzer, C. (2003), "Co-regulation of the media in Europe: European provisions for the establishment of co-regulation frameworks," *Media, Law and Policy*, **13** (1), 7–27.

Pan, P. P. (2005), "China cracks down on student web sites," *Washington Post*, March 24, A13.

Panagakos, A. N., and Horst, H. A. (2006), "Return to cyberia: technology and the social worlds of transnational migrants," *Global Networks*, **6** (2), 109–24.

Papacharissi, Z. (2004), "Democracy online: civility, politeness, and the democratic potential of online political discussion groups," *New Media and Society*, **6** (2), 259–83.

Papadakis, M. C. (2003), "People can create a sense of community in cyberspace," SRI International, Arlington, VA; available at www.sri.com/policy/csted/reports/sandt/it/Papadakis_IT_virtual_communities_issue_brief.pdf.

Paré, D. (2003), *Internet Governance in Transition: Who Is the Master of This Domain?* Lanham, MD: Rowman & Littlefield.

Park, S.-Y., and Yun, G. W. (2004), "The impact of internet-based communication systems on supply chain management: an application of transaction cost analysis," *Journal of Computer-Mediated Communication*, **10** (1), article 12.

Patomäki, H., and Teivanen, T. (2004), "The World Social Forum: an open space or a movement of movements?" *Theory, Culture and Society*, **21** (6), 145–54.

Pavan, E., and Diani, M. (2008), "Structuring online and offline discursive spaces of internet governance: insights from a network approach to map an emerging field," paper presented at the 3rd annual GigaNet symposium, Hyderabad, December 2.

Perrot, A. (2004), "Régulation et politique de concurrence dans les réseaux," *Économie publique*, **14**, article 11, http://economiepublique.revues.org/217.

Peyer, C. (ed.) (2005), *Who Pays for the Information Society? Challenges and Issues on Financing the Information Society*. Lausanne: Bread for All Publishers.

Pfanner, E. (2004), "Text-messaging the revolution: cellphones may have tipped the scales in Spanish election," *International Herald Tribune*, March 22, Finance, 11.

Phillips, D. J. (1996), "Defending the boundaries: identifying and countering threats in a Usenet newsgroup," *The Information Society*, **12** (1), 39–62.

Porter, M. E. (1990), *The Competitive Advantage of Nations*. New York: Free Press.

Poullet, Y. (2004), "Technologies de l'information et de la communication et 'co-régulation': une nouvelle approche?" in Poullet, Y., Wéry, P., Wynants, P., and De Streel, A. (eds.), *Liber Amicorum Michel Coipel*, 167–88. Brussels: Kluwer.

Preciado, B. (2000), *Manifeste contra-sexuel*. Paris: Balland.

Preece, J. (2000), *Online Communities: Designing Usability, Supporting Sociability*. Chichester, UK: John Wiley.

(2004), "Etiquette online: from nice to necessary," *Communications of the ACM*, **47** (4), 56–61.

Prempeh, H. K. (2006), "Marbury in Africa: judicial review and the challenge of constitutionalism in contemporary Africa," *Tulane Law Review*, **80** (4), 1239–323.

Price, M. E., and Verhulst, S. G. (2005), *Self-Regulation and the Internet*. The Hague: Kluwer Law International.

Prosser, T. (2005), "Regulatory contracts and stakeholder regulation," *Annals of Public and Cooperative Economics*, **76** (1), 35–57.

Proulx, S., and Latzko-Toth, G. (2000), "La virtualité comme catégorie pour penser le social: l'usage de la notion de communauté virtuelle," *Sociologie et sociétés*, **32** (2), 99–122.

(2005), "Mapping the virtual in social sciences: on the category of 'virtual community,'" *Journal of Community Informatics*, **2** (1), 42–52.

Proulx, S., Poissant, L., and Senecal, M. (2007), *Communautés virtuelles: Penser et agir en réseau*. Quebec City: Presses de l'Université Laval.

Qiu, J. L. (2000), "Virtual censorship in China: keeping the gate between the cyberspaces," *International Journal of Communications Law and Policy*, **4** (1), 1–25.

Raboy, M., and Landry, N. (2006), *Civil Society, Communication, and Global Governance: Issues from the World Summit on the Information Society*. New York: Peter Lang.

Raboy, M., Landry, N., and Shtern, J. (2010), *Digital Solidarities, Communication Policy and Multi-Stakeholder Global Governance: The Legacy of the World Summit on the Information Society*. New York: Peter Lang.

Radin, M. J. (2002), "Information tangibility," Public Law Research Paper no. 48, Stanford Law School; available at http://papers.ssrn.com/sol3/papers.cfm?abstract_id=357060.

(2006), "Boilerplate today: the rise of modularity and the waning of consent," *Michigan Law Review*, **104** (5), 1223–34.

Raymond, E. S. (2001), *The Cathedral and the Bazaar: Musings on Linux and Open Source by an Accidental Revolutionary*, rev. edn. Cambridge, MA: O'Reilly Media.

Reed, K. M. (2000), "From the great firewall of China to the Berlin firewall: the cost of content regulation on internet commerce," *The Transnational Lawyer*, **13** (2), 451–76.

Reidenberg, J. R. (1998), "Lex Informatica: the formulation of information policy rules through technology," *Texas Law Review*, **76** (3), 553–84.

Reiman, P. (2000), "In Congress electric: the need for on-line parliamentary procedure," *John Marshall Journal of Computer and Information Law*, **18** (4), 963–80.

Reynolds, T. (2007), *Internet Traffic Prioritisation: An Overview*. Paris: OECD.

Rheingold, H. (2000), *The Virtual Community: Homesteading on the Electronic Frontier*, rev. edn. Cambridge, MA: MIT Press.

(2002), *Smart Mobs: The Next Social Revolution*. Cambridge, MA: Perseus.

Rice, E. (1970), *The Foundations of Early Modern Europe, 1460–1559*. New York: W. W. Norton.

Rious, V., Glachant, J.-M., Perez, Y., and Dessante, P. (2009), "L'insuffisance des signaux de localisation pour la coordination entre la production et le transport d'électricité dans les systèmes électriques libéralisés," *Revue économique*, **60** (3), 819–29.

Robinson, M. (1996), "Governance," in Kuper, A., and Kuper, J. (eds.), *The Social Sciences Encyclopaedia*, 2nd edn., 347–8. London: Routledge.

Rochet, J., and Tirole, J. (2003), "Platform competition in two-sided markets," *Journal of the European Economic Association*, **1** (4), 990–1029.

(2007), "Two-sided markets: a progress report," *RAND Journal of Economics*, **37** (3), 645–67.

Rosanvallon, P. (2008), *La Légitimité démocratique: Impartialité, réflexivité, proximité*. Paris: Seuil.

Rosenau, J. N. (2003), *Distant Proximities: Dynamics beyond Globalization*. Princeton University Press.

(2006), *The Study of World Politics*, vol. I, *Theoretical and Methodological Challenges*. Abingdon, UK: Routledge.

(2007), *The Study of World Politics*, vol. II, *Globalization and Governance*. Abingdon, UK: Routledge.

Rosenau, J. N., and Czempiel, E. O. (1992), *Governance without Government: Order and Change in World Politics*. Cambridge University Press.

Rotenberg, M. (2001), "Fair information practices and the architecture of privacy (what Larry doesn't get)," *Stanford Technology Law Review*, 1 (February), article 1, http://stlr.stanford.edu/pdf/rotenberg-fair-info-practices.pdf.

Rustad, M. L., and Koening, T. H. (2005), "Rebooting cybertort law," *Washington Law Review*, **80** (2), 335–476.

Rydin, Y. (2007), "Re-examining the role of knowledge within planning theory," *Planning Theory*, **6** (1), 52–68.

Sabel, C., and Zeitlin, J. (2007), "Learning from difference: the new architecture of experimentalist governance in the European Union," European Governance Paper no. C-07-02, CONNEX, Mannheim; available at www.connex-network.org/eurogov/pdf/egp-connex-C-07–02.pdf.

Saltzer, R. H., Reed, D. P., and Clark, D. (1984), "End-to-end arguments in system design," *ACM Transactions on Computer Systems*, **2** (4), 277–88.

Samuelson, P. (2002), "Copyright, commodification, and censorship: past as prologue – but to what future?" in Netanel, N., and Elkin-Koren, N. (eds.), *The Commodification of Information*, 63–77. The Hague: Kluwer Law International.

Sang-Hun, C. (2008), "'Digital populism' sweeps South Korea," *International Herald Tribune*, June 18, Finance, 15.

Sappington, D. (2005), "Regulating service quality: a survey," *Journal of Regulatory Economics*, **27** (2), 123–54.

Saussier, S., and Glachant, J.-M. (2006), "Private and public partnership: recent developments," *Review of Industrial Organization*, **29** (1), 1–2.

Scharpf, F. W. (1999), *Governing in Europe: Effective and Democratic?* Oxford University Press.

Schemeil, Y. (2002), "Les biens publics premiers: Babel, côté tour et côté jardin," in Constantin, F. (ed.), *Les biens publics mondiaux: Un mythe légitimateur pour l'action collective?*, 101–31. Paris: L'Harmattan.

(2004), "Expertise and political competence: consensus making within the World Trade and the World Meteorological Organizations," in Reinalda, B., and Verbeek, B. (eds.), *Decision Making within International Organizations*, 77–89. London: Routledge.

Schemeil, Y., and Eberwein, W. D. (eds.) (2008), *Normer le monde*. Paris: L'Harmattan.

Schiavetta, S. (2004), "The relationship between e-ADR and article 6 of the European Convention of Human Rights pursuant to the case law of the European Court of Human Rights," *Journal of Information, Law and Technology*, **2004** (1), article 5, www2.warwick.ac.uk/fac/soc/law/elj/jilt/2004_1/schiavetta.

Schmithüsen, F. (2000), "The expanding framework of law and public policies governing uses and management in European forests," in Schmithüsen, F., Herbst, P., and Le Master, D. C. (eds.), *Forging a New Framework for Sustainable Forestry: Recent Developments in European Forest Law*, 1–27. Vienna: International Union of Forestry Research Organizations.

Schultz, T. (2005), *Réguler le Commerce électronique par la résolution des litiges en ligne: Une approche critique*. Brussels: Bruylant.

Schultz, W., and Held, T. (2004), *Regulated Self-Regulation as a Form of Modern Government: An Analysis of Case Studies from Media and Telecommunications Law*. Eastleigh, UK: John Libbey.

Schumpeter, J. A. (1954), *History of Economic Analysis*. Oxford University Press.

Schütz, C. (2005), *Der ökonomisierte Richter: Gewaltenteilung und richterliche Unabhängigkeit als Grenzen neuer Steuerungsmodelle in den Gerichten*. Berlin: Duncker & Humblot.

Schwartz, A., and Scott, R. (2003), "Contract theory and the limits of contract law," *Yale Law Journal*, **113** (3), 541–619.

Schwartz, J. (2002), "In the tech meccas, masses of people, or 'smart mobs,' are keeping in touch through wireless devices," *New York Times*, July 22, 4.

Schwitter, M., and Caoline, E. (2004), *The Role of International NGOs in the Global Governance of Human Rights: Challenging the Democratic Deficit*. Zurich: Schulthess.

Sédallian, V. (2005), "Responsabilité des prestataires techniques: le droit français," *Lex Electronica*, **10** (1), article 2, www.lex-electronica.org/articles/v10–1/sedallian.pdf.

Segal, I. (1999), "Contracting with externalities," *Quarterly Journal of Economics*, **114** (2), 337–88.

Select Committee on Science and Technology (2002), *What on Earth? The Threat to the Science Underpinning Conservation*, HL Paper 118(i). London: Stationery Office.

Senden, L. (2005), "Soft law, self-regulation and co-regulation in European law: where do they meet?" *Electronic Journal of Comparative Law*, **9** (1), article 3, www.ejcl.org/91/art91–3.html (accessed April 7, 2007).

Sharrock, L. M. (2001), "The future of domain name dispute resolution: crafting practical international legal solutions from within the UDRP framework," *Duke Law Journal*, **51** (2), 817–49.

Shirky, C. (2008), *Here Comes Everybody: The Power of Organizing without Organizations*. New York: Penguin Books.

Singh, J. P. (2008), *Negotiation and the Global Information Economy*. Cambridge University Press.

Slater, D. (2002), "Making things real: ethics and order on the internet," *Theory, Culture and Society*, **19** (5), 227–45.

Slaughter, A.-M. (2003), "Global government networks, global information agencies, and disaggregated democracy," *Michigan Journal of International Law*, **24** (3), 1041–74.

(2004), *A New World Order*. Princeton University Press.

Smeers, Y. (2005), "How well can one measure market power in restructured electricity systems?" Discussion Paper no. 2005050. Center for Operations Research and Econometrics, Louvain, Belgium.

Smith, C. B., McLaughlin, M., and Osborne, K. K. (1998), "From terminal ineptitude to virtual sociopathy: how conduct is regulated on Usenet," in McLaughlin, M., and Rafaeli, S. (eds.), *Network and Netplay: Virtual Groups on the Internet*, 95–112. Menlo Park, CA: AAAI Press.

Souter, D., MacLean, D., Akoh, B., and Creech, H. (2010), *ICTs, the Internet and Sustainable Development: Towards a New Paradigm*. Winnipeg: IISD; available at www.iisd.org/pdf/2010/icts_internet_sd_new_paradigm.pdf.

Spiller, P. T., and Liao, S. (2008), "Buy, lobby or sue: interest groups' participation in policy making: a selective survey," in Brousseau, E., and Glachant, J.-M. (eds.), *New Institutional Economics: A Guidebook*, 307–27. Cambridge University Press.

Spiller, P. T., Stein, E., and Tommasi, M. (2003), "Political institutions, policymaking processes, and policy outcomes: an intertemporal transactions framework," Design Paper no. DP1. Inter-American Development Bank, Washington, DC.

Spruyt, H. (1994), *The Sovereign State and Its Competitors: An Analysis of System Change*. Princeton University Press.

Stauffacher, D., and Kleinwächter, W. (eds.) (2005), *The World Summit on the Information Society: Moving from the Past into the Future*. New York: United Nations Publications.

Stenning, P. (2009), "Governance and accountability in a plural policing environment: the story so far," *Policing*, **3** (1), 22–33.

Stephenson, M. C. (2005), "Legislative allocation of delegated power: uncertainty, risk, and the choice between agencies and courts," Discussion Paper no. 506. Harvard Law School, Cambridge, MA.

Stevenson, J. H., and Clement, A. (2010), "Regulatory lessons for internet traffic management from Japan, the European Union and the United States: towards equity, neutrality and transparency," *Global Media Journal, Canadian Edition*, **3** (1), 9–29.

Stone, A. (1991), *Public Service Liberalism: Telecommunications and Transitions in Public Policy*. Princeton University Press.

Strowel, A., Ide, N., and Verhoestraete, F. (2001), "La directive du 8 juin 2000 sur le commerce électronique: un cadre juridique pour l'internet," *Journal des Tribunaux*, **6000**, 133–45.

Surowiecki, J. (2005), *The Wisdom of Crowds*. New York: Anchor Books.

Svantesson, D. J. B. (2005), "The characteristics making internet communication challenge traditional models of regulation: what every international jurist should know about the internet," *International Journal of Law and Information Technology*, **13** (1), 39–69.

Svensson, J. S., and Bannister, F. (2004), "Pirates, sharks and moral crusaders: social control in peer-to-peer networks," *First Monday*, **9** (6), article 4, http://131.193.153.231/www/issues/issue9_6/svensson/index.html.

Tacchi, J., Slater, D., and Hearn, G. (2003), *Ethnographic Action Research: A User's Handbook*. New Delhi: UNESCO; available at http://eprints.qut.edu.au/archive/00004399/01/4399.pdf.

Tate, J. (2001), "National varieties of standarization," in Hall, P. A., and Soskice, D. (eds.), *Varieties of Capitalism: The Institutional Foundations of Comparative Advantage*, 442–73. Oxford University Press.

Temple Lang, J. (2006), "Checks and balances in the European Union: the institutional structure and the 'Community method,'" *European Public Law*, **12** (1), 127–54.

Thessin, J. (2003), "Recent development: Department of Homeland Security," *Harvard Journal on Legislation*, **40** (2), 513–35.

Thévenot, L. (2007), "Reconnaissances: avec Paul Ricœur et Axel Honneth," in Delacroix, C., Dosse, F., and Garcia, P. (eds.), *Paul Ricœur et les sciences humaines*, 127–43. Paris: La Découverte.

Thomas, D. (2002), *Hacker Culture*. Minneapolis: University of Minnesota Press.

Thompsen, P. A., and Foulger, D. A. (1996), "Effects of pictographs and quoting on flaming in electronic mail," *Computers in Human Behavior*, **12** (2), 225–43.

Tierney, S. (2006), "The dangers and draw of online communication: pro-anorexia websites and their implications for users, practitioners, and researchers," *Eating Disorders*, **14** (3), 181–90.

Townes, M. D. (2011), "The spread of TCP/IP and the political origins of the internet," paper presented at the conference "Theorizing the web," College Park, MD, April 9; available at http://miles.oppidi.net/TownesTCPIP.TTW2011.pdf (accessed August 22, 2011).

Turner, F. (2006a), "How digital technology found utopian ideology: lessons from the first hackers' conference," in Silver, D., Massanari, A., and Jones, S. (eds.), *Critical Cyberculture Studies*, 257–69. New York: NYU Press.

(2006b), *From Counterculture to Cyberculture: Steward Brand, the Whole Earth Network, and the Rise of Digital Utopianism*. University of Chicago Press.

Twomey, P., Green, R., Neuhoff, K., and Newbery, D. (2005), "A review of the monitoring of market power: the possible roles of TSOs in monitoring for market power issues in congested transmission systems," Working Paper in Economics no. 0504. University of Cambridge.

Urfalino, P. (2007), "La décision par consensus apparent: nature et propriétés," *Revue européenne de sciences sociales*, **136**, 47–70.

US Census Bureau (2006), "E-stats: 2004 e-commerce multi-sector tables," US Census Bureau, Washington, DC, www.census.gov/econ/estats/2004/all2004tables.html.

Van Beijnum, I. (2007), "ARIN fights IP address trading as transition to IPv6 may get new deadlines," Ars Technica, August 2, http://arstechnica.com/news.ars/post/20070802-ipv4-is-a-democracy-ipv6-may-get-deadlines.html.

Van Schewick, B., and Farber, D. (2009), "Point/counterpoint: network neutrality nuances," *Communications of the ACM*, **52** (2), 31–7.

Verdure, C. (2005), "Les hébergeurs de sites web: victimes ou régulateurs de la société de l'information?" *Droit de la consommation/Consumentenrecht*, **68** (1), 31–52.

Vickers, J. (1997), "Regulation, competition and the structure of prices," *Oxford Review of Economic Policy*, **13** (1), 15–26.

Volti, R. (2006), *Society and Technological Change*, 5th edn. New York: St Martin's Press.

Von Hippel, E. (2005), *Democratizing Innovation*. Cambridge, MA: MIT Press.

Waddams Price, C., Brazier, K., Pham, K., Mathieu, L., and Wang, W. (2007), "Identifying fuel poverty using objective and subjective measures," Working Paper no. 07–11. Centre for Competition Policy, University of East Anglia, Norwich.

Wall, D. S., and Williams, M. (2007), "Policing diversity in the digital age: maintaining order in virtual communities," *Criminology and Criminal Justice*, 7 (4), 391–415.

Wallerstein, I. (1996), *After Liberalism*. New York: Free Press.

Wanamaker, A. (2006), "Censors in cyberspace: can Congress protect children from internet pornography despite *Ashcroft* v. *ACLU*?" *Saint Louis University Law Journal*, **50** (3), 957–94.

Weber, M. (1995 [1922]), *Economie et société*. Paris: Presse Pocket.

Weber, R. H. (2009), *Shaping Internet Governance: Regulatory Challenges*. Zurich: Springer.

Weber, R. H., and Menoud, V. (2008), *The Information Society and the Digital Divide: Legal Strategies to Finance Global Access*. Zurich: Schulthess Juristische Medien.

Weber, S. (2004), *The Success of Open Source*. Cambridge, MA: Harvard University Press.

Weinberg, J. (2000), "ICANN and the problem of legitimacy," *Duke Law Journal*, **50** (1), 187–260.

Wellman, B., and Haythornthwaite, C. (eds.) (2002), *The Internet in Everyday Life*. Oxford: Basil Blackwell.

Welser, H., Gleave, E., Fisher, D., and Smith, M. (2007), "Visualizing the signatures of social roles in online discussion groups," *Journal of Social Structure*, **8**, article 2, www.cmu.edu/joss/content/articles/volume8/Welser/.

Werbach, K. (2004), "Supercommons: toward a unified theory of wireless communication," *Texas Law Review*, **82** (4), 863–973.

WGIG (2005), *Report of the Working Group on Internet Governance*. New York: United Nations; available at www.wgig.org-WGIG-Report.html.

Whitaker, C. (2004), "The forum as open space," in Sen, J., Anand, A., Escobar, A., and Waterman, P. (eds.), *World Social Forum: Challenging Empires*, 111–21. New Delhi: Viveka Foundation.

Whybrow, P. C. (2005), *American Mania: When More Is Not Enough*. New York: W. W. Norton.

Williams, M. (2004), "Understanding King Punisher and his order: vandalism in an online community – motives, meanings and possible solutions," *Internet Journal of Criminology*.

Williamson, O. E. (1985), *The Economic Institutions of Capitalism*. New York: Free Press.

(1996), *The Mechanisms of Governance*. Oxford University Press.
Wilson, R. (2002), "Architecture of electric power market," *Econometrica*, **70** (4), 1299–340.
Wines, M., and LaFraniere, S. (2004), "Decade of democracy fills gaps in South Africa," *New York Times*, April 26, A1.
Winn, J. K. (2005), "Contracting spyware by contract," *Berkeley Technology Law Journal*, **20** (3), 1345–62.
(2006), "US and EU regulatory competition and authentication standards in electronic commerce," *Journal of IT Standards and Standardization Research*, **5** (1), 84–102.
Winn, J. K., and Webber, M. (2006), "The impact of EU unfair contract terms law on US business-to-consumer internet merchants," *The Business Lawyer*, **62** (1), 209–28.
Wright, S., and Street, J. (2007), "Democracy, deliberation and design: the case of online discussion forums," *New Media and Society*, **9** (5), 849–69.
WSIS (2003a), "Plan of action," Geneva, December 12; available at www.itu.int/wsis/docs/geneva/official/poa.html.
(2003b), "Declaration of principles: building the information society: a global challenge in the new millennium," Geneva, December 12; available at www.itu.int/wsis/docs/geneva/official/dop.html.
(2005), "Tunis agenda for the information society," United Nations, New York; available at www.itu.int/wsis/docs2/tunis/off/6rev1.pdf.
Wu, T. (2003a), "Network neutrality, broadband discrimination," *Journal of Telecommunications and High Technology Law*, **2** (1), 141–76.
(2003b), "When code isn't law," *Virginia Law Review*, **89** (4), 671–751.
Yamauchi, Y., Yokozawa, M., Shinohara, T., and Ishida, T. (2000), "Collaboration with lean media: how open-source software succeeds," in Kellogg, W. A., and Whittaker, S. (eds.), *Proceedings of the 2000 ACM Conference on Computer Supported Cooperative Work*, 329–38. New York: ACM Press.
Yang, G. (2006), "Activists beyond virtual borders: internet-mediated networks and informational politics in China," *First Monday*, **11** (9), article 5, http://firstmonday.org/htbin/cgiwrap/bin/ojs/index.php/fm/article/view/1609/1524.
Yardley, J. (2005), "A hundred cellphones bloom, and Chinese take to the streets," *New York Times*, April 25, A1.
Yoo, C. (2006a), "Network neutrality and competition policy: a complex relationship," in Lenard, T. N., and May, R. (eds.), *Net Neutrality or Net Neutering: Should Broadband Internet Services Be Regulated?*, 25–71. New York: Springer.
(2006b), "Network neutrality and the economics of congestion," *Georgetown Law Journal*, **94** (6), 1847–908.

Yu, P. K. (forthcoming), "Six secret (and now open) fears of ACTA," *SMU Law Review*, **64**; available at http://ssrn.com/abstract=1624813.

Zhao, H. (2004), "ITU and internet governance," draft input to the 7th meeting of the ITU Council Working Group on WSIS, Geneva, December 14.

Zittrain, J. (2003), "Internet points of control," *Boston College Law Review*, **44** (2), 653–88.

(2006), "A history of online gatekeeping," *Harvard Journal of Law and Technology*, **19** (2), 253–98.

(2008), *The Future of the Internet: And How to Stop It*. New Haven, CT: Yale University Press.

Index